Collective Bargaining Developments in Times of Crisis

Bulletin of Comparative Labour Relations

VOLUME 99

Founding Editor

The series started in 1970 under the dynamic editorship of Professor Roger Blanpain (Belgium), former President of the International Industrial Relations Association. Professor Blanpain, Professor Emeritus of Labour Law, Universities of Leuven and Tilburg, was also General Editor of the International Encyclopedia of Laws (with more than 1,600 collaborators worldwide) and President of the Association of Educative and Scientific Authors Authors. He passed away in October 2016.

General Editor

In 2015 Frank Hendrickx, Professor of labour law at the Faculty of Law of the University of Leuven (Belgium) joined as a co-Editor. Frank Hendrickx has published numerous articles and books and regularly advises governments, international institutions and private organisations in the area of labour law as well as in sports law. He is the Editor-in-Chief of the European Labour Law Journal and General Editor of the International Encyclopaedia of Laws.

Introduction

The Bulletins constitute a unique source of information and thought-provoking discussion, laying the groundwork for studies of employment relations in the 21st century, involving among much else the effects of globalization, new technologies, migration, and the greying of the population.

Contents/Subjects

Amongst other subjects the Bulletins frequently include the proceedings of international or regional conferences; reports from comparative projects devoted to salient issues in industrial relations, human resources management, and/or labour law; and specific issues underlying the multicultural aspects of our industrial societies.

Objective

The Bulletins offer a platform of expression and discussion on labour relations to scholars and practitioners worldwide, often featuring special guest editors.

The titles published in this series are listed at the end of this volume.

BULLETIN OF COMPARATIVE LABOUR RELATIONS - 99

Collective Bargaining Developments in Times of Crisis

Second Edition

Editor

Sylvaine Laulom

Contributors

Pierre-Emmanuel Berthier
Elisabeth Brameshuber
Judith Brockmann
Teresa Coelho Moreira
Kübra Doğan Yenisey
Nicola Gundt
Tamás Gyulavári
Jenny Julén Votinius
Gábor Kártyás
Fabienne Kéfer
Olivier Leclerc
Piera Loi
Yolanda Maneiro Vázquez
José María Miranda Boto
Cécile Nicod
Łukasz Pisarczyk
Felicia Rosioru
Katarzyna Wieczorek

General Editor

Frank Hendrickx

Founding Editor

Roger Blanpain

Wolters Kluwer

Published by:
Kluwer Law International B.V.
PO Box 316
2400 AH Alphen aan den Rijn
The Netherlands
E-mail: lrs-sales@wolterskluwer.com
Website: www.wolterskluwer.com/en/solutions/kluwerlawinternational

Sold and distributed by:
Wolters Kluwer Legal & Regulatory U.S.
920 Links Avenue
Landisville, PA 17538
United States of America
E-mail: customer.service@wolterskluwer.com

ISBN 978-94-035-0628-9

e-Book: ISBN 978-94-035-0638-8
web-PDF: ISBN 978-94-035-0648-7

Notes on Contributors

Pierre-Emmanuel Berthier, Professor of Labour Law, Université Lumière Lyon 2, France.

Elisabeth Brameshuber, Professor of Labour and Social Security Law, Universität Wien, Austria.

Judith Brockmann, Professor for Economic, Social and Labour Law, Universität Kassel, Germany.

Teresa Coelho Moreira, Associate Professor with Habilitation, School of Law, University of Minho, Portugal.

Kübra Doğan Yenisey, Professor of Labour and Social Security Law, Istanbul Bilgi University, Turkey.

Nicola Gundt, Associate Professor in Labour Law, Maastricht University, The Netherlands.

Tamás Gyulavári, Professor of Labour law, Pázmány Péter Catholic University, Labour Law Department, Budapest, Hungary.

Jenny Julén Votinius, Professor of Private Law, Faculty of Law, Lund University, Sweden.

Gábor Kártyás, Pázmány Péter Catholic University, Labour Law Department, Budapest, Hungary.

Fabienne Kéfer, Full Professor, University of Liège, Belgium.

Sylvaine Laulom, Advocate General, Cour de cassation, Professor of Law, Université Lumière Lyon 2, France.

Olivier Leclerc, CNRS Senior Researcher, Centre de Théorie et Analyse du Droit (CTAD UMR 7074), CNRS/University Paris Nanterre/Ecole normale supérieure, France.

Piera Loi, Professor of Labour Law, University of Cagliari, Italy.

Yolanda Maneiro Vázquez, Associate Professor of Labour Law and Social Security, Universidad de Santiago de Compostela, Spain.

José María Miranda Boto, Professor of Labour Law and Social Security, Universidad de Santiago de Compostela, Spain.

Cécile Nicod, Associate Professor of Labour Law, Université Lumière Lyon 2, France.

Łukasz Pisarczyk, Professor of Law, the University of Silesia in Katowice, Poland.

Felicia Rosioru, Associate Professor of Labour Law and Social Security, Babes-Bolyai University, Romania.

Katarzyna Wieczorek, PhD, Associate, Linklaters Warsaw, Poland.

Summary of Contents

Table of Contents

Introduction from the First Edition to the Second One

Sylvaine Laulom

I A NEW CONTEXT

In 2018, the first edition of the book, *Collective Bargaining Developments in Times of Crisis* was published.[1] The chapters included in the book were the results of research by the International Network for Labour Law Studies in times of Crisis (INLACRIS), financed by the European Commission (INLACRIS VS/2014/0532) with the participation of ASTREES.[2] The emerging network INLACRIS was set up for two previous projects and the results of the research presented follow on from them.[3] It gathers together experts on social issues – particularly social law – from different Member States of the European Union, as well as Turkey;[4] the aim was to analyse developments

1. S. Laulom (ed.), *Collective Bargaining Developments in Times of Crisis*, Bulletin of Comparative Labour Relations, 99 (2018).
2. Association Travail, Emploi, Europe, Société and Christophe Teisser, Project Manager at ASTREES.
3. M.-C. Escande-Varniol, et al. (eds), *Quel droit social dans une Europe en crise?* (Brussels: Larcier, 2012); S. Laulom, (ed.) *Which Securities for Workers in Time of Crisis*, European Labour Law Journal, 5 (Nos 3-4, 2014), Project VS/2012/0223.
4. Austria: Franz Marhold et Elisabeth Brameshuber, WU Vienna University of Economics and Business; Belgium: Auriane Lamine, Université catholique de Louvain; France: Christophe Teissier (ASTREES), Sylvaine Laulom, Marie-Cécile Escande Varniol, Florence Debord, Cécile Nicod, Pierre-Emmanuel Berthier, Carole Giraudet, University Lumière Lyon 2, Olivier Leclerc, Emmanuelle Mazuyer, CNRS, Center for Critical Legal Research (CERCRID UMR 5137); Germany: Judith Brockmann, Universität Hamburg; Greece: Aristea Koukiadaki, University of Manchester; Hungary: Tamás Gyulavári, Gábor Kártyás Pázmány Péter Catholic University in Budapest; Italy: Piera Loi, University of Cagliari; Netherlands: Nicola Gundt, University of Maastricht; Poland: Lukasz Pisarczyk, University of Warsaw; Portugal: Teresa Coelho Moreira, University of Minho; Romania: Felicia Rosiuru, Babes-Bolyai University, Cluj-Napoca; Slovenia: Barbara Kresal, University of Ljubljana; Spain: Yolanda Maneiro Vázquez, José María Miranda Boto, University of Santiago de Compostela; Sweden: Jenny Julén Votinius, University of Lund; Turkey: Kübra Dogan Yenisey, University of Bilgi; United Kingdom: Jeremias Prassl, University of Oxford.

in progress in the different Member States of the European Union related to the crises affecting the European Union (EU), in order to offer knowledge and expertise on these developments and as a way to propose innovative solutions. Another aim was to contribute to the continuous strengthening of relations between the academic world and social actors. The network is grounded in the asserted will of this collective of independent experts to contribute to the renewal of social policies in Europe in a way that respects people's rights and freedoms.

The aim of the research was to conduct a comparative analysis of developments in systems of collective bargaining in fifteen mainly EU countries (Austria, Belgium, France, Germany, Greece, Hungary, Italy, Netherlands, Poland, Portugal, Romania, Slovenia, Spain, Sweden, Turkey, United Kingdom). This was a broad range with countries with very different systems of industrial relations represented.

The term 'crisis', used in a very generic manner throughout the study, must be properly defined. Since the beginning, the EU has faced various crises. As early as the 1970s, the European Economic Community was forced to deal with the oil crisis and the end of a long period of economic growth. This situation certainly contributed to the adoption of the first European directives on the harmonisation of labour rights, devoted precisely to crises and company restructuring.

Since 2008, the EU has suffered a series of crises of unprecedented magnitude: the global financial crisis hit all European countries. It generated a series of crises: an economic crisis, an employment crisis (particularly among young people and older people), and a public debt crisis, with major social consequences including company closures and relocations, unemployment, increased poverty and inequality. Next came the migration crisis and the Brexit crisis. Since the publication of the first edition, other crises have emerged: the totally unexpected COVID-19 pandemic with its massive consequences, the energy crisis, the environmental crisis, and the Ukrainian war crisis followed by inflation.

In 2015, the then President of the European Commission, Jean Claude Juncker, already evoked the existence of a Europe in a polycrisis in which multiple economic, financial and social crises came together: '*There has been much talk in recent months of the Greek crisis, the refugee crisis and other crises. But in reality, Europe is confronted with a convergence of multiple complex, multi-stratisfactional crises coming from outside or within the European Union, and which are all happening at the same time.*'[5] As Felicia Rosioru quoted in her chapter '*crisis seems to be everywhere*'.[6] This general context of 'crisis' justified that the title of the second edition remains the same even if the crisis or crises are no longer of exactly the same nature.

To examine the reality of these crises and their various effects on the countries studied and look into the intricate causalities between these crises and developments

5. Speech by President Jean-Claude Juncker – EP Plenary session – Conclusions of the European Council meeting of 17 and 18 December 2015, https://ec.europa.eu/commission/presscorner/detail/en/ SPEECH_16_112.
6. L. Henderson, *What It Means to Say 'Crisis' in Politics and Law* (2014), http://www.e-ir.info/2014/03/05/what-it-means-to-say-crisis-in-politics-and-law/, accessed 2 September 2024.

in industrial relations systems would be an excessively ambitious undertaking. However, an analysis of European and national legislative and institutional discourses shows that a link is established between these 'crises' and a supposedly ideal configuration of industrial relations systems. Therefore, these crises have been used systematically to legitimise reforms which far from being cyclical, are intended to be structural.[7] Just after the financial crisis in 2011, J. Prassl concluded thus: '*what is perhaps the deepest crisis of employment law yet has been entirely overlooked: as labour markets continue to develop away from received paradigms; and worker-protective norms break down, the rhetoric of "financial crisis" and responses thereto have only served to increase moves into a deregulatory direction, instead of facing the key challenges at hand*'.[8]

The subject of this research is precisely to analyse the relationships between these 'discourses', these reforms and their consequences on the national systems of industrial relations.

The European response to the financial and employment crisis of 2008 was the primary focus of our research. This answer was very different from that of the late 1970s. Not only did the production of social legislation remain definitively at a standstill, but European legislation and national labour rights in particular were called into question. After the first few months of the crisis, when Member States used social 'shock absorbers', the emphasis was firmly placed on 'structural' labour market reforms and austerity measures. In this respect, the economic governance embodied in the European semester – the annual cycle for the coordination of economic policies – proved to be a formidable lever for influencing national labour rights, often towards a social regression and sometimes outside the scope of the EU's competences and outside the mechanisms of democratic representation of the EU.

The crisis that began in 2008 has thus legitimised not only an abstention on the part of social Europe but also a questioning of national social protections.

As regards collective bargaining, in the context of the 2008 financial crisis, the European economic governance, i.e., the 'European Semester' put in place during 2011, was a great incentive for Member States to decentralise their collective bargaining systems. One of the aims of the study was therefore to analyse these national developments, first of all in terms of the structure of the industrial relations systems, and then going beyond to look at this decentralisation and determine its real nature.

However, an essential change has taken place at the European level in this area since the publication in 2018 of the first edition, a change of such magnitude that it can be described as a paradigm shift. The adoption of the Directive on Adequate Minimum Wages (hereinafter 'the AMW Directive')[9] marks a true break with the post-financial crisis period as the EU is now focusing on the development and enhancement of strong

7. J. Prassl, *Contingent Crises, Permanent Reforms: Rationalising Labour Market Reforms in the European Union*, European Labour Law Journal, 211 (Nos 3 4, 2014) https://doi.org/10.1177/201395251400500303.
8. *Ibid.*, p. 230.
9. Directive (EU) 2022/2041 of the European Parliament and of the Council of 19 October 2022 on Adequate Minimum Wages in the European Union. L. Ratti, E. Brameshuber & V. Pietrogiovanni (eds), *The EU Directive on Adequate Minimum Wages* (Hart 2024).

sectoral collective bargaining systems in wage setting. Here again, this development is justified by the consequences of a crisis: '*The crisis caused by the COVID-19 pandemic is having a significant impact on the services sector, microenterprises and small enterprises, which have a high share of low-wage and minimum-wage earners. Minimum wages are therefore also important in view of the structural trends that are reshaping labour markets and which are increasingly characterised by high shares of precarious and non-standard forms of work, often including part-time, seasonal, platform and temporary agency workers. Those trends have led, in many cases, to an increased job polarisation resulting in an increasing share of low-paid and low-skilled occupations and sectors in most Member States, as well as to higher wage inequality in some of them. It is more difficult for workers with non-standard contracts to organise and negotiate for collective agreements*' (recital 11). Implicitly, the AMW Directive recognises the negative consequences of the decentralisation of collective bargaining: '*While strong collective bargaining, in particular at sector or cross-industry level, contributes to ensuring adequate minimum wage protection, traditional collective bargaining structures have been eroding during recent decades, due, inter alia, to structural shifts in the economy towards less unionised sectors and to the decline in trade union membership, in particular as a consequence of union-busting practices and the increase of precarious and non-standard forms of work. In addition, sectoral and cross-industry level collective bargaining came under pressure in some Member States in the aftermath of the 2008 financial crisis. However, sectoral and cross-industry level collective bargaining is an essential factor for achieving adequate minimum wage protection and therefore needs to be promoted and strengthened*' (recital 16).

These new crises, and this reorientation of European social policy towards collective bargaining, justify an update of the research published in 2018 to analyse the evolutions of collective bargaining in this new context.

For the first edition, in order to conduct a comparison, questionnaires were created on these different aspects, as well as national reports, which were discussed and debated in seminars and conferences. Comparison makes it possible to identify common trends and new, emerging issues in collective bargaining. It was not possible for the second edition to exactly follow the same methodologies. However, national reports have been updated and the questionnaire methodology was used, but on a lesser scale, since the aim was essentially to update the research. It should be stressed that the aim of this second edition is not to analyse the consequences of the successive crises that have occurred since 2008 on collective bargaining but rather to take up the conclusions of the first research and update them in the light of the current context.

II STRUCTURE OF THE BOOK

The book is organised around two building blocks. Part I presents some comparative perspectives both in terms of the structure of the industrial relations systems and in terms of subjects of collective bargaining, whether this be a classical theme of collective bargaining (wages and working time) or less traditional themes. Part II presents some national situations.

[A] Comparative Perspectives

In the first chapter of the book, S. Laulom (*From Decentralisation of Collective Bargaining to Re-centralisation of Industrial Relations Systems?*), using the national reports, shows that with the exception of the countries maintaining a centralised system of collective bargaining, decentralisation that is not controlled by sector level agreements rather amounts to a de-collectivisation of industrial relations, where collective bargaining has very limited powers to regulate the field of labour relations. The question raised by the adoption of the AMW Directive is, therefore, to determine how sectoral bargaining can be developed in countries where there is no such level of bargaining, or in countries where collective bargaining remains underdeveloped at all levels.

In Chapter 2, T. Gyulavári (*Chasing the Holy Grail? Stumbling Collective Bargaining in Eastern Europe and the Hungarian Experiment*), explains the reasons why Central and Eastern European countries have not developed an articulated system of collective bargaining. He also shows how the most recent attempts by the Hungarian government to develop collective bargaining at the company level, by encouraging employers to engage in negotiations to conclude derogating agreements, have not been successful.

In Chapter 3, P. Loi (*The function of sectoral collective agreements and the risk approach*) uses the risk theory to analyse the functions of collective agreements, especially with regard to wage risk. This perspective is particularly useful for understanding recent developments in European Social Policy. P. Loi analyses how the EU institutions have more recently dealt with the impact of global risks, like the COVID-19 pandemic and the digital transition, on workers' wages, in order to ascertain if sectoral collective agreements can still be considered regulatory tools capable of facing these risks. Notwithstanding the paramount importance of collective agreements especially at the sectoral level, in order to face wage risks for digital platform workers, at least two main obstacles can be highlighted: first of all, when digital platform workers are classified as employees, they have difficulties to be unionised because of their physical isolation and lack of continuity of their work. Second, there is a tendency of legal systems to raise questions about the conflicts between collective agreements for independent contractors (when digital platform workers are classified as independent contractors) and competition law. The way out of this regulatory dilemma could be either that the case law classifies all digital platform workers as employees in order to consider them inside the scope of application of collective agreements, or that collective agreements for digital platform workers, even if they are classified as self-employed, are exempted from the competition law rules.

The role played by the state in industrial relations systems varies greatly from country to country. The EU has encouraged the Member States to adopt measures to promote the decentralisation of collective bargaining and is now promoting the conclusion of collective agreements at the sectoral level. In order to transpose the directive on minimum wages, countries with a low collective bargaining coverage will have to adopt various measures to try to achieve the objectives set by the directive.

However, '*the mere promulgation of regulations does not automatically lead to compliant behaviour on the part of the actors at whom they are aimed*'. This is why, Chapter 4 by P.-E. Berthier and O. Leclerc *(Incentivising Collective Bargaining)* analyses precisely the different mechanisms that the States have been able to use as part of their social policy to encourage actors to negotiate. A typology distinguishing three types of measures is put forward (facilitation, reward and taxation). These rules are all too often overlooked by labour lawyers, despite their key role in effective collective bargaining and, ultimately, in the signing of collective agreements. In a European context where Member States are required to develop collective bargaining at the sectoral level, the analysis of these rules presents a particular interest.

In Chapter 5, N. Gundt, Ł. Pisarczyk and K. Wieczorek (*Negotiating Working Time in Times of Crisis and Twin Transition*) discuss the development of collective bargaining on working time and its legal framework since 2018 with special references to the phenomena which significantly affected the world of work (the twin transition: technological development and the pandemic) and leading tendencies in regulating working time, including shortening the working day and working week, increasing flexibilisation of working time and utilizing working time as an element of anti-crisis policies. Their conclusion is that the '*involvement of the social partners in anti-crisis activities as well as the development of the social dialogue in the post-pandemic era have confirmed the potential of collective bargaining in creating an appropriate framework for working time. Short-time work adopted with the participation of workers' representatives mitigated effectively the negative consequences of the pandemic. In the recent years collective bargaining contributed to further limitations in working hours. The social partners have been involved in developing four-day working week. Collective bargaining has also played an important role in flexibilizing working time at a level acceptable for both: companies and workers. Thanks to collective bargaining it is possible to extend the sphere of freedom of workers without excessive interfering with business activities. However, the importance of collective bargaining on working time varies significantly from country to country depending on statutory framework and factual position of a national social dialogue. Negotiating working time has been shifting from sectoral to company-level collective bargaining. Problems affecting trade unions may encourage the development of competences of elected representatives. A disturbing phenomenon is the development of employer's managerial prerogatives. At the same time the potential of collective bargaining in protecting against abuses in tech-based employment has not been fully utilized. To summarize, collective bargaining should remain a key instrument in reconstructing working time regulations as part of sustainable development of the employment relationship. It requires, however, both: creating a supportive legal framework by the state (e.g. by finding a balance between collective bargaining and managerial competences of employers) as well as adopting efficient strategies by the social partners (e.g. by counteracting abuses in the tech-based employment)*'.

Beyond developments related to collective bargaining systems and to the traditional subjects of collective bargaining, like working time and wages, our research also questioned the emergence of new issues for collective bargaining in Europe. Young people and older people are two categories particularly affected by the crisis and European institutions are encouraging social partners to address the employment issues affecting them. J. Brockmann and J. Julén Votinius demonstrate the specificities of each of these categories, how they are addressed by law and the policies of the EU, and the reasons why collective bargaining has struggled to date to address this subject. At a time when young people and older people represent serious societal issues, collective negotiation is struggling to address these subjects.

In Chapter 6, J. Julén Votinius (*Older Employees, Extended Working Lives and Collective Bargaining*) discusses some of many examples of how collective agreements in a constructive and applicable way can lead to the implementation of policy measures to promote extended working lives. However, this is not an easy task. The top-down active ageing policies stemming from EU and national policymakers, and also from the European social partner Framework Agreement, uncover a distance in relation to everyday practices in the workplace, and the positive narrative underlying the extended work-life policies does not resonate with employers and employees implementing and directly affected by these policies. While the rapid and ongoing prolongation of working lives in many EU Member States has been recognised and praised in the political debate, legislative reforms raising the retirement age and restricting early retirement have in many countries led to criticism and also significant protests from the public. Generally, retirement is considered a well-deserved freedom after a long working life and increased retirement age means cutting years off this freedom. Also, although people on average live longer, for many, this is not the same as years of good health. When working life is extended as a response to the increase in average life expectancy, there are growing risks related to deteriorating health and productivity – and these risks must to a large extent be borne by the individual employees and employers. Against this background, the importance of increased collective bargaining initiatives in the area of prolonged working lives is apparent. Social partner involvement has unmatched abilities to mitigate demands, expectations and actual prerequisites to ensure a balanced and tailored approach to the demographic and economic realities that are pressing for increased labour force participation in relation to older workers. It is however also crucial that collective bargaining initiatives are supported at the State level. Linking public funding to social partner initiatives means that the employers do not have to bear the (entire) economic risks and that more ambitious activities can be put in place. In this context, it is worth noting that research has also shown that, in addition to less costly measures, employers also tend to consider measures that are formulated in collective agreements.

In Chapter 7, J. Brockmann (*Collective Bargaining With Regard To Young Employees: Importance and Challenges*) focuses on collective bargaining with regard to young employees and gives examples of provisions in collective agreements targeting young employees. The role of the social partners and of collective bargaining is clearly emphasised by European policies when it comes to combating youth unemployment and promoting the labour market participation of young employees. By contrast, available data and information on collective bargaining with regard to young employees lead to the conclusion that collective agreements are of rather little importance.

Collective bargaining with regard to young employees' matters can be considered circumstantial. It seems to be complex and difficult to produce win-win situations in reconciling employers' and trade unions' interests. As long as employers do not experience any need in terms of qualifications or attractive labour conditions for young employees, and see their needs fulfilled by the supply side of the labour market, there is little motivation for them to collectively bargain on these matters. On the other hand, it might be attractive for employers to collectively bargain to downgrade labour conditions for young workers, which is particularly unattractive and might be counterproductive for trade unions. The social partners' scope for action might be limited in terms of the current European or national political and legal frameworks. However, facing the risks of young employees in the labour market by contributing to qualification and good quality employment opportunities for young employees can be considered crucial for the future of social partnership.

The last two chapters of the first part are not comparative as such but they are presenting two illuminating national situations of two very sensitive issues: the Multi-Employer situation and the organisation of social dialogue for platform workers.

In Chapter 8, G. Kártyás (*Multi-Employer Situations and Collective Bargaining: The Hungarian Cases*), borrowing from several case studies related to various productive structures (franchise networks, employee sharing, etc.) observed in Hungary, points to the multiple difficulties for workers and their representatives with the development of networks of companies. In particular, it is clear that the freedom accorded to companies to freely structure their activities must not lead, in practice, to depriving employees of their rights to collective bargaining. This presumably presupposes further work to point out the different regulations or existing national practices in a wide range of situations that form the basis of a harmonised approach to the difficulties encountered.

In Chapter 9, C. Nicod, (*Enhancing Working Conditions for Platform Workers through Social Dialogue: The French Example*) explains the French government's strategy towards platform workers. On the one hand, French authorities are convinced that the platform business model would not function if workers were allowed to become salaried employees and benefit from the protections set down by the Labour Code. So far, the French government recognises the need for and value of preserving this existing business model. As a result, they have, over the last few years, made every effort to bolster self-employed status by protecting it from the risk of requalification. On the other hand, they have also granted a number of guarantees for the working conditions and social rights of self-employed platform workers in order to stop platform workers from obtaining legal recognition of their 'employee status'. Among these guarantees, a framework for potential collective negotiations at the sectoral level has been defined in 2021. C. Nicod's conclusion is that '*since the implementation of these provisions, social dialogue between platform workers and platforms has been conducted by different stakeholders under highly varied conditions. Throughout 2022 and 2023, representatives were appointed and discussions held which led to several agreements that helped improve platform workers' working conditions. However, the situation remains unstable for various reasons including a crisis in the legitimacy of those bargaining, insufficient content in the agreements, and, now, the potential impact of the forthcoming European directive on platform work which is to introduce a presumption of employment for platform workers'.*

[B] National Outlook

Each chapter explores how national systems have been able to respond to European injunctions and have also responded to the new challenges posed by the COVID-19 pandemic and the emergence of new themes. These presentations demonstrate once again the extreme diversity of each industrial relations system. Some systems, such as the Austrian system (Chapter 10, E. Brameshuber, *The Continuous Importance of Sectoral Collective Bargaining in Austria*) appear to be unfailingly stable, while the Belgian system seems to be having more difficulty adapting (Chapter 11, F. Kéfer, *Wage moderation measures in times of crisis: the Belgian example*). Others appear to be resilient (Chapter 13, T. Coelho Moreira, *The Revival of Sectoral Collective Bargaining: The Portuguese Experience;* Chapter 15, Y. Maneiro Vázquez and J. M. Miranda Boto, *Collective Bargaining in Spain: The Road goes ever on),* while others appear to be particularly weak (Chapter 12, Ł. Pisarczyk, *Is a Revival of Collective Bargaining Possible? Polish Way from Neoliberalism to the Welfare State*; Chapter 14, F. Rosioru, *Collective Bargaining in Romania: The Aftermath of an Earthquake. A Fresh Start for Social Dialogue?*; Chapter 16, K. Doğan Yenisey, *A Retrospective Look at Turkish Decentralized Collective Bargaining: A Solution to Various Crisis?).*

Part I Comparative Perspectives

CHAPTER 1

From Decentralisation of Collective Bargaining to Re-centralisation of Industrial Relations Systems?

Sylvaine Laulom

Analysis of national developments in labour law since 2008 highlights a common trend: the decentralisation of industrial relations systems. This is a marked trend that is noted by observers of this period across the board: '*Finally, in some countries the crisis resulted in the adoption of new relationships between labour law rules, amounting to a decentralisation of collective bargaining. Company level collective bargaining has gained ground and the normative function of branch level collective agreements has become less important.*'[1]

This finding has been made by several other authors. For example, I. Schömann and S. Clauwaert state that '*a clear policy and/or ambition can be identified in many countries to decentralize collective bargaining, shifting from national/sectoral level to company level. The professed aim is to give businesses more flexibility and help them adjust to labour market conditions*'.[2]

This trend towards decentralisation is not new and predated the 2008 crisis. After World War II, the professional sectoral level was confirmed in many European countries as the favoured level for regulating labour relations and a space structuring labour relations;[3] the first trends towards decentralisation of collective bargaining, in

1. S. Laulom, et al., *How Has the Crisis Affected Social Legislation in Europe?*, ETUI Policy Brief, 2 (2012).
2. S. Clauwaert & I. Schömann, *The Crisis and National Labour Law Reforms: A Mapping Exercise*, ETUI Working paper 04 (2012). *See also* N. Brunn, K. Lörcher & I. Schömann, *The Economic and Financial Crisis and Collective Labour Law in Europe* (Oxford: Hart Publishing 2014).
3. A. Jacobs, *Collective Labour Relations*, in B. Hepple & B. Veneziani (eds), *The Transformation of Labour Law in Europe*, 201-231 (Oxford: Hart Publishing 2009).

particular in terms of regulating working time, appeared in the 1980s and the movement has since intensified, from 2008 onwards in particular.

From this point of view, while widely disseminated rhetoric has highlighted the need for labour market reforms to tackle the crisis, in reality, this is essentially a device permitting the legitimisation of processes already broadly underway prior to 2008. Another aspect of this decentralisation is apparent throughout this period: the emphasis placed hereafter on uncontrolled decentralisation of industrial relations systems at the expense of controlled decentralisation. New articulations of labour law standards have been implemented, granting precedence above all others to standards negotiated at the company level.[4]

These national developments have been broadly encouraged by the European Union (EU), particularly in the context of the 'European Semester'. Comparative studies reveal very varied forms of decentralisation of collective bargaining systems with very different consequences. However, it can be observed that the term decentralisation often masks a situation which is more one of de-collectivisation of labour relationships, namely the absence or rarity of collective regulation of labour relationships at a company level.

In the previous edition, we analysed the effect of these European and national policies on a number of national systems. The conclusion was that the consequences of these policies were far from uniform and that, in the end, the national systems showed a whole range of decentralisation. A few years later, the adoption of the Directive on Adequate Minimum Wages (hereinafter the AMW Directive)[5] constitutes a sharp break from the previous period, placing the emphasis on sectoral collective bargaining as the best means of defining decent wages. The definition of certain working conditions at the company level may still seem relevant when, for example, the issue of working time is at stake.[6] Nevertheless, the fact that the EU now strongly supports sectoral collective bargaining in the determination of minimum wages argues in favour of articulated systems of collective bargaining, where the sectoral level is combined with company levels. But how to rebuild or construct this level of bargaining? That is the challenge facing some EU countries today.

§1.01 THE EUROPEAN CONTEXT: A FUNDAMENTAL CHANGE

While the decentralisation of industrial relations systems was seen by the EU as a response to the 2008 financial crisis and its consequences, the EU is now encouraging Member States to support collective bargaining at the sectoral level.

4. A. Jacobs, *Decentralisation of Labour Law Standard Setting and Financial crisis*, in Hepple & Veneziani (eds), *supra* n. 3.
5. Directive (EU) 2022/2041 of the European Parliament and of the Council of 19 October 2022 on Adequate Minimum Wages in the European Union.
6. *See* in the volume, N. Gundt, Ł. Pisarczyk & K. Wieczorek, *Chapter 5. Negotiating Working Time in Times of Crisis and Twin Transition*, Maastricht University.

[A] A European Answer to the Financial Crisis: Decentralising Collective Bargaining

National developments have been taking place within a European context that strongly supports decentralisation of collective bargaining. Traditionally, and particularly since the 1980s under the leadership of Jacques Delors, the EU has supported action by social partners, in particular European social partners. Article 154 of the Treaty on the Functioning of the European Union (TFEU) which institutionalises the participation of European management and labour in the European decision-making process particularly attests to this support. However, the economic means of governance[7] have been implemented on the whole without any consultation with European social partners, to the extent that in 2013 the European Commission published a communication calling in particular for the strengthening of social dialogue.[8] Above all, these very governance mechanisms have revealed themselves to be formidable instruments of convergence between national policies. One of the consequences of the new economic governance is a massive intrusion into collective bargaining systems, encouraging their decentralisation. To put it simply, national policies in the euro area have not been able to use traditional monetary mechanisms to support national economies and European institutions have put the emphasis on wage restraint or decreasing labour costs to ensure that companies are competitive. The aim of decentralisation of collective bargaining is precisely that: to impact salary negotiations and decrease the cost of labour.[9]

It is within the framework of the European semester, an annual cycle of coordination of economic policies and the main pillar of this new governance, that the European Commission explicitly provides an incentive to Member States to contribute to the decentralisation of collective bargaining.

Each year, the European Commission analyses in detail the plans for Member States' macro-economic and structural budgetary reforms, providing them with recommendations for the following twelve to eighteen months. In this framework, euro

7. The terms of the new European economic governance refer to a set of rules and procedures that have been developed since 2008, but particularly since 2010, aimed at implementing more restrictive coordination of national economic policies. These rules were adopted in the framework of the 'six pack', (Directive 2011/85/EU, of 8 November 2011, on the requirements for budgetary frameworks of the Member States, JOUE, L 306 of 23.11.2011, p. 41), the 'two pack' (Regulation (EU) No. 473/2013, of 21 May 2013, on common provisions for monitoring and assessing draft budgetary plans and ensuring the correction of excessive deficit of the Member States in the euro area, JOUE, L 140 of 27.5.2013, p. 11) and the Treaty on Stability, Coordination and Governance (TSCG) (the TSCG is an intergovernmental agreement, signed by twenty-five Member States excluding the United Kingdom, the Czech Republic and Croatia). The six-pack strengthened the Growth Pact and introduced a new macroeconomic surveillance tool: the procedure on structural imbalances. The two-pack requires Member States in the euro area to submit their draft budget plans in mid-October for the following year, so an examination of budgetary policies can take place at an early stage and the European Commission's guidance can be taken into account prior to the adoption of national budgets.
8. COM(2013) 690 final, *Strengthening the social dimension of the economic and monetary union*, Brussels 2.10.2013.
9. *See* P. Loi, *Decentralisation of Wage Setting Mechanisms and Statutory Minimum Wage: Towards the End of Setoral Collective Bargaining?*, in S. Laulom, *Collective Bargaining in Times of Crises* (Kluwer 2018).

area countries are subject to specific obligations and, in particular, a sanctions mechanism has been defined for States that do not respect the recommendations issued as part of the alert mechanism. There are even greater restrictions for countries where European financial aid is deemed to be indispensable. In exchange for financial loans, these countries have been obliged to bring in major reforms, set out either in 'Memoranda of Understanding', with the troika composed of the EU, the ECB and the International Monetary Fund (IMF) (this is the case for Greece, Ireland and Portugal) or 'Stand-by Arrangements' with the IMF (in the case of Hungary, Lithuania and Romania).[10] Spain, which likewise benefited from aid to support its financial sector, was obliged to commit itself to the implementation of specific national recommendations in the context of the European semester.

All the Member States have therefore been subject to injunctions from the EU, and while the degree of restriction may vary, it is no longer a matter of entirely voluntary recommendations. Analysis of the subject of these recommendations[11] reveals a high number of them fall into the category of social policies. So while the TFEU Treaty explicitly places salaries outside the competence of the EU,[12] salary policy is one of the ongoing concerns of the European semester as salaries are the main adjustment variable for tackling economic imbalances and boosting competitiveness.[13] Taking salary-related action is basically taking action on collective bargaining, and decentralisation of collective bargaining is a central component of the structural reforms to labour markets that Member States are called upon to perform. Company-level collective bargaining, which must be separated from that at a sectoral level, must be encouraged.

Using just a few examples of the pressure brought to bear by the EU on the restructuring of collective bargaining, it is possible to cite the specific recommendations made to the Member States by the European Commission in the context of the European semester.

Thus for France in 2016, the Commission's diagnosis was that: '*the reforms carried out recently only gave employers a few options to derogate from sectoral agreements*'.[14] In Italy's case, the Commission found that '*second-level collective bargaining is not sufficiently widespread in Italy, which hinders the adoption, at a company level, of innovative solutions that could improve productivity and make*

10. D. Natali & B. Vanhercke, (eds), *Bilan social de l'Union européenne 2012, 14th Annual Report*, 190 (Brussels: ETUI, 2013).
11. S. Clauwaert, *The Country-Specific Recommendations (CSRs) in the Social Field. An Overview and Comparison Update Including the CSRs 2014-2015* (Brussels: ETUI, 2014).
12. We should revisit here the terms of Art. 153.5 TFEU under which, '*the provisions of this Article shall not apply to pay, the right of association, the right to strike or the right to impose lock-outs*'. Introduced by the Social Protocol of the Maastricht Treaty, this article excludes salary policies from European policies, at the precise moment when the Economic and Monetary Union is being put into place.
13. D. Natali & B. Vanhercke (eds), *Bilan social de l'Union européenne 2012, 14th Annual Report*, 192 (Brussels: ETUI, 2013).
14. COM (2016) 330 final, Brussels, 15.5.2016, *Recommendation on the 2016 national reform programme of France and delivering a Council opinion on the 2016 stability programme of France*.

salaries more reactive to labour market conditions'.[15] As some countries have never had or no longer have collective bargaining at a sectoral level and some countries have already reformed their system, the Commission does not provide, or no longer provides them with any incentive to carry out reforms in this area. Thus in 2014, the Commission found that the Spanish 2012 reform of the labour market had contributed to *'granting companies greater internal flexibility and limiting job losses, while giving priority to collective agreements at a company level and providing more opportunities for companies to derogate from a collective agreement'*.[16]

While it is difficult to establish direct causality between European recommendations, or more generally the objectives defined by the EU in the context of the European semester, and national legislative policies, it should be noted that the majority of States will sign up for this European scheme and propose reforms that are intended to be structural in terms of labour relations systems, where the aim is their decentralisation.[17]

[B] A New European Objective: Developing Sectoral Collective Bargaining

The AMW Directive, which enshrines the revival of industry-level collective bargaining, is part of a major development in the EU.

After the end of the Barroso Commission, the Juncker Commission certainly represented an important renewal of social Europe, epitomised by the adoption of the European Pillar of Social Rights, proclaimed at Gothenburg on 17 November 2017.

The measures adopted to implement the European Pillar of Social Rights have been numerous and rich in content.[18] The pandemic has not dampened the legislative momentum – quite the contrary.[19] It has prompted specific responses, like the adoption

15. COM (2016) 332 final, Brussels, 18.5.2016.
16. COM (2014) 410 final, Brussels, 2.6. 2014.
17. M.-C. Escande-Varniol, et al. (eds), *Quel droit social dans une Europe en crise?* (Brussels: Larcier, 2012). Clauwaert & Schömann, *supra* n. 2; A. Koukiadaki, I. Tavora & M. Martinez Lucio, *The Transformation of Joint Regulation and Labour Market Policy in Europe During the Crisis, Comparative Project Report* (University of Manchester, 2014). https://research.manchester.ac.uk/en/publications/joint-regulation-and-labour-market-policy-in-europe-during-the-cr, accessed 2 September 2024. *See also*, Conseil d'orientation pour l'emploi, *Les réformes des marchés du travail en Europe* (5 November 2015), https://www.vie-publique.fr/files/rapport/pdf/164000157.pdf, accessed 2 September 2024.
18. The EU has strengthened the legislative framework for posted workers (Directive (EU) 2018/957 of the European Parliament and of the Council of 28 June 2018 amending Directive 96/71/EC concerning the posting of workers in the framework of the provision of services; Regulation (EU) of 20 June 2019 establishing a European Labour Authority), gender equality (Directive (EU) of 29 June 2019 on work-life balance for parents and carers; Directive 2022/2381 of 23 November 2022 on improving the gender balance among directors of listed companies and related measures; Directive (EU) 2023/970 of 10 May 2023 to strengthen the application of the principle of equal pay for equal work or work of equal value between men and women through pay transparency and enforcement mechanisms) and working conditions (Directive (EU) 2019/1152 of 20 June 2019 on transparent and predictable working conditions in the EU).
19. On the European Social Policy during the pandemic, *see* S. Laulom, *Social Europe in Times of COVID-19*, 39(2) IJCLLIR, 159-174 (2023) https://doi.org/10.54648/ijcl2023010.

of the Support to mitigate Unemployment Risks in an Emergency (SURE) programme,[20] and its social consequences certainly reinforced the legitimacy of the directives adopted in highlighting the need for social protection for the most vulnerable workers. It may have encouraged the adoption of certain directives while opening up new fields of action. For example, the explosion of remote work during the pandemic undoubtedly created new workers' needs and called for a response, whether through legislative instruments or collective agreements.[21] Thus for P. Loi, the pandemic and the expansion of digital platform work could explain the change of perspective of the EU institutions as far as the role of sectoral collective agreements in wage setting.[22]

The AMW Directive embodies what many commentators consider to be a paradigm shift in the EU's social policy.[23] The particularity of this directive lies as much in its purpose as in its substance. While wages apparently fall outside the scope of EU social competences, the Directive represents the first-ever EU legislation aimed at ensuring minimum wages. However, before the adoption of the directive, this exclusion did not impede the EU from dealing with wages by the mechanisms of economic governance. From this point of view, the adoption of the directive implies a relocation of wages within social policy and even European social law.[24] The legislator was therefore under considerable pressure to manoeuvre on the margins of EU competence. Nor did the European Commission intend to call into question national systems based on the autonomy of the social partners, which are characterised, as in Sweden, Denmark and Italy, by the absence of a statutory minimum wage. This is one of the reasons why the directive neither defines a general right for all workers in the EU to a minimum wage, nor a specific and identical amount for this minimum wage.

When considering which regulatory sources could better guarantee adequate wages, the Directive clearly makes a preference for sectoral collective bargaining: '*sectoral and cross-industry level collective bargaining is an essential factor for achieving adequate minimum wage protection and therefore needs to be promoted and strengthened*' (recital 16). '*Well-functioning collective bargaining on wage-setting is an*

20. Council Regulation (EU) 2020/672 of 19 May 2020 on the establishment of a European instrument for temporary support to mitigate unemployment risks in an emergency (SURE) following the COVID-19 outbreak. On the SURE programme, *see* in this Volume, Chapter 3, P. Loi, *The Function of Sectoral Collective Agreements and the Risk Approach*.
21. After the European social partners have failed to reach an agreement on telework and workers' right to disconnect at the end of 2023, the European Commission has initiated the legislative procedure to regulate the right to disconnect, https://www.europarl.europa.eu/legislative-train/theme-employment-and-social-affairs-empl/file-al-legislative-proposal-to-the-commission-on-the-right-to-disconnect.
22. *See* in this Volume, Chapter 3, P. Loi, *The Function of Sectoral Collective Agreements and the Risk Approach*.
23. T. Müller & T. Schulten, *The European Minimum Wage Directive: A Milestone for EU Social Policymaking*, in B. Vanhercke, S. Sabato & S. Spasova (eds), *The European Union: State of Play 2023 – An Ambitious Implementation of the Social Pillar* (ETUI, 2024). For a full analysis of the Directive *see*: L. Ratti, E. Brameshuber & V. Pietrogiovanni (eds), *The EU Directive on Adequate Minimum Wages* (Hart 2024).
24. M. Schmitt, *La directive sur les salaires minimaux adéquats, ou la nouvelle politique sociale de l'Union européenne*, 233 RDTEur. (2023). C. Kilpatrick, *The Displacement of Social Europe: A Productive Lens of Inquiry*, 62 European Constitutional Law Review (2018) https://doi.org/10.1017/s1574019618000019.

important means by which to ensure that workers are protected by adequate minimum wages that therefore provide for a decent standard of living. In the Member States with statutory minimum wages, collective bargaining supports general wage developments and therefore contributes to improving the adequacy of minimum wages as well as the living and working conditions of workers. In the Member States where minimum wage protection is provided for exclusively by collective bargaining, their level as well as the share of protected workers are directly determined by the functioning of the collective bargaining system and the collective bargaining coverage. Strong and well-functioning collective bargaining together with a high coverage of sectorial or cross-industry collective agreements strengthen the adequacy and the coverage of minimum wages' (recital 22).

The directive's specificity also lies in its content. It is more like a methodological directive. Its degree of normativity is particularly low, so much so that one might wonder whether it does not borrow more from open methods of coordination and methods of economic governance than from traditional legislative techniques. This is particularly true of its provisions on the promotion of collective wage bargaining at the sectoral level.

The AMW Directive represents a radical departure from the previous period when States were invited to decentralise their collective bargaining systems. The preamble to the directive even implicitly criticises previous policy.[25]

The directive marks a major return to sectoral collective bargaining, which the Member States are invited to develop and support. The very ambitious objective is to achieve a collective bargaining coverage rate of 80%. For those Member States that do not currently meet this threshold, which is the case for most EU countries, an action plan will have to be drawn up, setting out a timetable for concrete measures. This plan will have to be reviewed regularly and communicated to the European Commission. With quantified targets, a timetable, regular national plans and monitoring by the European Commission, the borrowing from open methods of coordination is clear.

§1.02 TOWARDS DECENTRALISATION OF COLLECTIVE NEGOTIATIONS

Comparison of national experiences highlights very varied forms of decentralisation of collective bargaining systems with very different consequences.[26] In this regard, it is possible to distinguish three different groups of countries: those where it is not possible

25. *See* recital 16 of the preamble: '*While strong collective bargaining, in particular at sector or cross-industry level, contributes to ensuring adequate minimum wage protection, traditional collective bargaining structures have been eroding during recent decades, due, inter alia, to structural shifts in the economy towards less unionised sectors and to the decline in trade union membership, in particular as a consequence of union-busting practices and the increase of precarious and non-standard forms of work. In addition, sectoral and cross-industry level collective bargaining came under pressure in some Member States in the aftermath of the 2008 financial crisis. However, sectoral and cross-industry level collective bargaining is an essential factor for achieving adequate minimum wage protection and therefore needs to be promoted and strengthened.*'
26. All references to Austria, Belgium, Hungary, Poland, Portugal, Romania, Spain and Türkiye are taken from the chapters in this volume devoted to the analysis of national situations.

to talk of the decentralisation of a system because it is no longer or has never been centralised, systems where the sectoral level is still strong and finally systems where the State has been heavily involved first in helping to drive the decentralisation of collective bargaining with varying results. The aspect that sometimes distinguishes the second group from the third is the State's role, because a country may maintain a strong role at the sectoral level, while at the same time, the State may implement reforms aimed at decentralisation. This comparison highlights another trend which often masks the use of the term decentralisation: that of the de-collectivisation of industrial relations systems where in reality the absence of actors capable of negotiating at the company level should be observed.

[A] Absence of Decentralisation

The term decentralisation, frequently used to describe national systems of labour relationships, may refer to two distinguishable situations. On one hand, the term evokes the idea of evolution of a system where collective negotiation is relocated to the company level; on the other, the term likewise evokes a state where collective bargaining is to be situated mainly at a company level. Obviously, this is a very simplistic depiction, the degree of evolution, the articulation of the levels and the definition of the negotiation unit may appear in a wide range of configurations from State to State.

Türkiye, the United Kingdom, Hungary and Poland are categorised within the group of fully decentralised collective bargaining systems.[27]

However, it is debatable whether the term decentralisation is the most appropriate to describe the reality of these industrial relations systems. First, collective bargaining at a branch or sectoral level is kept to a minimum and sometimes even non-existent nowadays; consequently, there is no decentralisation of these systems. Second, collective regulation of labour conditions at a company level remains very low.

Thus in the United Kingdom, the challenge to the more centralised system of collective bargaining which took place in the 1980s did not really lead to the development of collective bargaining in private-sector companies where the rate of unionisation was decreasing. Labour conditions are, therefore, increasingly defined by the employer unilaterally, and it is even possible to ask whether collective laissez faire, the famous expression used by O. Kahn Freund to describe the British system of industrial relations,[28] has given way to laissez faire or to a law of the labour market.[29]

In Türkiye, the collective bargaining system has been broadly structured and developed by the State, and since 1982, collective bargaining has only taken place at

27. F. Traxler, *Bargaining (De)centralization, Macro Economic Performance and Control over the Employment Relationship*, 42(1) British Journal of Industrial Relations, 7 (2003) https://doi.org/10.1111/1467-8543.00259.
28. O. Kahn-Freund, *Labour Law*, in M. Ginsberg (ed.), *Law and Opinion in England in the 20th Century* (Stevens 1959).
29. R. Dukes, *The Labour Constitution: The Enduring Idea of Labour Law (Chapter: From Collective Laissez-Faire to the Law of the Labour Market)* (OUP, 2014).

the company level (the establishment, company or group of establishments). The last reforms took place in 2012 and were basically justified by the need to integrate international labour standards, namely International Labour Organization (ILO) Conventions Nos 87 and 98 and Articles 5 and 6 of the European Social Charter revised in 1996. Unlike the majority of Member States of the European Union, the economic situation was not invoked to justify the reforms: '*Nevertheless, despite Türkiye experiencing several economic crises -in 1994, 1999, 2001, 2009, and 2018 onwards it is notable that over the past forty years, collective agreements have not been considered either among the reasons for, or the solutions to, the economic crisis.*' In theory, decentralised bargaining should enable firms to negotiate agreements that reflect their unique circumstances, which could be particularly beneficial during times of rapid change. K. Doğan Yenisey demonstrates that '*instead, the situation in Türkiye reveals a disconnect between the potential flexibility of decentralized bargaining and the reality of rigid structures within the industrial relations framework. The industrial relations framework in Türkiye appears to be more rigid and less adaptive than the decentralized model would imply*'. She also notes '*that even during a humanitarian crisis like the pandemic, the content of collective agreements appears largely unaffected*'. The pandemic has therefore confirmed this lack of flexibility of these enterprise-level collective agreements.

Poland and Hungary demonstrate many common features. In these two countries, as elsewhere in the ten Member States of central and eastern Europe,[30] industrial relations systems are characterised by a low level of unionisation of employees and employers, fragmented and decentralised bargaining, low coverage of collective agreements, and limited bargaining autonomy of both employer associations and trade unions and the situation is not getting better. There are many reasons for this situation. There was no tradition of free collective bargaining during the communist period. Although legislation exists on paper, the practice could be different. This situation has rendered the reform more difficult than expected. Micro, small and medium enterprises dominate making the development of collective bargaining difficult. Like in Türkiye, divisions between and within employers' organisations and the trade union movement can also be an obstacle to the conclusion of collective agreements. In Poland, another obstacle to collective bargaining has been the limitation of its personal scope. Since the 1990s, the right to bargain collectively has been restricted to employees only (with some lesser exceptions). At the same time, the number of people working outside the employment relationship has increased significantly reaching the level of 2 million.

Although legally recognised, collective bargaining has not developed. Consequently, the Hungarian and Polish systems are characterised by the important role of the law in the regulation of labour conditions. As the law remains the main source of labour law due to the marginal role of collective bargaining, the objective of making working conditions more flexible of the neo-liberal agenda has been achieved by law and not by collective agreements. As a result, and '*not surprisingly, the legal framework*

30. *See* in this volume, Chapter 2, T. Gyulavári, *Chasing the Holy Grail? Stumbling Collective Bargaining in Eastern Europe and the Hungarian Experiment* and Chapter 12, L. Pisarczyk, *Is a Revival of Collective Bargaining Possible? Polish Way from Neoliberalism to the Welfare State.*

of collective bargaining has not been perceived as supportive to the development of collective bargaining at both: multi-company as well as company levels'. In Poland, the role of the State has thus been described as 'hostile neutrality'. At the same time, legislation has authorised negotiation of agreements with non-trade union actors, a situation which offers fewer guarantees, and which is likely to weaken trade union representation.

In Hungary like in Poland but with different goals, legislation has more recently intervened with the aim of developing collective bargaining. However, until now, legislative attempts to improve the situation have failed.

In Hungary, labour law was the subject of major reform in 2012 with the adoption of a new Labour Code, the aim of which was to achieve the most flexible employment market in the world. One of the mechanisms for rendering employment conditions more flexible has been the promotion of the role of collective agreements in labour regulations and making it very broadly possible for company collective agreements to derogate from the law, even where this is unfavourable. Nevertheless, the reform also restricted certain trade union rights and shifted several roles from trade unions to works councils. T. Gyulavári notes the failure of the reform, a failure demonstrated by the diminishing of collective agreement coverage. The incentive consists of derogation authorised by law: '*The legislator expected that the wide possibility of in pejus derogations (...) would increase collective agreement coverage, because employers would be motivated to conclude such agreements.*' However, as explained by T. Gyulavári, the reform certainly failed because it focused on only one problem regarding social partners – employer motivation – yet not even this goal was achieved. The employer's motivation has also been hindered by low and decreasing levels of employment protection. There has been no need to conclude collective agreements because the flexibilities allowed by the legislator were important. In addition, the weakening and general decline of trade unions contributed to the shrinking of collective bargaining.

In Poland, on 5 July 2018, the Law amending the Law on Trade Unions and some other laws was adopted. Both the 2018 reform and the anti-pandemic legislation were perceived as a chance to revitalise collective relations. Their results so far have been, however, disappointing. One of the aims of the 2018 reform was to recognise the freedom of association to some independent workers. However, '*The legislator eliminated the most obvious violations of freedom of association. At the same time no significant changes of the procedure of negotiating collective agreements have been adopted. The legislator either considered the extension of freedom of association as a sufficient remedy to the crisis of collective bargaining or was not interested in developing industrial relations. The policy of "hostile neutrality" remained in force*'. '*Taking into account the weakness and passivity of trade unions and reluctance of employers one could expect any improvement in collective bargaining. It is valid especially for collective bargaining for non-employees*'. '*First, the reform has not caused a significant increase in the union membership. The general tendency of decreasing the scope of collective bargaining has not been reversed either. To summarize, the 2018 reform, despite its scope and objective, has not caused an improvement in collective bargaining in Poland.*'

It is obvious that in these countries, the transposition of the Adequate Minimum Wages (AMW) is going to be challenging. For L. Pisarczyk, it will require not only 'new strategies of social partners but also a fundamental reconstruction of the legal framework'. The reconstruction of the legal framework should be adapted to each national situation. However, it is far from certain that national legislators have the political will to undertake such reforms.

[B] Maintaining a Centralised System of Collective Bargaining

Developments in national systems of labour relations and the major incentives that exist with regard to the decentralisation of collective bargaining must not mask the fact that some countries have not undergone such developments, or only to a very limited degree.

Within the range of countries studied, Austria, Germany, Belgium, Sweden and the Netherlands are in this situation, although their systems may be subject to a greater or lesser degree of pressure. These countries are all characterised by the fact that they have maintained a high level of unionisation (even if here once again, this rate might come down) and persistent abstentionism on the part of the State. Above all, the processes of decentralisation that exist remain controlled by high levels of collective bargaining and sectoral salary negotiations are still essential.

Austria is certainly the country where the labour relations system appears the most stable. Sectoral agreements still represent the main level of collective bargaining; it is at this level that minimum salaries are fixed and 95% of employees are covered by agreements at this level. Works councils agreements may only be entered into on matters defined under the law or if the sectoral agreement so authorises and they may not contravene the provisions of sectoral agreements. This is confirmed by E. Brameshuber: '*the Austrian system of sectoral collective bargaining has proved to be quite successful. It leads to a cartelising of wages, with hardly any sector of industry currently offering a minimum wage of less than EUR 1,700/month for a full-time position. The regulatory function of the cartelised wages should not be underestimated either, leading to a de facto perishing of low-performing companies in the long run. By bargaining the wages and working conditions for one sector rather than just a single employer, the employer's position especially is reinforced, thus leading to relatively low strike rates. In this way, the Austrian system provides for a very distinct peace function. Another important feature is its innovation function, which was particularly visible during the crisis of the years 2009/2010 as well as during the COVID-19 pandemic where important decisions to stabilise the labour market were taken at the level of sectoral collective bargaining. Thus, it seems highly unlikely that the system is going to change in the near future*'.

The Swedish system has also traditionally been depicted as a centralised system and this description is still valid, even though nowadays collective bargaining, particularly in relation to salaries, may take place at a decentralised level. '*In Sweden, collective bargaining has traditionally been described as highly centralized. This description is still valid. Nevertheless, the collective bargaining structure also contains significantly decentralized elements – particularly regarding bargaining on wages. The decisive steps towards this partial decentralization of collective bargaining in Sweden was not taken during the crisis years, but mainly in the early 1990s. Furthermore, this partial transition of the collective bargaining system is not a product of political decisions that have been implemented through legislation. Instead the development has taken place in the area of industrial relations, and its outcome has been operationalized in collective agreements.*'[31]

Finally, F. Kéfer notes that '*Belgium social dialogue has largely avoided the phenomenon of decentralisation observed elsewhere in Europe.*' However, the role of the State in wage setting has been much more important than in Austria, for example. '*The stalemate at the intersectoral level has led to increased State interventionism in the decision-making process for wage evolution. A twofold movement, paradoxical, can be observed: on the one hand, wage negotiation is being placed under State supervision, on the other hand, this interventionism is helping to revive social dialogue; indeed, once the margin has been set by the government, the social partners, who have failed to reach an agreement at the intersectoral level, regain control to negotiate the new wage benefits at the sectoral and company levels within the limits of the margin, and this according to their particularities.*'

For these countries, the implementation of the AMW Directive should not pose any particular difficulties. However, even if the Directive states as the rule that the Directive is '*without prejudice to the full respect for the autonomy of the social partners, as well as their right to negotiate and conclude collective agreements*' (Article 1.2),[32] Sweden like Denmark strongly opposed the adoption of the Directive. Bearing in mind the trauma caused by the Laval decision, Sweden fears that the Directive could have an impact on their collective bargaining systems.

[C] Legislative Intervention to Help Drive Decentralisation of Labour Relations Systems

The third group of countries (Italy, Spain, Portugal, Greece, Romania, Slovenia)[33] is characterised by legislative intervention, to a greater or lesser degree, aimed at decentralising industrial relations systems. The movement towards the decentralisation of collective bargaining, in itself, is not a recent phenomenon. What is new is the desire on the part of different regulators to prioritise the company level over the sectoral level as an answer to the financial crisis.

The notable common thread among these countries is the intervention, in some cases massive and in others repeated, by the State. Some reforms have been at the

31. J. Julén Votinius, internal report on Sweden, INLACRIS VS/2014/0532.
32. Furthermore Art. 1(4) stipulates that '*Nothing in this Directive shall be construed as imposing an obligation on any Member State: a) where wage formation is ensured exclusively via collective agreements, to introduce a statutory minimum wage; or b) to declare any collective agreement universally applicable.*'
33. *See* A. Koukiadaki, I. Tavora & M. Martinez Lucio, *Continuity and Change in Joint Regulation in Europe: Structural Reforms and Collective Bargaining in Manufacturing*, 22 European Journal of Industrial Relations, 1 (2016) https://doi.org/10.1177/0959680116643204.

demand of the European institutions, in particular in the context of the Memoranda of Understanding. For example, this is the case with Portugal and Greece. Social partners have sometimes been associated with reforms; however, in the majority of countries studied the main trade union organisations have been opposed to them.

The measures adopted in order to develop company collective bargaining are varied and more often than not a set of measures is adopted and combined. Despite certain specific national characteristics, there are some common traits.

A country's legislation may revise the conditions for signing collective agreements at a sectoral level. This is the case, for example, in Portugal and Romania, where new conditions of representativeness have led to a reduction in the number of agreements entered into at this level. Procedures aimed at extending sectoral agreements may also be reviewed and the options of extension reduced. A limit on the term of the duration of agreements made at a higher level may also be allowed. The favourability principle may be called into question or see its field of application reduced and the regulator may review the articulation of bargaining levels by granting company level the possibility of derogating from higher-level agreements in a way that is unfavourable to employees. The desire to develop collective bargaining at a company level also involves the acknowledgement of new actors in collective bargaining. In this way, elected or ad hoc representatives are sometimes granted the option of negotiating company agreements.

Thus, the State has intervened in the regulations governing articulations between collective agreements and employment contracts to prioritise company agreements.

This State intervention is of a kind to call into question the very collective autonomy of social partners. This is the case particularly when the regulator seeks to impose a certain type of articulation between collective agreement standards themselves, granting precedence to company agreements over sectoral collective agreements. This type of intervention has sometimes even been acknowledged as being contrary notably to basic ILO standards. In 2012, when discussing the reforms made in Greece at the request of several Greek trade union organisations, the ILO Committee on Freedom of Association found '*numerous, significant interventions against the principle of the inviolability of freely concluded collective agreements*' and an extensive deficit of social dialogue. '*The elaboration of procedures systematically favouring decentralized bargaining of exclusionary provisions that are less favourable than the provisions at a higher level can lead to a global destabilization of the collective bargaining machinery and of workers' and employers' organizations and constitutes in this regard a weakening of freedom of association and collective bargaining contrary to the principles of Conventions Nos. 87 and 98.*'[34]

The effects of reforms on these collective bargaining systems are very diverse. Examination of the results of the research carried out by Aristea Koukiadaki brings to light three groups of countries: countries where the collective bargaining system has collapsed (Greece, Romania), countries where the system is being eroded (Portugal,

34. 365th report of the committee on freedom of association, GB316-INS_9-1_[2012-11-0030-01]-Web-Fr.docx http://www.ilo.org/wcmsp5/groups/public/---ed_norm/---relconf/documents/meetingdocument/wcms_193264.pdf, pp. 286 et seq., accessed 4 September 2024.

Spain, Ireland, Slovenia) and countries where the system demonstrates continuity or resilience, such as Italy or France.

One of the major consequences of these reforms has been the sometimes drastic reduction of a sectoral level due both to the contraction of the field of application of sectoral agreements and the contraction of the subjects of negotiation. In Portugal, '*the number of employees covered by collective agreements fell from almost 1.9 million in 2008 to some 246,643 in 2014*'.[35] The conclusion for Portugal is '*the changes in the collective bargaining legal framework during the period of financial assistance did not promote organized decentralisation but a dramatic erosion of sector bargaining and coverage by collective agreements*'. The conclusion for Romania is still more pessimistic: '*The legislative intervention was brutal, without involving the social partners, and has ruined the social dialogue and the system the social partners had managed to build over the two decades, following the fall of communism. Decentralisation of collective bargaining to the lowest level has weakened the social acquis achieved so far by the trade unions at national and local level and affected sectoral collective bargaining. It has also lowered the standard of rights recognised so far, anchored in higher-level collective agreements.*'[36]

Another fairly general consequence and where there has not been parallel development of company-level collective bargaining. We might take Spain as an example. Post 2012, the law granted priority to company agreements. However, the option of negotiating at the company level has not been exercised. One of the reasons for this is related to the specific characteristics of the Spanish industrial base, which is comprised basically of small- and medium-sized companies. The size of the companies means that it is difficult for negotiation to take place at this level. The disappearance or weakening of negotiation space at a sectoral level results in an extension of the employer's unilateral decision-making power. This same observation has been made in Portugal.

Here again, the consequences of the change in European policy towards sectoral collective bargaining are varied. With the exception of Romania, in the other countries, the sectoral level has never disappeared and has rather remained at a more or less high level. The legislator has also been able to intervene to define more favourable measures for this level of negotiation.

In Portugal, since 2015 the government has been seeking to strengthen sectoral bargaining and the country has seen an increase in the number of agreements signed at this level, which has not been the case since 2012. This development can be supported by legislation whose objective has evolved to support the actions of the social partners. T. Coelho Moreira shows that '*the traditional tripartite concertation involving the government, employers, and trade unions is as a key framework supporting collective bargaining in Portugal*'. '*Legislative changes and historical resilience have fortified*

35. T. Coelho Moreira, *The Revival of Sectoral Collective Bargaining: The Portuguese Experience*, in S. Laulom (ed.), *Collective Bargaining in Times of Crisis* (Kluwer 2018).
36. F. Rosioru, *Collective Bargaining in Romania: The Aftermath of an Earthquake*, in S. Laulom (ed.), *Collective Bargaining in Times of Crisis* (Kluwer 2018).

collective bargaining mechanisms, ensuring their adaptability and continuity in the face of economic and social fluctuations'.

The situation is very different in Romania. The reforms introduced in 2011 have undermined an already weakened industrial relations system. However, a recent reform aims at reversing the situation. The main objectives of the Social Dialogue Act, adopted at the end of 2022, are to promote substantial and timely collective bargaining, to strengthen the role of social dialogue, particularly in wage setting, to encourage the participation of social partners in this process and to ensure consultations between the social partners and by the legislator. The legislative changes are very complex and the new regulation is too recent to assess its effectiveness or to highlight a visible improvement of social dialogue in Romania, a country where, currently, collective bargaining coverage is low and collective agreement usually contains very limited supplementary rights for the workers. Given the Social Dialogue Act's specific objectives to improve social dialogue and to enhance the capacity of social partners to engage in informed, substantial and timely collective bargaining, including on wage setting, the transposition of Directive 2022/2041 on AMW in the EU might constitute the relevant test to assess the practical relevance of the new regulation on social dialogue.

§1.03 CONCLUSION

In many EU Member States, the 2008 crisis provided grounds for a rarely equalled level of state intervention in the regulation of labour relations with an explicit aim: the decentralisation of collective bargaining. This movement began long before the crisis, but without a doubt intensified from 2008 onwards. However, the EU now recognises that when it comes to wages, it is the sectoral level that is best placed to guarantee a decent level of pay for employees, particularly the most precarious. These developments are not without their contradictions and they call into question the role that the State can or must play in the field of labour relations.

Traditionally, the State has intervened by means of various measures to support collective autonomy and favour an environment conducive to the development of collective bargaining. During 2008, State interventionism which, as we have seen, could be particularly intense, took new forms. It was not so much a matter of supporting actors and helping to drive collective agreement-making activity, as allowing businesses to conclude a certain type of agreement and take action with regard to the structures and indeed content of collective bargaining. The majority of reforms were of little interest to actors in collective bargaining, other than, in the absence of union organisations within the business, in terms of allowing negotiation with other actors without really giving them the means to engage in balanced negotiations.

The consequences of these policies had not been uniform. The decline in coverage by collective agreement can be dramatic, as has been the case in Greece and Romania. The main lesson is that the decline in the regulation of working conditions by the professional sector has not been twinned with the development of collective bargaining at a company level and that decentralisation that is not sector-led generally leads to the absence of a collective agreement, namely a de-collectivisation of labour relations. Today this is the situation in which Poland and Hungary find themselves.

In 2018, I concluded that '*In this context, comparative analysis indicates that another path could be taken by national policies which would consist in engaging in reflection on how best to develop and support the sector level. Changes in productive organisations that are currently taking place, which see the development of small and very small businesses, networked businesses and work via digital platforms likewise suggest this is the right approach.*' T. Gyulavári and L. Pisarczyk also conclude their analyses with the need to rebuild a collective bargaining system. There is no doubt that this reconstruction will require multiple, complex measures over a long period of time and that the outcome is far from certain. As a result, the question is necessarily raised as to the evolution of labour rights in the absence of collective regulation of labour conditions. The process of decentralisation has more often than not led to an extension of the employer's unilateral power where salaries and labour conditions are ever more frequently determined by direct negotiations between employer and employees, with the State becoming the sole guarantor of employee protection. Paradoxically, there is no certainty that the flexibilities sought by companies are necessarily achieved, except in terms of extending the employer's unilateral powers still further.

With the adoption of the AMW Directive, the EU, for the first time, is adopting an auxiliary legislation, i.e., legislation whose primary objective is to support the development of collective bargaining. Comparing the different systems also demonstrates the variety of national situations and the fact that each system is rooted in a specific historical socio-economic reality. From this perspective, what works in one country does not necessarily work in another. The directive itself takes account of this fact, leaving Member States a great deal of freedom. Its modus operandi, which looks like the open methods of coordination, with the obligation for Member States with a collective bargaining coverage rate below 80% to establish an action plan to promote collective bargaining to progressively increase the collective bargaining coverage rate, shall allow every Member States to take into account national tradition and practice. National Social Partners should also be involved in the drafting of these action plans. The fact remains that building a comprehensive system of collective bargaining is a difficult task, requiring multifactorial action and a clear determination on the part of both the legislator and the social partners.

A final question arises. The EU is not immune to a new reversal, which would see a return to austerity policies that are much less favourable to collective bargaining. While social Europe has always known good times and bad, a return to the policies that followed the 2008 crisis should not be an option. First, because the policies implemented during this period have proved ineffective and dangerous. Second, because new challenges caused by the green and digital transition cannot ignore the need to involve workers in the process of social transformation. Finally, because the recognition of sectoral collective bargaining is now enshrined in a legal instrument.

CHAPTER 2

Chasing the Holy Grail? Stumbling Collective Bargaining in Eastern Europe and the Hungarian Experiment

Tamás Gyulavári[*]

While industrial relations in central and eastern Europe exhibit certain differences across the ten European Union (EU) Member States, this group of post-socialist countries have many important things in common, such as the predominance of decentralised wage bargaining,[1] a low density of social partners and sparse collective agreement coverage. Hungary has long been an excellent example of all these attributes, since trade union membership and collective bargaining are low and declining, and sectoral collective bargaining hardly exists.

The new Hungarian Labour Code of 2012 therefore sought to increase the role of collective agreements in regulating employment relationships. Free derogation from the Labour Code was designed as the central measure to motivate employers to conclude collective agreements. Nevertheless, the reform restricted certain trade union rights and shifted several roles from trade unions to works councils. Diminishing collective agreement coverage shows the failure of the Hungarian experiment to increase collective agreement coverage by means of a single legal incentive.

This paper analyses first the attributes of industrial relations in central and eastern Europe, second the Hungarian situation, and third the details of the 2012 reform of Hungarian collective labour law. The central issue of the paper is whether the present low level of collective bargaining coverage might be increased at all in central

* The author is grateful to Erzsébet Berki, Gábor Kártyás, Barbara Kresal, Sylvaine Laulom, László Neumann, Lukasz Pisarczyk, Imre Szabó and Felicia Rosioru for their comments on the first edition of this chapter.

1. L. Funk & H. Lesch, *Industrial Relations in Central and Eastern Europe: Organisational Characteristics, Codetermination and Labour Disputes*, Intereconomics, 264 (September/October 2004).

and eastern European (hereinafter CEE) countries[2] – and if so, what reform measures could and could not work.

§2.01 WHY IS COLLECTIVE AGREEMENT COVERAGE LOW IN CEE COUNTRIES?

During the communist period, collective bargaining was not an essential mechanism for setting terms and conditions of employment. Generally, the state determined wages directly by wage scales, or indirectly by regulations. In countries such as Hungary and Poland (where there was a degree of decentralisation), limited collective bargaining at the company level took place, but, for instance, in Romania, there was no tradition of voluntary collective bargaining.[3] Moreover, sector-level bargaining never played an important role in most of the CEE countries before 1990, as collective bargaining had always taken place mainly at the company level.[4] For instance, in Poland before 1989 there was a system of sectoral collective agreements. They covered a large number of branches and employees. However, they were not a result of 'real' social dialogue (official trade unions were strictly connected with the political regime). After 1989, the whole structure collapsed and social partners were not encouraged to launch autonomous negotiations or to create a system of normal collective agreements.

Consequently, collective bargaining was a relatively new feature of the transitional model and was generally supported by a legal framework shortly after the political changes.[5] However, the absence of real collective bargaining before 1990 has rendered the reform in CEE countries more difficult than expected. Since the beginning of the 1990s, there have been repeated attempts to advance towards free collective bargaining. Although legislation exists on paper, actual practice is quite different, as collective agreements are still limited in number and the process is also often far from a dialogue of autonomous and independent social partners, as is common in western Europe.[6]

One indicator of the importance of collective bargaining is the proportion of employees affected by it – namely its coverage. Across the EU as a whole, more than six out of ten employees (61%) are covered by collective bargaining, although there are important variations between countries. Collective bargaining coverage is on average much lower in the EU-10 (CEE countries)[7] than in the EU-15 (Italy 97%, Austria 94%,

2. The CEE countries are defined in this paper exclusively as those joining the EU in 2004 (Czech Republic, Estonia, Hungary, Latvia, Lithuania, Poland, Slovakia, Slovenia), in 2007 (Bulgaria and Romania) and in 2013 (Croatia).
3. A. Trif, *Collective Bargaining in Eastern Europe: Case Study Evidence from Romania*, 13 European Journal of Industrial Relations, 241 (2007/2) https://doi.org/10.1177/0959680107078256.
4. *Industrial Relations in Europe 2010*, European Commission, 131 (2011).
5. J. Thirkell, R. Scase & S. Vickerstaff, *Changing Models of Industrial Relations in Eastern Europea and Russia*, in J. Thirkell, R. Scase & S. Vickerstaff (eds), *Labour Relations and Political Change in Eastern Europe: A Comparative Perspective*, 20 (London: UCL Press 2005).
6. G. Casale (ed.), *Social Dialogue in Central and Eastern Europe*, 17-20 (Budapest: ILO 1999).
7. Supplemented by the new CEE Member State, Croatia (EU-11 after 2013).

Spain 91%, Finland and France 90%, Sweden 89%).[8] Nevertheless, the coverage of collective agreements varies in CEE countries, from below 6% in Estonia to 79% in Slovenia,[9] where collective agreements were mandatory before 2006.[10] We find eight CEE countries in the last ten:

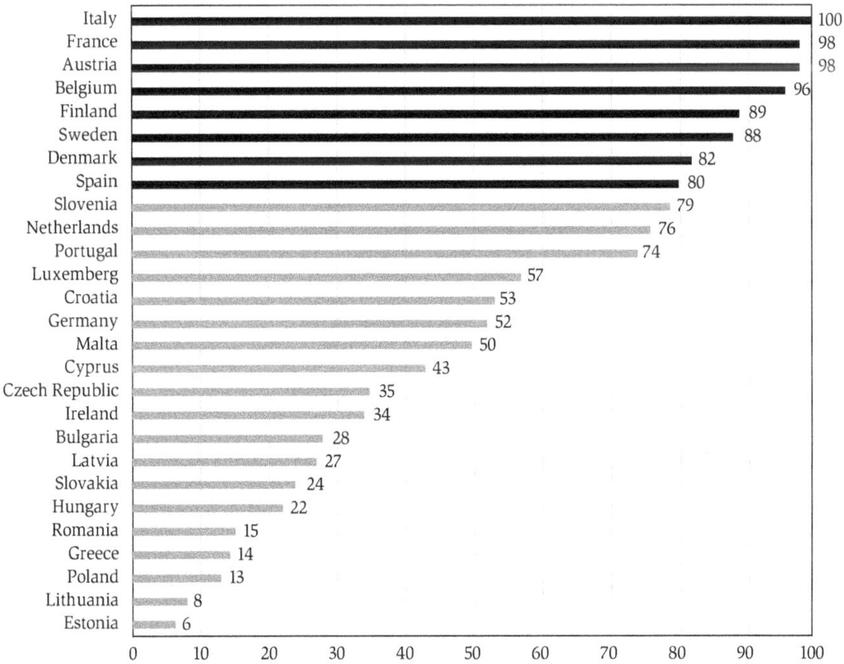

Source: OCED-AIAS ICTWSS database (ETUI, Minimum-wages directive – history in the making. 2022, https://www.etui.org/news/minimum-wages-directive-history-making).

The low(est) coverage in CEE countries, and the practical lack of it in some, is associated with several reasons, such as the decentralised (company-based) structure of collective bargaining and low level of organisation of employees and employers alike.[11] In the countries with low coverage, it is bargaining at company level that predominates. Almost by definition, company-level bargaining depends on union activity at the company level and is therefore more closely related to levels of union density. Divisions between and within employers' organisations and the trade union movement are also at the root of the failure to build an efficient system of collective bargaining. Employers in particular are often reluctant to negotiate with trade unions

8. Eurofound, *Collective Bargaining Coverage*, 15 December 2022, https://www.eurofound.europa.eu/en/european-industrial-relations-dictionary/collective-bargaining-coverage.
9. OECD, *Collective Bargaining Coverage*, https://stats.oecd.org/index.aspx?DataSetCode=CBC.
10. Trif, *supra* n. 3, 241.
11. Funk & Lesch, *supra* n. 1, 267.

in CEE countries.[12] Collective bargaining in the new Member States has actually declined with EU accession, at the company as well as sector level. In Poland, for instance, the decline in coverage has been constant: from 25% in 2000 to 18.9% in 2007 and 13.4% in 2019.[13]

As has already been mentioned above, the absolute lack or at least very weak presence of sector-level bargaining has always been a basic feature of collective bargaining in the CEE countries,[14] except Croatia, Slovenia and Romania.[15] However, in Romania collective bargaining was forcibly decentralised in 2011, resulting in a coverage rate that fell from 98% in 2011 to 35% after 2011, and as low as 15% in 2019.[16] Consequently, Slovenia and Croatia are the only present examples of considerable coverage in the entire region, however, even they do not reach the 80% threshold set by the Minimum Wage Directive in relation to special policy obligations.[17] In general, collective bargaining is most commonly practised at the enterprise level in CEE. Although there have been legislative attempts in several countries to promote collective bargaining at the industry level, the development of such bargaining is impeded by the lack of well-structured organisations on both sides of the industry and the lack of motivation on the employer side.[18] Industry-wide wage agreements tend to be most common in branches with monopolistic or oligopolistic structures, such as the energy sector and the railways.[19]

Evidently, trade union density is regarded as an important indicator of the ability of unions to negotiate collective agreements. Since 1990, trade union membership has decreased considerably in the post-socialist states, despite the reform of the previous communist employee associations and the founding of new ones. This development can largely be explained, first, by the revocation of the obligation to belong to a union; second, by the increase in unemployment; and third, by the increasing number of small and medium-sized enterprises that resulted from privatisation.[20]

Recent economic changes have also greatly contributed to dismantling representation on both sides of industry. The world of business has generally been transformed in the direction of a multitude of small and medium-sized enterprises in services. Small business structures have replaced the previously dominant corporate entities. Trade union presence is not merely fragmented, but largely non-existent in these new

12. Casale (ed.), *supra* n. 6, 17.
13. OECD, *Collective Bargaining Coverage*, https://stats.oecd.org/index.aspx?DataSetCode=CBC.
14. *See*, for example, Poland (P. Grzebyk, *Legal Position of Trade Unions in Polish Collective Labour Law: Enterprise-Based Trade Union*, Hungarian Labour Law E-Journal, 73-86 (2014/1)), http://www.hllj.hu.
15. G. Meardi, *Social Pacts: A Western Recipe for Central and Eastern Europe?, Warsaw Forum of Economic Sociology*, 2(3), 73-87. Retrieved from https://econjournals.sgh.waw.pl/wfes/article/view/446.
16. Eurofound, *Collective Bargaining in Europe in the 21st Century*, Luxembourg, 2015, https://www.eurofound.europa.eu/en/publications/2015/collective-bargaining-europe-21st-century, 42 (accessed 8 February 2017).
17. Directive (EU) 2022/2041 of the European Parliament and of the Council of 19 October 2022 on adequate minimum wages in the European Union. OJ L 275, 25.10.2022, pp. 33-47.
18. Casale (ed.), *supra* n. 6, 18.
19. Funk & Lesch, *supra* n. 1, 266.
20. *Ibid.*, pp. 264-265.

structures, with the exception of formerly state-owned larger companies. Given the large number of non-union companies and even non-union sectors (also lacking employers' associations), the essential conditions for collective bargaining are missing.[21]

Since 2000, trade union density has declined throughout the EU. However, the trend towards dwindling employee unionisation has been more pronounced in the CEE countries, for instance, in Estonia from 14% in 2000 to 6% in 2019.[22] The causes are manifold. In addition to the general trend towards de-industrialisation, growing unemployment and extensive migration to western Europe, legal obstacles to the recognition of trade unions, lack of institutional support of unions in key policy fields such as collective bargaining, and the marginalisation of unions in political decision-making all contribute to unions' waning organisational power.[23]

On the employers' side, a weakness in the industry associations can be observed. The main reasons for this are the short tradition of private employers in CEE, rivalries between different associations, and the structural changes in the economy.[24] Employers are more strongly organised in western Europe than in the EU-10. Organisational strength is very limited, for instance, in Poland, Hungary and Slovakia, although with a higher coverage rate than for trade unions.[25]

In consequence, industrial relations in the CEE countries (with very few exceptions like Slovenia) are characterised by weak employers' organisations and trade unions, fragmented and decentralised bargaining, and limited bargaining autonomy of both employer associations and trade unions.[26] Central and eastern European industrial relations contrast with the prevalent continental European, Scandinavian, and even Anglo-Saxon industrial relations models, although the latter is relatively close to the eastern European type in some respects. Kohl argues that a separate CEE transition model of industrial relations can thus be identified, distinct from other typologies dominant in the EU. While the initial situations may have been comparable, the results of social dialogue and union activities are clearly disparate.[27]

§2.02 DEVELOPMENT OF COLLECTIVE BARGAINING IN HUNGARY

In Hungary before 1990, the socialist Labour Code[28] and its many implementing decrees played the ultimate role in the regulation of both private and public employment relationships. Collective agreements could deviate from the Labour Code if the

21. H. Kohl, *Where Do Trade Unions Stand in Eastern Europe Today? Stock-Taking after EU Enlargement*, Internationale Politik und Gesellschaft, 111 (2008), http://library.fes.de/pdf-files/ipg/ipg-2008-3/09_a_kohl_gb.pdf (accessed 20 July 2017).
22. OECD, *Trade Union Dataset*, https://stats.oecd.org/Index.aspx?DataSetCode=TUD.
23. V. Glassner, *Central and Eastern European Industrial Relations in the Crisis: National Divergence and Path-Dependent Change*, *supra* n. 9, 160-161.
24. Funk & Lesch, *supra* n. 1, 264-265.
25. OECD Employment Outlook 2017, p. 136, https://read.oecd-ilibrary.org/employment/oecd-employment-outlook-2017_empl_outlook-2017-en#page138.
26. *Ibid.*, p. 158.
27. Kohl, *supra* n. 21, 112.
28. Act 2 of 1967.

few provisions specifically allowed it. Employment law was, therefore, *ius cogens* (as the main rule) and collective bargaining was in fact neglected.

In marked contrast, the 1992 Labour Code[29] in the newly regulated market economy aimed at providing statutory minimum standards that could be substituted and supplemented by collective agreements. Thus, collective agreements were designed to play a more important or even a substantial role in employment regulation. However, it was acknowledged, that both workplace and higher-level collective agreements would be concluded only slowly and gradually over a longer time. Thus, the adoption of the 'in favour principle', allowing only *in melius* derogations, filled the potential gap and cogent rules remained an exception.[30] *In pejus* derogation also existed in principle, though only within a marginal range. Sectoral collective bargaining was not specifically regulated by the Labour Code, but a separate law[31] regulated sectoral dialogue committees much later in 2009, which could conclude sectoral-level agreements.

Collective agreement coverage has been among the lowest in the EU at around 30% in recent decades,[32] without huge changes. There used to be a fairly high coverage of company agreements in an eastern European comparison, but case studies reveal that only a small proportion functioned as in developed market economies. Many company agreements are still far from being genuine negotiated agreements but are either defined unilaterally by the employer or, following state socialist traditions, simply repeat the law.[33]

Latest data reveals a slowly, but constantly shrinking coverage, which is presently around 20% concentrated at the company level.[34] The new coverage level, reflecting a decline in collective bargaining, is really one of the lowest in the EU.[35]

29. Act 22 of 1992 on the Labour Code.
30. Gy. Berke, *A munkaviszonyra vonatkozó szabályok (Regulation of employment)*, in Gy. Kiss, Gy. Berke, Z. Bankó & E. Kajtár (eds), *Emlékkönyv Román László születésének 80.* Évfordulójára, 68-70 (Pécs: PTE 2008).
31. Act 74 of 2009 on Sectoral Dialogue Committees.
32. In 2000 it was even as high as 51%, including all levels of collective agreements (L. Neumann, *Does Decentralised Collective Bargaining Have an Impact on the Labour Market in Hungary?*, 1 European Journal of Industrial Relations, 11-12 (2003)).
33. *Ibid.*, p. 12.
34. E. Berki, *Kollektív szerződések Magyarországon* (2012-2023), in T. Gyulavári & G. Kártyás, *A kollektív szerződéses lefedettség csökkenése Magyarországon 2012-2023*, 15 (2023), https://www.researchgate.net/publication/374675244_.
35. Eurofound comparative data: http://www.worker-participation.eu/National-Industrial-Relations/Across-Europe/Collective-Bargaining2 (accessed 25 January 2017).

Table 2.1 Rate of Employees under the Scope of Workplace Level Collective Agreements (% of All Employees)

	2014	*2015*	*2016*	*2017*	*2018*
Coverage of employees	24.59%	25.84%	25.99%	22.14%	18.18%

Source: Berki, *Kollektív szerződések Magyarországon* (2012-2023) In: T. Gyulavári & G. Kártyás, *A kollektív szerződéses lefedettség csökkenése Magyarországon 2012-2023*, p. 15, https://www.researchgate.net/publication/374675244, p. 16.

In spite of the establishment and detailed regulation of sectoral dialogue committees, sectoral collective bargaining has lacked vitality since 1990 and even after 2009 in Hungary. Just as in Poland,[36] if there is a collective agreement, it is typically concluded at workplace level. There have been only a few collective agreements with an extended scope over a sector. These agreements are concluded in sectors with a strong sectoral trade union and a smaller number of employers' organisations, such as construction, bakery, catering and electrical supply industries.[37] Such agreements do not regulate wages effectively, anyway, not only because their coverage is small but also because their contents are weak and the guarantees of implementation are doubtful.[38] However, even these sectoral agreements are not presently in force.

There are several related reasons explaining the weak regulatory function of collective agreements in Hungary. First, mass privatisation hampered the spread of collective agreements. The end of the socialist economic model based on large, state-owned 'socialist firms' considerably weakened trade unions and their capacity to enforce collective bargaining in the new private companies.[39] As a result of privatisation and economic changes, micro, small and medium workplaces became the dominant employers, presently accounting for over 70% of employees,[40] and the enforcement of the Labour Code is generally problematic in these workplaces.[41] Furthermore, it has not been feasible to conclude a collective agreement in the small firms due to the lack of trade unions and the strict rules of the former Labour Code on trade union representation.[42]

36. Grzebyk, *supra* n. 14.
37. Sz. Soósné Csikós, *A kollektív szerződés lefedettségi rátáját meghatározó tényezők*, Acta Juridica et Politica, PTE, Szeged, 31 (2005).
38. Neumann, *supra* n. 32, 12.
39. T. Laky, L. Neumann & D. Boda, *A privatizáció foglalkoztatási hatásai (Employment effects of privatization)* (Budapest, 2001).
40. Central Statistical Office (KSH), *A kis- és középvállalkozások helyzete hazánkban (Situation of small and medium enterprises)*, Statisztikai Tükör, 2 (2013/108), http://www.ksh.hu/docs/hun/xftp/stattukor/kkv12.pdf (accessed 17 January 2017).
41. T. Laky, *Az atipikus foglakozásokról (Atypical employment)* 14. http://docplayer.hu/932249-Laky-terez-az-atipikus-foglakozasokrol.html.
42. Article 33 of the 1992 Labour Code.

Evidently, trade union activity and collective bargaining are confined to companies of over 1,000 (75% coverage) or 500 employees (67%), but it is almost non-existent for those under 50 (11%) and particularly below 20 workers (0.1%).[43] Trade unions have been gradually confined to large state-owned (e.g., National Railways, Budapest Transport Company) and large, mostly multinational companies (e.g., Audi, GE, MOL). The weakness and decline of the Hungarian trade union movement can be explained by a set of factors, such as inadequate financial, scientific and organisational background, dependence on state support, service-oriented activities and low organisational potential of the society.[44] Trade unions are now old and tired, without new members even in their traditional fields, and more and more struggle to reach the 10% density required to conclude a collective agreement at many employers.

Figure 2.1 Trade Union Membership in Hungary (2001-2020)

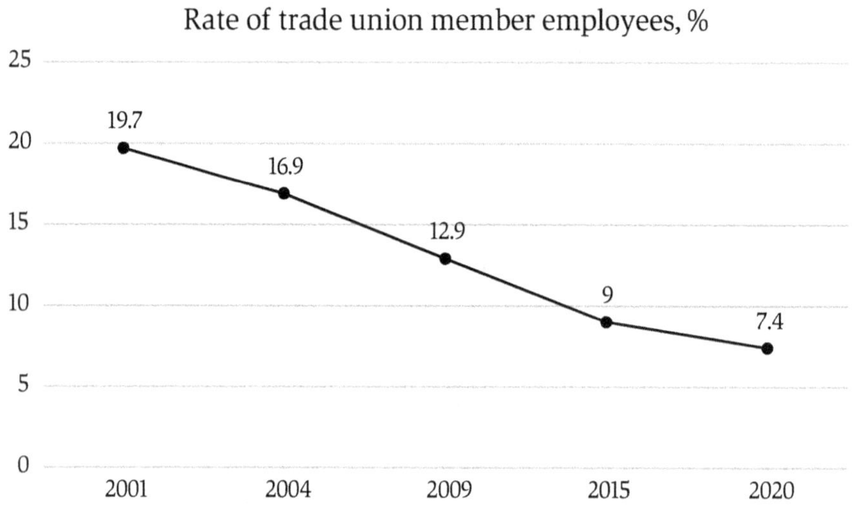

Source: Berki, *Kollektív szerződések Magyarországon* (2012-203) In: T. Gyulavári & G. Kártyás, *A kollektív szerződéses lefedettség csökkenése Magyarországon 2012-2023*, p. 15, https://www.researchgate.net/publication/374675244, p. 7.

43. Soósné Csikós, *A kollektív szerződés lefedettségi rátáját meghatározó tényezők, supra* n. 37, 48. Although this data is rather old, however, the problem is unchanged.
44. I. Krén, *A szakszervezetek helyzete Magyarországon (Situation of Trade Unions in Hungary)* 5 (Budapest: Friedrich Ebert Stiftung 2012).

However, the employers' side is also voluntary[45] and poorly organised.[46] Moreover, employers and their organisations have not been motivated by flexible employment regulation since 1990, which has even been 'further flexibilised' by the 2012 Labour Code (*see* table below). Before 2012, the old Labour Code allowed deviation via collective agreements to the benefit of employees (*see* details later). Therefore, employers were supposedly not really interested in amending the statutory rules if it meant employment conditions less favourable to them. Since the new Labour Code provides an even more flexible legal environment and free deviation from statutory provisions, employers seem to be rather satisfied with statutory minimums and thereby neglect derogations by collective agreement(s).[47]

As should be clear from the development of Hungarian collective bargaining, it is extremely difficult to reach tangible results without strong, prepared and motivated partners on both sides. On the employee side, we find weak, poor and declining trade unions that are motivated to conclude collective agreements, yet seem unable to achieve them. As for employers, they are in fact also poorly organised and not motivated by flexible labour law. Consequently, existing collective bargaining is restricted to large state-owned and multinational companies. However, the quality and practical effect of these existing agreements is somewhat questionable.

Therefore, the constant support of legal, institutional and financial strength of trade unions and employers' organisations is a precondition for an efficient national collective bargaining system. As a whole, the Hungarian model is an excellent illustration of the weaknesses and failures of collective bargaining in central and eastern Europe. Despite some national peculiarities, Hungary has a declining trade union movement, an undeveloped employers' organisation, respectively low collective agreement coverage and a recently flexibilised employment protection framework.[48]

45. Since 1 January 2012, companies and entrepreneurs have had to register at the relevant chamber of commerce. This mandatory registration costs an annual registration fee, but does not provide the same rights and obligations as those of full members of chambers. Employer organisations were hostile to the mandatory registration, since it does not give companies any benefit and could simply be considered a tax. It weakens companies' willingness to join employer organisations, which are based on the freedom of association (Eurofound 2017).
46. Eurofound, *Hungary Working Life Country Profile: Actors and Institutions*, https://www.eurofound.europa.eu/en/resources/article/2024/working-life-hungary (accessed 19 January 20 17). This figure is much lower, than the 40% indicated in table above in the first chapter.
47. Employers may be a party to workplace and also higher (sectoral, subsectoral) level collective agreements.
48. By contrast, in the Czech Republic there has been no significant attempt to reduce existing legal protection of employee or trade union rights, even under right-wing governments (Sz. Borbély & L. Neumann, *Similarities and Diversity in the Development of Wages and Collective Bargaining in Central and Eastern European Countries: A Comparison of Hungary, Slovakia and the Czech Republic*, in G. Van Gyes & Th. Schulten (eds), *Wage Bargaining under the New European Economic Governance*, 197-198 (Brussels: ETUI 2015)).

§2.03 LEGAL REFORM TO INCREASE COLLECTIVE AGREEMENT COVERAGE: 'FREE DEROGATION'

[A] Farewell to 'In Favour Principle'

The 'in favour principle' (Günstigkeitsprinzip, inderogability)[49] governs the relationship between law and collective agreements.[50] It means that legislation takes precedence over contractual regulation, as far as stipulations *in pejus* are concerned. This limitation on the freedom of contract of course is the very purpose and function of protective labour legislation. On the other hand, contracted provisions *in melius* have priority over statutory minimums.[51] Accordingly, collective agreements can in principle modify the law only *in melius* and not *in pejus* – i.e., they can only provide terms more favourable for employees. However, this general rule is usually subject to various levels of exceptions in national laws: the legislator frequently authorises collective agreements to derogate *in pejus* from certain statutory terms, sometimes with a limit.[52]

In the EU Member States, the 'in favour principle' is generally applied to deviation from the law by a collective agreement. However, Member States are divided into two clusters regarding *in pejus* derogations. In one group of Member States, only *in melius* deviations are allowed (from dispositive rules) for collective agreements, but in the other group, *in pejus* derogations are also possible from some (limited number of) statutory provisions. CEE countries adopted the German 'in favour principle' after 1990,[53] but legislation later gradually relaxed this strict rule by allowing *in pejus* derogations from some rules[54] of the Labour Code in some CEE countries (e.g., Czech Republic, Hungary, Slovakia and Slovenia).[55] At the same time, free (*in melius* and also *in pejus*) derogation has been a generally unknown hierarchy of labour law sources in the EU.

In Hungary, the 'in favour principle' was first adopted by the 1992 Labour Code, which meant a fundamental change at that time (*see* above). In the 1992 Labour Code, there were three kinds of exceptions to the general rule of *in melius* derogation. First, several provisions stated that any alteration to it is null and void (*ius cogens*). Second,

---

49. M. Freedland & N. Kountouris, *The Legal Construction of Personal Work Relations*, 151 (Oxford: Oxford University Press, 2011).
50. It may be assessed in relation to derogations by an employment contract as well, however, this context is not analysed here.
51. S. Evju, *The Relationship Between State Law, Collective Agreement and Individual Contract*, in Gy. Kiss (ed.), *Recent Developments in Labour Law* 21 (Budapest: Akadémiai Kiadó, 2013).
52. Italy is a good example for this system: T. Treu, *Labour Law in Italy*, 203 (The Netherlands: Kluwer Law International 2011).
53. Borbély & Neumann, *supra* n. 48, 196.
54. For instance, in Slovakia amendments to the Labour Code introduced in 2011 permitted collective agreements to worsen legal provisions in some areas, such as probation periods and overtime arrangements. However, the government elected in 2012 rejected these changes (*Ibid.*, p. 196.).
55. *Study on the characteristics and legal effects of agreements between companies and workers' representatives.* Final Report, DG Employment, Social Affairs & Inclusion, 2011, http://ec.europa.eu/social/main.jsp?catId=707&langId=en&intPageId=214, pp. 28-30 (accessed 20 July 2017).

the Labour Code in later amendments exceptionally allowed collective agreements to deviate to the detriment of employees (*in pejus*) from a few provisions, and the amendments to the Labour Code slightly increased the number of these derogations after the main harmonisation package in 2001 (e.g., on working time).[56] Third, there were statutory provisions which allowed for *in pejus* derogation only to a limited extent (e.g., maximum yearly hours of overtime).

The new Labour Code came into effect on 1 July 2012, replacing the previous law after twenty years.[57] Reorganisation of the hierarchy of labour law sources was the central element of the reform since rigidity of labour law was partly explained by low collective agreement coverage, which was attributed to the missing interest of employers by the government. The main aim of this conceptual change was, therefore, to enhance the role of collective agreements by radically widening the possibility of *in pejus* deviations from the Labour Code to make collective bargaining more attractive for employers.

Above all, the general rule was changed, since collective agreements may now derogate from most of the rules on both individual labour law[58] and collective labour law,[59] also to the detriment of employees (*in pejus* as well).[60] There are over fifty provisions allowing both *in melius* and *in pejus* derogation for collective agreements from the Labour Code. However, there are still three exceptions to this general rule (called 'absolute dispositivity'):

(a) Above all, there are over thirty cogent rules which do not allow any deviation (*ius cogens*). Only the second and third parts (Part 2 on employment relationships and Part 3 on collective labour relations) of the Labour Code are dispositive; all the other parts (Part 1 on general provisions, Part 4 on labour disputes and Part 5 on closing provisions)[61] are *ius cogens* (not any derogation allowed). Moreover, the general provisions concerning industrial relations and the rules on works councils within the third part of the Labour Code are also *ius cogens*.[62]
(b) Only *in melius* derogation is allowed by certain provisions (called 'relative dispositivity') – for example, in the entire chapter covering employer liability for damages incurred by the employee.
(c) Finally, a few statutory provisions allow for *in melius* and *in pejus* derogation only to a limited extent (called 'limited absolute dispositivity') – for example,

56. *See* especially Act No. 16 of 2001 on the amendment of the 1992 Labour Code concerning transposition of nine Directives.
57. Act No. 22 of 1992 on the Labour Code came into effect on the 1 July 1992.
58. Part 2, Articles 32-229.
59. Part 3, Articles 230-284.
60. Article 277 of the 2012 Labour Code.
61. Part I contains general provisions, Part IV is on labour disputes and Part V on closing provisions.
62. Section 277(3) The collective agreement: (a) may not contain derogations from Chapters XIX and XX; and (b) may not contain any restrictions concerning the provisions contained in sections 271-272.

the number of extra hours may be 250 per year, which may be raised to maximum 300 in the collective agreement.[63]

The system described above of a general rule and three exceptions[64] is quite complicated, so the exceptions are enlisted at the end of each chapter within the second and the third part of the Labour Code.[65]

This novel hierarchy of the Labour Code and collective agreements represents a radical change in dogma. As has been stressed, legislation has traditionally concerned itself with contractual regulation in the hierarchy of labour law sources, and this limitation on the freedom of contract followed from the purpose of labour legislation. The drastic expansion of *in pejus* derogations curtails this setup and may jeopardise the efficient functioning of protective labour law in an active collective bargaining system. As this measure was introduced in a very moderate collective bargaining environment (around one-third coverage), in this case, it does not seem to be a clear and present danger.

The legislator expected that the wide possibility of *in pejus* derogations outlined above would increase collective agreement coverage because employers would be motivated to conclude such agreements. This strategy was thus confined to a single measure: motivating employers. I will question below, first, if this single measure is sufficient in itself to reach this ambitious goal, particularly in the reformed employment law framework; and second, if employers have really become motivated by free derogation. Since collective agreement coverage dropped as a result of the reform (*see* data above), the ultimate question is – why did the reform fail?

[B] Is Motivation Enough to Affirm Collective Bargaining?

The first question here is whether the strategy was adequate in the light of its own goals and Hungarian labour market conditions. We cannot discard from our analysis the attributes of CEE countries described above, such as specifically: (a) declining trade unions; (b) poorly organised employer organisations; and (c) lack of sectoral collective bargaining.

As for the altered position of trade unions, there is some good news and more bad news. The good news is that the conceptual change described above may strengthen the bargaining position of trade unions, for they can demand more favourable conditions in crucial questions (e.g., wages) in exchange for accepting detrimental changes (e.g., working time). Furthermore, the new representation criterion of trade unions was declared to foster collective bargaining: a trade union will be entitled to conclude a collective agreement if its membership reaches 10% of all employees of a

63. Article 135(3) of the 2012 Labour Code.
64. For a detailed analysis: Gy. Berke, *The Collective Agreement in the New Labour Code*, in Gy. Kiss (ed.), *Trade Unions and Collective Agreements in the New Labour Code*, 122-127 (Budapest: Akadémiai Kiadó, 2015).
65. *See also* Art. 277 on further exceptions.

given employer.[66] However, this threshold seems to be quite high and unreachable for declining trade unions at more and more employers. As a consequence of rapidly declining trade union density, this limit will slowly become an increasingly relevant obstacle to the right to collective bargaining.

However, it is questionable whether the players on the two sides of the industry are prepared for active collective bargaining. On the employers' side, their organisations were not affected by the reform, so density remained at the former low level.

By contrast, the two-faced reform deliberately weakened trade unions. Further and even accelerated downfall of the trade union movement is clearly reflected by shrinking union membership, diminishing power and fewer collective agreements. Legislation substantially undermined unions' operating conditions (legal protection, time-off, financial support) and curbed trade union rights in the workplace.[67] For instance, the 2012 Labour Code curtailed working time exemption and legal protection of union activists.[68]

The workplace status of trade unions is also undermined by the promotion of works councils, often to the disadvantage of unions.[69] Works councils have been elected at employers of over fifty employees since 1992; however, their powers have been rather weak, without real teeth.[70] Therefore, the shift of rights towards works councils reveals the new concept of strengthening duality of the Hungarian industrial system. This policy is symbolised by the novel possibility that works councils may conclude collective agreements.[71] The new Labour Code allows a works council agreement concluded between the works council and the employer to function as a collective agreement under certain conditions.[72] Works council agreements may contain rights and obligations regarding employment relationships, if the employer is not covered by a collective agreement[73] and there is no representative trade union.[74] The only restriction regarding its contents[75] is that it cannot regulate wages.[76]

66. Article 276 of the 2012 Labour Code.
67. Borbély & Neumann, *supra* n. 48, 197-198.
68. A. Tóth, *The New Hungarian Labour Code: Background, Conflicts, Compromises* 9 (Friedrich Ebert Foundation Budapest, Working Paper, 2012).
69. It must be mentioned here that trade unions have traditionally had a dominant presence in works councils, which was incentivised by the representation criteria of the 1992 Labour Code based on the number of votes at works council elections.
70. Article 236 of the 2012 Labour Code.
71. The possibility of works council agreements replacing collective agreements was already in place between 1999 and 2002 (Art. 31 of the 1992 Labour Code).
72. Before the 2012 reform, works council agreements had a very different legal nature, since the law stipulated that only 'issues pertaining to the privileges of a works council and its relations with the employer' shall be set forth in such an agreement (Art. 64/A of the 1992 Labour Code amended in 1995).
73. As a result, the employer may conclude a normative works council agreement, should it fall under the scope of a subsector or sector level collective agreement.
74. Article 268 of the 2012 Labour Code.
75. Chapter XII, Articles 136-165.
76. This exception is mistaken, since higher wages usually compensate flexible provisions on working time or resting periods. Since such a pecuniary compensation is not allowed by the law, the conclusion of a balanced agreement may be frustrated (T. Gyulavári & G. Kártyás, *The Hungarian Flexicurity Pathway? New Labour Code after Twenty Years in the Market Economy*, 30-31 (Budapest: Pázmány Press 2015)).

Although the promotion of collective bargaining in medium-sized companies is a positive aim, the legal nature and potential practical effect of normative works council agreements are problematic. Works councils were designed to foster cooperation between employers and workers and to take part in the employers' decisions.[77] Participation seriously contradicts the attributes of collective bargaining, where employees' representatives confront the employer for better working conditions. Furthermore, works councils must not organise, support or obstruct strikes,[78] and the lack of collective action weakens their bargaining position.[79] In addition, only the chair of a works council enjoys protection against dismissal.[80] There is no data on the number of such agreements, but this new instrument is practically non-existent in the labour market probably due to the same reasons as those given for collective agreements.

The reform also failed regarding sectoral collective bargaining, though this was not even a declared objective of the government. Collective bargaining remained at workplace level, and the conclusion of sector-level collective agreements was not facilitated by the new legal and economic framework either, with the detailed rules still entirely missing from the Labour Code. As an exception to the lack of special provisions on sector-level collective agreements, the Labour Code regulates the relationship between higher (e.g., sector) and lower (e.g., workplace) level collective agreements. Although the new Labour Code retained the 'in favour principle' regarding their relationship, it added an important exception, opening the door to decentralisation of collective bargaining.

Accordingly, higher-level collective agreements may allow *in pejus* derogations in lower agreements by designating some rules for this purpose.[81] This new possibility may weaken the capability of higher-level collective agreements to standardise working conditions in an entire sector.[82] Thus, it may be considered a harmful legislative step, even if this opportunity is presently not exploited, due to the absolute lack of sectoral agreements.

Since motivation of employers was the central element of the reform, we must finally raise the question of whether at least this measure succeeded in encouraging employers to conclude collective agreements. Certainly, employers can change many of the rules of the Labour Code also *in pejus* through collective agreements, but the protective nature of the legal basis of derogation is a key issue here. As we can see, Hungarian employment protection has been rather flexible since even long before 2012, but the new Labour Code is one of the most flexible in a European comparison

77. Articles 235 and 262 of the 2012 Labour Code.
78. Article 266 of the 2012 Labour Code.
79. T. Gyulavári (ed.), *Munkajog (Labour Law)*, 53 (Budapest: Eötvös Kiadó, 2012).
80. Article 260(3)-(5) of the 2012 Labour Code.
81. Article 277 of the 2012 Labour Code.
82. G. Kártyás, *Kollektív szerződés (Collective Agreement)*, in Gyulavári (ed.), *Munkajog (Labour Law)*, *supra* n. 79, 491.

since the Orbán government has pursued a radical neoliberal reform including the flexibilisation of employment relations and the curtailing of union rights.[83]

Dropping collective agreement coverage after 2012 suggests that employers may be satisfied with the low level of employment protection and do not wish to give rights (e.g., extra payments) for *in pejus* derogations. Employers would be motivated, if *in pejus* derogations could somehow remarkably flexibilise employment conditions, such as working time and rest periods. Evidently, working time is the best example of this problem, as it has always been the main field of derogations to the benefit of employers since legal harmonisation of the Working Time Directive in 2001. Nevertheless, current provisions on working time and rest periods are extremely flexible. For example, the Labour Code widely allows work on six (sometimes even seven) days a week, twelve regular hours daily, and only one rest day monthly on a Sunday, in a reference period of four or even six months.[84] The only benefits of *in pejus* derogations would be a fifty-two-week reference period or a change in the work schedule within seven days of the start of scheduled working time.[85] In my opinion, setting higher statutory minimums and/or allowing specific *in pejus* derogations in workplace level or sectoral collective agreements on working time and rest periods would increase motivation of employers even in the present employment law framework. It would be a logical correction of the original strategy if the government seriously wants to increase the role of collective agreements. This policy may be promoted by the necessary harmonisation of the Minimum Wage Directive from 2024, which requires a framework of enabling conditions for collective bargaining and an action plan (in countries with coverage rate below 80%).[86]

Motivation may be hindered by the Labour Code on the trade union side as well by setting detailed rights at a fair level for employees and union officials. Working time reduction is an important benefit for union officials, and several extra payments or severance pay provide a solid statutory minimum for employees. Therefore, the employee side also automatically obtains some substantial advantages without collective bargaining. However, lowering this statutory protection would not increase in itself higher collective bargaining coverage, but it would reduce the level of protection both in individual and collective labour law.

It must be mentioned here that there is a special chapter in the Labour Code on so-called public companies in which the state (local government) has majority ownership. The evident purpose of these special provisions[87] was to prevent abuse by employment contracts or collective agreements, limiting deviations from statutory provisions, particularly on working time and termination of employment. It thus created a double employment regulation, one for public companies and the other for all other employers, a solution that raises the issue of unconstitutional difference in

83. I. Szabó, *Between Polarization and Statism: Effects of the Crisis on Collective Bargaining Processes and Outcomes in Hungary*, Transfer 213 (2013/2), http://journals.sagepub.com/doi/pdf/10.1177/1024258913480702 (accessed 18 January 2017).
84. Articles 99, 94, 105 of the 2012 Labour Code.
85. Articles 94(3) and 97(4)-(5) of the 2012 Labour Code.
86. Article 4.2.
87. Articles 204-207 of the 2012 Labour Code.

treatment. As a result, collective bargaining hardly exists in such public (service) companies. Moreover, in public employment laws, the right to collective bargaining is extremely limited, and the tendency leads towards the disappearance of bargaining.[88]

The failed Hungarian reform has some crucial messages for reformers in the region. In CEE countries, the starting situation is characterised by low collective agreement coverage, sporadic density of trade unions and employers' organisations, and a corresponding lack of efficient sectoral dialogue. Above and beyond statutory regulation, social partners on both sides should be strengthened to ensure their financial and professional stability and motivation. Sectoral dialogue may be incentivised by organisational improvement at the sectoral level and detailed regulation on sectoral collective bargaining. The Hungarian reform failed because it focused on only one problem regarding social partners – employer motivation – yet not even this goal was achieved. In addition, the weakening and general decline of trade unions contributed to the shrinking of collective bargaining.

§2.04 CONCLUSIONS: REASONS FOR DEPRESSED COLLECTIVE BARGAINING IN CEE COUNTRIES

CEE countries wished to copy the collective bargaining culture of western European Member States as an attractive model after 1990, just as in many other fields of law and life. They wished to reach a long-term high collective agreement coverage with substantial content, also at the sectoral level, with strong social partners. By contrast, thirty-three years later their social partners are the weakest, collective agreement coverage is still the lowest among EU Member States, and sectoral collective bargaining hardly exists. Certainly, there are some brighter exceptions, such as Slovenian social dialogue, but the overall picture is rather gloomy. The original aim of this legislation was good, as sectoral collective dialogue and strong social partners would help national economies and societies to work and live better and particularly to resist crisis situations. After this unsuccessful three decades, the feasibility of this project is doubtful.

Investigation of the reasons for this premature and nowadays even declining social dialogue system leads us directly to weaknesses of social partners: density, culture, experience and knowledge are missing on both sides. In addition, employer motivation is also hindered by low and decreasing levels of employment protection. It must be acknowledged that collective bargaining cannot improve in a flexibilised labour law environment with diminishing employee protection and trade union rights, and financially and professionally weak social partners.

Hungarian collective bargaining is a typical eastern European patient with all the above-mentioned symptoms. The meritorious aim of the 2012 reform was to increase collective agreement coverage. At the same time, the neoliberal labour law concept of the government consisted of diminishing employment protection and trade union

88. T. Gyulavári & G. Kártyás (szerk.), *A kollektív szerződéses lefedettség csökkenése Magyarországon 2012-2023*, 27, https://www.researchgate.net/publication/374675244.

rights,[89] plus motivation of employers by multiple options for *in pejus* derogation. The Hungarian lesson is that motivation as a single measure cannot work miracles, especially if employers have not become truly motivated in the end. The goal is attainable in the long term, but only complex legal measures and partnerships may help.

89. T. Gyulavári & L. Pisarczyk (2023), *Populist Labour Law Reforms in Hungary and Poland: Same Song, Different Melodies*, 39 International Journal of Comparative Labour Law & Industrial Relations, 49-70 (2023/1).

CHAPTER 3

The Function of Sectoral Collective Agreements and the Risk Approach

Piera Loi

§3.01 INTRODUCTION

What are the traditional regulatory models for managing social risks in labour law? How are other regulatory models designed for managing risks in other branches of law capable to influence the traditional regulatory models of labour law? Is collective agreement a regulatory tool suitable for managing social risks?

In the first part of this essay, we will briefly analyse risk management techniques, often used in business activities.

In the second part, we will consider risk-based regulatory techniques in labour law, keeping in mind that Labour Law and Social Security Law are branches of law where the risk-based regulatory techniques have already been tested. In particular, the insurance technique developed by social security law, where security from risks (old age, illness, and unemployment) derives from insurance and the principle of solidarity. In labour law, in addition to the insurance technique stemming from social security law, another regulatory technique is developed: the technique of mandatory provisions and fundamental rights. Fundamental rights can indeed be described as protection mechanisms from risks.

Finally, we will see how the European Union (EU) institutions have more recently dealt with the impact of global risks, like the financial crisis, the pandemic, the digital and environmental transition, on workers' wages, in order to ascertain if sectoral collective agreements can still be considered regulatory tools capable of facing these risks.

As will be seen later, in recent times the European legislator has extensively used risk management techniques, already widely tested in managing health and safety risks, in new fields such as data protection regulation, artificial intelligence regulation, and in defining due diligence obligations for transnational companies. It is worth analysing how the risk-based regulatory model can change not only the structure of the business but also the traditional regulatory models of labour law.

Examples of this regulatory technique are represented by Directive 89/381/EEC on health and safety at work (implemented by Legislative Decree 81/2008 on health and safety at work), Regulation (EU) 2016/679 on personal data protection, the Regulation on Artificial Intelligence, the proposal for a Directive on improving working conditions for platform workers, and the Directive on Due Diligence.

The risk perspective can also be useful for regulating discriminations, based on different prohibited factors. Adopting the risk perspective in discriminations can be helpful in making protection techniques from this risk more effective, when especially certain categories of workers are more exposed, particularly when discrimination arises from the use of artificial intelligence systems.

§3.02 THE MULTIPLE DEFINITIONS OF RISK AND RISK REGULATION TECHNIQUES

Despite the vastness of the literature on risk, it is not easy to identify a common definition of risk. 'Given the ubiquity of risk in almost every human activity, it is surprising how little consensus there is about how to define risk.'[1] The inability to give a univocal definition of risk is due to the variety of theories on risk and the contexts in which risk is studied and described.

In the economic and financial field, for example, since the publication of Frank Knight's seminal work, *Risk, Uncertainty, and Profit,*[2] the category of risk has been seen simultaneously as a threat but also as an opportunity and a possible justification for profits.

In other cases, business studies have reinforced the idea that although risk encompasses the concept of threat and danger, it can be measured and, as risk management theories affirm, organizational techniques can be developed to manage risks, primarily through their measurement and evaluation. The vast literature on risk management aims to demonstrate that such Enterprise Risk Management techniques are indeed capable of increasing the value and productivity of businesses.

According to Ulrich Beck, risk is the hallmark of modern society, not surprisingly defined as a risk society.[3] We are witnessing the decline of class society based on wealth, shifting to a risk society, as modern society is *'increasingly occupied with debating, preventing, and managing risks that it itself has produced'*.[4] The risks of modernity are characterized by their global nature (such as pandemics) and the

1. A. Damorodan, *Strategic Risk Taking: A Framework for Risk Management*, Upper Saddle River (NJ), Wharton School Pub., 2008, 5.
2. F. Knight, *Risk, Uncertainty, and Profit*, Boston MA, Hart, Schaffner and Marx; Houghton Mifflin, 1921.
3. U. Beck, *Risk Society: Towards a New Modernity*, London, Newbury Park, Sage Publ., 1992.
4. U. Beck, *Living in the World Risk Society*, Vol. 35 *Economy and Society*, 2005, 332.

modernity of their causes, as they are a product of industrialization and wealth production (such as environmental or financial risks).

Beck's analysis is of interest not only from a sociological perspective but also from an epistemological one: the risk-based approach presupposes a different reading of events and the social and economic reality to be regulated, as reality itself can be conceived in terms of risk. Risk is considered a fundamental characteristic of modernization as '*the social production of wealth systematically goes hand in hand with the social production of risks*'.[5] From the risk perspective even regulatory techniques need to be modified and legal systems are called upon to rethink the very modes of legal regulation, as the law itself produces risks by knowing, composing, and recomposing reality in terms of risk since: '*en soi rien n'est un risque [...] il n'y a pas de risque dans la réalité*'.[6]

Additionally, the dilemmas of distributive justice associated with the production of risks should be addressed, as not all subjects are equally exposed to the same risks in the labour market and not all are equally protected from social risks, as was evident during the financial crisis and the pandemic.

Labour law, borrowing the insurance technique from social security law, already has risk among its founding categories, and the same mandatory rights can be seen as techniques for protection from social risks. Besides that, labour law can be comprehensively described as a technique for rationalizing risks, defining, managing, and controlling risks, and at the same time for distributing risks, with the aim of ensuring worker security. In this sense, there is an inseparable link between risk and security[7] where the principle of security, from this point of view, is the general principle, established in the legal system, that underpins the action of the law in the construction of social rights, aimed at reducing or controlling risk.

When identifying the subjects who should bear the risks, both from a legal and economic point of view, each norm explicitly outlines a model of distributive justice. Distributive justice choices are, accordingly, manifested both in the selection and definition of risks and in the identification of the risk community, that is, the group of subjects exposed to the risk that the norm intends to protect from. Risks in labour law become 'social' because the collective dimension of such risks is relevant, not only for the single worker but also for a group of workers. As for the technique traditionally chosen by labour law, it should be reminded that traditionally labour law has defined a set of rights around the employee's status, outlining a status that protects the beneficiary from social risks.

In this framework labour law has not only provided the legal criterion for identifying the subjects of the insurance technique, i.e. the subordinate employment contract, but has also above all started a process of juridification of social risks and, in this perspective, fundamental social rights can be described as legal mechanisms for protecting employees from such risks.

5. Beck, *Risk Society: Towards a New Modernity*, *supra* n. 3, 19.
6. F. Ewald, *L'Etat Providence*, Paris, Grasset, 1986, 19-20.
7. N. Lhumann, *Risk: A Sociological Theory*, De Gruyter, Berlin, 1993, 19 ff., rejects this bipolar construction of the couple risk/security.

We Modern societies are witnessing the crisis of the legal criterion of subordination, whereas it's raising the exposure to social risks even for self-employed workers.

Workers, due to the very modes of conducting the employment relationship, are exposed to a series of social risks that can also stem from the functioning of the labour market or other markets such as the financial market. The financial crisis of 2008 is indeed a proof of how financial market risks produce labour market risks to which all workers have been exposed, albeit in different ways.[8]

Also the pandemic, as a global risk, has had devastating effects not only on public health but also on the labour market. We will see later that to address this latter type of risk, the EU adopted a specific instrument aimed at preventing unemployment and safeguarding employment generated by the pandemic, called SURE (Support to mitigate Unemployment Risks in an Emergency). Member States had access to SURE funds (although not all States used them) to finance job retention mechanisms that international analysts consider the key to economic recovery in Europe after the pandemic.

If we look at the protection techniques from risks traditionally developed by labour law, in most cases they consist in mandatory substantial provisions with the assignment of non-waivable rights to employees. In this sense, as we have said, social rights are themselves techniques for protecting from social risks. In more recent legislation, however, in response to the expansion and changing nature of risks, labour law has adopted, alongside the traditional methods defined by mandatory protection rules, a procedural method inspired by risk management techniques,[9] aimed at managing risk through processes of identification, evaluation, and management of risks. Businesses are subject to procedural obligations aimed at identifying, evaluating, and managing risks to minimize their negative impact on fundamental rights and, in the case of employment relationships, on fundamental social rights.

Risk management theories provide businesses with a risk management framework through complex quantitative and procedural methods for decision-making in situations of uncertainty, especially used in the financial field. These risk management methods assume the reduction of risk and, within certain limits, the inevitability and acceptance of risk. Business studies have reinforced the idea that although risk encompasses the concept of threat and danger, it can be managed to transform it into an advantage or to limit its negative impact. Through risk management theories, organizational techniques are developed and organized in phases, aimed at managing risks primarily through their measurement and evaluation, with a view to their prevention and minimization.

In recent years, a significant part of European legislation has adopted a regulatory approach inspired by risk management theories: the risks generated by business activities, are treated as negative impacts on the environment or as negative impacts on

---

8. P. Loi, *Risk: A New Paradigm to Face Market Challenges*, Vol. 3 *ELLJ*, 2014, 390 ff. https://doi.org/10.1177/201395251400500313.
9. K. Anderson, *The Uses and Abuses of Risk Management*, in *Times Literary Supplement Book Review*, 1997; D. Barlow, *The Evolution of Risk Management*, Vol. 4 *Risk Management*, 1993, 30-36; P. Bernstein, *Risk as a History of Ideas*, Vol. 51, No. 1, *Financial Analysts Journal*, 1995, 7-11 https://doi.org/10.2469/faj.v51.n1.1851; P. Berstein, *Against the Gods. The Remarkable Story of Risk*, New York, 1996.

fundamental rights stemming from the complex organization models chosen by companies in global value chains. The recent Directive on sustainability due diligence provides that the companies affected will have to take and implement a risk-based system to monitor, prevent, minimize or remedy human rights or environmental damages identified by the directive.[10]

At the same time, various degrees of risks to fundamental rights produced by digital innovation and the use of Artificial intelligence implemented by companies, should be identified, assessed, and minimized by companies through compliance procedures. These procedures are deemed to be not only capable of altering the organizational architecture of companies but can also affect the regulatory framework and enforcement systems and ensure the effectiveness of the rights protected by legal systems, particularly labour law. Although there is a general consensus among scholars on the need to adapt traditional regulatory tools to face the increasingly complex and rapidly changing phenomena (such as the expansion of Artificial Intelligence in workplaces or the environmental crisis), nonetheless there are concerns about relying on the automatization of corporate compliance systems to ensure the effectiveness of fundamental rights protection.[11]

The regulatory approach described has also been applied by the EU legislator in the context of the EU's digital transition, based on the belief that the digital transition brings significant advantages and new market opportunities, but also causes risks to fundamental rights of individuals and workers. The main acts using this approach are: the Artificial Intelligence Regulation,[12] the Data Governance Regulation,[13] the Digital Services Regulation,[14] and the proposal of[15] Directive on improving working conditions for platform workers. We have to remind, anyway, that this approach is nothing but new since it has already been used in the EU General Data Protection Regulation.[16]

Among the labour law traditional regulatory tools, also collective agreement can be described as a flexible tool aimed at facing social risks. Collective agreements adopt both regulatory methods in order to protect workers from social risks: either defining

10. Directive (EU) 2024/1760 of the European Parliament and of the Council of 13 June 2024 on corporate sustainability due diligence and amending Directive (EU) 2019/1937 and Regulation (EU) 2023/2859.
11. A. Aloisi & V. De Stefano, *Between Risk Mitigation and Labour Rights Enforcement: Assessing the Transatlantic Race to Govern AI-Driven Decision-Making Through a Comparative Lens*, Vol. 14 *ELLJ*, 2023, 303 https://doi.org/10.2139/ssrn.4337517.
12. Regulation (EU) 2024/1689 of the European Parliament and of the Council laying down harmonized rules on artificial intelligence and amending Regulations (EC) No. 300/2008, (EU) No. 167/2013, (EU) No. 168/2013, (EU) 2018/858, (EU) 2018/1139 and (EU) 2019/2144 and Directives 2014/90/EU, (EU) 2016/797 and (EU) 2020/1828 (Artificial Intelligence Act).
13. Regulation (EU) 2022/868 of the European Parliament and of the Council of 30 May 2022 on European data governance and amending Regulation (EU) 2018/1724 (Data Governance Act).
14. 2022/2065 of the European Parliament and of the Council of 19 October 2022, on a Single Market for Digital Services and amending Directive 2000/31/EC (Digital Services Act).
15. Proposal for a Directive of the European Parliament and of the Council on improving working conditions in platform work, COM/2021/762 final. The final text of the Directive have been approved by the Council the 14 October 2024.
16. Regulation (EU) 2016/679 of the European Parliament and of the Council of 27 April 2016 on the protection of natural persons with regard to the processing of personal data and on the free movement of such data, and repealing Directive 95/46/EC (General Data Protection Regulation).

fundamental rights that cannot be waived by the individual parties of the contract of employment, or defining procedures in order to evaluate, manage and minimize risks. In this chapter, we are interested in analysing more precisely the function of collective agreements, especially at sectoral level, in protecting workers from wage risks.

Observed from the risk management perspective, adopted so extensively by the EU legislator, collective agreements seem a very promising source of regulation: first of all because companies need to demonstrate that they have adopted compliance procedures in order to assess, prevent and minimize risks. In many ways, collective bargaining has, in different industrial relations systems, a complex proceduralized decision-making structure. Just think about the information and consultation procedures provided by EU legislation and national legislation in case of collective dismissals:[17] this is nothing but a procedure to assess the risk of unemployment for workers, which means collecting and evaluating quantitative and qualitative data. In the following phase of consultations, the parties involved (unions or workers' representatives and employers) evaluate how to reduce and minimize the risk of unemployment (through working time schemes, vocational training and so on). In a few words, it seems that companies should look at collective bargaining as a resource to implement more efficient risk management procedures.

§3.03 SECTORAL COLLECTIVE AGREEMENTS AS REGULATORY TOOLS TO PROTECT FROM WAGE RISKS

If we shift our analysis to evaluate which level of collective agreements is more suitable for implementing the risk management procedure, we should be cautious in giving a comprehensive answer. Much depends on the characteristics of risks that we are dealing with. The example of collective dismissals makes clear the necessity that a procedure of information and consultation, and the following collective bargaining, is activated at the company level, but the answer should be different if we are dealing with the wage risk. We should remember that workers are protected from the wage risk first of all by a fundamental right to sufficient and fair wages defined by legal sources at the international level, for example, by Article 7 of the UN Covenant on Economic, Social and Cultural Rights[18] and, at the EU level, as reminded by Principle No. 6 of the European Pillar of social rights and, at the national level, by Constitutions in different Member States.

---

17. Council Directive 98/59/EC on the approximation of EU countries' laws regarding collective redundancies.
18. The Covenant recognizes the right of everyone to the employment of just and favourable conditions of work which ensure, in particular:
    (a) Remuneration which provides all workers, as a minimum, with:
        (i) Fair wages and equal remuneration for work of equal value without distinction of any kind, in particular women being guaranteed conditions of work not inferior to those enjoyed by men, with equal pay for equal work.
        (ii) A decent living for themselves and their families in accordance with the provisions of the present Covenant.

When market events or other global risks produce negative impacts on the fundamental right to have minimum and adequate wages,[19] sectoral collective agreements could be considered regulatory tools aimed at protecting workers from wage risks, that is all the risks which could undermine the level of wage correspondent to the content of the worker's performance and to the adequacy of wage aimed at guaranteeing worker's dignity.

The EU Directive on minimum and adequate wages[20] highlights the importance of setting adequate wages, because adequate levels of minimum wages, as provided for in national law or collective agreements '*protect the income of workers, in particular of disadvantaged workers*' (recital 8).

The function of adequacy as established by collective agreements or by legislation is to protect from unpredictable downturns (market risks). The increasing in-work poverty in the Union over the past decades is explained by the recitals of the Directive on minimum and adequate wages (recitals 8 and 9) as an effect of economic downturns and economic crises hitting low-wage workers in particular, as they are more vulnerable to the consequences of such downturns. The role of adequate minimum wages in protecting such workers from such crises (like the COVID-19 pandemic or other market risks) is considered essential for the purpose of supporting a sustainable and inclusive economic recovery, which should lead to an increase in quality employment (recital 9). When considering which regulatory sources could better guarantee adequate wages, aimed at protecting workers from wage risks, the Directive clearly seems to make a preference for sectoral and cross-industry level collective bargaining, when saying '*sectoral and cross-industry level collective bargaining is an essential factor for achieving adequate minimum wage protection and therefore needs to be promoted and strengthened*' (recital 16). '*Well-functioning collective bargaining on wage-setting is an important means by which to ensure that workers are protected by adequate minimum wages that therefore provide for a decent standard of living*' (recital 22).

The preference of EU institutions towards sector or cross-industry level collective bargaining is evident in recital 16 of the Directive on adequate and minimum wages, which shows how the EU perspective on sectoral collective bargaining has deeply changed after the economic crisis of 2008 and after the pandemic of 2020: '*sectoral and cross-industry level collective bargaining came under pressure in some Member States in the aftermath of the 2008 financial crisis. However, sectoral and cross-industry level collective bargaining is an essential factor for achieving adequate minimum wage protection and therefore needs to be promoted and strengthened*'. *It follows saying that* '*strong collective bargaining, in particular at sector or cross-industry level, contributes to ensuring adequate minimum wage protection*'. Also, recital 22 expresses the same idea when saying that '*Strong and well-functioning collective bargaining together with a high*

19. On the concept of market correction mechanism of minimum wages *see* Z. Adams, *In search of Adequacy in Contemporary Labour Markets*, in L. Ratti, E. Brameshuber & V. Pietrogiovanni (eds), *The EU Directive on Adequate Minimum Wages. Context, Commentary and Trajectories*, Hart Publ., 2024, 14.
20. *See* a comprehensive commentary on the Directive by L. Ratti, E. Brameshuber & V. Pietrogiovanni (eds), *The EU Directive on Adequate Minimum Wages. Context, Commentary and Trajectories*, Hart Publ., 2024.

coverage of sectorial or cross-industry collective agreements strengthen the adequacy and the coverage of minimum wages.'

The path change of the EU institutions' attitude towards sectoral collective agreements and its central role in guaranteeing minimum and adequate wages can be found previously in the European Pillar of social rights proclaimed at Gothenburg on 17 November 2017.

The centrality of the European Pillar of social rights as far as minimum and adequate wages is recalled in recital 5 of the Directive. It recalls, first of all, that Principle No. 6 of the Pillar reaffirms workers' right to fair wages providing for a decent standard of living and ensuring adequate and minimum wages, in a way that provides for the satisfaction of the needs of the worker and his or her family in light of national economic and social conditions, while safeguarding access to employment and incentives to seek work.

As far as the prevention of in-work poverty all wages are to be set in a transparent and predictable way, according to national practices and respecting the autonomy of the social partners.

As far as the regulatory techniques, Principle No. 8 of the Pillar provides that the social partners are to be consulted on the design and implementation of economic, employment and social policies, according to national practices and that they are to be encouraged to negotiate and conclude collective agreements in matters relevant to them, while respecting their autonomy and the right to collective action. From this point of view, the Pillar does not make any preference as far as the level of collective agreements guaranteeing minimum wages, but in the EU Social Pillar Action Plan of 2021 when depicting the main challenges to be addressed is in-work poverty and inequality in EU, the EU Commission makes a link between two different phenomena: increasing share of low-paid and low-skilled occupations in EU labour markets from one side and the erosion of traditional collective bargaining structures in some countries, from another side. The erosion of collective bargaining structures in some countries is considered, as a consequence, one of the causes of the increasing share of low-paid and low-skilled occupations in EU labour markets. The Directive on adequate and minimum wages is precisely aimed at reducing the share of low-paid occupation using the lever of traditional collective bargaining and it seems that this time the EU Institutions have made their preferences clear, although respecting the tradition of Member States, it's talking about sectoral collective bargaining.

What seems striking is that the erosion of traditional collective bargaining structures during recent decades is considered by the EU institutions as *'due, inter alia, to structural shifts in the economy towards less unionised sectors and to the decline in trade union membership, in particular as a consequence of union-busting practices and the increase of precarious and non- standard forms of work'*.[21] Researches on the main causes of the erosion of collective bargaining structures during recent decades, confirm only partially this view. EU policies after the economic crisis of 2008 were mainly

21. This opinion was already shared by researchers in the field of collective bargaining in many EU Member States *see* T. Müller, K. Vandaele & J. Waddington, *Collective Bargaining in Europe: Towards an Endgame*, ETUI, 2019.

directed at emphasizing the role of decentralized collective bargaining in order to enhance the flexibility needed by enterprises, especially in wage setting, as a crisis exit strategy to structural shifts in the economy towards less unionized sectors and to the decline in trade union membership, in particular as a consequence of union-busting practices and the increase of precarious and non-standard forms of work.[22]

In this framework, two main phenomena are relevant in explaining the change of perspective of the EU institutions as far as the role of sectoral collective agreements in wage setting: the pandemic and the expansion of digital platform work. Both phenomena can be interpreted in terms of risks capable of producing negative impacts on wages with the contemporary loss of the central role of collective agreements as the main source of regulation.

First of all, the digital platform work is relevant because it has produced a high risk of exclusion of digital platform workers from the boundaries of the traditional collective bargaining wage setting due to their classification as independent workers, whereas the pandemic has demonstrated its disruptive effects on the continuity of wages. In the next paragraphs, we will analyse the policies adopted by the EU institutions to protect wages facing these two global risks, and in this case, we will see that the regulatory role of collective bargaining at sectoral level is reinforced.

§3.04 THE EU AND THE RISK PERSPECTIVE DURING THE PANDEMIC: THE CASE OF SURE

Global risks, such as the COVID-19 pandemic, capable of indiscriminately affecting very large categories of individuals, bring back the issue of insuring workers from the risk of unemployment caused by global-scale events like pandemics, financial crises, or climate crises in unprecedented terms. These are, in fact, global risks that produce an impact on the labour market and create additional risks, such as unemployment, which in turn can lead to income risks. Like all types of risks, the risk of unemployment can be managed through an insurance-type system: therefore, in the case of involuntary unemployment, the worker will receive unemployment benefits based on their insurance seniority. Alternatively, it can be managed in terms of risk prevention and reduction, with systems aimed at preventing and reducing the risk of unemployment.

The EU, through the SURE programme,[23] has sought to address the risk of unemployment (and the consequent wage risk) in a novel way, through a mechanism of financing public policy systems of working hours reduction, known as Short Time Work Arrangements (STWA). These kinds of schemes have been used in some Member States for a long time. In a certain number of Member States (like Estonia, Greece, Cyprus, Malta and Sweden), STWA were not used to respond to drops in labour demand caused by an economic downturn, and workers could only get the regular unemployment schemes. Through this programme, the EU has adopted a

22. *See* S. Laulom (ed.), *Collective Bargaining Developments in Times of Crisis*, Kluwer Law Int., 2018.
23. Council Regulation (EU) 2020/672 of 19 May 2020 on the establishment of a European instrument for temporary SURE following the COVID-19 outbreak.

specific policy to face a global risk like the pandemic which is soundly based on the solidarity principle.

A key point to note is the legal basis of EU Regulation 2020/672, which introduced the SURE mechanism: the legal basis is Article 122, paragraph 1 of the Treaty on the Functioning of the European Union (TFEU), where the principle of solidarity (or spirit of solidarity) among Member States is identified as the basis that, from a legal perspective, allows for the bypassing of the no bail-out clause. It is therefore worth highlighting, in our opinion, the EU's choice to base this instrument for supporting national passive employment policies (even in the form of a loan) on the principle of solidarity, which underpins every system of mutualizing social risks. As will be seen, in this intervention, the European legislator distributed the risk of job loss caused by the pandemic crisis – a risk that affected all Member States, and although not equally, all categories of workers – among all Member States, including those that, by their own choice, did not access the loans.

The EU, through the agreement of the Member States expressed in the choice of a binding and immediately effective instrument such as the Regulation, acts as a guarantor to investors for the payment, at maturity, of the bonds issued to cover the loans granted under SURE. Although not all Member States have used SURE and therefore did not request loans from the EU to finance either short-time work schemes (STWA) or support measures for self-employed workers or health-related measures, all Member States have recognized the EU's role as a guarantor in the issuance of social bonds.

With the SURE Regulation, the EU implemented a EUR 100 billion intervention aimed at providing financial support to Member States, in the form of loans granted under favourable conditions by the EU to Member States, for the purpose of activating short-time work schemes to mitigate the risks of unemployment. It is worth noting that all Member States, even those that did not access the measure, signed bilateral guarantee agreements that enabled the EU to raise loans from the market under very favourable conditions to finance SURE. This is indicative of a solidarity among States that quickly proved its effectiveness. On 22 September 2020, after the signing of the guarantee agreements by all Member States, the Commission accelerated the activation of the SURE instrument for the nineteen Member States that accessed the funding: Belgium, Bulgaria, Croatia, Cyprus, Czech Republic, Estonia, Greece, Hungary, Ireland, Italy, Latvia, Lithuania, Malta, Poland, Portugal, Romania, Slovakia, Slovenia, and Spain. More than 90% of the funding was disbursed between October 2020 and May 2021.

This involves the issuance of social bonds, issued and guaranteed by the EU, to enable the collection of funds in the financial market at rates that individual Member States would not have been able to obtain on their own. Given the EU's good credit rating, the European Commission, in its second semi-annual report on the impact of SURE, estimates that by using SURE, beneficiary Member States have saved approximately EUR 8.2 billion in interest payments.[24] The funds were raised in the market through the purchase of bonds by investors, who were potentially interested not only in the profitability of the financial product itself but also in its social purpose, which was to finance tools for reducing working hours (or similar measures) to avoid mass layoffs in response to the health crisis. After raising funds through various issuances of social bonds, the States (though not all of them) then requested and obtained loans from the EU to varying degrees, to finance national measures for reducing working hours or other similar measures.

The SURE mechanism can ultimately be described as a system of social risk-sharing (the risk of job loss due to the health crisis) through the financial market. While these types of bonds are not high-risk and therefore do not guarantee very high returns, they do meet the financial markets' need to allocate excess liquidity. The sale of social bonds on the market thus allows for at least partial distribution of the social risk of job loss within the financial market.

The issuance of social bonds follows the procedures outlined in the EU SURE Social Bond Framework, which incorporates the guidelines set out internationally by the Social Bond Principles Voluntary Process Guidelines for Issuing Social Bonds, adopted by the International Capital Market Association (ICMA).[25] Despite their non-binding nature (as they are guidelines), these principles provide fairly precise indications of the characteristics that social bond issuances must have, defined as '*any type of bond instrument whose proceeds are exclusively applied to finance or refinance, in whole or in part, new and/or existing social projects, and in any case are aligned with the four core components of the Social Bond Principles,*' which are: (1) the use of proceeds; (2) the process for project evaluation and selection; (3) the management of proceeds; (4) reporting activities.[26]

These are essentially relevant pieces of information provided by the issuers of social bonds to investors. Among the components of Social Bonds, the use of the proceeds from the bond issuance within Social Projects is crucial, '*which must be adequately described within the legal documentation of the bond. All projects qualified as Social Projects should clearly deliver social benefits, which should then be assessed and, where possible, quantified by the issuer*'. Among the categories of Social Projects that are described by way of example are those '*related to job creation and programs designed to prevent or mitigate unemployment resulting from socio-economic crises*'. This social objective is clearly aligned with the purposes of the SURE instrument outlined in Article 1, paragraph 2, of EU Regulation 2020/672, which allows '*the*

24. EU Commission, Report from the Commission to the European Parliament, the Council, the Economic and Financial Committee and the Employment Committee Report on the European instrument for Temporary Support to mitigate Unemployment Risks in an Emergency (SURE) following the COVID-19 outbreak pursuant to Art. 14 of Council Regulation (EU) 2020/672, Brussels, 22.9.2021, COM(2021) 596 final, 3.
25. ICMA (International Capital Market Association), *Social Bond Principles Voluntary Process Guidelines for Issuing Social Bonds*, June 2020, available in https://www.icmagroup.org/assets/documents/Regulatory/Green-Bonds/June-2020/Social-Bond-PrinciplesJune-2020-090620.pdf.
26. ICMA, *supra* n. 25, 3.

financing, primarily, of short-time work schemes or similar measures aimed at protecting employees and the self-employed, and thus reducing the incidence of unemployment and loss of income, as well as funding certain health-related measures, particularly in the workplace'.

§3.05 THE WAGE RISK OF DIGITAL PLATFORM WORKERS: WHICH ROLE FOR SECTORAL COLLECTIVE BARGAINING?

The risk of remuneration, as the risk of its continuity and intangibility, is one of the main social risks associated with the performance of a working activity. Insurance systems, protecting workers from the occurrence of such risk, are represented by rights, often of an inalienable nature, on the definition of a minimum wage, on the intangibility of remuneration, on the certainty of the criteria for its calculation and structure.

In the field of digital economy and platform-based work, scholars report serious violations of fundamental principles regarding remuneration both at national and international level.[27] Despite the prevailing narrative that tends to describe platform workers as "gig workers", who take on small jobs to supplement family income or to occupy only part of their day, some empirical studies, such as the one on Amazon Mechanical Turk personnel in India and the USA, describe a completely different reality.[28] For 38% of American workers on Amazon Mechanical Turk and 49% of Indian workers on the same platform, crowdworking is the sole source of income, which increases their exposure to remuneration risk.

Regarding the ways in which remuneration is defined, it is important to highlight the fact that in defining the type (whether time-based or piecework), the contractual imbalance between workers and platforms is most evident. Furthermore, the absence of a collective representation structure for workers' interests in the negotiation of remuneration implies a unilateral definition of remuneration by the digital platform, resulting in changes to contractual and remuneration conditions that are simply notified to workers through the applications used to perform the work. Particularly in crowdworking, the risk of remuneration is emphasized: although the methods of defining remuneration vary depending on the type of service provided and the type of crosourcer, on some platforms like Amazon Mechanical Turk, the micro-tasks performed by turkers (the so-called HITs such as small translations, content moderation on social media, photo tagging, etc.) are compensated by Requesters (the clients of the final services reassembled by the platform into a unified service) with a few cents of a dollar for each task performed, paid into a virtual account opened by AMT for each worker. What does the risk of remuneration mean for the worker? Their payment is

27. J. Berg, *Income Security in the On-Demand Economy: Findings and Policy Lessons from a Survey of Crowdworkers*, ILO Conditions of Work and Employment Series, No. 74, 2016; C. Degrise, *Digitalisation of the Economy and Its Impact on Labour Markets*, ETUI WP n. 2016.02, 35 ff.
28. K. Hara et al., *Worker Demographics and Earnings on Amazon Mechanical Turk: An Exploratory Analysis*, ACM digital Library, 2019, available at https://dl.acm.org/doi/abs/10.1145/3290607.3312970.

withheld until the Requester has accepted the service, noting that there is no obligation on the part of the Requester to justify the refusal of the service. The Requester can thus accept the micro-task and pay the Turker, or reject it, meaning that the worker, despite having performed the task, will not receive the agreed compensation. Workers have difficulties in challenging unfounded or illegitimate refusals of services on the AMT platform and what is particularly significant, beyond the immediate lack of payment, is the indirect damage caused to the worker by the refusal. Refusals indeed affect the worker's reputation on the platform: it is correctly noted that workers are anonymous and are identifiable on AMT only through a numerical string, thus their only real asset is their reputation, which allows them to receive more and better-paid HITs. Many workers complete thousands of HITs solely to improve their reputation and gain access to better-paid HITs: hence, one can understand the harm caused by unjustified refusals of services by Requesters. Data from surveys conducted among AMT and Crowdflower workers show that 94% of workers have had services refused by Requesters, resulting in payment refusals.[29]

The transfer to the worker of the economic risk typically borne by the entrepreneur is also evident in the remuneration technique adopted by other platforms that operate by emphasizing competition among an indefinite number of potential workers, who simultaneously perform the same task for the Requester, who will choose the most satisfactory service, which will also be the only one to be paid. Remuneration based on a bid or auction in the platform's internal crowdwork market can lead the Requester to select the worker who will perform the task based on the lowest offer (in terms of requested compensation), thus creating a system of downward competition among workers, allowing companies to use the lowest-cost labour available in the digital services market without having to bear the risks of physical relocation.[30] The absence of a regulatory mechanism such as a collective agreement which not only balances contractual power but also serves an anti-competitive function among workers, exposes digital platform workers to a greater risk of remuneration, reinforcing the importance of defining a minimum wage through collective bargaining.

Regarding the different types of remuneration, many digital platforms choose the pay-as-you-go or piecework method.[31] Other platforms prefer the first-come-first-served technique, where only the worker who performs the task first will be paid. In some cases, the platform pays the worker who performed the service for the Requester, or the latter pays the compensation while the platform takes a commission on the executed transaction, but reserves the right to pay it only if the service is satisfactory. In the absence of union representation to protect crowdworkers from remuneration

29. Berg, *supra* n. 27, 15; *see* K. Hara & Y. Tanaka, *Understanding Crowdsourcing Requesters' Wage Setting Behavior*, ACM digital library, 2022, available at https://dl.acm.org/doi/10.1145/3491101.3519660.
30. M. Gramham, et al., *Digital Labour and Development: Impacts of Global Digital Labour Platforms and the Gig Economy on Worker Livelihoods*, Vol. 23, No. 2 *Transfer*, 2017, 1 ff. https://doi.org/10.1177/1024258916687250.
31. A. Alkhatib, M.S. Bernstein & M. Levi, *Examining Crowd Work and Gig Work Through the Historical Lens of Piecework*, Proceedings of the 2017 CHI conference on human factors in computing systems, 2017.

risks, AMT crowdworkers started to use a browser plugin (Turkopticon) by which they share information about Requesters, their reliability (including payment reliability) with other crowdworkers, functioning as a rating system. This system should lead crowdworkers to avoid working for unreliable Requesters. For workers, reputation currently appears to be the only tool to counterbalance the power of Requesters and platforms. Although Turkopticon is a weak alternative to a traditional system of collective interest representation, it nevertheless helps create some collective awareness among these workers by providing them with essential tools to respond to possible abuses through the same rating techniques used to evaluate workers' performance. In the absence of a collective bargaining system, there is, therefore, a huge power disparity between the parties in the field of remuneration.

The issue of digital platform worker remuneration is often addressed within the framework of subordinate work and minimum wage, so the path to recognizing a minimum wage seems to lie in the worker's classification as an employee. It is indeed true that while for many workers, using apps and platforms is a way to supplement their income by using their free time, for many others, it is their only source of income.[32] Therefore, it is reasonable to consider the perspective of a minimum wage. In this sense, the issue of remuneration, when viewed from the perspective of risk, leads to the assertion that – regardless of the legal classification of the relationship established between workers and platforms – the issue of how to guarantee digital platform workers a minimum level of economic security must be addressed. This security could come from either ensuring a minimum number of microtasks or guaranteeing a base wage plus a piece-rate component.

Another relevant issue is that of evaluating and quantifying remuneration: remuneration is normally paid in relation to working hours, which is the main criterion used in subordinate work to quantify the volume of the work done, whereas there is a noticeable disconnection between remuneration and working hours in most wage systems in the digital economy. In digital platform work, the issue of evaluating, including for remuneration purposes, the time spent searching for work and performing all preliminary activities before starting the work itself is presented in an unprecedented way. Research indicates that platform workers spend a significant portion of their time 'looking for work', that is, searching for microtasks to complete or waiting for assignments. For every hour of work performed, crowdworkers spend an average of eighteen minutes on unpaid work – time spent not only searching for more work but also reading reviews of Requesters to ensure they are reliable, reading instructions on how to perform the task, or passing tests to qualify for the task. These practices lead to a vast quantity of unpaid digital platform work.[33]

When calculating the average hourly wage received, even though piecework, it is undoubtedly lower due to the unpaid time spent on ancillary activities required to perform the task.

---

32. Berg, *supra* n. 27, 6.
33. V. Pulignano, et al., *Does It Pay to Work? Unpaid Labour in the Platform Economy*, ETUI Policy Brief, 15, 2021.

Another issue, not adequately addressed, is the remuneration of data produced by workers during the performance of their tasks, which is essentially ceded for free to the employer. Scholars who focus on these issues strive for Unions' information rights to access to platform's activity, that finally could end up in a collective agreement,[34] with the result of understanding the use of data and, in this sense, assessing its possibility of compensation. This highlights the challenges faced by platform workers in terms of compensation, particularly regarding unpaid time and the value of data produced during their work.

§3.06 WAGE RISK FOR DIGITAL PLATFORM SELF-EMPLOYED WORKERS AND THE ROLE OF COLLECTIVE AGREEMENTS

We have seen that the exclusion of digital platform workers from the boundaries of the traditional collective bargaining wage-setting mechanisms is mainly due to their classification as independent workers.

All EU Member States have faced the rise of independent work as figures show remarkable numbers in different sectors,[35] but surely the expansion of independent work is even more relevant in the area of the gig economy, due to the organization models chosen by digital platforms all over the world, claiming their preference for a network of independent contractors. The tendency of relegating digital platform workers into the realm of self-employment is declared to be ridiculous, by the English judge in Aslam & Farrar,[36] but in the end could deprive a huge number of workers of labour law and social security protections and, what is more relevant to discuss in this paper, from their collective rights and the possibility of signing collective agreements.

Many researchers have underlined the dramatic consequences on the ever-growing number of digital platform workers of the classification conflicts, because of the difficulties of applying the criteria developed, either by national courts or by the CJEU, to distinguish genuine self-employment from bogus self-employment and employee status. As a matter of fact, those who are classified as independent contractors are totally excluded, in almost all the legal systems in EU Member States, from the labour law protections and especially from the wage-setting mechanisms of collective agreements. The gig economy has amplified the inner contradictions of the traditional binary division between the employee status and the independent worker status and the tendency to relegate digital platform workers into the realm of self-employment, which in the end could deprive a huge number of workers of labour law and social security protections and, what is more relevant, of their collective rights and the possibility of signing collective agreements.

34. Z. Adams & J. Wenckebach, *Collective Regulation of Algorithmic Management*, Vol. 14 *ELLJ*, 2023, 211 ff. https://doi.org/10.1177/20319525231167477.

35. *See* Eurostat data extracted 18 April 2024, available at https://ec.europa.eu/eurostat/statistics-explained/index.php?title=Employment_statistics_within_national_accounts#Evolution_by_sector.

36. *Uber BV v. Aslam & Others* [2018] EWCA Civ 2748; *Uber B.V. and Others v. Mr Y Aslam and Others*, 26 October 2016, IRLR, 2017, 4; Employment Appeal Tribunal, *Uber B.V ._and_Others-_v._Mr_Y_Aslam_and_Others*, _UKEAT_0056_17_DA.

The definition of an intermediate legal category between self-employed and employee status, as adopted in some Member States, in some cases has been demonstrated to be a possible solution. Examples of this solution could be found in the Italian legal system, which has adopted a third legal category for a very long time, known by the acronym of co.co.co., regulated by Article 409 of the civil procedure code, already in 1975 was introduced a specific type of independent work characterized by the continuity of the activity, the personal performance of the work and the coordination with the organization of the enterprise. This category of self-employed workers, from the very beginning, was given the right to a special social security scheme and the right to claim rights before labour law Courts instead of Civil Law Courts.

More recently the intermediate category of '*collaborazioni etero-organizzate*' has been introduced, in the Italian legal system, by Article 2, D.Lgs. 81/2015: the worker's activity is performed personally, is continuous and is organized by the client. Originally that definition was completed by the fact that the organization by the client could be dependent on the time and place of the performance, but since 2019 any reference to time and place has been amended (Article 2, D.Lgs. 81/2015 was amended by Law No. 128/2019). Following Article 2 of D.Lgs. 81/2015 the category of hetero-organized worker is entitled to the same labour law and social security rights as the employee category. The same Law No. 128/2019 provides that digital platform workers delivering goods (more frequently food) on behalf of others, in urban areas using bikes or motor vehicles, are included in its scope of application if their work is organized by the digital platform; workers can be classified as hetero organized workers, meaning that digital platform workers, as all other hetero organized workers, are recognized all the labour law and social security rights and, as a consequence, collective agreements at sectoral level can set their wages.

This means that if digital platform workers are classified either as employees or as hetero-organized workers they are entitled to the same labour law and social security rights. Whereas if they are classified as co.co.co. they are entitled simply to social security rights and, in case of litigation, the same procedural rules for employees' litigation, will apply.

Also, Austrian labour law recognizes an intermediate category of workers between employees and self-employed (persons with a similar status to employees or '*Dienstnehmeranliches*') but it is social security law that first recognized the right to a social security protection to the category of '*Freie Dienstnehmer*', whereas all the attempts made to enlarge the spectrum of social rights to be recognized to that category have been brought under the severe scrutiny of the Austrian Constitutional Court.[37]

In Spain, an intermediate category, between the employee and the self-employed status, is the TRADE ('*trabajador autónomo económicamente dependiente*') a self-employed person whose income (at least 75%) depends on one single employer. On the basis of this strong economic dependence, the law recognizes the TRADE a special legal status with a social security protection and some labour law rights (indemnities in

37. F. Marhold, *Social Protection of Contingent Work: Austria and the Full coverage Social Insurance System*, in E. Ales, O. Deinert & J. Kenner (eds), *Core and Contingent Work in the European Union. A Comparative Analysis*, Hart, 2017, 233 ff.

case of unlawful dismissal, holidays, maternity leave) similar to that recognized to employees and, what is most important, some collective rights.[38] Article 13 of the LETA[39] states that TRADE representatives can sign collective agreements which can regulate the mode, time and place of their activities and the other general conditions of the contract. This category of collective agreements. in this case, will be subject to specific rules as far as their general applicability but, nonetheless, they fulfil the same function as the other collective agreements.

Notwithstanding the paramount importance of collective agreements especially at the sectoral level, in order to face wage risks for digital platform workers, at least two main obstacles can be highlighted: first of all, when digital platform workers are classified as employees, they have difficulties to be unionized because of their physical isolation and lack of continuity of their work. Second, there is a tendency of legal systems to raise questions about the conflicts between collective agreements for independent contractors (when digital platform workers are classified as independent contractors) and competition law. The way out of this regulatory dilemma could be either that the case law classifies all digital platform workers as employees in order to consider them in the scope of application of collective agreements, or that collective agreements for digital platform workers, even if they are classified as self-employed, are exempted from the competition law rules.

The EU institutions, aware of these negative perspectives, have pursued both the classification path and the exemption of collective agreements for self-employed from competition law rules.

As far as the first path goes the proposal of a Directive on working conditions of digital platform workers have among its aims '*to combat false self-employment in platform work and to facilitate the correct determination of the employment status*' (recital 26) and in this respect '*Member States should have appropriate procedures in place to prevent and address misclassification of the employment status of persons performing platform work*' (recital 26). The introduction of a legal presumption of subordination in Article 5 by which '*The contractual relationship between a digital labour platform and a person performing platform work through that platform shall be legally presumed to be an employment relationship when facts indicating control and direction*' means that collective agreements are the main source of regulations, also as far as wages, of digital platform work.

We have to highlight the fact that a variety of collective agreements have been signed in different Member States regulating digital platform work[40] and sectoral

38. A.P. Pazos Pérez, *Régimen jurídico del trabajo por cuenta propia con especial referencia al trabajador autónomo económicamente dependiente (TRADE)*, Vol. 21 *Dereito*, 2012, 63 et seq.; E. Sánchez Torres, *The Spanish Law on Dependent Self-Employed Workers: A New Evolution in Labour Law*, Vol. 31 *CLLPJ*, 2010, 231.
39. Ley 20/2007, 11 July 2007, Estatuto del trabajo autónomo (LETA).
40. J.M. Miranda Boto & E. Brameshuber (eds), *Collective Bargaining and the Gig Economy: A Traditional Tool for New Business Models*, Hart Publ., 2023.

collective agreements have, although slowly and not with the same results, tried to catch up their role in setting minimum wages[41] with very promising results.[42]

As far as the second path chosen by the EU Institutions is concerned, we should first of all remember the attitude taken by the CJEU in the *FNV* case, apparently dismantling the *Albany* jurisprudence.

The CJEU since the *Albany* case defined the effects and also the functions of collective agreements stating that 'it *is beyond question that certain restrictions of competition are inherent in collective agreements between organisations representing employers and workers. However, the social policy objectives pursued by such agreements would be seriously undermined if management and labour were subject to Article 85(1) of the Treaty when seeking jointly to adopt measures to improve conditions of work and employment*'. Here the CJEU identified the collective agreements functions, as acquired by the EU social policy objectives, in being '*measures to improve conditions of work and employment*'[43] and at the same time to guarantee the protection of Article 28 of the Charter of Fundamental Rights of the EU. Conversely, at the same time, has identified the possible negative effects of collective agreements, that is the production of certain restrictions of competition, considered inevitable consequences of the social regulation. The CJEU confirmed in other cases after *Albany*[44] the collective agreements exemption from Article 101 TFEU until the discussed case *FNV* in which the same exemption seems to be recognized not to all collective agreements signed by organizations acting in the name and on behalf of self-employed, but only to the collective labour agreement which directly contributes to the improvement of the employment and working conditions of substitute musicians classified as 'false self-employed'.[45]

It could be helpful to rethink the multiple functions of collective agreements in order to find a way out in the apparently trapped legal argumentation raised not only by the CJEU in the *FNV* case[46] but also at the national level, that any collective agreement defining the working conditions of independent workers could imply a violation of competition laws. In this uncertain framework from one side labour law scholars indicate the theoretical approaches that could bring to the recognition of a fundamental right to collective bargaining for avoiding an infringement of Article 101

41. *See* D. Perez Del Prado, *The Personal Dimension of Collective Bargaining in the Gig Economy: The Spanish Perspective*, in J.M. Miranda Boto & E. Brameshuber (eds), *Collective Bargaining and the Gig Economy: A Traditional Tool for New Business Models*, Hart Publ., 2023, 179 ff.
42. *See* the case of the recently-signed autonomous collective agreement for food delivery work in Sweden in N. Selberg, *Autonomous Regulation of Work in the Gig Economy: The First Collective Bargaining Agreement for Riders in Sweden*, Vol. 14 *ELLJ*, 2023, 609 ff. https://doi.org/10.1177/20319525231178980.
43. Judgment of the CJEU of 21 September 1999, *Albany International BV v. Stichting*, case C-67/96, paras 54-60.
44. Judgment of the CJEU of 21 September 1999, joined cases C-115/97 to C-117/97, *Brentjens*, para. 57; Judgment of the CJEU of 21 September 1999, Case C-219/97, *Drijvende Bokken*, para. 47; Judgment of the CJEU of 12 September 2000, case C-180/98 to C-184/98, *Pavlov and Others*, para. 67; Judgment of the CJEU of 21 September 2000, case C-222/98, *Van der Woude*, para. 22 Judgment of the CJEU of 3 March 2011, case C-437/09, *AG2R Prévoyance*, para. 29.
45. Judgment of the CJEU of 4 December 2014, case C-413/13, *FNV Kunsten Informatie en Media*, para. 29.
46. Judgment of the CJEU of 4 December 2014, case C-413/13, *FNV Kunsten Informatie en Media*.

TFEU[47] and from another side the EU Commission in its Guidelines on the application of Union competition law to collective agreements regarding the working conditions of solo self-employed persons[48] seems to exclude that collective agreements for solo self-employed infringe Article 101 TFEU, when self-employed lack bargaining power exactly as employees (recital 8 and 9).

If we take a look at the Union's vision on the issue of collective agreement's function, as declared by the European Trade Union Confederation (ETUC) Resolution on Priorities for the Coordination of Collective Bargaining and Wage Policies, collective agreement's function can be summarized in the necessity of reducing the growing imbalances of power inside the contract of employment; in guaranteeing, especially at sectoral level, the highest degree of solidarity among workers, since collective bargaining is a barrier against downward competition on wages and precarious working condition.[49] The collective agreements' functions of avoiding downward competition on wages and precarious working conditions and of guaranteeing solidarity among workers could be, nonetheless, undermined if the ETUC Resolution didn't put clearly as a priority of collective bargaining, the implementation of the objectives set in the Social Pillar, to cover remuneration of precarious workers and certain categories of self-employed.[50]

In order to exclude the conflict between competition law and collective agreements for independent workers, we should underline the collective agreements' more relevant functions which are the rebalancing of unbalanced powers inside an employment relationship, and the competition regulatory function avoiding downward practices, especially for wages. The fact that the collective agreement sets wages for a group of workers, especially at the sectoral level, is at the centre of the discussion when applied to collective agreements signed for independent workers. Notwithstanding the fact that these are to be considered the most important relevant functions, we believe that other functions of collective bargaining should be evaluated and other approaches could be put forward.

The argument to support the idea of collective agreements for self-employed, with an exemption to competition law, is that collective agreements, at the sectoral level, can have a different function when considered from the point of view of the risk theory. As we have seen modern societies are characterized by the production of risks (social, environmental, financial) and the production of wealth is systematically accompanied by the production of risks. This factual description can be turned into an epistemological analysis if we think that nothing in itself is a risk and everything can be a risk.[51] The insurance activity to protect from risks does not consist in a simple activity

47. E. Brameshuber, *A Fundamental Right to Collective Bargaining for Economically Dependent, Employee-Like Workers*, in J.M. Miranda Boto & E. Brameshuber (eds), *Collective Bargaining and the Gig Economy: A Traditional Tool for New Business Models*, Hart Publ., 2023, 227 ff.
48. EU Commission, Guidelines on the application of Union competition law to collective agreements regarding the working conditions of solo self-employed persons, 2022/C 374/02.
49. ETUC, *Resolution on Priorities for the Coordination of Collective Bargaining and Wage Policies*, adopted on the 25/06/2018, available in https://www.etuc.org/fr/node/17190.
50. ETUC, *supra* n. 49, priority 4.
51. *See* Ewald, *L'Etat Providence*, *supra* n. 6.

of ascertaining the existence of risks but in 'producing' risks, either by a private institution or by the Welfare State, and the effect is that insurance, together with other risk management techniques is, first of all, a way of redistributing risks. From this perspective, social security law sources and labour law sources can be seen as legal instruments to ascertain and distribute social risks and social rights as the mechanisms of protection from risks.

From this perspective, also collective agreements can be considered instruments for identifying risk communities and, through the solidarity principle, for sharing social risks and mutualising the costs of protecting from social risks. That is why collective agreements, also for self-employed characterised by economic dependence and vulnerability, operate as protective shields from traditional social risks (old age, sickness maternity) and from new risks (wage risk, classification risk, personal data risk).

On one hand, the solidarity principle enshrined in the collective agreements is precisely the reason that can justify the exemption of self-employed collective agreements from the scope of Article 101 TFEU,[52] if we stick to the usual scheme of the CJEU legal argumentation. On the other hand, if we are searching for new forms of solidarity in social security systems, in order to include subjects traditionally excluded from the communities sharing social risks, we should reverse the CJEU legal reasoning in the *FNV* case. We should, then, start from the described collective agreement's function of identifying risk communities, to ascertain in which cases a limitation of the solidarity principle is admissible by the competition law principles. As a matter of fact, the solidarity principle is not only recognized as a fundamental principle in the constitutional tradition of many Member States but also at the EU level, since Article 2 TEU explicitly refers to the solidarity principle and Chapter IV (Articles 27-38) of the Charter of Fundamental Rights of the EU is entitled to solidarity as the cornerstone of all social rights.

52. Judgment of the CJEU of 3 March 2011, case C-437/09, *AG2R Prévoyance*, para. 47.

CHAPTER 4

Incentivising Collective Bargaining

Pierre-Emmanuel Berthier & Olivier Leclerc

§4.01 INTRODUCTION

The mere promulgation of regulations does not automatically lead to compliant behaviour on the part of the actors at whom they are aimed. Accordingly, the provision of rules on collective bargaining does not guarantee the public authorities that they will actually be implemented by the social partners. How can public authorities manage to get employers, employees and union organisations to agree to engage in collective bargaining and sign collective agreements? How can political impetus towards collective bargaining be effectively translated into a change in bargaining practices in companies and professional sectors?

Until now, labour lawyers have provided three different responses to this question. The first response consists in making collective bargaining obligatory at the company level. The obligation to negotiate is not in itself an obligation to reach an agreement. However, it is implicitly supposed that at least part of the negotiations will lead to collective agreements. This procedure can be found in place in several European countries. Under the French Labour Code, employers must engage in regular negotiations on an ever-increasing number of subjects within the company.[1] During the negotiation period, the employer loses the power to take unilateral action on the matters that are the subject of the negotiation.[2] Thus, it is hoped that, by making negotiation compulsory, collective agreements will finally be concluded.

1. Negotiation must be undertaken every year with regard to pay, working hours, the sharing of added value created by the company, professional equality between men and women and quality of work (Art. L. 2242-1 of the French Labour Code). In companies with more than 300 employees, the employer must, every three years, open negotiations on the management of employment and career paths (Art. L. 2242-2 of the French Labour Code).
2. Article L. 2242-4 of the French Labour Code.

The second response given by labour lawyers consists of pointing out that the very decision to conclude collective agreements falls outside the scope of the law and is a matter of interest to sociologists and economists. Notions such as 'trade union cultures' (more or less reformist), the 'balance of power' (more or less favourable) and the 'economic interests' of the parties to the agreement are particularly highlighted. In short, labour law regulations allow collective bargaining and put the relevant organisational framework in place, but the decision whether they wish to sign any agreements is left to the social partners. From this perspective, legal analysis can only relate to the context of the actions but not to the actions themselves.

Between these two approaches – one concerned with the obligation to negotiate collective agreements, the other advocating that the signing of collective agreements falls outside the remit of legal analysis – some authors have highlighted the possibility of implementing reflexive regulations. Adherence to the law arises not only from fear of sanctions but also from the integration of rules into the instruments created by social actors themselves, rooted in self-regulation. As Simon Deakin, Colm McLaughlin and Dominic Chai put it:

> reflexive regulation offers a critique of voluntarist approaches on the one hand and 'command and control' forms of law on the other. Voluntarist approaches which assume that the interests of business will automatically align themselves with the wider public good are seen as ignoring a range of barriers to this occurring, including externalities and related forms of market failures. The 'command and control' approach, in contrast, is criticised as involving excessive reliance on prescriptive controls. (...) Regulation should aim instead to be reflexive in the sense of both responding in its form and content, to social contexts, and in triggering a range of responses from social actors which can form the basis for effective self-regulation.[3]

Reflexive regulations are also found in the field of collective bargaining. There are many examples of companies adopting good conduct guides to negotiation or undertaking to hold periodic discussions on one subject or another.

All three of these ways of looking at the relationship between collective bargaining law and the signing of collective agreements by the social partners are present, to varying degrees, in current legislation in European countries. In addition to these approaches, this chapter draws attention to a fourth, incentive-based method of bringing rules into operation. Incentives are a well-known part of economic theory. The theory of incentive agreements has undergone significant development by focusing on establishing financial mechanisms that incite rational economic agents to adopt certain behaviour that is deemed desirable.[4] The theory behind incentive thus constitutes a serious attempt to take account of the limited rationality of economic agents and asymmetries of information. Within an employment relationship, it seeks, above all, to establish a salary level capable of inciting workers not to lower their productivity to the

3. S. Deakin, C. McLaughlin & D. Chai, *Gender Inequality and Reflexive Law: The Potential of Different Regulatory Mechanisms*, *in* L. Dinkens (ed.), *Making Employment Rights Effective. Issues of Enforcement and Compliance*, 115-137 (Oxford: Hart Publ., 2012), p. 119.
4. There is an extraordinarily number of published texts. For a classic introduction, *see* J.-J. Laffont & J. Tirole, *A Theory of Incentives in Procurement and Regulation* (MIT Press, 1993).

detriment of the employer.[5] Outside of the flourishing field of law and economics, this approach has had a limited impact on labour law for a long time. In past research, we both have seek to characterise incentive-based rules of law.[6] Incentive rules are legal provisions that leave players the choice of adopting one course of action or another, but which aim to make the desired course of action more attractive. Incentives do not impose; they allow for a particular form of behaviour and encourage its adoption on the basis of the supposed interests of the beneficiary of the rule. It is expected that beneficiaries abide by the rule not because they are obliged to do so and would be sanctioned if they did not, but because they are interested to do so. This approach creates a new space for legal analysis, which can focus not only on what the law imposes or prohibits but also on the legal techniques used to encourage certain actions.

In this chapter, we examine the rules of law that provide an incentive to social partners to enter into collective agreements. We suggest that labour law is not limited to *imposing the bargaining* of collective company agreements: it also implements mechanisms that *provide incentives to enter into* collective agreements. These rules are all too often overlooked by labour lawyers, despite their key role in effective collective bargaining and, ultimately, in the signing of collective agreements.

Incentive mechanisms can work in favour of both decentralisation and centralisation of collective bargaining. In numerous European countries, collective bargaining law has displayed an ever-greater tendency towards decentralised collective bargaining.[7] On a European scale, a general trend has emerged towards collective bargaining centred on the company and the establishment.[8] Decentralised collective bargaining is believed to be more in line with the financial situation of the companies and to better serve the wishes of employees and their representatives. The backdrop of the economic crisis experienced by Europe since the late 2000s has accentuated this trend, making collective bargaining a preferred tool for national legislations seeking to adapt to ongoing economic changes.[9] Conversely, however, trends towards the centralisation of

5. *See* Janet L. Yellen's seminal paper, *Efficiency Wage Models of Unemployment*, Vol. 74, No. 2 American Economic Review, 200-205 (1984).
6. P.-E. Berthier, *Les normes incitatives du droit du travail* (mémoire HDR, Université Lyon 2, 2021); A.-L. Mazaud, *Les mécanismes d'incitation à conclure des accords collectifs dans les ordonnances de septembre 2017*, La Semaine juridique – Social, 1232 (2018); P.-E. Berthier, *Les incitations légales*, 1680 Semaine sociale Lamy, 36 (2015); O. Leclerc & T. Sachs, *Gouverner par les incitations. La diffusion d'une logique incitative dans le droit du travail*, 2 Revue française de socio-économie, 171 (2015). *See also* S. Leroy, *Droit social et incitations: contribution à l'étude des transformations de la normativité juridique* (thèse Université Paris Nanterre, 2014); V. Pietrogiovanni, *Le sanzioni positive nel diritto del lavoro*, (Universita degli studi di Bari Aldo Moro, 2013).
7. For an overview, *see* the contribution of Sylvaine Laulom in this issue.
8. Harry C. Katz, *The Decentralization of Collective Bargaining: A Literature Review and Comparative Analysis*, Vol. 47, No. 1, ILR Review, 3-22 (1993) https://doi.org/10.1177/001979399304700101; A. Lyon-Caen & A. Perulli (eds), *Trasformazioni dell'impresa e rapporti di lavoro*, (Padova: Cedam, 2004).
9. B. Hepple & B. Veneziani (eds), *The Transformation of Labour Law in Europe. A Comparative Study of 15 Countries 1945-2004* (Oxford: Hart Publ., 2009); G. Loy (ed.), *Diritto del lavoro e crisi economica. Misure contro l'emergenza ed evoluzione legislativa in Italia, Spagna e Francia* (Roma: Ediesse, 2011); M.-C. Escande-Varniol, et al., *Quel droit social dans une Europe en crise?* (Bruxelles: Larcier, 2012); E. Peskine, *La célébration de l'accord collectif d'entreprise. Quelques enseignements de la loi relative à la sécurisation de l'emploi*, 5 Droit social, 438-445 (2014).

collective bargaining can also be detected, as illustrated by the Directive of 19 October 2022 on adequate minimum wages in the European Union (EU).[10] This Directive, which encourages States to adopt a statutory minimum wages with the aim of achieving decent living and working conditions (Article 1), recommends strong collective bargaining, '*in particular at sector or cross-industry level*' (recital 16 and Article 4.1.a): '*sectoral and cross-industry level collective bargaining is an essential factor for achieving adequate minimum wage protection and therefore needs to be promoted and strengthened*' (recital 16). The directive aims to achieve the widest possible coverage of collective agreements, and to this end sets a target rate of 80% (Article 4.2). In its terms, '*strong and well-functioning collective bargaining together with a high coverage of sectorial or cross-industry collective agreements strengthen the adequacy and the coverage of minimum wages*' (recital 22).

Based on French labour law, the article presents a typology of incentives in collective bargaining law. We identify three incentive mechanisms. *Facilitation* seeks to *facilitate* collective bargaining conditions for employers or unions (§4.02). It entails removing material obstacles that could deter actors from entering into discussions and reaching agreement. *Retribution* consists in *compensating* actors who have actually signed a collective agreement (§4.03). For example, an employer may receive a 'bonus' for signing an agreement permitting the employment of young workers. *Taxation* consists in *taxing* companies who do not engage in the negotiation of a collective agreement (§4.04). In this case, the incentive consists in making the undesirable situation more expensive (but without making it illegal).

§4.02 FACILITATION

Facilitation refers to a rule of law designed to make the conduct set out by law more simple. Facilitation is aimed at simplifying the reputation of collective bargaining with a view to making it more attractive – a clear contrast to the unwieldiness and complexities sometimes attributed to it. Collective bargaining may indeed well appear costly, demanding and risky; negotiators may be lacking or unwilling to engage in negotiations. Facilitation is aimed at removing these obstacles. The Directive 2022/2041 of 19 October 2022 on adequate minimum wages in the EU relies on such a mechanism. It requires Member States to '*promote the building and strengthening of the capacity of the social partners to engage in collective bargaining on wage-setting, in particular at sector or cross-industry level*' (Article 4.1). This entails '*facilitating the exercise of the right to collective bargaining on wage-setting*', protecting '*workers and trade union representatives from acts that discriminate against them in respect of their employment on the grounds that they participate or wish to participate in collective bargaining on wage-setting*', protecting the latter '*against any acts of interference by*

10. *See* Dossier in *Italian Labour Law e-Journal*, Vol. 14, No. 1 (2021); Luca Ratti, *The Sword and the Shield: The Directive on Adequate Minimum Wages in the EU*, Vol. 52, No. 2, Industrial Law Journal, 478-500 (2023) https://doi.org/10.1093/indlaw/dwad001; G. Bargain, *Le salaire minimum adéquat. À propos de la directive (UE) 2022/2041 du 19 octobre 2022*, Revue de Droit du travail, 404 (2023).

each other or each other's agents or members in their establishment, functioning or administration' (Article 4.1). In States where the rate of collective bargaining coverage is less than 80%, governments are required to define an '*action plan to promote collective bargaining*' (Article 4.2).

In France, facilitation is mainly aimed at removing two obstacles: the lack of information available to parties and a lack of availability on the part of trade union negotiators.

Lack of information can be a disincentive to negotiation and is the target of various types of facilitation. A union or employer may, for example, be unfamiliar with the various forms of collective bargaining or unaware of the legal consequences of signing an agreement. In France, a number of measures have been taken to make collective bargaining accessible to the greatest number of companies – especially the smallest – and to the trade unions. For example, the Combrexelle report[11] recommended that 'standard collective agreements' be drawn up in professional sectors for use by small companies. Also with a view to education, a law passed on 8 August 2016 stipulated that 'employees, employers or their representatives can benefit from joint training aimed at improving social dialogue practices in companies'.[12] However, the system has proved ineffective when employers and trade unions are not prepared to support it.[13] The very idea of joint training conveys the image of a peaceful 'social dialogue', far removed from the struggles and strategies inherent in collective bargaining. It is in this sense that the mechanism arouses the mistrust of the trade unions, who are worried that it is a means for employers' organisations to influence the course of current or future negotiations.[14] For all these reasons, the success of these training offers has been marginal: only a dozen of them were held between the beginning of 2018 and the summer of 2021, and only five branch agreements have implemented the scheme.[15] This situation reflects the limited initial relevance of the training system proposed by the law, which consists of attempting to co-train players who defend divergent interests. In terms of the educational objective pursued, the facilitation provided for under French law reveals therefore glaringly inappropriate.

However, lack of information is not the only material obstacle to collective bargaining. The unavailability of actors, in particular the unions, is also an issue for facilitation. The time spent on collective bargaining within the company, if unsalaried, can be an obstacle to union negotiators, who have to interrupt their work in order to join in the negotiations. French law grants union representatives the right to absent themselves from their work, without loss of pay, so they can fulfil their union role.[16] These supplementary hours allow union representatives and employees called upon to

11. J.-D. Combrexelle (dir.), *La négociation collective, le travail et l'emploi*, 89 (France stratégie, September 2015).
12. Articles L. 2212-1 et seq. of the French Labour Code.
13. Cf. Ch. Thuderoz, *Les 'formations communes syndicats/entreprises'. Sociographie d'un dispositif à repenser*, 493 RDT (2021).
14. *Ibid.*
15. *Ibid.* The professional sectors concerned are road transport, open-air hotels, telecommunications, air transport and mechanical glassmaking.
16. Articles L. 2143-13 et seq. of the French Labour Code.

take part in negotiations to prepare for it without loss of salary and without needing to use the monthly delegated hours to which they are entitled. The employer has to pay for both the time spent preparing for negotiations and the actual working hours. The aim is to put the participants in a position to fulfil the role that is expected of them: to enter into negotiations and reach an agreement.

§4.03 RETRIBUTION

Retribution differs from facilitation.[17] In terms of collective bargaining, a 'retribution' is given once a collective agreement has been signed. It compensates the parties who have actually signed an agreement and provide them with a benefit. To this end, it sometimes consists of providing a financial advantage [A] and, in some cases, reducing the legal constraints that may be a burden to the employer [B].

[A] Financial Advantage

Some provisions of French law provide for financial incentives for signing a collective agreement. These incentives may pursue different objectives. In most cases, they are aimed at achieving the objectives that public policies pursue in terms of employment through collective bargaining. The agreements sought are designed to keep the workers most affected by unemployment in employment or training. In France, it is now possible, under a collective agreement, to reduce severance pay payable to an employee taken on under a fixed-term contract in exchange for 'preferential access' to vocational training.[18] Sometimes incentives are linked to the company's projected employment plan and may, in this context, appear to be inconsistent with other measures in existing law. This is the case for exemptions from social security contributions and income tax on compensation paid to an employee who volunteers to leave the company. These exemptions benefit the employer only when voluntary departures take place within the context of a collective agreement on managing employment and professional career paths.[19] The law makes a direct link between a management planning agreement and the termination of the employment contract. This makes it difficult to support the view of the *Cour de cassation* that the legality of the redundancy procedure is independent of compliance with the procedural obligations relating to employees skills planning.[20] Specifically, it is difficult to maintain that employment management and redundancy procedures do not serve the same 'purpose', when the law expressly envisages, through such an incentive, the termination of

17. N. Bobbio, *De la structure à la fonction. Nouveaux essais de théorie du droit*, trad. et présentation D. Soldini (Paris: Dalloz, 2012), 56.
18. Article L. 1243-9 of the French Labour Code.
19. These exemptions were first introduced by Art. 16 of the 2007 Social Security Financing Act. They are now found in Art. L. 242-1 of the Social Security Code and eighty duodecies of the General Tax Code.
20. Soc., 30 September 2009, Bull. civ. V, n° 217; D. 2010, p. 679, obs. A. Fabre. This means that a job protection plan is valid even though the employer has not complied with its consultation and negotiation obligations in terms of management planning.

the employment contract as a possible objective of the management planning process.[21]

[B] Relief from Legal Constraints

Other forms of retribution involve alleviating the legal constraints weighing on the employer and granting them additional powers. In that case, the incentive consists of granting employers the benefit of more flexible legal rules than if they had not signed an agreement.

In France, this technique of encouraging collective bargaining involves derogating from the law or from a broader collective agreement. When a derogatory agreement is signed, the employer benefits from a system that makes fewer demands on him – while not being necessarily more favourable to employees – than is established by law. Derogatory agreements can cover various aspects of employment relationships, whether in relation to salaries, regulation of working hours or part-time work, including to rules governing redundancy on economic grounds. Since 2013, the law has allowed collective agreements to introduce major derogations from the rules governing redundancies. Thus, '*internal mobility agreements*' and '*employment preservation agreements*' were established, with considerable scope for derogation from the law. '*Internal mobility agreements*' provided for the geographical mobility of employees within the company. '*Employment preservation agreements*' permitted a temporary reduction in wages or an increase in working hours without any increase in pay. In return, the employer committed not to proceed with redundancies for the duration of the agreement. All of these agreements had one thing in common: even if employees were to refuse to sign up to them, they would still be made redundant without benefiting from the rules governing collective redundancies. However, in 2017 these agreements were removed from French legislation and replaced by the possibility of concluding '*collective performance agreements*'.[22] The approach adopted for these collective agreements differs from that of its predecessors on a number of points. First, when an employee refuses the application of a collective performance agreement concluded within the company, the law rules out the qualification of 'economic redundancy' and, with it, all the guarantees inherent in this category of redundancy. Second, the collective performance agreement does not necessarily require the employer to commit to maintaining employment.[23]

For its part, the employer is encouraged to conclude such an agreement, as this will enable them to exercise their power within a less heavy and less demanding legal framework. However, the legal advantages granted to the employer may infringe

21. *Contra* F. Favennec-Héry, *Du droit du licenciement au droit de l'employabilité du salarié*, 3 SSL n° 1291; G. Bélier & S. Guedes da Costa, *GPEC/PSE: deux dispositifs autonomes*, *ibid.*, 8.
22. Ord. n° 2017-1385 of 22 September 2017; Art. L. 2254-2 of the French Labour Code.
23. The latter are not the intended beneficiaries of legal incentives. The employer is the only one who can decide what to put on the bargaining table. The unions' incentive to consent to the agreement arises not from the law, but from the commitments made during the negotiation of such an agreement.

employees' fundamental rights. For instance, a law of 17 August 2015 had already removed the employer's obligation to reassign employees made redundant when they refused to apply an employment preservation agreement. Employers are therefore no longer under any obligation to find out whether a job is available and to offer it to the employee before making him or her redundant, as the law requires them to do in principle for all redundancies. The conclusion of a collective performance agreement rules out redundancy and, with it, the obligation to redeploy employees in other jobs and to provide them with the training they may need to fill them. However, according to the case law of the French Constitutional Court, the right to reassignment derives from the 'right to employment' protected by the preamble to the French Constitution.[24] The exclusion of reassignment for a redundancy that is not attributable to the employee but to the 'operation of the company' is therefore questionable. In effect, this amounts to ruling out the right to reassignment in the event of dismissal which, although not qualified as being 'economic' by the law, is nonetheless based on a reason unrelated to the employee personally.[25]

The unions, for their part, may be encouraged to sign such an agreement because of a promise made by the employer not to make redundancies or to limit the number of redundancies. However, this overlooks the fact that the collective agreement itself is subject to the agreement of each individual employee, and that each refusal will result in a further redundancy. It is therefore quite possible that the application of such an agreement would actually increase rather than reduce the number of redundancies. The example of a collective agreement concluded in a company located in France[26] ('Mahle-Behr') demonstrates that this arrangement may result in the opposite effect to that expected by the trade unions. An employment preservation agreement had been signed in July 2013, by the majority representative trade unions within the company, in order to avoid the loss of 102 jobs. 162 employees then refused to implement the agreement. These employees were therefore made redundant without being able to claim the guarantees usually provided for in the event of large-scale redundancies. A so-called employment maintenance agreement therefore leads to larger-scale redundancies than those contemplated before it was signed. The incentive can therefore lead to disappointment when the signing of a collective agreement does not bring its signatories the expected benefits or, worse still, leads to the opposite result to the one sought.

24. Cons. const., 7 August 2008, No. 2008-568 DC.
25. Under the terms of the law, a collective performance agreement is concluded in order to 'meet the needs linked to the operation of the company or with a view to preserving or developing employment' (Art. L. 2254-2 of the Labour Code). The reasons for the agreement are therefore economic in nature, and not inherent to the individual employee, even if the reason for dismissal following the employee's unwillingness to accept the agreement is, according to the law, based on a 'specific reason'.
26. *See* P. Adam, *Le 'prodigieux' accord de maintien de l'emploi. Escapade en pays de Rouffach*, 1611 SSL (23 December 2013).

§4.04 TAXATION

'Taxation' is familiar in economists' discussions on incentives.[27] It can be referred to under a variety of headings – 'contributions', 'penalty' or 'malus' – and can be applied in a wide range of areas.[28] A tax is aimed at making undesirable conduct more onerous. It consists of taxing the party who does not accomplish an act expected of it. From this point of view, taxes have very close links with criminal sanctions which are also a reaction on the part of the law to undesirable conduct (theft, impediment, discrimination, etc.).

There are, however, two aspects that distinguish taxation from a criminal sanction. Unlike a criminal sanction, taxation is much more predictable in terms of *amount*. While a criminal sanction can vary depending on the judge's assessment of the severity of the offence – as compensation might vary according to the prejudice caused to a victim – taxation varies on the basis of predefined, quantifiable criteria, such as a company's workforce or the percentage of its total payroll. 'Taxation' does not have the connotations that a sanction does either. Under a taxation system, undesirable conduct is not necessarily 'illegal' or 'prohibited', it is simply costlier. In terms of collective bargaining, taxation consists of making employers pay a certain amount when they do not engage in negotiation with the unions, or when they fail to uphold the agreement resulting from such negotiation. The few examples, past or present, that we have identified in France show that taxation can either be in addition to a criminal sanction, or replace it.

Taxation sometimes seeks to augment criminal sanctions, the dissuasive nature of which can be debated. Thus, French companies with at least fifty employees who have not engaged in annual collective bargaining on workforce salaries are subject to taxation,[29] in addition to any criminal sanction to which they might be subject for having failed to respect this obligation to negotiate.[30] In other cases, taxation replaces sanctions. This was the case in France where companies with at least 300 employees were subject to a financial 'penalty' when they failed to engage in negotiations on the implementation of the 'generation contract'[31] aimed at boosting the employment of young people.

Taxation is a good illustration of an incentive-based approach. It does not find those who fails to negotiate or respect a collective agreement guilty of either a civil or

27. In France, well-known economists have proposed replacing the damages that an employer can be ordered to pay when deciding redundancy without genuine, serious grounds for doing so, with a specific, predetermined 'tax': O. Blanchard & J. Tirole, *Protection de l'emploi et procédures de licenciement*, Report by the Economic Analysis Council (Paris: La documentation française, 2003).
28. In addition to the incentives to negotiate a collective agreement, an example of this is the tax that may be due by a French company that does not employ, or employs very few disabled people compared to its total workforce (Art. L. 5212-9 of the French Labour Code).
29. Article L. 2242-7 of the French Labour Code.
30. Article L. 2243-1 and L. 2243-2 of the French Labour Code. Failure to respect this obligation to negotiate is punishable by a fine of EUR 3,750 and a one-year prison sentence. In practice, only the fine is imposed by the courts, and usually for less than the maximum amount.
31. Article L. 5121-9 of the French Labour Code (abrogated in 2017).

criminal offence. It leaves it to them to decide what is most advantageous for them, by comparing the tax cost with the cost of negotiation or the ensuing costs of an agreement resulting from such negotiation.

§4.05 CONCLUSION

This article highlights the use of incentive mechanisms to prompt the signing of collective agreements. This type of regulation constitutes a 'soft' option for achieving the signing of a collective agreement. Rather than obliging social partners to enter into collective agreements, the law is conceived such that it is rational for them to want to do so. From the point of view of the public authorities, incentive-based mechanisms offer a major advantage: they enable a result to be obtained (the signing of collective agreements) without interfering in the employer's management decisions. While forcing social partners to sign agreements would contradict contractual freedom, incentives mean that such courses of action can be encouraged without the application of any constraints. The perspective of negotiating and reaching agreement appears indeed more in line with the employers and employees' interests. Signing a collective agreement does not become obligatory; it simply becomes more rational.

In France, incentives to sign collective agreements basically relate to the management of employment within a company, with a view to, or in the context of, economic difficulties, and working conditions. The most 'offensive' agreements relating to working conditions, in particular to salary and working hours, are still those rooted in financial justification. In other cases, incentives can be related to employment of certain categories of workers (young or old). The incentive to sign collective agreements can thus be seen as a means of boosting an employment policy without forcing employers to recruit particular categories of workers. As a result, employment policies are implemented by the 'softer', but by no means less genuine, process of incentive. Incentives are used to support an employment policy that is implemented directly at the company level.

In most cases, the majority of incentives favouring the signing of collective agreements are aimed at employers as well as at employees. The signing of a collective agreement appears as a condition for allowing them to benefit from certain advantages or avoid certain inconveniences. For example, French Labour Code states that '*in order to improve the professional development of employees on a fixed-term contract, a collective agreement at branch or company level can both cap the amount of compensation when the contract comes to an end at 6% [rather than 10%], while offering consideration to these employees, particularly in the form of preferential access to professional training*' (Article L. 1243-9 of the Labour Code). In this case, the incentive benefits both the employer (reduction in social charges) and employees (improved professional training). However, identifying the beneficiary of the incentive is sometimes much less clear-cut. For example, in order to encourage the implementation of collective performance agreements,[32] the French labour law stipulates that employees

32. Article L. 2254-2 of the French labour Code.

who refuse the application of the provisions of the agreement to their employment contract may be made redundant. The law stipulates that their redundancy takes the form of a dismissal based on a 'specific reason', not an economic one. The right to economic redundancy is also waived whatever the number of employees involved and even if, in total, they exceed the thresholds for definition as collective redundancy. Is the incentive designed by the law aimed at the employee or at the employer? Predetermination of the redundancy system applicable in the event of an employee's refusal to apply the agreement allows the employer to benefit from a less onerous redundancy regime. At the same time, the incentive is extended towards the employee who is incited to accept the implementation of the agreement (and thus the mobility clause), under the threat of redundancy.

Interestingly, no retribution given directly to the unions could be identified in France. The incentive to conclude collective agreements always seems to be aimed at employers and employees, presumably on the assumption that this will lead them to encourage trade unions to conclude agreements. This situation might explain by the fact that providing unions with a direct incentive to sign collective agreements could give rise to an unlawful inequality of treatment between trade unions. For example, in France, retributing a union simply because it is more inclined than another to sign an agreement would not constitute legitimate grounds for such a disparity.[33] Two additional arguments can be raised. First, in so far as employers have the power to influence employment, they must be the main target of the incentives. In the examples given, the retribution is not given to encourage *both parties* to reach agreement, but to encourage the employer to accept the obligation to maintain employment and retain employees as an essential part of the decision-making process. In turn, the unions will already be encouraged to take the decision to sign the agreement by the promise made to them in relation to maintaining employment and/or salary level, without the need to promise them further retribution. Secondly, the role of unions would arguably be called into question if they were acknowledged as having a vested interest in the signing of an agreement. It is indeed difficult to reconcile the idea that unions represent the collective interests of employees with the idea that they could be guided towards 'rational' behaviour by incentives, particularly those of a financial nature. This interest might diverge from the professional interests of the workers that they represent.

33. The French Court of Cassation holds that the '*principle of equality is a constitutional rule, and does not allow an employer to subsidise one representative union and not another, on the basis of whether or not they have signed a collective agreement or convention*' (Cass., Soc. 29 May 2001, *Bull. civ.* V, No. 185).

CHAPTER 5

Negotiating Working Time in Times of Crisis and Twin Transition*

Nicola Gundt, Łukasz Pisarczyk & Katarzyna Wieczorek

§5.01 INTRODUCTION

Working time has constantly remained among the key topics covered by labour legislation and collective bargaining.[1] Indeed, one of the focal points in the early development of labour law concerned the reduction of the number of working hours.[2] Economic and organizational changes which have occurred since 1970s entailed a parallel tendency – the flexibilization of working time[3] understood as adjusting working hours to variable companies' needs.[4] The expectation of greater flexibility has

* This article is co-financed by Narodowe Centrum Nauki (the National Science Centre in Poland), project No. 2019/33/B/HS5/02067.

1. *See* more S. Lee, D. McCann & J.C. Messenger, *Working Time Around the World: Trends in Working Hours, Laws and Policies in a Global Comparative Perspective*, ILO, Routledge, 2007, pp. 24 et seq.
2. *See, e.g.*, L. Golden, *A Brief History of Long Work Time and the Contemporary Sources of Overwork*, Journal of Business Ethics, 2009/84(2), pp. 217-227 https://doi.org/10.1007/s10551-008-9698-z. S. De Spiegelaere & A. Piasna, *The Why and How of Working Time Reduction*, European Trade Union Institute, Brussels, 2017, pp. 11 et seq.; J. Messenger, *Working Time and the Future of Work*, International Labour Office, Geneva, 2018, p. 2. However, this is true mainly for developed countries and rather not for developing ones. The gap between countries remains significant (S. Lee, D. McCann & J.C. Messenger, *Working Time Around the World: Trends in Working Hours, Laws and Policies in a Global Comparative Perspective*, ILO, Routledge, 2007, p. 39).
3. International Labour Organization, *Hours of Work. From Fixed to Flexible*, International Labour Office, Geneva, 2005; J. Messenger, *Working Time and the Future of Work*, International Labour Office, Geneva, 2018, p. 15.
4. C. Lang, S. Clauwaert & I. Schömann, *Working Time Reforms in Times of Crisis*, European Trade Union Institute, Brussels, 2013, p. 6 underline that working time is treated as a key adjustment mechanism applied in the labour market reforms, predominantly to satisfy employer's needs for cost reductions and greater flexibility.

been particularly strong during crises which affected the world economy in recent decades.[5] The economic recovery and the end of the pandemic have offered an opportunity to reconstruct the employment relationship in a way more favourable for workers, in particular by enabling them to reconcile work and private (family) life.[6] However, at the same time the law is confronted with new challenges caused by technological developments (the Fourth Industrial Revolution)[7] and extensive use of atypical forms of employment[8] not covered by the protection arising from the labour law[9] which may limit rather than expand the sphere of freedom of working people.[10] In some European countries, a crucial role in regulating working time has been played by collective bargaining.[11] The world of work has undergone a profound twin transition (digital and environmental). The role of the law and collective bargaining is to make this transition fair and sustainable.[12] Working time and work day arrangements are important elements in these transitions on both sides: for employers, having a say in when and how much employees should work (and be paid) is crucial for their entrepreneurial freedom and the possibility of smoothly running the company, for workers, being able to rely on a certain income and/or working time patterns allows for planning other responsibilities such as care.

The article discusses the development of collective bargaining on working time and its legal framework since 2018 with special references to the phenomena which significantly affected the world of work (technological development, pandemic) and

5. *See, e.g.*, V. Glassner, M. Keune & P. Marginson, *Collective Bargaining in a Time of Crisis: Developments in the Private Sector in Europe*, Transfer 2011/17(3) https://doi.org/10.1177/1024258911406378; A. Kümmerling & S. Lehndorff, *The Use of Working Time-Related Crisis-Response Measures During the Great Recession*, International Labour Office, ILO, Geneva, 2013.
6. Eurofound, *Working Time in 2021-2022*, Publications Office of the European Union, Luxembourg, 2023, p. 2. The improvement is also associated with the implementation of EU standards, in particular Work-life Balance as well as Transparent and Predictable Working Conditions directives.
7. For more *see, e.g.*, D.M. Vicente, S. de Vasconcelos Casimiro & C. Chen (eds), *The Legal Challenges of the Fourth Industrial Revolution*, vol. 57, ICLCFIR 2022, Law, Governance and Technology Series, Springer, Cham, 2022.
8. OECD, *Self-Employment Rate (Indicator)*, 2023, https://data.oecd.org/emp/self-employment-rate.htm.
9. For more *see, e.g.*, B. Waas & Ch. Hießl (eds) *Collective Bargaining for Self-employed Workers in Europe*, Alphen aan den Rijn, Wolters Kluwer, 2021.
10. Compare J. Prassl, *Humans as a Service: The Promise and Perils of Work in the Gig Economy*, Oxford University Press, 2018.
11. Working time issues have been regulated in 85% of analysed collective agreements (International Labour Organization, *Social Dialogue Report 2022. Collective Bargaining for an Inclusive, Sustainable and Resilient Recovery*, Geneva, ILO, 2022, pp. 80-81). *See also* L. Golden, *A Brief History of Long Work Time and the Contemporary Sources of Overwork*, Journal of Business Ethics, 2009/84(2), p. 218 https://doi.org/10.1007/s10551-008-9698-z; S. Lee, D. McCann & J.C. Messenger, *Working Time Around the World: Trends in Working Hours, Laws and Policies in a Global Comparative Perspective*, ILO, Routledge, 2007, p. 10. However, the impact of collective bargaining on working time regulatory framework differs from country to country. It is also to underline that the situation of European countries is unique compared to the rest of the world (p. 151).
12. ILO' Centenary Declaration for the Future of Work; International Labour Organization, *Work for a Brighter Future: Global Commission on the Future of Work*, Geneva, ILO 2019; European pillar of social rights (2017). Interinstitutional Proclamation on the European Pillar of Social Rights (O.J. *C 428, 13.12.2017)*.

leading tendencies in regulating working time, including shortening the working day and working week, increasing flexibilization of working time and utilizing working time as an element of anti-crisis policies. The text is an extended and updated version of the chapter *Negotiating Working Time in Times of Crisis.*[13]

§5.02 UNDERSTANDING THE DEVELOPMENT OF WORKING TIME REGULATIONS: FUNDAMENTAL RIGHTS, LEGISLATION AND COLLECTIVE BARGAINING

The development of collective bargaining on working time must be seen in a broader perspective of fundamental rights and challenges facing the functioning of contemporary society. The right to rest, leisure and reasonable limitation of working hours constitutes a key element of just and favourable conditions of work ensured by international standards (Article 7 of the International Covenant on Economic, Social and Cultural Rights) and the European Union (EU) law (Article 31.2 ChFR). Working conditions should respect worker's health, safety and dignity (Article 31.1 ChFR). As a result, the economic and technological development is not an end in itself. It should remain human-orientated[14] contributing to the implementation of fundamental workers' rights. Any development which is not accompanied by the improvement in working conditions cannot be treated as a real progress.[15] Improving the position of workers can materialize, *inter alia*, by enlarging their sphere of freedom. Time outside work can be used for rest and leisure, to exercise other fundamental rights, including the right to personal and family life. It contributes to the protection of workers' health, too.[16] Technological and economic developments allow to maintain the profitability and competitiveness of enterprises while reducing working time.[17] The link between long working hours and productivity is considered to be a 'myth'.[18] Not surprisingly, the demands to shorten the working day and/or working week have recently become an important element of the International Labour Organization's (ILO's) strategy[19] and

13. Ł. Pisarczyk, *Negotiating Working Time in Times of Crisis* in *Collective Bargaining Development in Times of Crisis,* (ed.) S. Laulom, Wolters Kluwer 2018. The analysis is based on general surveys and articles as well as a number of national reports (Austria, Hungary, the Netherlands, Poland, Portugal and Romania).
14. ILO's Centenary Declaration for the Future of Work; International Labour Organization, *Work for a Brighter Future: Global Commission on the Future of Work*, Geneva, ILO 2019.
15. Compare ILO's resolution concerning the second recurrent discussion on social dialogue and tripartism, 2018.
16. J. Messenger, *Working Time and the Future of Work*, International Labour Office, Geneva, 2018, p. 26.
17. *See* S. Lee, D. McCann & J.C. Messenger, *Working Time Around the World: Trends in Working Hours, Laws and Policies in a Global Comparative Perspective,* ILO, Routledge, 2007, p. 149. Decreasing working hours may even contribute do improve the efficiency of work. It should, however, constitute a part of a package aimed at improving the quality of jobs (p. 150).
18. J. Messenger, *Working Time and the Future of Work*, International Labour Office, Geneva, 2018, p. 12.
19. *See* Reduction of Hours of Work Recommendation, 1962 (No. 116). The principle of the progressive reduction of normal hours of work may be given effect through laws or regulations, collective agreements, or arbitration awards, by a combination of these various means, or in any

a demand raised by workers and their representatives.[20] Moreover, organizing personal and family life (work-life balance) is facilitated by stable and predictable schedules of working time. Work-life balance policies may also require worker-orientated flexibility.[21]

However, the workers' sphere of freedom has been threatened by technological development (tech-based employment, remote work).[22] Working outside employer's premises entails the risk of extending factual working hours and blurring the borderline between work and privacy.[23] The privacy and well-being of workers may be invaded by the technology.[24] The role of the law and collective bargaining is to safeguard fundamental workers' rights and to prevent abuses.[25] At the same time, economic and organizational needs of companies must be taken into account. European companies must remain competitive in the global market.[26] Reducing working hours is, to a certain extent, not only a legal but rather also an economic issue. Companies must be ready to decrease the number of working hours while at the same time maintaining or even improving wages, leading to a financial burden.[27] Furthermore in several countries, the labour market is overheated, which means that the lack of (other) qualified personnel is an obstacle to reducing working hours for those already employed. Unbalanced changes in working time standards may affect business and lead to redundancies and insolvencies.[28] Therefore companies should have the possibility to adjust working hours to variable needs for work (flexible working time) unless

other manner consistent with national practice, as may be most appropriate to national conditions and to the needs of each branch of activity (Art. I.3 Reduction of Hours of Work Recommendation).

20. *See, e.g.*, European Trade Union Confederation, *Growing Europe-Wide Demand for Four-Day Week*, https://www.etuc.org/en/growing-europe-wide-demand-four-day-week.
21. S. Lee, D. McCann & J.C. Messenger, *Working Time Around the World: Trends in Working Hours, Laws and Policies in a Global Comparative Perspective*, ILO, Routledge, 2007, pp. 75 et seq.
22. Compare J. Prassl, *Humans as a Service: The Promise and Perils of Work in the Gig Economy*, Oxford University Press, 2018.
23. For more *see, e.g.*, I.V. Borges, *R2D: The Right to Disconnect from Work*, in *The Legal Challenges of the Fourth Industrial Revolution*, (eds) D.M. Vicente, S. de Vasconcelos Casimiro & C. Chen, vol. 57, ICLCFIR 2022, Law, Governance and Technology Series, Springer, Cham, 2023.
24. J. Messenger, *Working Time and the Future of Work*, International Labour Office, Geneva, 2018, p. 19.
25. Compare M. Lamannis, *Collective Bargaining in the Platform Economy: A Mapping Exercise of Existing Initiatives*, ETUI, Brussels, 2023, p. 27.
26. Compare European pillar of social rights (2017). Interinstitutional Proclamation on the European Pillar of Social Rights (O.J. C 428, 13.12.2017).
27. Eurofound, *Working Time in 2021-2022*, Publications Office of the European Union, Luxembourg, 2023, p. 10.
28. According to the Reduction of Hours of Work Recommendation measures for the progressive reduction of hours of work should be worked out and implemented in a manner suited to the particular national circumstances and the conditions in each sector of economic activity. They should take into account, *inter alia:* (a) the level of economic development attained and the extent to which the country is in a position to bring about a reduction in hours of work without reducing total production or productivity, endangering its economic growth, the development of new industries or its competitive position in international trade, and without creating inflationary pressures which would ultimately reduce the real income of the workers; (b) the progress achieved and which it is possible to achieve in raising productivity by the application of modern technology, automation and management techniques (Arts I.6 and 7).

it does not interfere with workers' fundamental rights and adopted policies like work-life balance.

As a result, working time regulations should be perceived as a compromise between the protection of workers and the expectations of companies which have to adapt their businesses to the economic and technological environment. The controversial 2024 Greek reform increasing the number of working hours has been explained as an attempt to increase productivity and overcome the consequences of the economic crisis.[29] Collective bargaining remains a unique instrument enabling the maintenance of the link between the market and social development[30] as regards the number of working hours and their organization. Collective agreements negotiated by employers and workers' representatives enable a real compromise and social equilibrium. Moreover, collective bargaining has the potential to tailor working time solutions to the needs of various sectors and companies.[31] It may implement various policies, like work-life balance,[32] and contribute to the enforcement of working standards including the enforcement of the right to be offline.[33] As a result, collective bargaining may play the role of a bridge between work efficiency and increased workers' rights. An example is the consent of workers' representatives to flexible arrangements of working time in return for a general reduction of working hours[34] (e.g., in Germany).[35] However, collective bargaining can only fulfil this role on condition that the social partners adopt new, adequate policies adjusted to the realities of the twin transition. The social partners including trade unions, are in the process of adopting strategies adjusted to the labour market affected by such phenomena as technological development, platform work and the growing importance of atypical form of employment, including self-employment.[36] Although some successes have already been achieved,[37] it is a process that is still ongoing.

---

29. M. Race, *Greece Starts Six-Day Working Week for Some Industries*, https://www.bbc.com/news/articles/czd9g7yzn4jo.
30. The ILO's Declaration on Fundamental Principles and Rights at Work, 1998.
31. International Labour Organization, *Social Dialogue Report 2022. Collective Bargaining for an Inclusive, Sustainable and Resilient Recovery*, Geneva, ILO, 2022, p. 18.
32. E. Voss & H. Riede, *Digitalisation and Workers Participation: What Trade Unions, Company Level Workers and Online Platform Workers in Europe Think*, European Trade Union Institute, Brussels, 2018, p. 16.
33. M. Lamannis, *Collective Bargaining in the Platform Economy: A Mapping Exercise of Existing Initiatives*, European Trade Union Institute, Brussels, 2023, p. 27.
34. S. Lee, D. McCann & J.C. Messenger, *Working Time Around the World: Trends in Working Hours, Laws and Policies in a Global Comparative Perspective*, ILO, Routledge, 2007, p. 100; International Labour Organization, *Social Dialogue Report 2022. Collective Bargaining for an Inclusive, Sustainable and Resilient Recovery*, Geneva, ILO, 2022, p. 82.
35. T. Schulten & R. Bispinck, *Varieties of Decentralisation in German Collective Bargaining: Experiences from Metal Industry and Retail Trade. WP CSDLE 'Massimo D'Antona'.INT – 137/2017.* [Working Paper], pp. 21-22.
36. *See, e.g.*, F. Roşioru, *The 'Smart' Trade Union: New Strategies for a Digitalised Labour Market* in *Collective Bargaining and the Gig Economy*, (eds) E. Brameshuber & J.M. Miranda Boto, Hart Publishing 2022.
37. J. Waddington, T. Müller & K. Vandaele, *Conclusion: Trade Unions Picking Up the Pieces from the Neoliberal Challenge*, in *Trade Unions in the European Union. Picking Up the Pieces of the Neoliberal Challenge*, (eds) J. Waddington, T. Müller & K. Vandaele, Brussels, Peter Lang 2023, pp. 1108-1109.

Legal provisions concerning working time can be divided into two groups.[38] First, they set up, directly or indirectly, the number of working hours on a daily, weekly and yearly basis (maximum daily and weekly working hours, rest periods, days off). Second, they regulate the distribution of working hours within days, weeks and reference periods (schedules of working time). The law usually distinguishes between normal (regular) working hours which are to be performed by the worker and overtime work.[39] Limits, arising from the law or collective agreements, can be imposed on both. As a rule, overtime work is subject to additional restrictions (the conditions of performance, extra compensation).[40]

The EU directive on working time[41] merely aims at minimum harmonization and therefore still leaves much room for the Member States. National laws on working time usually play a dual role. First, they set up the number of working hours and the length of rest periods. Second, they create a framework for organizing the process of work. For instance, they provide for organizational solutions that can be used by social partners (e.g., working time accounts) as well as set up maximum reference periods for the calculation of working hours. The social partners may regulate working time either as a part of collective autonomy (in areas not regulated) or on the basis of a statutory authorization (e.g., deviating from statutory standards). Collective bargaining on working time can be conducted at various levels: cross-sectoral (national), sectoral, company and plant/establishment. National agreements may constitute a sui generis social pact empowering the state to undertake legislative action.[42] Agreements concluded at sectoral level, due to their scope of application, concern usually more general issues like harmonizing the number of working hours (usually weekly working time)[43] and basic organizational constructions (e.g., time banking accounts) while schedules of working time are usually adopted in companies and establishments. However, the division is not sharp. In a traditional hierarchy of labour law sources sectoral

38. C. Lang, S. Clauwaert & I. Schömann, *Working Time Reforms in Times of Crisis*, European Trade Union Institute, Brussels, 2013, p. 7, distinguish three main tendencies: (1) allowing employers to extend working time duration; (2) allowing employers to shorten time duration; and (3) allowing the employers to accommodate the allocation of working hours according to their needs.
39. *See, e.g.*, S. Lee, D. McCann & J.C. Messenger, *Working Time Around the World: Trends in Working Hours, Laws and Policies in a Global Comparative Perspective*, ILO, Routledge, 2007, pp. 7 et seq.
40. For more *see* S. Lee, D. McCann & J.C. Messenger, *Working Time Around the World: Trends in Working Hours, Laws and Policies in a Global Comparative Perspective*, ILO, Routledge, 2007, pp. 11 et seq. Overtime compensation is a very popular topic of collective bargaining – around 51 % of analysed agreements have concerned this issue (International Labour Organization, *Social Dialogue Report 2022. Collective Bargaining for an Inclusive, Sustainable and Resilient Recovery*, Geneva, ILO, 2022, p. 81).
41. Directive 2003/88/EC of the European Parliament and of the Council of 4 November 2003 concerning certain aspects of the organization of working time (OJ L 299, 18.11.2003, pp. 9-19), hereinafter referred to as 'Directive 2003/88'.
42. *See, e.g.*, V. Glassner & M. Keune, *Crise et politique sociale: la rôle des accords collectifs*, Revue Internationale du Travail 2012/4, p. 388.
43. Eurofound, *Working Time in 2021-2022*, Publications Office of the European Union, Luxembourg, 2023, pp. 13 et seq.

agreements prevailed over company-level arrangements. Company-level social partners may be authorized to adapt sectoral standards to local conditions. Thanks to derogation clauses they may also modify provisions of sectoral or branch agreements.[44] In some countries (e.g., France) this relationship has been modified by recognizing the sui generis primacy of company-level agreements (El-Khomri law).[45] Some aspects of working time can be regulated in sectoral collective agreements unless there are no provisions of company-level agreements.

The composition of structures (units) negotiating working time depends on various factors, including the level of negotiations (sectoral versus company-level negotiations) national model of the social dialogue as well as the factual situation of trade unions. Sectoral, branch or regional agreements have been concluded mainly with trade unions. Employers are usually represented by their organizations. An exceptional solution is representation by economic chambers based on obligatory membership (Austria).[46] The structure of the company-level social dialogue in EU countries is much more complex. The competences to act on behalf of workers are divided between trade unions and elected bodies. The position of elected bodies varies from country to country. In some systems regulating working time is considered to be a part of company matters negotiated with elected bodies, e.g., work councils (Austria, Germany).[47] Moreover, collective agreements concluded with trade unions (*Tarifvertrag*) may authorize employers and work councils to regulate matters reserved for *Tarifvertrag* by means of company-level arrangements (*Betriebsvereinbarung*).[48] In other systems, the involvement of elected bodies in negotiating working time can be a response to the lack of trade union structures at appropriate (e.g., company) levels (Poland, Romania). In Poland, where the position and competences of work councils remain limited, the law provides for negotiating collective agreements on working time with employees' representatives elected according to the rules adopted in a company (when there are no trade unions).[49] Irrespective of differences between the Member States, the role of elected bodies in negotiating working time, in particular the

44. International Labour Organization, *Social Dialogue Report 2022. Collective Bargaining for an Inclusive, Sustainable and Resilient Recovery*, Geneva, ILO, 2022, p. 59.
45. The El Khomri law (2016) concerned such issues as the duration of working time (daily and weekly) and overtime work. *See* Ch. Vigneau, *Negotiation Working Time in Time of Crisis: The 'El Khomri Law'*, in *Collective Bargaining Development in Times of Crisis,* (ed.) S. Laulom, Wolters Kluwer 2018.
46. §4 the Austrian Labour Constitution. For more *see, e.g.*, V. Glassner & J. Hoffmann, *Austria: From Gradual Change to an Unknown Future,* in *Collective Bargaining in Europe: Towards an Endgame*, (eds) T. Müller, K. Vandaele & J. Waddington, vol. 1, European Trade Union Institute, Brussels 2019, pp. 33-51.
47. §97 the Austrian Labour Constitution; 87 the German Workplace Constitution Act.
48. Company agreements concluded with elected bodies are considered to be sources of labour law but are situated lower than traditional (typical) collective agreements. *See, e.g.*, §7 the German Law on Working Time.
49. If workers are not represented by trade unions, collective agreements concerning selected aspects of working time are concluded with employee representatives elected according to the rules determined at a given enterprise (establishment). The potential scope of the regulation is relatively broad. It covers the extension of calculation periods (up to twelve months). The law does not regulate the election procedure of representatives. Ad hoc representatives do not enjoy any protection against dismissal or other actions undertaken by the employer. As a result, the

organization of working hours, is usually greater than in negotiating other working conditions, for instance, remuneration.

The actual role of collective bargaining in regulating working time depends significantly on the development of the social dialogue in various countries. There is a fundamental difference between the West and the East as regards intensity and coverage by collective bargaining. In Central and Eastern European Countries (CEEC) the coverage remains low or very low which is valid in particular for multi-company (sectoral) bargaining.[50] The weakness of collective bargaining limits its usefulness as an instrument to achieve social equilibrium – also in the field of working time. The differentiation in the development of collective bargaining is reflected by a factual number of annual working hours in EU countries: which is lower in the West and higher in the East.[51] In some Western countries (e.g., Denmark) collective bargaining has established a comprehensive legal framework for working time while in the CEEC, due to the weakness of collective bargaining, the role of the legislation increases significantly. The relaxation of statutory standards and increasing flexibility in countries where collective bargaining remains underdeveloped could pose a significant threat to workers' rights.[52]

Collective bargaining agreements on working time, in particular in countries where its factual importance is limited, can be supplemented or even replaced by other legal instruments, including internal acts and instructions issued by companies and individual employment contracts. The regulatory power of corporate acts may be derived from managerial competences of the employer. Employers perceive corporate acts issued unilaterally as more flexible and adaptable to the needs of companies. However, unilateral employer's acts, even if they emerge after consulting workers' representatives[53] do not guarantee a necessary balance between management and labour. Therefore, they cannot usually be used as an effective instrument to restructure working time (the scope of flexible solutions that can be introduced in this way being limited).[54] They also constitute a challenge for collective bargaining. In some countries,

---

regulation does not guarantee a balance between social partners and may lead to the destruction of the traditional model of social dialogue.

50. Eurofound, *Collective Bargaining Coverage*, https://www.eurofound.europa.eu/en/european-industrial-relations-dictionary/collective-bargaining-coverage.
51. Eurofound, *Working Time in 2021-2022*, Publications Office of the European Union, Luxembourg, 2023.
52. S. Lee, D. McCann & J.C. Messenger, *Working Time Around the World: Trends in Working Hours, Laws and Policies in a Global Comparative Perspective*, ILO, Routledge, 2007, pp. 143-144 and 151.
53. *See* Art. 104^2 the Polish Labour Code.
54. Polish law provides for internal regulations concerning the organization of work. They must be issued by employers with at least fifty employees. Any employer of twenty or more workers is obliged to issue the regulations on request of the trade unions. By means of internal regulations, it is possible to introduce the extension of daily working hours, flexible working time (without working hours), shift work or the extension of yearly limit of overtime work. However, it is not possible to introduce reference periods longer than four months, intermittent work or variable working hours. The above-mentioned solutions must be accepted by trade unions in collective agreements. For work rules, *see* more M. Włodarczyk, in *Outline of Polish Labour Law System*, (ed.) K.W. Baran, Wolter Kluwers 2016, pp. 109-110.

(e.g., Hungary),[55] flexibilization was connected with extending individual autonomy and freedom of contracts. It was based on assumption that employers and workers can best adapt working conditions to the current situation. The freedom, however, is usually apparent because of the domination of employers who is able to protect its own interests with a potential detriment to workers' rights.[56] Collective bargaining remains the best instrument to strike a balance between the needs of companies and protection of workers, in particular to introduce legal mechanisms characterized by a high level of flexibility which may affect the traditional model of the employment relationship.

A special case of working time management and bargaining is anti-crisis measures adopted in the event of serious disruptions in the functioning of the economy and society (the world economic crisis, pandemic). The consequences of major crises (such as the pandemic) exceed the possibilities of individual entities to protect their own interests. Affected companies are threatened by redundancies or even insolvencies. As a result, workers could lose jobs or face tougher employment conditions. Only larger communities, especially the state, have adequate resources to counteract this kind of global crisis effectively. To protect the social equilibrium, the state should provide companies and workers with the necessary support.[57] Among popular anti-crisis solutions which involve working time are: (1) suspending employment relationships; (2) short-time work; (3) wage subsidies; (4) increasing flexibility in work organization (e.g., more flexible working hours). The aim is to preserve employment by enabling companies to adjust working hours and economic activity.[58] Although aimed at preserving employment the anti-crisis legislation cannot disregard the current protection of workers whose position during the crisis becomes even weaker. While adopting short-time work or flexible schedules of working hours, the state should always be mindful of the necessity to keep protecting the fundamental human and employment rights of workers.[59] The role of collective bargaining is, again, searching for an equilibrium in creating and adopting anti-crisis measures.[60] The social partners may limit the application of short-time work, e.g., in return for freezing remuneration for a

55. T. Gyulavári T, *COVID-19 and Labour Law: Hungary*, Italian Labour Law E-Journal 2020/13(1S), pp. 1-3.
56. J. Prassl, *Humans as a Service. The Promise and Perils of Work in the Gig Economy*, Oxford, 2018, pp. 52 et seq., 68-69.
57. Economic and social consequences of the crisis have been divided between employers, employees and the State. Sometimes the State takes on the burden of the crisis, like in France, Germany, Italy and Spain (e.g., T. Sachs, *Regards comparés sur le droit social à l'épreuve du covid-19*, Revue de Droit du Travail 2020/4, p. 273).
58. T. Müller, T. Schulten & J. Drahokoupil, *Job Retention Schemes in Europe During the COVID-19 Pandemic: Different Shapes and Sizes and the Role of Collective Bargaining*, Transfer: European Review of Labour and Research, 2022/28(2), p. 249, https://doi.org/10.1177/10242589221089808.
59. Among the pillars of anti-crisis actions, the ILO indicates protecting workers in the workplace as well as supporting jobs and incomes (ILO Monitor, *COVID-19 and the World of Work*, 5th edn, Briefing Note, 30 June 2020, p. 14). *See also* G. Davidov, *A Purposive Approach to Labour Law*, Oxford University Press, 2016, p. 2. The support provided to businesses (employers) cannot be treated as being equivalent to providing support to employees.
60. Of course, the general assumption about the balance of bargaining power must be confronted with the actual position of workers' representation. Collective agreements may also contribute

certain period, increase short-time payments or provide for additional entitlements for affected workers.

Theoretically, a role in regulating certain aspects of working time could be played by transnational company agreements (TCAs) negotiated by multinational companies since the 1980s.[61] It was hoped, especially in CEEC where collective bargaining undergoes a deep crisis, that transnational agreements would contribute to the unification of employment conditions, including working time.[62] However, the significance of the TCAs in this area has remained limited. First of all, the provisions of TCAs are characterized by a certain generality. They focus rather on fundamental workers' rights or restructuring matters.[63] As a result, provisions concerning working time have been rather unique.[64] Moreover, there are significant differences between companies acting in various Member States. Multinational companies which have searched for cheaper labour opportunities are not interested in increasing costs of work. At the same time companies from CEEC have built their position thanks to lower labour costs while the approach of local trade unions has remained passive.[65] Moreover, in recent years the idea of transnational bargaining has weakened significantly. There are very few agreements negotiated recently. As a result, one should not expect TCAs to become a real instrument of regulating working time. Working time remains a domain of traditional bargaining which take place at sectoral or company level.[66] Companies from CEEC will not be encouraged by central managements to improve significantly working time standards.

---

to employee income protection, e.g., by increasing benefits offsetting the loss of some remuneration (in short-time work *see, e.g.*, J. Brockmann, *Regards comparés sur le droit social à l'épreuve du covid-19: Allemagne*, Revue de Droit du Travail 2020/4, p. 284).

61. *See, e.g.*, I. Schömann, *Transnational Company Bargaining in Search of a Legal Framework*, in: *Transnational Collective Bargaining at Company Level: A New Component of European Industrial Relations?*, ETUI 2012.
62. S. Adamczyk & B. Surdykowska, *The Importance of Transnational Company Agreements from the Perspective of Industrial Relations in the New Member States: The Polish Case*, in *Transnational Company Agreements: A Stepping Stone Towards a Real Internationalisation of Industrial Relations?*, (ed.) S. Leonardi, Rome 2012, p. 108.
63. Eurofound, *Transnational Company Agreement*, https://www.eurofound.europa.eu/en/european-industrial-relations-dictionary/transnational-company-agreement.
64. V. Glassner, *Transnational Collective Bargaining in National Systems of Industrial Relations*, in: *Transnational Collective Bargaining at Company Level: A New Component of European Industrial Relations?*, ETUI 2012, pp. 81-82.
65. *See, e.g.*, I.T. Berend, *Social Shock in Transforming Central and Eastern Europe*, Communist and Post-Communist Studies 2007/40(3), pp. 269-280 https://doi.org/10.1016/j.postcomstud.2007.06.007; M.A. Orenstein & B. Bugarič, *Work, Family, Fatherland: The Political Economy of Populism in Central and Eastern Europe*, Journal of European Public Policy 2020/29(2), pp. 176-195 https://doi.org/10.1080/13501763.2020.1832557.
66. V. Glassner, *Transnational Collective Bargaining in National Systems of Industrial Relations*, in: *Transnational Collective Bargaining at Company Level: A New Component of European Industrial Relations?*, ETUI 2012, pp. 81-82.

§5.03 A RETURN TO A TRADITIONAL PATH: THE ROLE OF COLLECTIVE BARGAINING IN REGULATING THE LENGTH OF WORKING TIME

A technological development and increased work efficiency make it possible to shorten working hours. However, shortening working time is a complex and long-term process that requires weighing the economic situation of employers and the interests of workers. In addition to the legislation, collective bargaining, which is an expression of inter-group compromise, can play a large role in shortening working hours.
How much people work is determined by several factors. The most important are the concept of working time (periods included in working time), the number of regular working hours as well as the conditions of performing overtime work. The number of working hours is calculated on various basis: daily, weekly and yearly. Reducing or extending working hours is usually associated with reducing or extending weekly working time which is considered a basic measurement of the length of work.[67] Extending daily working hours within an unchanged weekly limit could be perceived as flexibilization rather than as the extension of working hours *sensu stricto*. Weekly working time is usually calculated in reference periods. The number of working hours per year is influenced not only by weekly working time but also by the number of days off: annual leave, holidays, and other days off. Moreover, the law provides for rest periods (daily and weekly) which may supplement or modify regulations concerning working hours.

The basic standards of defining working time have been developed by the *acquis communautaire*. According to the concept formulated by the Tribunal, working time covers every period during which the worker is obliged to remain at the employer's disposal (not only on the employer's premises).[68] These periods cannot be excluded from working time or calculated in a way that is less favourable than working time *sensu stricto*.[69] The social partners may, however, extend the concept of working time to include periods which are not clearly periods during which the employee remains at the employer's disposal (e.g., additional breaks).[70] Defining working time in collective agreements may be particularly relevant for non-employees who are not covered by the protection arising from labour law. For instance, in the case of delivery riders the social

67. Compare S. Lee, D. McCann & J.C. Messenger, *Working Time Around the World: Trends in Working Hours, Laws and Policies in a Global Comparative Perspective*, ILO, Routledge, 2007, pp. 11 et seq.
68. *See* the judgments of the Court of Justice of 3 October 2000, in the case C-303/98, *Sindicato de Médicos de Asistencia Pública (Simap) v. Conselleria de Sanidad y Consumo de la Generalidad Valenciana* and of 9 September 2003, in the case C-151/02 *Landeshauptstadt Kiel v. Norbert Jäger* and of 21 February 2018, in the case C-518/15 *Ville de Nivelles v. Rudy Matzak*.
69. Judgment of the Court of 1 December 2005 in the case C-14/04 *Abdelkader Dellas and Others v. Premier ministre and Ministre des Affaires sociales, du Travail et de la Solidarité*.
70. Eurofound, *Working Time in 2021-2022*, Publications Office of the European Union, Luxembourg, 2023.

partners may provide that their time spent waiting for deliveries will be treated as working time.[71]

As regards the length of working time, it is limited by rest periods and maximum weekly working time (forty-eight hours). However, many European legislations still provide for normal daily and/or weekly working time (Austria, France, Germany,[72] Hungary, Netherlands, Poland, Portugal and Romania). The main reference point is usually regular weekly working time which amount to forty hours or less.[73] Work performed beyond this threshold is treated, as a rule, as overtime. The relationship between the law and collective bargaining is usually governed by the *favor laboratoris* principle. The social partners may reduce the number of working hours and/or extend rest periods. Modifications *in peius* are exceptional and may occur where a statutory limit is set up at a relatively low level – far below the traditional forty-hours working week. In France, where the statutory weekly working time amounts to thirty five hours[74] subject to overtime which legal framework has been flexibilized over recent years.[75] The social partners may increase a weekly limit of working hours.[76] In 2022, the average collectively agreed normal weekly working hours amounted to 35.7.[77] The increase of working hours by collective agreements is also allowed when it is justified by a special nature of work, e.g., if work is not performed constantly but the worker remains ready to provide service (Austria,[78] Germany).[79] In other Member States the law provides only for rest periods and maximum working time – with or without overtime (Cyprus, Denmark, Ireland, Malta).[80] The social partners, at various levels, may adopt more favourable conditions. In countries without regular weekly working time, they are responsible for setting up the maximum number of working hours. In Austria, Denmark or Germany, in private sector, regular weekly working time is set up by collective agreements.[81] The social partners may also establish a protective

71. Platforms have adopted various solutions (M. Lamannis, *Collective Bargaining in the Platform Economy: A Mapping Exercise of Existing Initiatives*, European Trade Union Institute, 2023, p. 43).
72. In Germany, daily working time cannot exceed, as a rule, eight hours (§3 the Law on Working Time).
73. Eurofound, *Working Time in 2021-2022*, Publications Office of the European Union, Luxembourg, 2023, p. 13.
74. Article L 3121-27 the French Labour Code.
75. https://travail-emploi.gouv.fr/droit-du-travail/duree-et-temps-de-travail.
76. https://www.service-public.fr/particuliers/vosdroits/F1911.
77. Eurofound, *Working Time in 2021-2022*, Publications Office of the European Union, Luxembourg, 2023, p. 14.
78. §3 the German Law on Working Time.
79. §7 the German Law on Working Time. Daily working time can be extended by a collective agreement beyond ten hours.
80. Eurofound, *Working Time in 2021-2022*, Publications Office of the European Union, Luxembourg, 2023, p. 13.
81. S. Lee, D. McCann & J.C. Messenger, *Working Time Around the World: Trends in Working Hours, Laws and Policies in a Global Comparative Perspective*, ILO, Routledge, 2007, p. 34; https://www.bmi.bund.de/DE/themen/oeffentlicher-dienst/beamtinnen-und-beamte/arbeitszeit/arbeitszeit-node.html.

framework for non-employees, e.g., for platform workers by setting up either maximum working hours or maximum number of services per day/week.[82]

A natural tendency in the development of working time to reduce the number of working hours was disrupted by the world economic crisis. One of the reactions to the crisis was extending working time to reduce the cost of work. Previously employed workers worked longer for the same salary while the employer did not have to recruit new people. The increase in working hours was accomplished either by legislation (e.g., the Portuguese public sector extended from thirty-five to forty) or by means of collective agreements.[83] An increase in working hours was usually of a temporary nature.[84] The improvement of the economic situation restored a long-lasting tendency to maintain or reduce working time. Particularly in 2021/22, collective agreements show a tendency to reduce working hours (again). An important role has been played by multi-company agreements which have the potential to cover large groups of workers.[85] The shortening has been reported, *inter alia,* in Austria (private care sector) and Portugal (municipal suppliers of water). Decreasing weekly working hours, like in some sectors in Italy, can be combined with flexible arrangements. Of course, there are still examples of extending working hours due to economic and technical reasons, e.g., by withdrawing from previous more favourable arrangements (e.g., the Finnish paper sector).[86]

Nonetheless, the general tendency is once again, to reduce working time by collective agreements. In 2021, the average working week set up in the form of collective bargaining amounted to 38.1 hours. Not surprisingly, the role of collective bargaining in shortening working hours is greater in the West than in the CEEC. Collectively agreed weekly working time in Nordic countries, the Netherlands and Germany is below thirty-eight hours. In Czechia (the lowest level among CEEC) and Italy it was 38 hours, in Spain 38.4, in Austria 38.5 while in Ireland 39 and in Portugal 39.4 hours.[87] In Italy, working time in some sectors has been reduced to the level below the legislative threshold (e.g., thirty-nine hours in the logistics sector).[88,89] In other CEEC, collective bargaining plays rather a margin role in shortening working time.

82. *See, e.g.,* T. Jaspers, B. Mądrzycki & Ł. Pisarczyk, *Collective Bargaining in Technology-Based Employment*, Bialystok Law Review 2024/2, p. 46 https://doi.org/10.15290/bsp.2024.29.02.04.
83. A. Kümmerling & S. Lehndorff, *The Use of Working Time-Related Crisis-Response Measures During the Great Recession*, International Labour Office, Geneva, ILO, 2013, pp. 11-12.
84. European Trade Union Confederation, *35-Hour Week Restored in Portuguese Public Sector*, https://www.etuc.org/en/35-hour-week-restored-portuguese-public-sector.
85. International Labour Organization, *Social Dialogue Report 2022. Collective Bargaining for an Inclusive, Sustainable and Resilient Recovery*, Geneva, ILO, 2022, p. 70. In systems based on multi-company negotiations the coverage by collective agreements is around 70% while in countries where company-level negotiations dominate is only around 15% (International Labour Organization, *Social Dialogue Report 2022. Collective Bargaining for an Inclusive, Sustainable and Resilient Recovery*, Geneva, ILO, 2022, p. 70).
86. Examples mentioned in Eurofound, *Working Time in 2021-2022*, Publications Office of the European Union, Luxembourg, 2023, pp. 8-9.
87. Eurofound, *Working Time in 2021-2022*, Publications Office of the European Union, Luxembourg, 2023, pp. 2, 14.
88. https://www.rivermate.com/guides/italy/working-hours.
89. For more details about shortening working hours in selected sectors *see* Eurofound, *Working Time in 2021-2022*, Publications Office of the European Union, Luxembourg, 2023, pp. 15 et seq.

Consequently, usual working hours (including overtime and absence) in the CEEC is also clearly higher than in the 'old' Member States.[90]

A decrease in working hours can also be part of a broader strategy initiated or adopted by the state and aimed at changing the ratio between work and private life. A symbol of progress is a four-day working week.[91] Although discussed since the 1970s, it became particularly interesting after the pandemic which stimulated various forms of flexible working time. A four-day working schedule may be implemented with or without reduction in working hours (condensed working week).[92] Germany has been testing the system 100-80-100.[93] Decrease in the working time to 80% will be accompanied with maintaining both: productivity as well as the remuneration. The pilot system connected with 10% reduction in working time was also adopted in Spain. The reduction could be introduced at a company level by social partners. The aim of the project was to evaluate the influence of a four-day week on productivity in small and medium enterprises (SMEs).[94] An opposite strategy has been adopted in Greece. The new law which entered into force on 1 July 2024 allowed a six-day working week and extending weekly working hours to forty-eight. However, the extension is possible only in specific industries (operating on a permanent basis), under specific conditions and are optional for workers.[95] Nonetheless the amendment is considered inconsistent with contemporary trends to increase workers' well-being and therefore criticized, e.g., by trade unions.[96]

Annual working time can be shortened by provisions of collective agreements increasing: (a) annual paid leave; and/or (b) the number of additional days off (holidays).[97] Again, such provisions are far more often concluded by companies in western Europe.[98]

A new challenge connected with the length of working time has been caused by technological development. Although the definition of the employment relationship in

90. Eurofound, *Working Time in 2021-2022*, Publications Office of the European Union, Luxembourg, 2023, pp. 19 et seq.
91. *See* T. Campbell, *The Four-Day Work Week: A Chronological, Systematic Review of the Academic Literature*, Management Review Quarterly 2023/74(1).
92. H. Chung, *A Social Policy Case for a Four-Day Week*, Journal of Social Policy 2022/51(3), pp. 551-554 https://doi.org/10.1007/s11301-023-00347-3; T. Jahal, E. A. Bardoel & J. Hopkins, *Could the 4-Day Week Work? A Scoping Review*, Asia Pacific Journal of Human Resources 2023, p. 2 https://doi.org/10.1111/1744-7941.12395.
93. Euronews, *Germany Launches Major 4-Day Workweek Trial Amid Labour Shortage*, https://www.euronews.com/next/2024/02/02/germany-launches-major-4-day-workweek-trial-amid-labour-shortage.
94. Eurofound, *Working Time in 2021-2022*, Publications Office of the European Union, Luxembourg, 2023, p. 9.
95. M. Race, *Greece Starts Six-Day Working Week for Some Industries*, https://www.bbc.com/news/articles/czd9g7yzn4jo.
96. S. Meredith, *Greece Becomes First EU Country to Introduce a Six-Day Working Week*, https://www.cnbc.com/2024/07/02/greece-becomes-first-eu-country-to-introduce-a-six-day-working-week.html.
97. Eurofound, *Working Time in 2021-2022*, Publications Office of the European Union, Luxembourg, 2023, p. 26.
98. Eurofound, *Working Time in 2021-2022*, Publications Office of the European Union, Luxembourg, 2023, p. 23.

the tech-based economy has not been formally changed,[99] the use of technology may lead to a – hidden – increase in working hours. This increase, which may or may not be visible, is due to the blurred boundaries between private life and work life, e.g., in telework. People working outside the employer's premises and using modern technologies may easily perform work in their private time work which is beyond the control of the employer and remains unregistered. In some cases extra work meets informal expectations of companies but is difficult to control and to prove. A large number of teleworkers is available or/and expected to be available in their free time.[100] At the same time only some European countries adopted legislation referring directly to the right to disconnect[101] while in others the general rules on working time apply. An important role in enforcing the right to disconnect can be played by collective bargaining at sectoral and company-level.[102] For instance, collective agreements may establish monitoring procedures aimed at implementing the mechanisms provided for either by the law or by the social partners.[103]

The situation may change when the legal framework for distant work is rebuilt. Initiatives to ensure an effective right to disconnect have been undertaken at various levels. On 21 January 2021, the European Parliament adopted a resolution with recommendations to the Commission on the right to disconnect.[104] On 20 June 2020, European social partners concluded the Agreement on Digitalization.[105] When the negotiations of the European social partners on a legally binding framework agreement on telework had failed, the Commission initiated the legislative procedure to regulate the right to disconnect.[106] The amendments in legal frameworks have been adopted or debated in various Member States.[107]

§5.04 THE ROLE OF COLLECTIVE BARGAINING IN ORGANIZING AND FLEXIBILIZING WORKING TIME

A constant development trend in working time is its increasing flexibility. The idea of flexibilizing working time is to adjust work performed by workers to the actual needs

99. Compare European Parliament resolution of 21 January 2021 with recommendations to the Commission on the right to disconnect.
100. *See* I.V. Borges, *R2D: The Right to Disconnect from Work*, in *The Legal Challenges of the Fourth Industrial Revolution*, (eds) D.M. Vicente, S. de Vasconcelos Casimiro & C. Chen, vol. 57, ICLCFIR 2022. Law, Governance and Technology Series, Springer, Cham 2023, footnote 11.
101. Eurofund, *Right to Disconnect in the 27 EU Member States*, 2020, pp. 15 et seq.
102. M. Lamannis, *Collective Bargaining in the Platform Economy: A Mapping Exercise of Existing Initiatives*, European Trade Union Institute, 2023, p. 27.
103. D. Mangan, E. Gramano & M. Kullmann, *An Unprecedented Social Solidarity Stress Test*, European Labour Law Journal 2020/11(3) https://doi.org/10.1177/2031952520934585.
104. European Parliament resolution of 21 January 2021 with recommendations to the Commission on the right to disconnect.
105. https://www.etuc.org/system/files/document/file2020-06/Final%2022%2006%2020_Agreement%20on%20Digitalisation%202020.pdf.
106. https://www.europarl.europa.eu/legislative-train/theme-employment-and-social-affairs-empl/file-al-legislative-proposal-to-the-commission-on-the-right-to-disconnect.
107. Eurofund, *Right to Disconnect in the 27 EU Member States*, 2020, pp. 15 et seq.

of companies and to increase the efficiency of the employment relationship.[108] The more changeable and unpredictable the process of work, the more flexibility in organizing working hours is needed.[109]

On the one hand, the continuing flexibilization of working time may be treated as a price that employees have to pay to maintain their employment.[110] On the other hand, the protective dimension of working time standards should not be overlooked.[111] From this perspective, the most dangerous systems are those in which the worker cannot be sure as regards the number of working hours (work on-call, zero-hours contracts).[112] At the same time, flexible schedules of working time may be an obstacle in organizing private and family life of workers.[113] As a result, the point is to strike a balance between organizational needs of employers on the one hand and the protection of workers, on the other.[114] Member States shall take the measures necessary to ensure that an employer who intends to organize work according to a certain pattern takes account of the general principle of adapting work to the worker, with a view, in particular, to alleviating monotonous work and work at a predetermined work-rate, depending on the type of activity, and of safety and health requirements, especially as regards breaks during working time.[115]

Organizing working hours can be perceived as a field of competition between the employer's managerial power and the competences of the social partners. This relationship is shaped differently in various Member States. Again, this is collective bargaining which can reconcile the needs of both parties. Regulating schedules of

108. J. Messenger, *Working Time and the Future of Work*, International Labour Office, Geneva, 2018, p. 15.
109. Flexible working time arrangements have been provided for by 53% of analysed collective agreements (International Labour Organization, *Social Dialogue Report 2022. Collective Bargaining for an Inclusive, Sustainable and Resilient Recovery*, Geneva, ILO, 2022, p. 83).
110. The (temporary) worsening of working conditions may contribute to the improvement of the employer's position and the protection of workplaces (e.g., B. Hepple, *Four Approaches to the Modernisation of Individual Employment Rights*, in *Changing Industrial Relations & Modernisation of Labour Law: Liber Amicorum in Honour of Professor Marco Biagi*, (eds) R. Blanpain & M. Weiss, Kluwer Law International 2003, pp. 184-185).
111. The right to reasonable working hours may be treated as a fundamental employee right guaranteed by the main international documents and conventions. Article 24 Universal Declaration of Human Rights provides that everyone has the right to rest and leisure, including reasonable limitation of working hours. According to Art. 7 International Covenant on Economic, Social and Cultural Rights, everyone has the right to leisure and reasonable limitation of working hours, as well as remuneration for public holidays. Article 2 European Social Charter obliges the Parties to provide for reasonable daily and weekly working hours and for public holidays with pay; the working week should be progressively reduced to the extent that the increase of productivity and other relevant factors permit. When it comes to the EU standards Art. 31.2 Charter of Fundamental Rights declares that every worker has the right to limitation of maximum working hours, to daily and weekly rest periods. Finally, one should not overlook the standards arising from the ILO's conventions.
112. J. Messenger, *Working Time and the Future of Work*, International Labour Office, Geneva, 2018, p. 17.
113. Compare S. Lee, D. McCann & J.C. Messenger, *Working Time Around the World: Trends in Working Hours, Laws and Policies in a Global Comparative Perspective*, ILO, Routledge, 2007, pp. 69 et seq.
114. Article 10 of the Directive 2019/1152.
115. Article 13 of the Directive 2003/88.

working time by means of collective agreements increases the level of stability and predictability. The use of collective mechanisms is justified especially when work organization may be particularly burdensome for workers, e.g., due to its unpredictability. Therefore, some forms of organizing working time require the consent of workers' representatives. Collective bargaining has been playing a role in particular in balancing working time, adopting variable working hours and working time accounts as well as in extending calculation periods of working time.

On-call work and zero-hours contracts protect the economic interests of employers to the greatest extent. At the same time due to the lack of a stable number of working hours, the workers bear an important part of economic risk, thus modifying the paradigm of the employment relationship. It can also be detrimental to the health and personal life of workers.[116] In some Member States, on-call work can be provided for in individual employment contracts (sometimes under specific conditions). In Austria, on-call work can be allowed via collective agreements.[117] Moreover, even if accepted by law on-call work can be limited by collective agreements. The social partners may agree that each employment contract must provide for a fixed amount of work (meaning non-flexible number of contract hours, the prohibition of on-call work), may establish conditions which must be met to apply on-call work or set up a minimum number of working hours.[118]

An important instrument of flexibilizing the process of work is balancing daily working time. Some Member States have not established a norm of regular daily working hours. The organization of work is limited by rest periods. In other Member States, daily limits have been maintained. However, it is usually possible to exceed the daily limit (e.g., from eight to ten hours) which is balanced by shortening working hours on other days or additional days off. Domestic legislation may provide for substantial (e.g., if it is justified by a specific nature of work)[119] and/or formal conditions of the extension. In particular, the extension may depend on the decision of the social partners. In France, daily working time which, as a rule, cannot exceed ten hours, can be extended in a collective agreement to twelve hours.[120] In Germany, collective agreements may provide for daily working time exceeding ten hours if the worker remains ready for work.[121]

Increasing the daily number of working hours may constitute part of establishing a four-day working week without reducing the number of working hours (condensed

116. J. Messenger, *Working Time and the Future of Work*, International Labour Office, Geneva, 2018, p. 17.
117. In Austria, sectoral collective agreements can permit on-call duty to be agreed for thirty days within a period of three months.
118. M. Lamannis, *Collective Bargaining in the Platform Economy: A Mapping Exercise of Existing Initiatives*, European Trade Union Institute, 2023, pp. 42-43.
119. In Poland, collective agreements may extend daily working hours up to twelve if justified by the nature of the work (Art. 135 the Polish Labour Code). In special cases, an extension to sixteen (readiness to work) or even twenty-four hours (security staff) is possible. However, these solutions can be applied not only in collective agreements but also in internal regulations issued unilaterally by the employer (Arts 136 and 137 the Polish Labour Code).
120. https://www.service-public.fr/particuliers/vosdroits/F1911.
121. §7 the German Law on Working Time.

working week).[122] The Belgian Labour Deal of 3 October 2022 empowered the social partners to introduce a four-day working week without limiting the number of working hours. The result is achieved by increasing daily working hours to a necessary level (e.g., to ten).[123] In Austria, some collective agreements provide for a similar mechanism which can be implemented at the company level with the consent of works councils or, if there is no works council, with an employee's consent (daily working time can be extended to ten hours).[124] In Portugal, however, trade unions refused to accept such a construct aiming at parallel reducing both: days of work and weekly working hours.[125]

Another way of (temporarily) raising the working time is the use of overtime, the extent to which this is possible depends on statutory limits and collective agreements. A common solution is to authorize the social partners to increase the number of extra hours (Austria, France, Poland).[126] The social partners may also be entitled to diminish the compensation payable for overtime work (France).[127] Conversely, they may also limit the use of overtime by establishing additional conditions for the use, setting up the maximum number of extra hours or decreasing the compensation for overtime work. The social partners may be entitled to provide work on days declared free from work by the legislation. In Germany, collective agreements may, under specific circumstances, modify some rules concerning work on Sundays and holidays.[128] At the same time, collective agreements may limit night or Sunday (holiday) work.

A special form of the organization of working hours is work time banks (accounts). These allow the accumulation of hours of work to be used when justified by the employer's needs (though there can also be part of working hours dedicated to the employee).[129] Working time banks (accounts) may be introduced by means of typical collective agreements or agreements concluded with work councils (in Austria, France, Germany, the Netherlands and Portugal).[130] In some countries (Portugal), they

122. H. Chung, *A Social Policy Case for a Four-Day Week*, Journal of Social Policy 2022/51(3), p. 553 https://doi.org/10.1017/s0047279422000186.
123. Eurofound, *Working Time in 2021-2022*, Publications Office of the European Union, Luxembourg, 2023, p. 5.
124. Eurofound, *Working Time in 2021-2022*, Publications Office of the European Union, Luxembourg, 2023, p. 9.
125. Eurofound, *Working Time in 2021-2022*, Publications Office of the European Union, Luxembourg, 2023, p. 10.
126. In Austria, the law allowed a maximum of five overtime hours per week; collective agreements may extend this number up to ten for workers who work in restaurants, bars, the hotel business, transport or communication. In Poland, the yearly maximum of working hours may be extended above the level of 150 hours (provided for by the Labour Code).
127. According to the 'El Khomri' Law the compensation for overtime work could be reduced to 10%.
128. §12 the German Law on Working Time.
129. A. Kümmerling & S. Lehndorff, *The Use of Working Time-Related Crisis-Response Measures During the Great Recession*, International Labour Office, Geneva, ILO, 2013, p. 18-20.
130. Working time accounts are used to a broad extent in Germany, where they are treated as an important form of the flexibilization of the work process. In Austria, collective agreements may allow for time credits to be carried over to the next reference period. The date must be determined within four weeks or time credit use is to be granted within thirteen weeks. Otherwise, a worker may either determine the date of use autonomously, provided that he/she observes a notice period of four weeks and the date does not conflict with any compelling

have been allowed or developed in connection with the economic crisis. Some Member States (e.g., Poland) consistently refuse to accept this form of flexibilizing working time.

The idea of variable working hours is to differentiate working hours on various days in particular to start work earlier than it had been started on a previous day which is important due to the calculation of daily working time and daily rest within twenty-four hours.[131] Collective agreements may provide for a differentiation of starting and ending work on different days. They may also authorize workers to decide about work start time in the framework set up in the agreement, e.g., workers may decide about staring work between 7 and 10 a.m. In Poland, collective agreements may provide for starting work at different hours. Then work undertaken in the previous twenty-four working hours is not treated as overtime.[132] A special way to achieve variable working hours is resigning from adopting patterns (schedules) of working time and introducing task-oriented employment.[133] Working without schedules is usually treated as an exception from the traditional model of organizing working time. The social partners may be authorized to accept the application of task-oriented work (e.g., in cases justified by the nature of work). They may also limit this type of work either directly (by an explicit provision) or indirectly (by setting up schedules of working time). In some countries, collective agreements may also deviate from the principle of uninterrupted work by adopting intermittent working time – with a break not included in the working time in Poland.[134]

Finally, collective agreements implement specific schedules of working time binding in whole companies or internal entities.[135] Collective schedules of working time increase the predictability of work and protection of workers. However, in the framework set up by the law the social partners may adapt days and hours of work to real employer's needs deviating from the typical 'workweek'.[136] 'Corridors' of working hours is an example. For instance, in Germany, the social partners differentiate weekly working time for groups of workers within a given framework (e.g., between thirty and forty hours) in a reference period. A similar mechanism has been applied by the social partners in Denmark.[137] Apart from the days guaranteed by the law as non-working

operational requirements, or claim cash compensation. For more *see* A. Kümmerling & S. Lehndorff, *The Use of Working Time-Related Crisis-Response Measures During the Great Recession*, International Labour Office, Geneva, ILO, 2013, pp. 21-23.

131. Article 5 Directive 2003/88.
132. Article 129 the Polish Labour Code.
133. Austria: flexitime (flexible daily starting and ending times) is introduced by means of plant-level agreement. Poland: flexible working hours, including task-orientated employment, may be introduced not only by means of collective agreements (but also in an individual way – at the employee's request).
134. Article 139 the Polish Labour Code.
135. *See* C. Lang, S. Clauwaert & I. Schömann, *Working Time Reforms in Times of Crisis*, European Trade Union Institute, Brussels, 2013, p. 24.
136. J. Messenger, *Working Time and the Future of Work*, International Labour Office, Geneva, 2018, p. 14.
137. A. Kümmerling & S. Lehndorff, *The Use of Working Time-Related Crisis-Response Measures During the Great Recession*, International Labour Office, Geneva, ILO, 2013, pp. 23-24.

days (Sundays, public holidays) collective bargaining may be responsible for determining, as a part of schedules of working time, working days and days off. At the same time collective agreements may provide for specific days (e.g., Saturdays) free from work in a company as well as limit night and Sunday work also by providing extra compensation.[138] Collective schedules of working time may be either required by the law or agreed autonomously by the social partners. Negotiating schedules of working usually takes place at a company level. However, the autonomy of company-level social partners may be limited by multi-company collective agreements providing for, e.g., rest periods on specific days, e.g., during weekends.

The level of working time flexibility depends largely on the length of the reference periods within which average working hours are to be balanced. In some legislation averaging working hours is permitted only through collective bargaining[139] while in others is also available by means of other legal instruments, e.g., the employer's decision. A symbol of flexibility is 'annualized' working time which allows one to adapt working hours to a changeable demand for work over a year.[140] Minimum requirements concerning reference periods have been set up by the EU law. However, Directive 2003/88, under specific conditions, provides for the possibility to derogate from these standards, by means of collective agreements (Article 18):

(a) concluded at the national or regional level or, in conformity with the rules laid down by them, by means of collective agreements or agreements concluded between the two sides of industry at a lower level; or
(b) in Member States in which there is no statutory system ensuring the conclusion of collective agreements or agreements concluded between the two sides of industry at national or regional level by way of collective agreements or agreements concluded between the two sides of industry at the appropriate collective level.

This authorization has been widely utilized among the Member States.[141] For instance, German law provides for a general possibility to extend reference periods by means of collective agreements and further (extraordinary) extension in specific sectors and branches is also possible.[142]

138. International Labour Organization, *Social Dialogue Report 2022. Collective Bargaining for an Inclusive, Sustainable and Resilient Recovery*, Geneva, ILO, 2022, p. 90.
139. S. Lee, D. McCann & J.C. Messenger, *Working Time Around the World: Trends in Working Hours, Laws and Policies in a Global Comparative Perspective*, ILO, Routledge, 2007, p. 126.
140. S. Lee, D. McCann & J.C. Messenger, *Working Time Around the World: Trends in Working Hours, Laws and Policies in a Global Comparative Perspective*, ILO, Routledge, 2007, p. 100.
141. Austria: maximum one year; can be extended by means of collective agreements. Hungary: four or six months; can be extended up to twelve months. Germany: collective agreements may introduce different reference periods than those determined by the law. Romania: can be extended by collective agreements for up to six/twelve months. In Poland as a rule, reference periods cannot exceed four months; collective agreements may extend reference periods up to twelve months (the law adopted in 2013 to increase the level of flexibility). Longer reference periods cannot be introduced by means of regulations adopted by the given employer.
142. §7 the German Law on Working Time.

§5.05 A REACTION TO THE PANDEMIC: SHORT-TIME AND OTHER ANTI-CRISIS MEASURES

The pandemic caused unprecedented market disruptions. Legal measures adopted to protect life and health (social distancing, closure of entire economic sectors) could have resulted in bankruptcies, liquidations and redundancies. Stabilizing the (national) economy during these times required an extraordinary reaction from the state and social partners. The Anti-crises measures taken, were generally aimed at supporting companies to overcome difficulties, in particular by reducing costs of work, and, as a consequence, to preserve jobs during the crisis. It seemed at that time that direct interests of employees have been set aside to ensure further operation of their employing units. During the pandemic, social partners were involved in negotiating protective measures at cross-sectoral (national) and sectoral levels,[143] mainly in industries particularly affected by the lockdown (e.g., tourism, hospitality, restaurants, and services).[144] Further, they participated in implementing short-time work and flexible work orders at a company level.

One of the most popular methods of preserving employment during the crisis is constant short-time work.[145] The idea of short-time work is to reduce the number of working hours with a proportionate reduction in pay when work performed by workers cannot be used effectively.[146] The extreme form of reducing working time – which was also used – is the suspension of the employment relationship for a specific period (usually part of a year), leading to a reduction in working hours from a broader

143. Austria: compensation for short-time work and implemented by the Labour Market Services (M. Risak, *COVID-19 and Labour Law: Austria*, Italian Labour Law E-Journal 2020/13(1S), p. 2). Thanks to adopted measures the workers affected by short-time are compensated at the level of 80-90%. Denmark: the state financed temporary salary compensation scheme to employers facing the risk of large-scale redundancies (M. Soested & N. Videbaek, *COVID-19 and Labour Law: Denmark*, Italian Labour Law E-Journal 2020/13(1S), p. 3). The agreement provided for a payment of a part of salaries by the State (75% of the salary up to approximately EUR 4,000). The agreement concluded for public employees provided, *inter alia*, for the obligation to take remaining holidays or time off in lieu of up to five days. A separate agreement was concluded for employees in public sector. Italy: comprehensive regulation of employment matters (A. Perulli, *Regards comparés sur le droit social à l'épreuve du covid-19: Italie*, Revue de Droit du Travail 2020/4, p. 277). Spain: extension of employment and income protection (R.G. Gordillo, *Covid-19 and Labour Law: Spain*, Italian Labour Law E-Journal 2020/13(1S), p. 3).

144. M. Soested & N. Videbaek, *COVID-19 and Labour Law: Denmark*, Italian Labour Law E-Journal 2020/13(1S), p. 3. In cooperation with the largest trade unions and employer organizations the system of professional trainings for employees affected by the lockdown was established. Salaries paid by the employers are to be reimbursed from the State and union funds. There are negotiations to extend the system on other sectors (p. 4). The company IG Metall proposed to establish a four-day work week in some branches to avoid redundancies. Italian social partners have concluded an agreement, *inter alia*, with banks (A. Perulli, *Regards comparés sur le droit social à l'épreuve du covid-19: Italie*, Revue de Droit du Travail 2020/4, p. 277).

145. *See* more C. Lang, S. Clauwaert & I. Schömann, *Working Time Reforms in Times of Crisis*, European Trade Union Institute, Brussels, 2013, pp. 20 et seq.

146. *See* more J. Messenger & N. Ghosheh (eds), *Work Sharing During the Great Recession: New Developments and Beyond*, Edward Elgar, 2013.

perspective (furlough schemes).[147] The remuneration lost by workers was, however, compensated – fully or partially – from external sources, e.g., state budget, social insurance.[148] In some countries special funds were created which were funded through contributions paid by the employers.[149] As a result, complex systems of short-time work, combining private and public elements, was created. An alternative for short-time work and furlough schemes is wage subsidy which consists of providing support for hours worked. Wages subsidies allows avoiding the reduction of working hours. All these forms of support together are called job retention schemes.[150]

The public support was justified by the fact that problems caused by a global recession or pandemic could not be solved by the parties to the employment contract or even by the social partners only. As a result, public support was needed to restore an economic and social equilibrium and uphold consumption within the societies. Although criticized as an interference with free market and not effective,[151] short-time work has been used in various European countries for a long time. During the global economic crisis short-time work was developed even in the countries where such solutions had not previously been provided or had been evaluated sceptically before the crisis, e.g., the Netherlands.[152]

Lockdowns and other obstacles in running businesses during the pandemic required the application of short-time work to a much greater extent. At the same time,

---

147. T. Müller, T. Schulten & J. Drahokoupil, *Job Retention Schemes in Europe During the COVID-19 Pandemic: Different Shapes and Sizes and the Role of Collective Bargaining*, Transfer: European Review of Labour and Research, 2022/28(2), p. 251, https://doi.org/10.1177/1024258922108 9808.
148. Compare M. Tiraboschi & S. Spattini, *Anti-crisis Labour Market Measures and Their Effectiveness Between Flexibility and Security*, in *Labour Regulation in the 21st Century: In Search of Flexibility and Security*, (eds) T. Davulis & D. Petrylaitė, Cambridge Scholars Publishing 2012, p. 196; A. Kümmerling & S. Lehndorff, *The Use of Working Time-Related Crisis-Response Measures During the Great Recession*, International Labour Office, Geneva, ILO, 2013, pp. 12-14.
149. The finest example of the application of short-time is Germany. In Austria, the Employment Promotion Act 2009 made it possible to conclude short-time work agreements for a maximum duration of eighteen months where a company faces economic difficulties. The French law on short-time work was enacted in 2013 on the basis of a transsectoral collective agreement. *See also* J. Messenger & N. Ghosheh (eds), *Work Sharing During the Great Recession: New Developments and Beyond*, Edward Elgar 2013.
150. T. Müller, T. Schulten & J. Drahokoupil, *Job Retention Schemes in Europe During the COVID-19 Pandemic: Different Shapes and Sizes and the Role of Collective Bargaining*, Transfer: European Review of Labour and Research, 2022/28(2), pp. 250-251, https://doi.org/10.1177/10242589 221089808.
151. *See* more C. Lang, S. Clauwaert & I. Schömann, *Working Time Reforms in Times of Crisis*, European Trade Union Institute, Brussels, 2013, pp. 22-23, referring to the objections against the instrument discussed: e.g., the negative influence of short-time work on the situation of so-called outsiders (non-employees). Supporting 'insiders' (employees), the countries cannot invest enough in efficient labour market policies.
152. Compare V. Glassner & M. Keune, *Crise et politique sociale: la rôle des accords collectifs*, Revue Internationale du Travail 2012/4, p., pp. 386-394.

there was a need to protect workers' interests by compensating the loss of remuneration. Short-time systems enjoyed a warm welcome from the labour market in numerous Member States (e.g., Germany, France, Italy, Poland, Spain, and Sweden).[153] European countries applied all solutions: short-time work (with reduced pay for shorter work periods)[154] the suspension of the employment relationship[155] as well as wage subsidies. Despite differences in techniques and scale of applying job retention schemes it was undoubtedly the most spectacular example of using this idea in practice. In particular in the first phase of pandemic even one-third or more workers in various member states were covered by job retention schemes.[156] Though, the negative consequences of short-time work may exceed beyond mere loss of remuneration in the months of reduced working time and hinder the career advancement.[157] In Germany, short-time work schemes were considered a key instrument protecting workers against the negative consequences of the pandemic crisis.[158]

Usually, the precondition to obtain the financial support is the involvement of workers' representatives (trade unions or elected bodies) resulting in various working time arrangements.[159] However, in some countries, the role of collective bargaining in implementing short-time work was limited by recognizing the employer's unilateral prerogatives to limit the number of working hours or to suspend the employment

153. *Flash Reports on Labour Law, Summary and Country Reports*, Publication Office of the European Union, Luxembourg, 2020, pp. 1-3. https://ec.europa.eu/social/main.jsp?pager.offset=35&catId=1307&langId=en; J. Brockmann, *Regards comparés sur le droit social à l'épreuve du covid-19: Allemagne*, Revue de Droit du Travail 2020/4, pp. 282-283; Ch. Gaglione, I. Purificato & O. Rymkevich, *COVID-19 and Labour Law: Italy*, Italian Labour Law E-Journal 2020/13(1S), p. 3; C. Johansson, *COVID-19 and Labour Law: Sweden*, Italian Labour Law e-Journal 2020/13(1S), p. 3 (the mechanisms had been hardly used before the pandemic crisis). The crisis entailed even some procedural changes (A. Guamán & J.M. Sánchez, *Regards comparés sur le droit social à l'épreuve du covid-19: Espagne*, Revue de Droit du Travail 2020/4, p. 280).

154. *Flash Reports on Labour Law, Summary and Country Reports*, Publication Office of the European Union, Luxembourg, 2020, pp. 1-3. https://ec.europa.eu/social/main.jsp?pager.offset=35&catId=1307&langId=en.

155. T. Novitz, *COVID-19 and Labour Law: United Kingdom*, Italian Labour Law E-Journal 2020/13(1S), p. 6. The idea of 'furlough' (a total suspension of the employment relationship) was compensated by the British Government paying 80% of the pre-crisis wages, but no more than GBP 2,500 (plus tax-related costs) to employees only.

156. T. Müller, T. Schulten & J. Drahokoupil, *Job Retention Schemes in Europe During the COVID-19 Pandemic: Different Shapes and Sizes and the Role of Collective Bargaining*, Transfer: European Review of Labour and Research, 2022/28(2), pp. 254 et seq., https://doi.org/10.1177/10242589221089808.

157. *See, e.g.*, S. Vogtenhuber, N. Steiber & M. Mühlböck, *The Lasting Earnings Losses of COVID-19 Short-Time Work*, Research in Social Stratification and Mobility, 89, 2024, https://doi.org/10.1016/j.rssm.2024.100889.

158. B. Fitzenberger & U. Walwei, *Short-Time Work During the COVID-19 Crisis: Lessons Learned*, Institute for Employment Research, 2023, https://doku.iab.de/forschungsbericht/2023/fb0523en.pdf.

159. T. Müller, T. Schulten & J. Drahokoupil, *Job Retention Schemes in Europe During the COVID-19 Pandemic: Different Shapes and Sizes and the Role of Collective Bargaining*, Transfer: European Review of Labour and Research, 2022/28(2), p. 259, https://doi.org/10.1177/10242589221089808.

relationship (e.g., Portugal, Spain).[160] Unilateral procedures are flexible and effective. They do not guarantee, however, the equilibrium necessary to balance the needs of companies and the protection of workers. It can be achieved by means of collective bargaining. As a result, collective bargaining remained the basic way to reduce working time during the crisis[161] in particular in the second stage of the pandemic. The vast majority of anti-crisis agreements were concluded at the company level. Exceptionally, authorization by sectoral agreements was required.[162] When a company did not meet the criteria for public support sometimes social partners negotiated short-time work without financial compensation for workers.[163] During the pandemic, the law offered also various forms of allocating work to make the functioning of companies more flexible.[164] 'Corridors' of working time were used to a greater extent.[165] Usually, the legislation required the conclusion of a collective agreement to implement patterns of working time which may primarily affect workers' interests. Another form of limiting costs was cutting off overtime work which could be done, e.g., by means of collective agreements. The social partners could also provide for obligatory holidays or holiday shutdowns. Time off could be used, e.g., to organize vocational training or to requalify workers.[166] In general, the pandemic increased working time flexibility. Collective bargaining played an important role in improving the position of workers, e.g. by increasing the level of allowances granted to compensate the remuneration lost.[167]

Anti-crisis measures were introduced through either regular collective agreements or special covenants provided for by the law because of the pandemic. The agreements were concluded with various worker representatives: (1) trade unions; (2) elected bodies: (a) permanent bodies with a stable structure (e.g., workers councils), (b) representatives elected ad hoc, e.g., only for specific procedures; while sometimes (3) the consent of the majority of employees (workers) was required. Although numerous countries retained trade union priority or even trade union exclusivity, the pandemic seemed to be a factor stimulating collective bargaining with non-union

---

160. D.C. Martins, *COVID-19 and Labour Law: Portugal*, Italian Labour Law E-Journal 13(1S), p. 2; R.G. Gordillo, *COVID-19 and Labour Law: Spain*, Italian Labour Law E-Journal 2020/13(1S), pp. 1-2.
161. In some countries, short-time work cannot be introduced unilaterally by employers. For instance, in Germany an agreement with either trade unions or work councils was required. Similar solution was adopted in Sweden: C. Johansson, *COVID-19 and Labour Law: Sweden*, Italian Labour Law e-Journal 2020/13(1S), p. 4.
162. For instance, in Sweden while adopting short-time work: C. Johansson, *COVID-19 and Labour Law: Sweden*, Italian Labour Law e-Journal 2020/13(1S), p. 4.
163. A. Kümmerling & S. Lehndorff, *The Use of Working Time-Related Crisis-Response Measures During the Great Recession*, International Labour Office, Geneva, ILO, 2013.
164. International Labour Organization, *Social Dialogue Report 2022. Collective Bargaining for an Inclusive, Sustainable and Resilient Recovery*, Geneva, ILO, 2022, p. 22.
165. A. Kümmerling & S. Lehndorff, *The Use of Working Time-Related Crisis-Response Measures During the Great Recession*, International Labour Office, Geneva, ILO, 2013, p. 24.
166. A. Kümmerling & S. Lehndorff, *The Use of Working Time-Related Crisis-Response Measures During the Great Recession*, International Labour Office, Geneva, ILO, 2013, pp. 10-11, 25.
167. T. Müller, T. Schulten & J. Drahokoupil, *Job Retention Schemes in Europe During the COVID-19 Pandemic: Different Shapes and Sizes and the Role of Collective Bargaining*, Transfer: European Review of Labour and Research, 2022/28(2), pp. 261-262, https://doi.org/10.1177/10242589221089808.

bodies.[168] This is valid for implementing short-time work as well as – even to a greater extent – flexible schedules of working hours. Involving non-union bodies in certain decision-making process during the pandemic was a reflection of hitherto tendencies to enhance their rights in countries where the trade union participation rate (popularity of the works councils) is low[169] and the choice comes down to negotiation with a non-union elected body or none.

Last but not least, the pandemic crisis was unique in terms of the personal scope of actions undertaken. In some countries, assistance was provided to workers engaged otherwise than under an employment relationship and even the self-employed at the statutory level.[170] One example is covering non-employees with work suspension programmes or reducing the number of working hours, but also subsidizing their jobs.[171] Of course, this may lead to a conflict with economic freedoms, especially in the context of wages.[172] However, certainly, this crisis highlighted the real market position of numerous workers who are not employees and the need to protect them. Consequently, it may change the perception of non-workers, including self-employed, and strengthen the tendency to guarantee their collective rights due to their real bargaining power restoring the social equilibrium.[173]

§5.06 CONCLUSIONS

For many years, the world of work has been evolving under the pressure of social, economic and technological changes. The last decade has been full of challenges related to the dual transition fueled by technological changes and environmental concerns legislation. The legal framework of human work must be adjusted to a changing environment. An important role in this transition has been played by working time regulations. A constant tendency is an increasing flexibility of working time

168. About the phenomenon itself *see, e.g.*, M. Biagi & M. Tiraboschi, *Forms of Employee Representational Participation*, in *Comparative Labour Law and Industrial Relations in Industrialized Market Economies*, (ed.) R. Blanpain, Kluwer Law International, pp. 466 et seq.
169. *See, e.g.*, Eurofound, Trade Union Density, https://www.eurofound.europa.eu/en/european-industrial-relations-dictionary/trade-union-density.
170. *See, e.g.*, I. Florczak, *COVID-19 and Labour Law: Poland*, Italian Labour Law E-Journal 2020/13(1S), pp. 3-4; R.G. Gordillo, *COVID-19 and Labour Law: Spain*, Italian Labour Law E-Journal 2020/13(1S), p. 3, p. 2; C. Johansson, *COVID-19 and Labour Law: Sweden*, Italian Labour Law e-Journal 2020/13(1S), p. 4.
171. Such a bipartite mechanism was adopted in Belgium to support the income of self-employed and dependant self-employed and a tripartite agreement was adopted in Denmark (*see, e.g.*, The Trade Union Advisory Committee to the OECD, *COVID19 Crisis: Mapping Out Trade Union and Social Partners' Responses*, 30 June 2020, https://tuac.org/news/covid19-crisis-mapping-out-trade-union-and-social-partners-responses/).
172. *See, e.g.*, T. Gyulavári, *Collective Rights of Platform Workers: The Role of EU Law*, Maastricht Journal of European and Comparative Law 2020/27(4), pp. 9-16 https://doi.org/10.1177/1023263x20932070; V. Deskalova, *The Competition Law Framework and Collective Bargaining Agreements for Self-Employed: Analysing Restrictions and Mapping Exemption Opportunities*, in *Collective Bargaining for Self-Employed Workers in Europe*, (eds) B. Waas & Ch. Hießl, Alphen aan den Rijn, Wolters Kluwer 2021, pp. 19-51.
173. Compare with the decision of European Committee of Social Rights *ICTU v. Ireland*, 123/2016 (12 September 2018).

reflected by balancing working hours, variable schedules of working time and extended reference periods. The world economic crisis and the pandemic entailed enormous distortions that threatened social equilibrium and required extraordinary intervention from states. The recovery of the economic situation opened the possibility of reconstructing working time in a way that extended workers' sphere of freedom. At the same time, new challenges have been provoked by technology which affects the privacy of workers. The role of the legal framework is to eliminate abuses and to find an appropriate balance between the needs of companies and the protection of workers. An important role in reconstructing working time regulations should be played by collective bargaining based on the balance of power between management and labour.

The involvement of the social partners in anti-crisis activities as well as the development of the social dialogue in the post-pandemic era have confirmed the potential of collective bargaining in creating an appropriate framework for working time. Short-time work adopted with the participation of workers' representatives mitigated effectively the negative consequences of the pandemic. In recent years, collective bargaining contributed to further limitations in working hours. The social partners have been involved in developing a four-day working week. Collective bargaining has also played an important role in flexibilizing working time at a level acceptable for both: companies and workers. Thanks to collective bargaining it is possible to extend the sphere of freedom of workers without excessively interfering with business activities. However, the importance of collective bargaining on working time varies significantly from country to country depending on the statutory framework and factual position of a national social dialogue. In some countries negotiating working time has been shifting from sectoral to company-level collective bargaining. Problems affecting trade unions may encourage the development of competences of elected representatives. A disturbing phenomenon is the development of employer's managerial prerogatives. At the same time, the potential of collective bargaining in protecting against abuses in tech-based employment has not been fully utilized. To summarize, collective bargaining should remain a key instrument in reconstructing working time regulations as part of the sustainable development of the employment relationship. Collective bargaining is the best way to balance employer's managerial needs and striving to ensure decent working conditions for workers. It requires, however, both: creating a supportive legal framework by the state (e.g., by finding a balance between collective bargaining and managerial competences of employers) as well as adopting efficient strategies by the social partners (e.g., by counteracting abuses in tech-based employment). This lesson needs to be learned.

CHAPTER 6

Older Employees, Extended Working Lives, and Collective Bargaining

Jenny Julén Votinius

§6.01 INTRODUCTION[1]

The ageing of Europe's population has and increasingly will continue to have fundamental implications for the labour market. Starting from legislation and policies on the European Union (EU) and national level, this chapter argues that collective bargaining may considerably contribute to mitigating the interests at stake in relation to the ageing workforce, due to its unique ability to offer tailor-made solutions - an ability that is particularly important when it comes to older employees, as this group is characterized by an unusually high level of heterogeneity.

For labour law, in the last decades, the ageing population in Europe has brought to the fore questions on age discrimination and ageism, along with a pressing need to enable and encourage employees to stay longer in the labour market before retiring. Collective bargaining for older employees takes place within a legal and policy framework where the ban on age discrimination in EU law together with active ageing in EU policy forms an important part of the background. As regards age discrimination, EU law feeds into national legislation in a very direct and specific way - not least through the case law of the Court of Justice of the European Union (CJEU) on the Equal Treatment (framework) Directive 2000/78/EC. This is in contrast with the policy agenda on active ageing and extending working lives; although this agenda is strongly promoted by the EU, almost all the details are left to the Member States.

1. This chapter has been carried out within the framework of the research project 'Prolonged Working Lives, Older Workers, and Dismissals. A Study of the Dynamics between Employment Protection, Non-discrimination, and Collective Bargaining', funded by the Swedish Research Council for Health, Working Life, and Welfare (Forte). I thank all colleagues in the INLACRIS team for input and comments. All errors remain mine.

Drawing on labour market research and using national examples of collectively bargained solutions in the area of longer working lives, the chapter shows that effective strategies to meet the challenges of an ageing workforce can translate into collective agreements and thus become a part of everyday life in the workplace. Although in the last two decades, a significant and increasing expansion of social partner's activities can be seen in the area, the chapter claims that there is an important unused potential in collective bargaining for targeting the situation of older workers, and suggests that it would be rational for both employers and trade unions to increase their engagement in the area of collective bargaining for older employees. This is particularly important given the difficulties in integrating labour market realities and balancing the interests of employers and workers against the not-always-aligned interests of policymakers at the EU and national level.[2]

§6.02 THE GREYING WORK FORCE OF EUROPE[3]

The demographic development of Europe, just like the rest of the world, is characterized by longer lifespans, decreased birth rates, and, still for another few years, a growing population.[4] The demands associated with an ageing population involve a changing economic situation.[5] Along with the increased demand for services such as medical care, senior housing and elder care, an increasingly smaller share of the population is becoming responsible for supporting more and more people.[6] In the upcoming years, it is anticipated that the EU's population will begin to decline while the share of elderly people will continue increasing in relation to the population of working age, resulting in a sharp increase in the old-age dependency ratio in all

2. M. Sánchez & P. Díaz, 'Active Ageing Policy in Challenging Production Environments: A Case Study Involving Social Partners in Spain' European Journal of Ageing 19 (2021) 3:509-519 https://doi.org/10.1007/s10433-021-00650-6.
3. Below, sections 2-4 partly draw upon my previous research published in J. Julén Votinius, 'Age Discrimination and Labour Law in Sweden', in A. Numhauser-Henning & M. Rönnmar (eds), *Age Discrimination and Labour Law: Comparative and Conceptual Perspectives in the EU and Beyond* (Kluwer Law International, Alphen aan den Rijn 2015), J. Julén Votinius, 'Intersectionality as a Tool for Analysing Age and Gender in Labour Law', in S. Manfredi & L. Vickers (eds), *Challenges for Active Ageing: Equality Law and the Workplace* (Palgrave Macmillan 2016), and J. Julén Votinius & M. Rönnmar, 'Intergenerational Aspects of Elder Law: Conflict, Solidarity – or Ambivalence', in A. Numhauser-Henning & M. Rönnmar (eds), *Elder Law: Evolving European Perspectives* (Edward Elgar 2017).
4. The most aged populations are in the developed countries. In developing countries, population ageing has begun rather recently; W. Thompson, 'Population' American Journal of Sociology 34 (1929) 959 https://doi.org/10.1086/214874; J.C. Caldwell, *Demographic Transition Theory* (Springer 2006) 307f. *World Population Ageing 2023. Challenges and Opportunities of Population Ageing in the Least Developed Countries* (United Nations 2023).
5. For a broader picture of the challenges associated with the ageing population, *see* S. Harper, 'The Challenges of Twenty-First-Century Demography', in C. Torp (ed.), *Challenges of Ageing. Pensions, Retirement and Generational Justice* (Palgrave Macmillan 2015). Cf. W. Lutz, W. Sanderson & S. Scherbov, 'The Coming Acceleration of Global Population Ageing' Nature 451 (2008) 716.
6. In January 2023, within the EU, there were 33.4 persons aged 65 and over per 100 persons of working age (15-64 years). In 2060, this number is expected to be 53, and in 2100 it is expected to be 59.7 (Eurostat, Population Projections in the EU, March 2023).

Member States over the coming decades.[7] In this setting, where society is presented with major challenges, the support and promotion of longer working lives become of crucial political importance. Simply put, there is a need to make people stay longer in the labour market to support themselves and to continue their financial contribution to the societal systems.

In the political discourse on the ageing workforce, as well as in policies and actions directed towards older employees in the European context, older workers are primarily understood as the share of the workforce that is in the early end of their working life. The Active Ageing Index, launched by the European Commission and the United Nations Economic Commission for Europe (UNECE), takes into account people from the age of 55.[8] Also, the case law of the CJEU on age discrimination reflects the idea that the critical age with regards to employment is the period starting in the early end of a person's working life; the case law mainly concerns employees from the age of just above fifty years of age and older.[9]

The heterogeneity of the group referred to as older employees cannot be stressed enough. The diversity that this group displays is vast and could almost be described in terms of polarization. In that respect, the older employees diverge from all other groups in the labour market. An important share of persons in high or top positions in society are persons who would be defined as older employees - may it be in politics, in management and or in working life. On a more general level, older employees form an important part of what has been described as the well-protected insiders of the labour market, that is persons who hold permanent employment, high level of employment protection, accrued rights and privileges based on seniority, and, consequently, a precedence of position over other employees.[10]

But this is only one side of the coin. On the other side, quite oppositely, older employees form a precarious group in the labour market.[11] In this group, we find the largest number of people with outdated competencies, people with age-related health problems and people with disabilities caused by a long and hard working life. Here we also find the unemployed persons who have the most severe difficulties in getting employment. For a person who has reached the age of 50, unemployment implies a serious risk of never returning to working life. Moreover, older employees are at the highest risk of exposure to ageism and age discrimination. Research has shown that older women employees comprised one group of workers perceived as being at the

7. European Commission, *2024 Ageing Report: & Budgetary Projections for the EU Member States (2022-2070) Institutional Paper 279, April 2024* (Publications of the European Union 2024).
8. The index was launched in 2012 in the European Year for Active Ageing and Solidarity between Generations. European Centre Vienna, *Active Ageing Index Concepts, Methodology and Final Results. Methodology Report Submitted to European Commission's DG Employment, Social Affairs and Inclusion, and to Population Unit, UNECE* (Vienna, 2013).
9. Cases C-144/04 *Werner Mangold* (52 years), C-152/11 *Odar* (54 years), C-447/09 *Prigge* and case C-286/12 *Commission v. Hungary* (60 and 62 years respectively), cases C-499/08 *Ingeniørforeningen i Danmark*, C-411/05 *Palacios de la Villa*, C-388/07 *Age Concern*, C-45/09 *Rosenbladt*, the joint cases C-159/10 and C-160/10 *Fuchs* and *Köhler*, cases C-141/11 *Hörnfeldt*, C-341/08 *Petersen*, and joined cases C-250/09 and C-268/09 *Georgiev* (all 65, 67 or 68 years).
10. Cf. Nicola Gundt's contribution in this issue.
11. Votinius (2016), *supra* n. 3.

highest risk for precarious work within the EU, before groups such as interns, apprentices, women in general, older workers in general, and women who are pregnant or returning from maternity leave.[12] Already in 2013, AGE Europe noted that age was quickly becoming the most commonly perceived disadvantage in the labour market and that this particularly applies to older women 'who are among those most affected by the crisis and one of the groups most likely to lose their job and be unable to find new employment'.[13]

During the years following the Great Recession, in many EU countries, the level of insecurity in the labour market increased dramatically.[14] From an immediate labour market participation perspective, the negative effects of the economic crisis could be observed primarily in relation to young employees, among whom unemployment rose sharply during the crisis years. For older workers who had a firm foothold in the labour market, the crisis did not affect their position, however, older employees in precarious positions were hit very hard – this group was more or less pushed out from the labour market. The COVID-19 recession played out quite differently. As is normally the case, young persons were hit much harder than others in terms of labour market opportunities, older workers in the EU were not affected in the same way as after the financial crisis in 2008, although there were great discrepancies between labour market sectors.[15]

A division between insiders and outsiders in the labour market can be seen in all age groups. But for older employees, the contrast is unusually clear. This is to a large extent because the position that an older person has reached in the labour market at the entry of the early end of his or her working life is a result of the working life that this person has had so far. Successful careers tend to result in a position as a well-protected insider, while the opposite applies to a person whose path in working life has been less

12. S. McKay, et al., *Study on Precarious Work and Social Rights. Carried Out for the European Commission (VT/2010/084)* (Working Lives Research Institute, London Metropolitan University 2012).
13. AGE, *Contribution to the European Commission's Assessment of the Transposition and Application of Employment Equality Directive (2000/78/EC)*, 2013. There is growing recognition of the insight that age and gender synergize in ways that tend to discriminate against women, S. Spedale, C. Coupland & S. Tempest, 'Gendered Ageism and Organizational Routines at Work: The Case of Day-Parting in Television Broadcasting' Organization Studies 35 (2014) 11:1585 https://doi.org/10.1177/0170840614550733; W. Loretto, C. Duncan & P.J. White 'Ageism and Employment: Controversies, Ambiguities and Younger People's Perceptions' Ageing and Society (2000) 20:279, 285 and 296 https://doi.org/10.1017/s0144686x00007741; and J. McMullin, 'Theorizing Age and Gender Relations', in S. Arber & J. Ginn (eds), *Connecting Gender and Ageing: A Sociological Approach* (Open University Press 1995).
14. S. Laulom, E. Mazuyer & C. Escande Varniol (eds), *Quel droit social dans une Europe en crise?* (Larcier 2012); S. Laulom, 'Dismissal Law under Challenge: New Risks for Workers' European Labour Law Journal 5 (2014) 3-4:231 https://doi.org/10.1177/201395251400500304; C. Degryse, M. Jepsen & P. Pochet, *The Euro Crisis and Its Impact on National and European Social Policies* (ETUI 2013); C. Barnard, 'The Financial Crisis and the Euro Plus Pact: A Labour Lawyer's Perspective' Industrial Law Journal 41 (2012) 98 https://doi.org/10.1093/indlaw/dws002.
15. Eurofound, *Recovery from COVID-19: The Changing Structure of Employment in the EU* (Publications Office of the European Union, Luxembourg 2022).

straightforward. Although young employees typically are hit the hardest by unemployment and following labour law reforms after periods of crisis, effects relating to the dismantling of employment security are a concern for every employee, especially for employees who belong to a group that typically is perceived as less attractive in the labour market – such as older employees.[16] Within EU law, the longstanding tradition of legislation to safeguard the fundamental principles of equal treatment and non-discrimination in working life can provide a barrier against unfair management decisions. The following section introduces the relevant provisions of EU discrimination law, with a particular focus on older workers.

§6.03 THE EU BAN ON AGE DISCRIMINATION IN WORKING LIFE

The area of non-discrimination has largely evolved in the context of gender equality in working life, which has had a place on the social policy agenda within the EU since the 1970s (although progress has been slow). A comprehensive body of secondary legislation and case law on sex discrimination began to develop in the 1970s, mainly on the basis of the provision in the Treaty of Rome regarding equal pay for men and women.[17] The promotion of gender equality also appears in policy documents such as the European Pillar of Social Rights and the Gender Equality Strategy (previously the Community Action Programmes on equal opportunities for men and women), as well as in several recommendations and resolutions from the Council.[18] Many times, these soft-law documents have expressed a more progressive approach than the binding law.[19]

In 2000, following the Treaty of Amsterdam, the existing directives on sex discrimination were accompanied by directives prohibiting discrimination on the grounds of racial or ethnic origin, religion or belief, disability, sexual orientation – or age. Through ratification of the Lisbon Treaty, and its coming into force in 2009, promotion of equal treatment and the combatting of discrimination were acknowledged as a key aim of the EU, and the fundamental right to equality became protected under the Charter of Fundamental Rights of the European Union (CFREU) and the

16. J. Prassl, 'Contingent Crises, Permanent Reforms: Rationalising Labour Market Reforms in the European Union' European Labour Law Journal 5 (2014) 3-4:211 https://doi.org/10.1177/201395251400500303; Eurofound, *Employment Trends and Policies for Older Workers in the Recession* (2012).
17. E. Ellis & P. Watson, *EU Anti-discrimination Law* (2nd ed., Oxford University Press 2013).
18. European Parliament, Council of the European Union, European Commission, 2017, *Solemn Declaration on the European Pillar of Social Rights*, Principle 2, along with Principles 3, 11, 15 and 18 and A Union of Equality: Gender Equality Strategy 2020-2025. *See also*, *Labour and skills shortages in the EU: an action plan*, COM(2024) 131 final.
19. P. Foubert, *The Legal Protection of the Pregnant Worker in the European Community: Sex Equality, Thoughts of Social and Economic Policy and Comparative Leaps to the United States of America* (Kluwer Law International, 2002) 214. C. McGlynn, 'Reclaiming a Feminist Vision: The Reconciliation of Paid Work and Family Life in European Union Law and Policy' Columbia Journal of European Law 7 (2001) 242.

European Convention of Human Rights (ECHR).[20] Today, the prohibitions against age in working life are found in the Employment Equality Directive 2000/78.[21]

The Employment Equality Directive 2000/78 distinguish between *direct* discrimination and *indirect* discrimination. The former is at hand when a person is being subjected to less favourable treatment which is associated with a protected ground, such as age.[22] The latter regards the case where the employer applies a condition or criterion that appears neutral, but in fact puts persons belonging to a protected group at a particular disadvantage, and where the criterion cannot be justified with reference to an objectively acceptable aim. A possibility for justification is built into the very construction of indirect discrimination, but normally direct discrimination is allowed in only the few cases that are specifically enumerated in the directive. However, in relation to direct discrimination on the grounds of age, the possibilities for exemptions are particularly comprehensive; in fact, the possibilities for justification are similar to what otherwise applies in cases of indirect discrimination.[23] In relation to age, premise 25 of the Equal Treatment Framework Directive 2000/78 emphasizes the importance of distinguishing between 'differences in treatment which are justified, in particular by legitimate employment policy, labour market and vocational training objectives, and discrimination which must be prohibited'. Accordingly, Article 6 justifies differential treatment on the grounds of age for various employment policy objectives.[24] To be permitted, differential treatment must be deemed appropriate and necessary, but in its case law, the CJEU imposes very undemanding requirements on Member States to prove that measures that disadvantage older workers actually provide the labour market benefits that are claimed as their justification.[25] It is clear that many times, collective and public interests that stem from the function of the labour market and societal considerations may be given priority over the interest of non-discrimination on the grounds of age.

20. Treaty of the European Union, Art. 3, Charter of Fundamental Rights of the European Union, Chapter III, particularly Arts 21 (non-discrimination), 23 (equality between men and women) and 25 (the rights of the elderly), and European Convention on Human Rights, Art. 14 and Protocol No. 12.
21. Council Directive 2000/78/EC establishing a general framework for equal treatment in employment and occupation; European Parliament and Council Directive 2006/54/EC.
22. Article 2, Directive 2000/78/EC and Art. 2.1, Directive 2006/54/EC.
23. Cf. A. Numhauser-Henning, 'The EU Ban on Age-Discrimination and Older Workers: Potentials and Pitfalls' International Journal of Comparative Labour Law and Industrial Relations 29 (2013) 4:391-414 https://doi.org/10.54648/ijcl2013025. J. Julén Votinius, 'Rule of Law Discourses in Swedish Labour Law' Scandinavian Studies in Law 69 (2023) 377-392 https://doi.org/10.53292/32f26f7c.02211413. S. Robin-Olivier, 'Modernizing EU Anti-discrimination Law to Better Combat Discrimination against Older Workers', in J. Julén Votinius & M. Rönnmar, *Older Workers, Active Ageing, and the Future of Work* (Kluwer Law International, forthcoming 2024).
24. Article 6.1, Directive 2000/78/EC, interpreted by the CJEU in numerous cases.
25. J. Fudge & A. Zbyszewska, 'An Intersectional Approach to Age Discrimination in the European Union: Bridging Dignity and Distribution?', in A. Numhauser Henning & M. Rönnmar (eds) *Age Discrimination and Labour Law. Comparative and Conceptual Perspectives in the EU and Beyond* (Kluwer Law International 2015).

§6.04 THE ACTIVE AGEING AGENDA IN EU EMPLOYMENT POLICIES

Before the introduction of the prohibition on age discrimination in 2000, old age was a fairly invisible matter in the EU labour law context.[26] The recognition of age as grounds for discrimination coincided with a general shift within the EU, towards policies that more actively addressed the looming demographic change in Europe.[27] In a short time, ageing and the situation of older persons became a central component of EU agendas regarding policies for employment and economic growth, embodied in the key concept of *active ageing*.[28] EU policy discourses on active ageing have been described as comprising two contrasting models.[29] The first, and predominant, model focuses on extending working life; this model is based on considerations about productivity and economic growth.[30] The other model has been less influential on the EU level but has been a leading one for WHO and the UN. It is much more comprehensive, in that it has an equal focus on including quality of life, mental and physical well-being, and social participation.[31] To an increasing extent, and in conjunction with an increased overall focus on sustainability matters and with particular emphasis added in the aftermath of the COVID-19 events, the EU policy actions have moved towards a convergence

26. Council Directive 2000/78/EC establishing a general framework for equal treatment in employment and occupation. Earlier measures on older workers in the EU are few, and all have the form of non-legally binding acts. A very early example is the Council Recommendation 82/857/EEC on the principles of a Community policy with regard to retirement age, 27. Cf. Ellis & Watson (2013), *supra* n. 17, M. Bell, *Anti-discrimination Law and the European Union* (Oxford University Press 2002), N. ten Bokum & P. Bartelings (eds), *Age Discrimination Law in Europe* (Kluwer Law International, 2009).
27. *Towards a Europe for All Ages* COM (1999) 221; *Europe's response to World Ageing* COM (2002) 143; *Confronting demographic change: a new solidarity between the generations* COM (2005) 94; *The demographic future of Europe – From challenge to opportunity*, COM (2006) 571; Council Resolution 6226/07 Opportunities and challenges of demographic change in Europe; *Dealing with the impact of an ageing population in the EU (2009 Ageing Report)* COM (2009) 180.
28. Already in 1999 and 2000, the EU set out the Stockholm target to ensure that half of those aged 55-64 were in employment by 2010, and the Barcelona target to increase actual retirement age by five years by 2010. In the 2010 EU's growth and job strategy 'Europe 2020', active ageing was addressed in the flagship initiative towards full employment – the 'Agenda for new skills and jobs' *Europe 2020, A Strategy for Smart, Sustainable and Inclusive Growth*, COM (2010) 2020 final. European Commission White Paper: An Agenda for Adequate, Safe and Sustainable Pensions, COM (2012) 55 final. A. Walker & T. Maltby, 'Active Ageing: A Strategic Policy Solution to Demographic Ageing in the European Union' International Journal of Social Welfare 21 (2012) 117 https://doi.org/10.1111/j.1468-2397.2012.00871.x. *See also*, C. Krekula, *European Union Extended Working Life Policies: On Pension Systems, Public Finances and Biopolitical Disciplining*, Lives Working Paper 2020/77.7.
29. L. Foster & A. Walker, 'Active and Successful Aging: A European Policy Perspective' The Gerontologist 55 (2015) 1:83 https://doi.org/10.1093/geront/gnu028; E. Carmel, K. Hamblin & T. Papadopoulos, 'Governing the Activation of Older Workers in the European Union' International Journal of Sociology and Social Policy 27 (2007) 9/10:387 ttps://doi.org/10.1108/01443330710822084.
30. K. Hamblin, 'Changes to Policies for Work and Retirement in EU15 Nations (1995-2005): An Exploration of Policy Packages for the 50-Plus Cohort', International Journal of Ageing and Later Life (2010) 5:513 https://doi.org/10.3384/ijal.1652-8670.105113.
31. O. Sinyavskaya, 'The Future of Active Ageing and Related Needs for Research', in K. Leichsenring & A. Sidorenko (eds) *A Research Agenda for Ageing and Social Policy* (Edward Elgar Publishing 2024). L. Foster & A. Walker, 'Gender and Active Ageing in Europe' European Journal of Ageing 10 (2013) 3 https://doi.org/10.1007/s10433-013-0261-0.

between these two models. One example is the Green Paper of Ageing launched by the European Commission in 2021, which spans a great area of matters including healthy living, lifelong learning, longer working lives, sustainable pensions, sufficient health-care and long-term care for older people.[32] Still, however, the overall emphasis is still very much on promoting labour market opportunities and enhancing employment conditions and employability of older employees. So does the European Pillar of Social Rights proclaimed jointly by the European Parliament, the European Council and the European Commission at the Social Summit for Fair Jobs and Growth in November 2017 grant workers a right to a working environment adapted to their professional needs and which enables them to prolong their participation in the labour market.[33] The political efforts to extend working lives have paid off. Within the EU, the median employment rate for the age group 55-64 years has increased steadily every year from a median of 35% in 2000, and 45% in 2011 to nearly 64% in 2023.[34]

Although often presented as emancipatory and empowering for older workers, in the end, policies to extend working lives are primarily motivated by interest related to state finances including the sustainability of welfare and pension systems.[35] Consequently, the EU Pension Adequacy Report 2024 emphasizes the extension of working lives as essential for preserving the sustainability and adequacy of pension systems and concludes that while positive incentives and flexible retirement possibilities are difficult to evaluate, changes to the pensionable age and restrictions on early retirement are measures with a direct impact.[36] However, longer life expectancy does not necessarily mean more healthy years, and the realities of increasing employment rates among older workers may also involve a deterioration in quality of life. The European Commission High-level Group on the Future of Social Protection and of the Welfare State in the EU, notes in its report of 2023 that increasingly more people struggle to be able to work up to the pension age as Member States close pathways to early retirement and raise the pensionable age. The report calls for a more nuanced approach involving better and more flexible working arrangements along with preventive measures to avoid people withdrawing from the workforce prematurely. In addition, working beyond the statutory pension age should be possible for those who choose to do so, although no one should be forced by inadequate or encouraged by social security exemptions.[37]

---

32. European Commission, Green Paper on Ageing. Fostering solidarity and responsibility between generations COM(2021) 50 final.
33. Interinstitutional Proclamation on the European Pillar of Social Rights (2017/C 428/09).
34. Eurostat, Europe 2020 Employment Indicators, 64/2020 – 21 April 2020, and Eurostat, Employment rate of older workers, age group 55-64, updated 13 June 2024.
35. This aspect has been analysed thoroughly in C. Krekula & S. Vickerstaff, 'The "Older Worker" and the "Ideal Worker": A Critical Examination of Concepts and Categorisations in the Rhetoric of Extending Working Lives', in A. Ní Léime et al. (eds), *Extended Working Life Policies* (Springer 2020).
36. European Commission, *The 2024 Pension Adequacy Report: Current and Future Income Adequacy in Old Age in the EU* (Publications Office of the European Union, 2024), 69 f.
37. European Commission High-Level Group of Experts, *The Future of Social Protection and of the Welfare State in the EU* (Publications Office of the European Union, 2023), 53 f.

The European Commission Action Plan for the European Pillar of Social Rights sets out that by 2030, at least 78% of the population aged 20 to 64 should be in employment. However, in this context, the Action Plan also includes a commitment to extend the length of working life. The Commission advocates a review of the concept of the 'working age population' which at present covers persons from 20 to 64 years. As working lives are lengthening across the EU due to ageing and policy reforms, the Commission announces that it will undertake analytical and statistical work with a view to adjusting the current indicator in the context of the review of this Action Plan.[38] As an integrated part of the European employment policy, the understanding of active ageing and extended working lives is closely connected to the discourse on employability and its emphasis on the responsibility of the individual employee to achieve and maintain his or her own power of attraction in the labour market.[39] The concept of employability also encompasses a requirement to adjust to ever-new and increasing changes and insecurities in the labour market, in relation to which policies for deregulation in order to allow for more flexibility for employers are seen as key.[40] In line with this approach, the European Commission Action Plan on Labour Skills and Shortages adopted in March 2024, stressed the decline in the working-age population in the EU since 2009 and the expected further decline combined with increased demand for healthcare and long-term care services in the years to come, emphasizes the need to encourage the employment of older workers, including through reforms of pension systems.[41]

In the realization of active ageing in the meaning of extended working lives, the social partners are attributed an important role. The Social Pillar Action Plan calls on the social partners to accelerate its implementation and swiftly make its principles a reality.[42] Along the same lines, the labour skills and shortages action plan specifically highlights the importance of social partner's involvement in meeting its demands and realising the identified measures, including those related to older workers. Already in 2017, the European Social Partners concluded a Framework Agreement on Active Ageing and Inter-generational Approach, to be implemented by the national social partners by March 2020.[43] Acknowledging the shared commitment of employers, employees, and their representatives to active ageing, the agreement sets out to increase awareness and provide approaches promoting active ageing, ensure a healthy,

---

38. European Commission, *The European Pillar of Social Rights Action Plan*, COM (2021) 102 final, 6.
39. A. Fejes, 'Discourses on Employability: Constituting the Responsible Citizen' Studies in Continuing Education 32 (2010) 89; P. Moore, *The International Political Economy of Work and Employability* (Palgrave Macmillan 2010); B. Casey, 'The Implications of the Economic Crisis for Pensions and Pension Policy in Europe' Global Social Policy (2012) 12:246 https://doi.org/10.1177/1468018112455633.
40. J. Julén Votinius, 'Having the Right Attitude: Cooperation Skills and Labour Law' The International Journal of Comparative Labour Law and Industrial Relations 28 (2012) 2:223 https://doi.org/10.54648/ijcl2012014.
41. *Labour and skills shortages in the EU: An action plan,* COM (2024) 131 final.
42. European Commission, *The European Pillar of Social Rights Action Plan*, COM (2021) 102 final, 4.
43. Autonomous Framework Agreement on Active Ageing and an Inter-generational Approach, concluded on 8 March 2017 between BusinessEurope, CEEP, UEAPME and ETUC.

safe and productive working environment, foster life-cycle approaches enabling people to remain in work until legal retirement age and promote the transfer knowledge and experience between generations at the workplace. Unlike the EU institutions, the Framework Agreement does not use the concept of extended working lives but aims to enable people to remain in work 'until legal retirement age'. While this may thus be understood as rejecting early retirement policies, it should be stressed that the Framework Agreement does not express support for increased retirement ages. On the contrary, the interpretative guidelines for the agreement specifically mention 'the – regrettable – fact that in most countries the legally established pension age has been raised'.[44] At the national level, the Framework Agreement has been implemented using a variety of tools and measures. In addition to awareness-raising and information dissemination efforts, these include collective agreements, tripartite agreements and legislative initiatives. Some of these were already in place and others are new and emerging, many of them covering broad themes such as occupational health and safety, skills development and labour supply, but with some specifically targeting older workers.[45]

§6.05 EXTENDED WORKING LIVES AND COLLECTIVE BARGAINING ON A NATIONAL LEVEL

[A] Regulatory Approaches and Strategies to Promote Extended Working Lives

Policies for active ageing, including the fostering of extended working lives, are to varying extent pursued on a national level in all of the countries in Europe.[46] While the situation of older employees is high on the agenda in countries like Sweden, Finland, Denmark, Germany and the Netherlands, the matter has drawn much less political attention in Poland, Bulgaria, Slovenia, Slovakia, Romania, Greece and Hungary.[47] The following section presents some examples of how collective bargaining activities have added to the development of national labour market approaches to active ageing. As always, it is important to emphasize that the Member States differ in terms of their regulation of working life, not least as regards the role of the social partners, as well as

44. Interpretation Guide, European Social Partners' Autonomous Framework Agreement on Active Ageing and an Inter-generational Approach, p. 4.
45. Framework Agreement on Active Ageing and an Inter-generational approach, Final Implementation Report November 2021.
46. For a detailed overview of national approaches to active ageing, *see* A. Zaidi & D. Stanton, *Active Ageing Index 2014. Analytical Report*, United Nations Economic Commission for Europe, Geneva, and European Commission, Directorate General for Employment, Social Affairs and Inclusion (Brussels 2015).
47. European Parliament *Ageing policies: Access to Services in Different Member States* (2021). A. Walker & A. Zaidi, 'New Evidence on Active Ageing in Europe' Intereconomics 51 (2016) 3:139-144 https://doi.org/10.1007/s10272-016-0592-0, European Agency for Safety and Health at Work, *Analysis Report on EU and Member State Policies, Strategies and Programmes on Population and Workforce Ageing* (Luxembourg Publications Office of the European Union 2016).

the interaction between labour law and industrial relations. All Member States have introduced at least some form of statutory regulation to promote extended working lives.[48] Normally, statutory law provides the general framework, and in many cases also financial incentives, while the social partners to varying degrees contribute to the detailed design and implementation. In a number of countries, comprehensive tripartite agreements have been concluded to introduce longer working life strategies. This is the case in, for instance, Finland, Denmark, Belgium, Ireland, Germany and France.[49] In some countries, such as France, Germany and Denmark, the social partners have also concluded sectoral-level agreements in the matter, beyond the statutory framework.

Research as well as policy documents on active ageing point to a number of key factors in the promotion of longer working lives, although the consistent increase of older persons in employment in many EU Member States during the last decade has been to a great extent attributed to the abolishing or penalising of early retirement[50] The conceptualization of these key factors varies in different descriptions and there is a lack of coherent terminology.[51] The following section is structured around three policy areas comprising factors that are recurrently highlighted in the extended working lives discourse (although the exact phrasing may vary): working conditions and work organization, workforce and career development, and age awareness and attitudes in the workplace. An important policy area that will not be discussed below is the general health status of older workers. The interaction between health issues and longer working lives also provokes complex questions for labour law. The work environment tends to impact the health status of employees throughout their careers, which in turn affects how long they stay in working life. Though this life-course approach is important, this chapter focuses only and specifically on the situation of older employees. In the following, matters relating to the work environment are considered within the area of working conditions and work organization. Arrangements specifically intended to promote the health of older persons are not discussed here, as such arrangements primarily relate to policies on health and medical care, and thus primarily belong outside the area of labour law and collective bargaining.

48. European Parliament *Ageing Policies: Access to Services in Different Member States* (2021). Eurofound, *Role of Governments and Social Partners in Keeping Older Workers in the Labour Market* (Dublin 2013).
49. Eurofound (2013), *supra* n. 48. Cf. C. Claisse, C. Daniel & A. Naboulet, 'Les accords collectifs d'entreprises et plans d'action en faveur de l'emploi des salariés âgés' (157) *Document d'études. Direction de l'animation de la recherche, des études et des statistiques*, DARES 2011.
50. R. Konle-Seidl, 'Retention and Re-integration of Older Workers into the Labour Market: What Works?' (IAB-Discussion Paper 17/2017), Institute for Employment Research, Nuremberg, Germany.
51. C.E. Edge, A.M. Cooper & M. Coffey, 'Barriers and Facilitators to Extended Working Lives in Europe: A Gender Focus' Public Health Reviews 38 (2017) (2) https://doi.org/10.1186/s40985-017-0053-8; A. Blackham, *Extending Working Life for Older Workers Age Discrimination Law, Policy and Practice* (Hart Publishing 2016); Eurofound (2013), *supra* n. 48; European Commission, *European Employment Observatory Review, Employment Policies to Promote Active Ageing 2012* (Publications Office of the European Union, Luxembourg 2012); R. Gould, et al., *Dimensions of Work Ability. Results of the Health 2000 Survey* (ETK, Kela, KTL, FIOH 2008).

[B] Working Conditions, Work Organization and Part-Time Pension Schemes

Measures related to work organization that may have a positive impact on extending working lives include policies to promote flexible work and working time, adjusting workplaces and tasks to match the capacities of the employees, along with special arrangements to lighten the workload of older workers.[52]

In certain cases, the requirement for reasonable accommodation of employees with disabilities in Article 5 of Equal Treatment Framework Directive 2000/78 may impose a statutory obligation on the employer to adjust the working conditions to the needs of an older employee. As stated by the CJEU in the cases *HK Denmark* and *Chacón Navas*, the only decisive factor for the definition of disability is that it refers to a physical, mental or psychological impairment that hinders the participation of the person concerned in professional life for a long time.[53] The cause of the impairment is thus not relevant. The requirement for reasonable accommodation may include not only an obligation for the employer to provide for special aids, especially if the impairment relates to functional capacity but also for adjustments of work tasks or their redistribution between employees in a workplace. Even if the impairment only means an inability to work full-time, it constitutes a disability within the meaning of the Directive. In an individual case, a national court may find that an obligation to reduce working hours for the disabled employee would impose a disproportionate burden on the employer. As a matter of principle, however, the Directive does not exclude the possibility that a reduction in working hours can be a suitable measure to meet the requirement of reasonable accommodation.[54]

The statutory requirement for reasonable accommodation of disabled employees very clearly shows how adjusted working conditions and work organization can contribute to prolonging someone's working life. It bears noting that the current EU strategy for the rights of persons with disabilities specifically underlines the increased prevalence of disabilities that come with age.[55] However, the requirement is limited to employees with a disability and only covers measures to allow the employee to carry out the work despite the impairment caused by that disability. By contrast, extended working-life policies cover all employees above a certain age, and when addressing working conditions and work organization, these policies typically seek to create incentives to remain in working life by facilitating the working situation of these employees in various ways.

To make a real difference in prolonging working lives, it must to some extent be possible to tailor adjustments of working conditions to the individual employee. Thus, whereas the framework for these policies can be set at the national or sectoral level, the

---

52. Eurofound (2013), *supra* n. 48, 13.
53. Joined Cases C-335/11 and C-337/11 *HK Denmark*, case *Chacón Navas* C-13/05. Cf. Numhauser-Henning (2013).
54. Joined Cases C-335/11 and C-337/11 *HK Denmark*.
55. In fact, almost half of persons aged above 65 reports some form of disability, Strategy for the rights of persons with disabilities 2021-2030, COM (2020) 101 final, p. 3.

details of the adjustment measures are normally set at the workplace level. One way in which the social partners have opened up for individual modifications of working conditions in some cases is to introduce the possibility for older employees to trade other privileges for time off. For instance, the collective agreement between the Federation of the Finnish Technology Industries and the Finnish Metal Workers' Union contains a clause on the seniority bonus – an extra top-up of the wage after a certain number of years in service. In addition, the collective agreement allows for individual agreements between the employer and employees whereby the latter can exchange their seniority bonus or a part thereof for corresponding time off.[56] Similar practices can be found in the Netherlands, where the construction industry agreement allows workers of 55 years and older to request a four-day working week (thirty-two hours) instead of claiming other rights to leave, such as extra paid vacation due to age.[57] In the Netherlands generally, provisions on the adjustment of working conditions to spare older workers are found in collective agreements in various sectors of industry, which include exemptions from night shifts, shift work and on-call duties.[58] Other examples can be found in Spain, where some collective agreements exempt older workers from particularly strenuous work, including rotating shifts, whereas others require individualized measures with a comprehensive analysis and evaluation with the involvement of occupational medicine experts for all workers above a certain age.[59] In marked contrast to protection against strenuous shifts, or the option to trade other benefits for a reduction in working time, a number of Member States also provide the right to a part-time pension at a certain age. Part-time pension schemes can contribute to prolonging working lives, as the possibility to partly step down can serve as an alternative to full retirement, thus enabling those who want to stay in working life a bit longer to do so. There is a wide variety of solutions for partial retirement within the EU.[60] Schemes set by national legislation sometimes cover all employees, such as the Austrian schemes for partial retirement and partial pension. In other cases, such as the German Altersteilzeitgesetz, statutory law provides a voluntary framework to which companies may or may not accede. It is common to develop statutory schemes in consultation with the social partners, and for most partial retirement schemes, the details can be modified in collective agreements.[61]

56. Clause 14.4.3 of the Collective agreement between the Technology Industry Employers of Finland and Industrial Union 6 February 2023-30 November 2024.
57. Chapter 6, section 5 of the Collective Agreement for the Construction & Infrastructure Sector [cao Bouw & Infra 2024]. A. Rutten, *Essays on Work and Retirement*, Center for Economic Research (Tilburg University 2023).
58. Chapter 4, section 2.9 of the Collective Agreement for Dutch Universities 1 April 2023-30 June 2024, whereby employees over the age of 57 at their own request, and with effect from 1 January 2025, may be exempt from working night shifts.
59. Section 41 of the Collective Agreement for Cemex Spain Operations, S.L.U. 2022, and section 44.4. of Collective Agreement IV Saint-Gobain Isover Ibérica, SL.
60. Eurofound, *Extending Working Lives Through Flexible Retirement Schemes. Partial Retirement* (Publication office of the European Union 2016).
61. For example, the Austrian scheme for partial retirement (Altersteilzeit) stipulated in section 27 of the Unemployment Insurance Act (AVIG as well as the scheme for a partial pension (Teilpension), stipulated in section 27a of the same Act, has been adjusted in some collective agreements).

There are also examples of partial retirement schemes established by collective agreements only, for instance, in the Netherlands and Denmark. In Sweden, collectively bargained partial pensions have existed in the state sector since 2003, and since 2006 for employees in the municipal and county sectors. In 2013, the social partners in the private sector concluded collective agreements on extensive rights to apply for partial retirement for large industry, construction and transport, from the age of 60 or 62.[62] An application for partial retirement can be denied only for considerable disruptions that cannot be easily reduced or eliminated by the employer, who must consider the possibility of relocating the worker to enable their partial retirement, even if the relocation requires certain vocational training. The explicit purpose of these agreements is to create conditions for generational renewal. Some years after this agreement, in 2017, following tough negotiations, the social partners in the private service sector concluded a collective agreement on flexible retirement, resulting in virtually the entire labour market since then being covered by collective agreements on partial retirement or flexible retirement.[63] The coverage has increased further though the collective arrangement in the state sector has been renegotiated in 2023 to cover a larger group of employees and partly modified rights.'[64] Several studies have been undertaken to investigate the effect of part-time pension schemes on the length of working lives.[65] The results do not offer any distinct support for a positive correlation between part-time pension schemes and prolonged working lives. There are methodological difficulties in measuring the impact of part-time pension schemes, as ideally, their output should be compared with a hypothetical situation where the scheme did not exist.[66] More importantly, the effects of part-time retirement schemes can be measured from different perspectives. Thus, while such schemes might have a positive impact on the share of older employees in the workforce, their impact on the average total number of years in employment might be insignificant. Studies have questioned the benefit of introducing part-time pension schemes, due to the risk that part-time

62. Information nr 4/2013 1(7) Appendix 7 and 8, Gemensam kommentar Deltidspension l Teknikarbetsgivarna och IF Metall, Gemensam kommentar Deltidspension Teknikarbetsgivarna och Unionen/Sveriges Ingenjörer. Cf Swedish National Mediation Office, *Annual report 2013*, Stockholm 2014, 32 and Handbook on collectively agreed occupational pensions and insurance 2024 (Avtalat 2024).
63. Agreement of the 22 February 2017 on Flexpension in Service Companies between Almega and Engineers of Sweden, Unionen and SEKO. The Swedish Pensions Agency, Flexpension och delpension – En översikt inom de fyra stora avtalsområdena. Ref. no. 2017-247, 2017, https://www.pensionsmyndigheten.se/content/dam/pensionsmyndigheten/blanketter---broschyrer---faktablad/publikationer/rapporter/20171/Flexpension och delpension.pdf.
64. Agreement of 5 May 2023 between Arbetsgivarverket and OFR, Saco-S, Trade Union in services and Communication, amending PA 16 Pension Agreement in the State Sector, https://www.arbetsgivarverket.se/globalassets/arbetsgivarverket/avtal-och-skrifter/avtal/pa-16-pensionsavtal/overenskommelse-om-andringar-i-pa16-forhandlingsprotokoll-20230505.pdf.
65. Bustos, E., Partial Retirement and Labor Supply: Evidence from Swedish Collective Bargaining Agreements, IFN Working Paper No. 1495, 2024, https://www.ifn.se/media/0fyclblz/wp1495.pdf. For different ways to approach the matter, *see* Eurofound (2016), *supra* n. 60. *See also* P. Berg, et al., 'Can Policy Facilitate Partial Retirement? Evidence from Germany', Discussion Paper No. 9266, IZA 2015.
66. M. Takala & N. Väänänen, 'Does Part-Time Pension Extend Working Lives? A Finnish Case Study' Reports 05, Finnish Centre for Pensions 2016, 27.

work might crowd out full-time work without increasing the overall working-time output.

[C] Lifelong Learning and Mobility in the Labour Market

The policy area of lifelong learning and mobility in the labour market is a matter for all ages and does not concern older employees specifically. In the discourse on extended working lives, however, lifelong learning including digital upskilling has been identified as a key area. It is therefore important to note that older employees have significantly more limited opportunities for training and development than younger employees in most counties.[67] Lack of willingness on the employers' side to invest in older employees, along with the reluctance of older employees to adapt to the changing requirements for workplace performance, have been identified as factors that hamper strategies for training and skills improvement opportunities for the ageing workforce.[68]

In May 2009, a strategic framework for European cooperation in education and training was adopted. The framework sets as a benchmark that by 2020 at least 15% of adults aged 25 to 64 years old should participate in lifelong learning.[69] It has proved difficult for all but a few Member States to meet this benchmark.[70] In 2014, the EU average of adults in lifelong learning schemes was just below 11%, and in 2015 this average did not increase. In fact, in some EU countries, the 2015 average was lower than the year before, and in comparison with 2012, adult learning participation rates fell in fourteen Member States.[71] As for 2020, Sweden, the Netherlands, Germany, Hungary, Austria, and display high participation rates, whereas those in Romania, Poland, Bulgaria, and Greece are low or very low. In 2020, the 2009 strategic framework was replaced with the European Skills Agenda, setting new objectives to be met in 2025 and 2030.[72]

---

67. S. Vickerstaff, C. Phillipson & W. Loretto, 'Training and Development: "The Missing Part of the Extending Working Life Agenda?"' Public Policy Aging Report 25 (2015) 4:139-142 https://doi.org/10.1093/ppar/prv018, U. Leber, J. Stegmaier & A. Tisch, 'Altersspezifische Personalpolitik: Wie Betriebe auf die Alterung ihrer Belegschaften reagieren', *IAB-Kurzbericht* 13/2013, Nürnberg, 8 S, Chartered Institute of Personnel and Development CIPD, *Creating Longer, More Fulfilling Working Lives. Employer Practice in Five European Countries*, Policy Report 2016, 32. J. Schmitz, 'Companies and Old Workers. Obstacles and Drivers of Labour Market Participation in Recruitment and in the Workplace', in S. Scherger (ed.) *Paid Work Beyond Pension Age: Comparative Perspectives* (Palgrave Macmillan 2015).
68. G. Martin, et al., 'In the Name of Meritocracy: Managers' Perceptions of Policies and Practices for Training Older Workers' Ageing & Society (2014) 34:992-1018 https://doi.org/10.1017/s0144686x12001432.
69. Council conclusions of 12 May 2009 on a strategic framework for European cooperation in education and training ('ET 2020'), Annex I, Reference levels of European average performance ('European Benchmarks').
70. European Parliament, *Ageing Policies: Access to Services in Different Member States* (2021).
71. Eurostat, *Adult Learning Statistics* (June 2017).
72. European Commission, European Skills Agenda for sustainable competitiveness, social fairness and resilience COM(2020) 274 final.

Within the EU as a whole, employers provide around one-third of non-formal education and training.[73] In the 2020 Skills Agenda, the European Commission emphasizes the need to work in close partnership with employers. The Commission furthermore commits to promoting the participation of social partners in labour market projections and the identification of training needs to develop skills intelligence.[74]

In most EU Member States, lifelong learning strategies focusing on vocational training are drawn up in consultation with the social partners, or in tripartite arrangements. The social partners can then choose to conclude sectoral or local collective agreements to set the framework for the company level.[75] One example is the sectoral agreement for the Finnish Facilities Services Sector. In order to secure and increase the supply of competent workforce in the branch associations, the agreement recommends that employees should have opportunities to participate in education that supports and develops their professional skills and that the education should be provided at the expense of the employer.[76] Another example specifically targeting older employees is the agreement between the German metalworkers' trade union and the employers in the information technology sector, concluded as part of an initiative to improve employment and employability for persons aged above 50 years, i.e., by offering individually designed comprehensive training opportunities.[77] In France, collective agreements at branch and company levels very often include provisions directed specifically towards older employees. This is to a large extent a result of the statutory obligation for social partners that applied between 2003 and 2017, to negotiate on the employment of older workers. The most common themes in these collective agreements are career development and the promotion of skills and qualifications.[78]

In 2022, two landmark cross-sectoral agreements on work-life security, transition and employment protection were concluded in Sweden. These so-called Main Agreement extends the established structure providing support in case of redundancy to cover also employees who are in employment and who want to strengthen their future labour market position.[79] The agreements are supported by new legislation on public

73. Eurostat, Adult learning statistics – characteristics of education and training. Statistics Explained. Data extracted in June 2024.
74. European Commission, European Skills Agenda for sustainable competitiveness, social fairness and resilience COM(2020) 274 final.
75. The frequency and coverage of such agreements vary greatly between the Member States. Eurofound, *Contribution of Collective Bargaining to Continuing Vocational Training* (Dublin 2009).
76. Collective Labour Agreement for the Facilities Services Sector, 1 March 2023-31 March 2025, Real Estate Employers Services United PAM.
77. IT 50 Plus, a joint initiative between IG Metall and BITKOM. Cf. 'e-Skills in Europe, Germany, Country report' (2014), within the project for the European Commission *e-Skills for Jobs in Europe. Measuring Progress and Moving Ahead.*
78. Ministère du Travail, du Plein emploi et de l'Insertion, *Édition 2023 Direction générale du travail La négociation collective en 2022*, 361.
79. The bargaining process was pursued by a few powerful parties in the private sector. Initially, the social-partner agreement was signed only by the private employer Confederation of Swedish Enterprise and the white-collar confederation PTK. Several trade unions in the blue-collar federation LO considered that the agreement brought deteriorations for their members without providing anything substantial in return. Later, a couple of large LO unions joined the

funding, which was adopted along with a bill on reformed employment protection legislation.[80] In 2023, additional similar main agreements were concluded in the private sector, and in parallel, several parties in the public and private sectors updated their transition agreements in line with the legislative changes following the 2022 agreements. Transition agreements and sectoral collective agreements to support employees in cases of redundancy have covered the labour market since the early 70s. Although not targeting older workers specifically, the agreements are especially important to this group, for whom unemployment implies a serious risk of never re-entering the labour market. Under these agreements, Job Security Councils (trygghetsråd) established by the social partners, provide financial support, career planning and counselling to find a new job in the event of restructuring.[81] The new agreements, concluded in 2022, replace the transition agreements and extend their content providing those who are already employed with comprehensive support in the form of guidance, education and generous study grants and loans along with a right to study leave.[82]

[D] Age Awareness and Attitudes Towards Older Employees

In addition to measures to alleviate working conditions, introduce incentivizing benefits and create opportunities for professional development, key strategies to promote longer working lives include workplace arrangements to make the situation of older employees more visible. By increasing employer knowledge regarding the needs that may occur in later working life, and allowing older employees themselves to articulate and contribute to resolving the challenges that come with age, such arrangements also help to counteract ageism and prevent age discrimination. The

social-partner agreement and then the entire LO, but each member union would choose LO whether to sign the national cross-sectoral collective agreement that would result from the social-partner agreement. The national cross-sectoral collective agreement was signed in the summer of 2022. In 2023, LO and PTK had signed in total six similar main agreements with employers' organizations in the private sector, and in parallel, several parties in the public and private sectors had updated their transition agreements in line with the legislative changes following from the 2022 Main Agreement. *See* further, Swedish National Mediation Office, *Annual Report 2022* (Stockholm 2023) 14 ff.

80. For a thorough description of the reform and the process leading up to it, *see* M. Rönnmar & A. Iossa, *CODEBAR. Comparisons in Decentralised Bargaining: Towards New Relations Between Trade Unions and Works Councils? Swedish Country Report* (2022).
81. Government Report SOU 2002:59, 37. K. Ahlberg & N. Bruun, 'Sweden: Transition Through Collective Bargaining', in T. Blanke & E. Rose (eds), *Collective Bargaining and Wages in Comparative Perspective: Germany, France, the Netherlands, Sweden and the United Kingdom* (Kluwer Law International, Alphen aan den Rijn 2005). M. Rönnmar, 'Intergenerational Bargaining: Sweden – Country Report', Report to the EU-project 'Intergenerational Bargaining: Towards Integrated Bargaining for Younger and Older Workers in EU Countries (iNGenBar)' (2014).
82. Without interfering with the existing education support system and nor with company-specific training funded by the individual employer, the agreements allow persons who have worked for a certain number of years to take study leave to pursue an education to strengthen their position in the labour market with a grant replacing a large part of the income, and with the possibility to take up an additional study loan.

adoption of a statutory, tripartite or collectively bargained framework for such awareness-raising policies serves to create a readiness to adjust the working situation for employees in their late working life. This expectation, in turn, fosters a general anticipation that employees actually should stay longer in work.

Age management strategies primarily target persons who are already in employment. However, measures to increase the recruitment of older employees can also be a part of a comprehensive age management strategy. Some EU Member States have introduced schemes to encourage employers to hire employees above a certain age. Early examples can be found in the Spanish combination of social security bonuses and hiring benefits, the *contrat de génération* scheme in France and hiring subsidies in the Netherlands.[83] Later examples are the Portuguese 2019 law on 'contract generation' whereby companies receive subsidies when simultaneously hiring a person in his or her first job and a long-term unemployed person aged 45 years old or older.[84] This initiative was the result of a tripartite agreement in 2018 between the social partners and the Portuguese Government, in the Standing Committee for Social Concertation.[85] Likewise, in 2019, the Belgian Parliament of the German-speaking Community introduced subsidize schemes for the hiring of persons 45 and 54 years, and 55 and 65 years, respectively.[86] Strategies to address approaches towards older members of the workforce are the core of age management.[87] This includes recruitment policies towards older jobseekers, but equally important are measures such as consultations, planning

83. The Spanish *Programa Extraordinario de Activación para el Empleo* providing benefits for long-term unemployed workers and labour intermediation policies was recognized in the national framework collective agreement signed by the main employers' organizations and the two main trade unions, which encourages the social partners at the sectoral level to promote the recruitment of, e.g., workers over 45, taking into account the public system of hiring bonuses Chapter I, Point h) of *III Acuerdo para el Empleo y la Negociación Colectiva*, 8 June 2015, between CEOE & CEPYME and CCOO & UGT. The French contrat de génération scheme introduced in 2013 required the social partners to conclude a collective agreement under which companies may recruit a younger worker on a permanent employment contract and at the same time keep on (or hire) an older worker, S. Robin-Olivier, 'Age Discrimination and Labour Law in France', in A. Numhauser-Henning & M. Rönnmar (eds), *Age Discrimination and Labour Law: Comparative and Conceptual Perspectives in the EU and Beyond* (Kluwer Law International, Alphen aan den Rijn 2015). Until 2018, employers in the Netherlands employers could apply for a subsidy when training or hiring an unemployed person over 50, Regeling van de Minister van Sociale Zaken en Werkgelegenheid van 26 September 2013, 2013000129478, tot verstrekken van subsidie voor scholing en plaatsing van oudere werklozen (Regeling scholing en plaatsing oudere werklozen), Stcrt. 2013, 27343, applicable until 1 January 2018. *See* M. Kullmann, 'Extended Working Life: The Dutch Government Response' European Labour Law Journal 7 (2016) 1:31-51 https://doi.org/10.1177/201395251600700103.
84. Decree No. 112-A/2019 on Contract-Generation, Diário da República 12 April 2019.
85. Economic and Social Council (CES) (2018): Tripartite agreement on combating precarious work and labour market segmentation and promoting greater dynamism in collective bargaining.
86. Dekret zur AktiF und AktiF Plus-Beschäftigungsförderung am 28. Mai 2018 durch Parlament der Deutschsprachigen Gemeinschaft.
87. On attitudes towards older employees *see*, for instance, C. Ulander-Wänman, 'Swedish Collective Agreements and Employer's Willingness to Hire and Retain Older Workers in Employment' Journal of Working Life Studies 6 (2016) 2:61-79, C.T. Kulik, S. Perera & C. Cregan, 'Engage Me: The Mature-Age Worker and Stereotype Threat' Academy of Management Journal 59 (2016) 6:2132-2156 https://doi.org/10.19154/njwls.v6i2.4972, M. Carlsson & S. Eriksson, *The Effect of Age and Gender on Labour Demand: Evidence from a Field Experiment*, Working Paper 2017:8, IFAU.

and individually targeted measures for employees of a certain age. Some examples of such targeted measures have already been discussed above, in §6.02 on working conditions and §6.03 on workforce development. But there are also examples of how collective bargaining can introduce comprehensive structures for planning and consultation with older employees in the workplace. In Denmark, the importance of age management practices is long established among the social partners. Since 2009, the collective agreement in the public sector has provided for *senior conversations*, a voluntary dialogue with the employer on how the job demands of older workers can be met to satisfy both parties. To accommodate the needs of the employer and the individual employee, the agreement includes particular senior employment contracts with reduced working time or modified job content, and schemes that allow for financial incentives or extraordinary pension contributions to employees who choose to stay on longer in employment for a certain number of years.[88] Similarly, under the title Prolonging Working Careers, the collective agreement between the Federation of Finnish Technology Industries and the Finnish Metal Workers' Union (also mentioned above, in §6.02) states that the employer shall discuss with employees attaining the age of 58 the available measures for helping an older employee to cope at work. In addition, the agreement refers to the technology industries' career-span scheme publication for examples of measures that can be taken.[89] Along the same lines, several collective agreements in France provide so-called end-of-career interviews.[90]

§6.06 DISCUSSION AND FINAL REMARKS

The topic of extended working lives is high on the EU employment policy agenda. In many Member States, the need to meet the challenges of an ageing workforce has an important impact on policy-making and regulatory development. The crucial role of the social partners in this development has repeatedly been stressed. Indeed, the development in the last decade has shown that strategies for accommodating the challenges that come with an ageing workforce successfully can translate into collective agreements. This chapter discusses some of many existing examples of how collective bargaining in a constructive and applicable way can lead to the implementation of policy measures to promote extended working lives. At the same time, empirical studies in recent years have shown that implementing such measures can be more

88. Chapter 1, section 4 of Rammeaftale om Seniorpolitik, 2021. Cf. M. Barslund, *Extending Working Lives: The Case of Denmark*, CEPS Working Document No. 404, 2015. Other studies indicate is a discrepancy among the Danish companies in terms of the recognition of the problem and practical action. *See*, for instance, H. Jensen & R. Juul Møberg, 'Age Management in Danish Companies: What, How, and How Much?' Nordic Journal of Working Life Studies 2 (2012) 3:49-66 https://doi.org/10.19154/njwls.v2i3.2363.
89. Clause 31.1.10 of the Collective agreement between the Technology Industry Employers of Finland and Industrial Union 6 February 2023-30 November 2024.
90. Ministère du Travail, du Plein emploi et de l'Insertion, *Édition 2023 Direction générale du travail La négociation collective en 2022*, 361. *See*, among many others, Accord GEPP de la Société Vitréenne d'Abattage (SVA) Jean Rosé (secteur agroalimentaire) de juillet 2022 and Accord SCNF Collectif Relatif aux Dispositifs d'Accompagnement de Fin de Carrière, Version d'avril 2024.

difficult than expected. This has been explained by the fact that the top-down active ageing policies stemming from EU and national policymakers, and also from the European social partner Framework Agreement uncover a distance in relation to everyday practices in the workplace and that the positive narrative underlying the extended work-life policies does not resonate with employers and employees implementing and directly affected by these policies. While the rapid and ongoing prolongation of working lives in many EU Member States has been recognized and praised in the political debate, legislative reforms raising the retirement age and restricting early retirement have in many countries led to criticism and also significant protests from the public. Generally, retirement is considered a well-deserved freedom after a long working life and increased retirement age means cutting years off this freedom.[91] Also, although people on average live longer, for many, this is not the same as years of good health.[92] When working life is extended as a response to the increase in average life expectancy, there are growing risks related to deteriorating health and productivity – and these risks must to a large extent be borne by the individual employees and employers.

Against this background, the importance of increased collective bargaining initiatives in the area of prolonged working lives is apparent. Social partner involvement has unmatched abilities to mitigate demands, expectations and actual prerequisites to ensure a balanced and tailored approach to the demographic and economic realities that are pressing for increased labour force participation in relation to older workers. It is however also crucial that collective bargaining initiatives are supported at the State level. When facing the upcoming ageing of the workforce, typically employers tend primarily to consider measures that are financially and practically low in cost.[93] Thus, adjustments in the working conditions, such as ergonomic measures or reduction in working time, are more likely to take place than employability-increasing practices such as vocational training. At first sight, this approach from the employer is only logical. As explained by Schmitz, from the perspective of human resource capital theory, the expected outcome for employers (and also employees) of an investment in training decreases with the age of the employee.[94] What might be more difficult to see is that investments in training and other employability-increasing measures have a significant potential to pay off, as the employer can avoid the costs of early retirement and the hiring and training of new employees. Linking public funding to social partner initiatives means that the employers do not have to bear the (entire) economic risks and that more ambitious activities can be put in place. In this context, it is worth noting

91. A.S. Grødem & R.H. Kitterød, 'Older Workers Imagining Retirement: The Collapse of Agency, or Freedom at Last?' Ageing and Society 42 (2022) 10:2304-2322 https://doi.org/10.1017/s0144686x20002044. B. Apouey, 'Conditions of Existence and Subjective Perceptions of Retirement: Quantitative Evidence from France' Ageing and Society 42 (2022):564-587 https://doi.org/10.1017/s0144686x20001002. Sánchez & Díaz (2021), *supra* n. 2.
92. Krekula & Vickerstaff (2020), *supra* n. 35.
93. M. Fleischmann, F. Koster & J. Schippers, 'Nothing Ventured, Nothing Gained! How and under Which Conditions Employers Provide Employability-Enhancing Practices to Their Older Workers' The International Journal of Human Resource Management 26 (2015) 22:2908-2925 https://doi.org/10.1080/09585192.2015.1004100.
94. Schmitz (2015), *supra* n. 67.

that research has also shown that, in addition to less costly measures, employers also tend to consider measures that are formulated in collective agreements.[95]

The impact of collective bargaining in the context of promoting extended working lives is highly significant; it has a clear potential to make a difference, and a unique ability to provide tailor-made solutions. In addition, also from a strategic perspective, it would be rational for both employers and trade unions to increase their engagement in collective bargaining for older employees. Collective bargaining enables the social partners to direct the measures towards areas that matter to them, which are not always the same as those that matter to the public policymaker. To illustrate this, the Swedish collective agreements on part-time retirement, first put in place in 2013, provide an example. There seems to be scientific evidence that part-time pensions can extend working careers for certain groups in the sense that people within these groups actually stay longer in working life than they would otherwise have done. Nevertheless, there is little support for the positive impact on public finances. On a macroeconomic level, it is probably more efficient if people continue to work full-time for a somewhat shorter period instead of working a number of additional years on a part-time basis.[96] To counteract the effects of the ongoing demographic shift, working-life reforms should increase the overall working-time output by imposing a positive effect on income levels and tax revenues. From the perspective of public finances, this renders part-time pension schemes less interesting. Looking at the matter from the perspective of the social partners, however, the situation comes out differently. The explicit aim of the collective agreement was not primarily to contribute to the public finances, but to provide for generational renewal. In the promotion of knowledge transfer or the retaining of skills and experience within business, part-time pension schemes have the potential to play a key role. Collective bargaining has an important potential to contribute to the strategies of extended working lives in ways that let the social partners impact significantly on the future shaping of labour and skills supply, which in the Swedish setting also can be seen in the legislative reforms following the ground-breaking 2022 Main Agreement on work-life security, transition and employment protection. Social partners' involvement in active ageing could therefore be seen as a way to not only pursue their interest in this specific area but also to generally advance their positions and influence on labour market developments.

95. Fleischmann, Koster & Schippers (2015), *supra* n. 93.
96. Takala & Väänänen (2016), *supra* n. 66, 27. Cf. A.L. Gustman & T.L. Steinmeier, 'Projecting Behavioral Responses to the Next Generation of Retirement Policies' Research in Labour Economics 28 (2008), 237-253 https://doi.org/10.3386/w12958.

CHAPTER 7
Collective Bargaining with Regard to Young Employees: Importance and Challenges

Judith Brockmann

Young employees can be considered a vulnerable group that has been particularly hit by the various crises in the past years, i.e., the so-called financial and economic crisis and the COVID-19 crisis and their effects on the labour market. This paper focuses on collective bargaining with regard to young employees and gives examples of provisions in collective agreements targeting young employees. The role of the social partners and of collective bargaining is clearly emphasised by European policies when it comes to combating youth unemployment and promoting the labour market participation of young employees. By contrast, available data and information on collective bargaining with regard to young employees lead to the conclusion that collective agreements are of rather little importance. The paper explores possible legal and factual reasons. *Inter alia*, these are not only the functioning of the European legal framework but also the labour market situation, and the structure and functioning of trade unions.

§7.01 INTRODUCTION

Youth unemployment and the raising of young employees' labour market participation are major concerns in European Union (EU) policy and for the Member States.

Young or future employees are a vulnerable group when it comes to labour market participation and precarious working conditions. Youth can be conceived as a specific risk factor in the labour market.[1] Youth unemployment rates doubled in

1. Jenny Julén Votinius, *Young Employees: Securities, Risk Distribution and Fundamental Social Rights*, (3-4) 5 European Labour Law Journal 366, 367 (2014) https://doi.org/10.1177/201395251400500312; European Commission, *Joint Employment Report 2017 as Adopted by the EPSCO Council on 3rd March 2017*, 28, https://data.consilium.europa.eu/doc/document/ST-6887-2017-INIT/en/pdf (accessed 19 August 2024).

several Member States and even rose to over 50% in 2014 in certain Member States such as Greece[2] and Spain.[3] They have significantly decreased since then but have risen in the meantime due to the COVID-19 pandemic and remain notably higher than the overall unemployment rates in nearly all Member States.[4] In addition, young persons have been particularly struck by unemployment during the COVID-19 pandemic, compared to other groups.[5] Although the overall unemployment rate has roughly halved since 2013,[6] around one in three young people aged 15-24 in Greece[7] and Spain[8] are still unemployed. Of course, labour market situations vary in the different Member States,[9] but independently of the general labour market situation, low-skilled young people have particular problems entering the labour market.[10] This is all the more true for Member States with difficult labour market situations.[11] Vulnerability is not only limited to unemployment but also concerns precarious employment relationships and working conditions.[12] Young employees are significantly more often employed in non-standard forms of employment, such as on

2. Statista, *Greece: Youth Unemployment Rate from 2004 to 2023*, 2024, https://www.statista.com/statistics/812053/youth-unemployment-rate-in-greece/; and https://eures.europa.eu/living-and-working/labour-market-information/labour-market-information-greece_en (accessed 19 August 2024).
3. Statista, *Spain: Youth Unemployment Rate from 2004 to 2023*, 2024, https://www.statista.com/statistics/813014/youth-unemployment-rate-in-spain/ (accessed 19 August 2024).
4. Eurostat, *Unemployment Statistics, Monthly Data, June 2024*; https://ec.europa.eu/eurostat/statistics-explained/index.php?title=Unemployment_statistics#Youth_unemployment (accessed 18 July 2024).
5. Eurofund, *Becoming Adults: Young People in a Post-pandemic World: Research Report*, 2024, https://www.eurofound.europa.eu/en/publications/2024/becoming-adults-young-people-post-pandemic-world (accessed 18 July 2024); OECD, '*Youth and COVID-19: Response, Recovery and Resilience*', *OECD Policy Responses to Coronavirus (COVID-19)* at 6 et seqq. (Paris 2020), https://doi.org/10.1787/c40e61c6-en (accessed 18 July 2024). *See also* ETUC, *Time for Quality Jobs, Report*, February 2021, https://etuc.org/sites/default/files/press-release/file/2022-01/Report%20youth%20questionnaire%20-%20Feb2021.pdf (accessed 18 July 2024).
6. Statista, *Youth Unemployment Rate in the European Union as of April 2023, by Country*, 2024, https://www.statista.com/statistics/613670/youth-unemployment-rates-in-europe/ (accessed 19 August 2024).
7. Statista, *Greece: Youth Unemployment Rate from 2004 to 2023, supra* n. 2.
8. Statista, *Spain: Youth Unemployment Rate from 2004 to 2023, supra* n. 3; *see also* Gobierno de España, *Informe Jóvenes y Mercado de Trabajo No 40, 2023T4*, 2024, https://www.mites.gob.es/ficheros/ministerio/sec_trabajo/analisis_mercado_trabajo/jovenes/2024/Informe-Jovenes-Num40-Marzo-2024.pdf (accessed 19 August 2024).
9. *Draft Joint Employment Report from the Commission and the Council accompanying the Communication from the Commission on the Annual Growth, Survey 2015, Brussels 20 November 2014*, COM (214) 9 final, 5.
10. *See* Eurofund, *supra* n. 5, 7 et seq., https://www.eurofound.europa.eu/en/publications/2024/becoming-adults-young-people-post-pandemic-world (accessed 18 July 2024); and Hans Dietrich, *Youth Unemployment in the Period 2001-2010 and the European Crisis: Looking at the Empirical Evidence*, 19(3) Transfer 305-324 (2013) https://doi.org/10.1177/1024258913495147.
11. Eurofund, *supra* n. 5. For example, *Council Recommendation of 12 July 2016 on the 2016 National Reform Programme of Portugal and delivering a Council opinion on the 2016 Stability Programme of Portugal*, (2016/C 299/26), No. 10, 111. For a general overview *see* European Commission, DG Employment, Social Affairs and Inclusion, *Mutual Learning Programme, Thematic Paper: What Works for the Labour Market Integration of Youth at Risk*, 4 et seq. (2016).
12. Julén Votinius, *supra* n. 1, at 366.

part-time, temporary or temporary agency contracts.[13] They often earn less than the average employee,[14] that raises legal questions concerning age discrimination.[15] Youth unemployment and precarious working conditions are a concern in different respects, especially because of long-term scarring effects. They raise the risk of ongoing precarious working arrangements,[16] and long-term unemployment.[17] Consequently, they lead to higher poverty risks,[18] including negative effects on old-age provisions and pension shortfalls. In addition, they may have more or less severe consequences for the social structure.[19]

Policies and measures to promote youth employment are manifold. They are developed at a European as well as a national level by the Member States. European activities in favour of youth employment are included in the framework of different European policies, especially the reinforced European Youth Guarantee (EYG), to name only the most important. European policies address not only Member States but also the social partners. Social partners' action is of course not only institutionally embedded in the regulatory legal framework of collective bargaining in the relevant

---

13. *See* Janine Leschke, *Has the Economic Crisis Contributed to More Segmentation in Labour Market and Welfare Outcomes?*, ETUI Working Paper 2012.02; Frank Tros & Maarten Keune, *Intergenerational Bargaining in the EU: Comparative Report*, at 6 (2016) with further references, http://uva-aias.net/nl/research-projects/ingenbar (accessed 19 August 2024); ILO, *Non-standard Employment Around the World: Understanding Challenges, Shaping Prospects*, 135 et seq. and 140 (2016), https://www.ilo.org/sites/default/files/wcmsp5/groups/public/@dgreports/@dcomm/@publ/documents/publication/wcms_534326.pdf (accessed 20 August 2024).
14. This might be due to special youth minimum wages foreseen by collective agreements (*see infra* §7.03[A]) or national legislation. Statutory minimum wages are adjusted for young employees in Belgium, Cyprus, France, Ireland, Luxembourg, Malta and the Netherlands, *see* Eurofound, *Minimum Wages in 2024: Annual Review*, at 8 (Minimum wages in the EU series, Publications Office of the European Union 2024). For example, Dutch law provides a youth minimum wage that was applicable up to the age of 23, *see* Frank Tros, *Inter-generational Bargaining: Towards Integrated Bargaining for Younger and Older Workers in EU Countries: The Netherlands – Country Report*, at 14, http://uva-aias.net/nl/research-projects/ingenbar (accessed 19 August 2024) but has been reconducted to the age of 20; For the actual rate visit https://www.government.nl/topics/minimum-wage/minimum-wage-amounts-as-of-2024 (accessed 19 August 2024); the National Minimum Wages Act of 2000 of the Republic of Ireland provides lower minimum wages for young employees up to the age of 20 years and special trainee rates. The German Minimum Wages Act of 2014 (MiLoG) does not apply to persons aged under 18 without having accomplished any vocational or professional education according to Art. 22(2) MiLoG.
15. Opinion of the European Economic and Social Committee on the equal treatment of young people in the labour market (own-initiative opinion) (2023/C 293/08).
16. ILO, *supra* n. 13, at 137 et seq.; Maarten Keune, *YOUnion Final Report: Trade Unions and Young Workers in Seven EU Countries*, at 6 et seq., https://moodle.adaptland.it/pluginfile.php/21128/mod_resource/content/2/Maarten%20Keune%20%28UVAAIAS%29%20-%20Trade%20unions%20and%20young%20workers%20in%20seven%20EU%20countries%20%28comparative%20report%29.pdf (accessed 19 August 2024).
17. *See* Achim Schmillen & Matthias Umkehrer, *The Scars of Youth: Effects of Early-Career Unemployment on Future Unemployment Experience*, IAB Discussion Paper 6/2013.
18. Matthias Umkehrer, *The Impact of Changing Youth Employment Patterns on Future Wages*, IAB Discussion Paper 31/2015.
19. ILO, *supra* n. 13, at 138, 143.

Member State and in the current economic situation[20] but also depends on – diverse – industrial relations traditions and on the current situation and power of the social partners.[21]

After some definitions concerning the target group 'young employees' (§7.02), the paper offers examples of collective bargaining issues regarding young employees from different Member States (§7.03). As far as data and information are available, collective bargaining seems to be of little importance when it comes to young employees as a target group. This may be explained by different legal and current conditions at the EU level and in the Member States (§7.04). But the legal framework is only one possible explanation. In reality, the reasons for the marginal role of collective bargaining with regard to young employees are manifold (§7.05). Important factors may also be found in the current labour market situation and in the structure and functioning of trade unions.

§7.02 WHO ARE 'YOUNG EMPLOYEES'?

Talking about young employees as a group of stakeholders in collective bargaining, the paper concentrates on collective bargaining agreements that include special provisions for young employees. These provisions might act in favour of young employees, e.g., involving special training or mentorship, rules or quotas for the intake of young employees. But they might also lead to a downgrading of labour conditions for young employees, with, e.g., lower minimum wages in order to make employing them more attractive for employers thanks to reduced labour costs.

It must be taken into account that 'young employees' are far from being a legally defined group. This is true for the age structure and their limits as well as for the social structure. When speaking of young employees, one should be aware that there is no clear or legal concept defining a certain age group. Its extent depends on the policy context. European statistics usually understand by 'young workers' or 'young employees' persons aged 15 to 24.[22] In this paper, the term will be used in this sense, unless it is defined differently. In European policies, definitions might either be more restrictive[23] or wider.[24] For example, the reinforced Youth Guarantee applies to young people under the age of 30; compared to the original instrument, the EYG of 2013,

20. Kurt Vandaele, *Trade Unions' 'Deliberative Vitality' Towards Young Workers: Survey Evidence Across Europe*, at 16, 35, in Andy Hodder & Lefteris Kretsos (eds), *Young Workers and Trade Unions: A Global View* (Palgrave Macmillan 2015).
21. *See* Orestis Papadopoulos, *Economic Crisis and Youth Unemployment: Comparing Greece and Ireland*, 22(4) European Journal of Industrial Relations 409, 419 (2016) https://doi.org/10.1177/0959680116632326 for a general appreciation. *See also* Tros & Keune, *supra* n. 13, at 26.
22. Eurostat, *Glossary: Youth Unemployment*, 2024, https://ec.europa.eu/eurostat/statistics-explained/index.php?title=Glossary:Youth_unemployment (accessed 18 August 2024). *See also* Dominique Anxo, *Entry and Exit Patterns from the Labour Force: A European and Live-Course Perspective*, at 17, 18 et seq., in Ann Numhauser-Henning & Mia Rönnmar (eds), *Age Discrimination and Labour Law. Comparative and Conceptual Perspectives in the EU and Beyond* (Kluwer Law International 2015).
23. The Council Directive 94/33/EC of 22 June 1994 on the protection of young people at work, for example, targets young workers aged under 18 years.

which focused on people up to the age of 25,[25] the target group has been widened. However, this is binding neither for the Member States and national legislation nor for the social partners.[26] Various examples show that the notion of young employees may be enormously extended. Depending on the objective pursued, national legislation sometimes defines the group of young employees reaching up to the age of 29[27] or 30[28] years. For the purposes of this paper, we will just consider the definition employed by the ruling bodies, i.e., the legislature and/or the social partners, considering their competences.

Finally, young employees are far from being a homogeneous group. They are diverse in terms of, e.g., their level of education (from school dropouts to tertiary education),[29] professional situation[30] and experience (individuals with or without a degree looking for internships or their first jobs, others having their first professional experiences), and migration background. The paper will concentrate on those engaged in the labour market, i.e., young employees currently employed or unemployed and looking for a job. For this reason, it will specifically not consider the group known as 'NEETs' (neither in employment nor education and training).[31]

§7.03 EXAMPLES OF COLLECTIVE BARGAINING WITH REGARD TO YOUNG EMPLOYEES

Collective bargaining on young employees' matters is not monitored systematically, so for most Member States, reliable data is not available and more empirical research in this field would be desirable. That said, examples of collective agreements with special provisions concerning young employees can be found[32] and some key issues can be

24. For example, the survey on the group of NEETs targets persons between 15 and 29 years of age, *see* Eurostat, *Statistics on Young People Neither in Employment nor in Education or Training*, May 2024, https://ec.europa.eu/eurostat/statistics-explained/index.php?title=Statistics_on_young_people_neither_in_employment_nor_in_education_or_training (accessed 20 August 2024).
25. Council of the European Union, Council Recommendation of 22 April 2013 on establishing a Youth Guarantee, OJ C 120/1, 26 April 2013.
26. *See supra* n. 16 for statutory youth minimum wages and *infra* §7.03[A] for collectively bargained youth wages.
27. For example, Cyprus, *National Reform Programme 2017, Europe 2020 Strategy for: Smart, Sustainable and Inclusive Growth*, 8, https://commission.europa.eu/document/download/10123eda-f658-49d1-a4d1-29fc48f13ca7_en?filename=2017-european-semester-national-reform-programme-cyprus-en.pdf (accessed 19 August 2024).
28. *See also* on the example of Portugal Margherita Bussi & Leonard Geyer, *Youth Guarantees and Recent Developments on Measures Against Youth Unemployment: A Mapping Exercise*, 37 (ETUI 2013).
29. Educational qualifications cannot prevent especially structural unemployment, but still seem to be the best insurance against unemployment, *see* ILO, *supra* n. 13, at 143 as well as Keune, *supra* n. 16, at 7.
30. Tros & Keune, *supra* n. 13, at 12.
31. For an in-depth analysis, *see* Bussi & Geyer, *supra* n. 28, at 18 et seq.; and Eurofound, *Exploring the diversity of NEETs*, 2016, https://op.europa.eu/en/publication-detail/-/publication/00c83c68-472a-11e6-9c64-01aa75ed71a1/language-en (accessed 17 August 2024).
32. Also thanks to the research on intergenerational bargaining within the iNGenBar project: *Intergenerational Bargaining: Towards Integrated Bargaining for Younger and Older Workers in*

identified. Some of them are well known, such as youth wages [A], targets for the intake of young employees or job guarantees for apprentices [B], and vocational education and training (VET) matters [C]. But with regard to demographic changes, young employees are also an important group to be considered when it comes to intergenerational bargaining that focuses on both young and older employees [D].

[A] Youth Wages

In some Member States, particularly where no statutory minimum wage is provided by national legislation, special youth wages are foreseen by collective agreements.[33] This is the case where stipulations provide lower wages for young employees (as a defined age group) compared with 'adult professional' workers. The logic underlying youth wages is to render youth employment more attractive for employers by reducing labour costs.[34]

Youth wages exist, e.g., in Belgium, where mandatory national minimum wages have been fixed by national collective agreements within the National Labour Council (CNT/NAR) since 1975. Until 2013 the agreements provided special youth wages. Since then, the minimum wage has basically applied from the age of 18 years onwards, but there are still increments combining age and seniority criteria up to the age of 21. Furthermore, the conventional minimum wages do not apply for young employees under the age of 18 and those employed on special student contracts or apprenticeship programmes even beyond the age of 18.[35]

Similar examples are reported in Sweden, where minimum wages are not fixed by statutory rules but by social partners and are subject to collective agreements at different levels.[36] (Lower) youth minimum wages are common for young employees aged 16 to 19 years. In addition, periods of professional experience acquired before the age of 18 or 19 may not be taken into account for the purposes of wage calculation.[37]

EU Countries, financed by the European Commission; DG Employment, Social Affairs and Inclusion; Social Dialogue, Industrial Relations (VS/2013/0353), http://uva-aias.net/nl/research-projects/ingenbar (accessed 19 August 2024). For more examples, *see also* Inga Pavlovaite, *Getting Young Workers on Board of the European Pillar of Social Rights (ESPR)* (ETUC 2021), at 31 et seqq.; https://www.etuc.org/sites/default/files/page/file/2021-08/ESPR_research%20report_ETUC.pdf (accessed 19 August 2024).

33. However, youth pay discrimination also exits in legal provisions; therefore, ETUC called Member States to act against youth pay discrimination, ETUC Press Release 31 July 2024, https://www.etuc.org/en/pressrelease/eu-must-follow-uk-action-against-youth-pay-discrimination (accessed 19 August 2024).
34. *See, e.g.,* Julén Votinius, *supra* n. 1, at 381 et seq.; Keune, *supra* n. 16, at 7.
35. *See* Conseil National du Travail/Nationale Arbeitsraad 2024, *Salaire Minimum,* https://cnt-nar.be/fr/dossiers-thematiques/salaire-minimum; and *Montants des CCT,* https://cnt-nar.be/fr/documents/montants-des-cct (accessed 19 August 2024) with further references.
36. Mia Rönnmar, *Intergenerational Bargaining: Towards Integrated Bargaining for Younger and Older Workers in EU Countries, Sweden: Country Report* (2014), at 5 et seq., http://uva-aias.net/nl/research-projects/ingenbar (accessed 19 August 2024).
37. Jenny Julén Votinius, *Age Discrimination and Labour Law in Sweden,* at 292 with further references, in Ann Numhauser-Henning & Mia Rönnmar (eds), *Age Discrimination and Labour Law. Comparative and Conceptual Perspectives in the EU and Beyond* (Kluwer Law International 2015); *see also* Petter Hällberg & Christian Kjellström, *Collective Agreements and Minimum*

When it comes to the allowances for apprentices foreseen by collective agreements in the field of VET (*see infra*), they are usually lower than statutory or conventional minimum wages. That said, it must be considered that the object of apprenticeship contracts is not work but professional training. In this respect, they are not comparable to youth wages.

[B] Intake of Young Employees

Collective agreements may contain provisions to directly facilitate the integration of young employees into the labour market in the form of job guarantees. However, their extent may vary considerably. For example, sector-level collective agreements may provide numbered targets for the intake of young employees or former apprentices. They can thus be understood as declarations of intent, as they are usually not legally binding or at least not enforceable. This may be different when it comes to job guarantees for apprentices who have completed their VET (*see infra*). Job guarantees for young employees may also be linked to the employment or early retirement of older employees; examples will be given in the context of intergenerational bargaining (*see infra*).

For example, Swedish law provides special collective agreements to promote the employment of young people, the so-called introduction agreements. The state regulation results from a tripartite negotiation process and provides financial subsidies when young employees are hired in the application of an introduction agreement.[38] These collective agreements deal with the hiring of young employees and combine it with education, training and supervision.[39]

[C] Qualification of Young Employees and VET

The qualification of young employees is another important subject, especially when employers need to find qualified workforce. Collective agreements may provide a wide range of skills enhancement, training on the job, mentorship and/or supervision of young employees. The importance of collective bargaining depends mainly on the VET systems of the Member States.[40]

In countries with an established (dual) VET system, status, working and learning conditions in companies are traditionally subject to collective bargaining. This is especially true for Germany and Austria.[41] The collective agreements traditionally fix

Wages: A report from the Swedish National Mediation Office (Medlingsinstitutet 2020), https://www.mi.se/app/uploads/Minimum_wages_eng.pdf (accessed 19 August 2024).

38. *See in detail* Rönnmar, *supra* n. 36, at 19 et seq.
39. *See infra* §7.04.
40. Jason Heyes, *Vocational Education and Training and the Great Recession: Supporting Young People in a Time of Crisis*, ETUI Report 131, at 56 (2014).
41. Moreover, the social partners are usually represented in the bodies that are in charge of administration and control of VET; *see* for Germany: Arts 77, 82 and 92 Berufsbildungsgesetz (BBiG) (Germany); for Austria: Arts 19, 31-31d Berufsausbildungsgesetz (BAG).

allowances for apprentices[42] but may include guarantees to hire young workers after they have completed their VET or at least agree quotas for the intake of former apprentices. The employer's side invokes principally the need to find and bind qualified workforce and to make a return on investments in VET as motives for this kind of guarantee.[43] But in Italy too, for example, occupational standards for VET and other forms of apprenticeships are subject to collective agreements.[44]

[D] Intergenerational Bargaining

Regarding demographic changes in the active labour force, intergenerational bargaining seems to be an interesting approach for the social partners. Rather than bargaining separately for the young and the old, intergenerational bargaining is characterised by a more holistic and work-life-cycle-orientated approach.[45] Even if collective bargaining and the provisions seem to particularly focus on the concerns of older employees,[46] life-cycle-orientated rules are appropriate to meet young employees' interests at least in a medium- or long-term perspective.[47] Occasionally, collective agreements may also link the employment or intake of a young employee to either the maintenance or the (early) retirement of an elder employee. The idea of intergenerational bargaining is not new. For example, Italian law has provided instruments to promote collectively bargained 'generational relay schemes' since 1984, though they have scarcely been used in practice.[48] This also seems to be true for recently assessed forms of intergenerational bargaining.

In France, there has been a certain tradition in the actions of social partners and labour market policies to facilitate the employment of young employees by linking them to the leave of older employees.[49] In 2013, a statutory law[50] – preceded by a

42. Article 17 of the German BBiG (*supra* n. 41) even allows for collective agreements to deviate from the statutory VET minimum wages in peius; *see* Thomas Günther, *Die Angemessenheit der Ausbildungsvergütung im Lichte der gesetzlichen Mindestausbildungsvergütung*, Neue Zeitschrift für Arbeitsrecht, 805 (2023).
43. Antonio Brettschneider, *Intergenerational Bargaining: National Report Germany* (2014), http://uva-aias.net/nl/research-projects/ingenbar (accessed 19 August 2024).
44. Lisa Rustico & Roberto Pedersini, *iNGenBar: Inter-generational Bargaining Towards Integrated Bargaining for Younger and Older Workers in EU Countries*, Italy Country Report, 9, http://uva-aias.net/nl/research-projects/ingenbar (accessed 19 August 2024).
45. *See also* Julén Votinius, in this issue, Part I, Chapter 6, *Older Employees, Extended Working Lives, andCollective Bargaining* (*supra*).
46. Bundesanstalt für Arbeitsschutz und Arbeitsmedizin (ed.), *Altersdifferenzierte und alternsgerechte Betriebs- und Tarifpolitik: Eine Bestandsaufnahme betriebspolitischer und tarifvertraglicher Maßnahmen zur Sicherung der Beschäftigungsfähigkeit*, inqa-Report 42, at 167 et seq., (2011).
47. This is true for flexible part-time solutions or long-term working-time accounts, *see* Brettschneider, *supra* n. 43, at 30.
48. Rustico & Pedersini, *supra* n. 44, at 6.
49. Dominique Méda, Michèle Tallard & Jean-Louis Renoux, *Intergenerational Bargaining, Country Report: France*, 5 et seq., http://uva-aias.net/nl/research-projects/ingenbar (accessed 19 August 2024).
50. Former Articles L5121-9 et seq. Code du travail.

national collective agreement[51] – introduced the legal framework of a 'generation contract' (contrat de génération).[52] The law aimed to facilitate the access of young employees to open-ended contracts, to hire and maintain the contracts of older employees and to secure the transmission of knowledge and competences between both groups.[53] It provided financial subsidies for small and medium enterprises (SMEs) hiring a young employee on the basis of an open-ended contract linked to the maintenance or conclusion of a contract with an older employee. The law also aimed to promote collective bargaining and obliges the employer to establish an action plan on the employment of young and older employees and the modes of knowledge transmission in the company if no collective agreement was concluded at the sectoral or company level.[54] Two reports assessed the instrument and its application and showed that the government's expectations were far from being met.[55] Even if a growing number of sectoral-level agreements had been concluded, and the scope of their application extended by decree,[56] they tended to repeat the legal provisions set by the law. Indeed, agreements may often have included numbered targets for the intake of young or the maintenance of older employees, but they were usually not legally binding and had to be understood as a declaration of intent. Company-level agreements tended to copy the content of sector-level agreements, so the social partners did not seem to make active use of their regulating power for rule setting.[57] Finally, the instrument was abolished by the so-called Ordonnances Macron in 2017.[58]

In Germany, around 2010 a new type of collective agreement was emerging, the so-called demography-related collective agreements (Demografie-Tarifverträge), at a sectoral as well as a company level. These are the product of autonomous collective bargaining and are not incentivised by statutory rules. One important aim of demography-related collective agreements is to guarantee a performant workforce in times of age-related fluctuation. In this sense, they may provide a guarantee of the employment of a certain number of apprentices, former apprentices or other young employees, sometimes directly linked to the retirement of an older employee.[59] Moreover, sectoral-level agreements provide for a set of possible measures to be

51. Accord National Interprofessionnel du 19 octobre 2012 relatif au contrat de génération, https://irshare.eu/wp-content/uploads/2024/07/FR-accord-national-interprofessionnel-du-19-octobre-2012-relatif-au-contrat-de-generation_1357536972.pdf (accessed 28 October 2024).
52. Méda, Tallard & Renoux, *supra* n. 49, at 22.
53. Former Article L5121-6 Code du travail.
54. It depends on the company's size whether one or both provisions apply, DARES, *L'aide à l'embauche en contrat de génération: Une incitation à pérenniser l'emploi des jeunes*, DARES Etudes No. 025 (Mars 2015).
55. *Ibid.*
56. For a full list, *see* https://travail-emploi.gouv.fr/le-contrat-de-generation (accessed 7 October 2024).
57. Cour de Comptes, *Rapport public annuel 2016, Tome I: les observations, version intégrale*, at 66 et seq., https://www.ccomptes.fr/sites/default/files/EzPublish/02-contrat-generation-RPA2016-Tome-1.pdf (accessed 28 October 2024).
58. Article 9 II of the Ordonnance n° 2017-1387 du 22 septembre 2017 relative à la prévisibilité et la sécurisation des relations de travail, JORF n°0223 du 23 septembre 2017.
59. The same mechanism can be found in the former 'contrat de génération' in France. The important difference is that the instrument is not provided by German statutory rules and unlike in France, public financial subventions are not available.

activated either by company-level agreements or at the plant level by single employers and works councils. Despite their relative prevalence, the impact of demography-related collective agreements seems to be limited, as their application at company level is not very popular for various reasons.[60] The relevant provisions appear to have been maintained or renegotiated, but the current shortage of skilled labour means that partial retirement arrangements hardly meet employers' interests anymore.[61]

The conclusion of a collective agreement containing a 'generation pact' in 2018 has also been reported from the Netherlands.[62] However, this example did not set a precedent, the instrument has explicitly been discontinued in 2023.[63] In contrast, current collective agreements in Spain show that such regulations are very much up to date.[64] They may be considered a concretisation of the V Agreement for Employment and Collective Bargaining (V AENC) for the years 2023, 2024, and 2025 that provides for the promotion of the recruitment of young workers in order to address youth unemployment.[65]

[E] Interim Conclusions

Examples of collective bargaining concerning young employees' matters can be found in any structural collective bargaining setting, i.e., autonomous as well as incentive-induced[66] and mandatory collective bargaining structures. Collective bargaining concerning young employees takes place on all levels, i.e., national, sectoral and company,[67] and can also be found in European group-level agreements.[68] However,

60. Brettschneider, *supra* n. 43, at 48 et seq.
61. *See*, e.g., https://www.evg-online.org/fileadmin/Tarif/Tarifrunde_2023/SCHLICHTUNG/23-08-09_Aushang_Besondere_Teilzeit.pdf (accessed 19 August 2024).
62. ETUC, *A Better Life for Young and Old(er)*, https://www.etuc.org/en/better-life-young-and-older (accessed 20 August 2024).
63. CAO 2023, Art. 16, https://www.fnv.nl/getmedia/bff3dd8c-056d-4e24-988f-bfb617e76016/1100-stichting-fokus-exploitatie-cao-1-1-2023-tm-31-12-2023-v30112023.pdf?ext=.pdf&dtime=20240424105248 (accessed 19 August 2024).
64. Article 26 of the Convenio colectivo de la empresa Lufthansa, Líneas Aéreas Alemanas en España as acknowledged by the Spanish Ministerio de Trabajo y Economía Social, the 25 December 2023, BOE-A-2024-684, https://www.boe.es/diario_boe/txt.php?id=BOE-A-2024-684 (accessed 19 August 2024).
65. Chapter III, 2 of the V Acuerdo para el Empleo y la Negociación Colectiva, as acknowledged by the Spanish Ministerio de Trabajo y Economía Social, 19 May 2023, BOE-A-2023-12870, https://www.boe.es/diario_boe/txt.php?id=BOE-A-2023-12870 (accessed 19 August 2024).
66. *See* in this issue Pierre-Emmanuel Berthier & Oliver Leclerc, Part I, Chapter 4, *Incentivising Collective Bargaining* (*supra*).
67. For an in-depth analysis of different bargaining levels, *see* Sylvaine Laulom, in this issue, Part I, Chapter 1, *From Decentralisation of Collective Bargaining to Re-centralisation of Industrial Relations Systems? (supra)*.
68. *See* the example of the European Framework Agreement of the Groupe Safran (Accord cadre européen en faveur de l'insertion professionnelle des jeunes) concluded on 28 March 2013, http://safran-cfdt.fr/wp-content/uploads/2014/03/Accord-Cadre-Europeen-Developpement-25-03-2015.pdf or http://fo-safran.com/wp-content/uploads/2016/03/Accordcadreeuropéen-VF.pdf (accessed 19 August 2024).

following the different national or comparative reports, collective bargaining does not play an important role when it comes to young employees' matters.[69]

VET can be considered an important field for collective bargaining. But this seems to be true only if the social partner's involvement in the VET system is well established and if collective bargaining agreements are part of it. This seems to be the case in Austria and Germany. However, it is doubtful whether these are suitable as a model for other Member States, considering the wide variety of educational and collective bargaining systems. Austria and Germany have a long tradition of highly advanced dual VET systems, combining school and on-site training.

The intake of young employees seems to be rather important considering the demographic structure of the workforce. This is particularly true when employers are seeking generational (knowledge) transfer.

Finally, collective bargaining also seems to play a role when it comes to lowering labour conditions for young employees. This is often based on the conviction that alleviated charges for employers and less employment protection will improve employment opportunities for young workers. Thus, the latter end up depending on the general labour market situation. In other respects, lowering the labour conditions by collective agreements will contribute to precarious employment arrangements and may finally turn against trade unions (*see infra*).

§7.04 THE INSTITUTIONAL FRAMEWORK: CHALLENGES FOR COLLECTIVE BARGAINING WITH REGARD TO YOUNG EMPLOYEES' MATTERS

Collective bargaining depends on many factors, and the legal framework is only one of them. Both the European and national legal conditions must be considered. The national traditions and structures of social dialogue and industrial relations play an important role.[70] Furthermore, the labour market situation and the functioning and structures of trade unions must be taken into account.

[A] European Policies

The involvement of the social partners seems to be one of the key concerns of the EU when it comes to labour market policies. This is to be expected, as the promotion of the social partners is foreseen by the treaties in the context of employment regulation, especially in Articles 151, 154 and 155 Treaty on the Functioning of the European Union (TFEU). It is stressed in most policy documents concerning employment strategies, labour market reforms and the combating of youth unemployment/

69. This appraisal is unanimously shared by all the experts engaged in the INLACRIS network as well as the social partners' representatives from different Member States that have been involved in the present research.
70. *See, e.g.*, Papadopoulos, *supra* n. 21, at 410 et seq.

increasing of young employees' labour market participation.[71] Thus, in policy fields dealing with young employees or job seekers, social partners are not explicitly or necessarily involved with the furthering of the policies on a European or national level. Instead, they are named as stakeholders in these fields, along with other institutions, the Member States, business and civil society. Social partners have occasionally been consulted at the European level, e.g., with the development of the *Quality Framework for Traineeship*.[72]

With the introduction and establishment of the European Semester,[73] the EU has adopted soft law strategies on the one hand[74] and combined them with financial policies and instruments on the other.[75] This can be illustrated with regard to the Youth Employment Support package[76] and the (reinforced) EYG[77] and its implementation mechanism.[78] The implementation is based on typical measures of the open method of co-ordination (OMC),[79] i.e., choices are left to the Member States as to the establishment of good practices and financial incentives.[80] At the same time, financial policies such as austerity measures or the goals and assessments in the European Semester framework focus on measures taken by the Member States. Member States, or rather their governments, are held liable towards the EU and its institutions. This leads to

71. *See only* European Commission, Communication from the Commission, *Europe 2020: A strategy for smart, sustainable and inclusive growth Brussels*, 3.3.2010 COM (2010) 2020 final; Council of the European Union, *Council Recommendation of 22 April 2013 on establishing a Youth Guarantee*, OJ C 120/1, 26 April 2013; European Commission, *Draft Joint Employment Report from the Commission and the Council accompanying the Communication from the Commission on the Annual Growth Survey 2016*, Brussels, 26.11.2015 COM (2015) 700 final; European Commission, *Draft Joint Employment Report from the Commission and the Council accompanying the Communication from the Commission on the Annual Growth Survey 2017*, Brussels, 16.11.2016, COM (2016) 729 final; European Commission, n. 6, at 28.
72. Beryl ter Haar & Mia Rönnmar, *Intergenerational Bargaining, EU Age Discrimination Law and EU Policies: An Integrated Analysis*, 13, http://uva-aias.net/nl/research-projects/ingenbar (accessed 19 August 2024).
73. Regulation (EU) 2024/1263 of the European Parliament and of the Council of 29 April 2024 on the effective coordination of economic policies and on multilateral budgetary surveillance and repealing Council Regulation (EC) No. 1466/97, L 2024/1263.
74. *See* Paul Copeland & Beryl ter Haar, *A Toothless Bite? The Effectiveness of the European Employment Strategy as a Governance Tool*, 23(1) Journal of European Social Policy, at 21, and 27 (2013) https://doi.org/10.1177/0958928712463157.
75. *See* Manfred Weiss, *European Employment Policies: A Critical Analysis of the Legal Framework*, 8(2) European Labour Law Journal, at 111, and 113 (2017), with further references https://doi.org/10.1177/2031952517712117.
76. Communication from the Commission to the European Parliament, the Council, the European Economic and Social Committee and the Committee of the Regions 'Youth Employment Support: a Bridge to Jobs for the Next Generation' COM/2020/276 final.
77. Council Recommendation of 30 October 2020 on A Bridge to Jobs – Reinforcing the Youth Guarantee and replacing the Council Recommendation of 22 April 2013 on establishing a Youth Guarantee 2020/C 372/01.
78. *See* Edoardo Ales, *The European Employment Strategy as Enhanced Coordination: A Holistic Approach to the EU Social Commitment*, 8(2) European Labour Law Journal, 122 et seq. (2017) with further references https://doi.org/10.1177/2031952517712123.
79. Arne Pilniok, *Governance im europäischen Forschungsförderverbund*, at 208 et seq. (Mohr Siebeck 2011); Arthur Benz, *Accountable Multilevel Governance by the Open Method of Coordination?*, 13 European Law Journal, 505-522 (2007) https://doi.org/10.1111/j.1468-0386.2007.00381.x.
80. *See* Copeland & ter Haar, *supra* n. 74, passim.

Member State-driven measures (i.e., by legislators or governments) to fulfil the goals,[81] which may leave little space for collective bargaining.[82] In this sense, measures taken by the Member States seem to be far more important.[83]

When it comes to the procedures provided within the European Semester, it is remarkable that youth unemployment has been an important issue in the Country Specific Recommendations (CSR) in 2015/16, despite having been barely mentioned in earlier CSRs. However, the European recommendations were very general and did not and do not systematically assess the implementation of the EYG or the social partners' involvement in this regard.[84] Today, the topic of youth unemployment is generally mentioned in the national reports, but not addressed in the CSRs.[85]

The social partners' involvement in the procedures of the European Semester by the European Commission and by the Member States, i.e., especially the elaboration of the National Reform Programmes (NRPs) or National Recovery and Resilience Plans (RRPs) and the CSR in the Member States has been analysed over the years with varying results. It shows that the level of involvement differs a lot in the Member States.[86] Obviously, no general participation procedures have been established in the Member States, but participation depends on the issues at stake.[87]

---

81. As Leclerc stated: 'Labour law reform seems to be one of the few policy instruments available to governments in the eurozone [sic!] with which to reassure the financial markets and to avoid the downgrading of their sovereign debt by the credit rating agencies. In that sense, labour market reform seems to work as a signal to the financial markets of the willingness of individual States to act positively for the sake of their economies.' – Olivier Leclerc, *Which Securities for Workers in Times of Crisis? Challenges and Perspectives*, 5(3-4) European Labour Law Journal, at 410, 414 (2013) https://doi.org/10.1177/201395251400500314.
82. *See* Copeland & ter Haar, *supra*, n. 74, passim.
83. In this sense also Kurt Vandaele, *Union Responses to Young Workers Since the Great Recession in Ireland, the Netherlands and Sweden: Are Youth Structures Reorienting the Union Agenda?*, 19(3) Transfer, 381, 395 (2013), Tros, *supra* n. 14, at 40 et seq., and Vanessa Beck & Glynne Williams, *iNGenBar: Inter-generational Bargaining: Towards Integrated Bargaining for Younger and Older Workers in EU Countries – UK Country Report*, http://uva-aias.net/nl/research-projects/ingenbar, at 14 et seq. (accessed 19 August 2024).
84. The courant CSR all contain the phrase 'The systematic and effective involvement of local and regional authorities, *social partners* [emphasis added] and other relevant stakeholders remains important for the successful implementation of the recovery and resilience plan, as well as other economic and employment policies going beyond the plan, to ensure broad ownership of the overall policy agenda.' *See, e.g.*, Council Recommendation on the 2023 National Reform Programme of France and delivering a Council opinion on the 2023 Stability Programme of France, SWD (2023) 610 final, recital 27.
85. With exception of Spain, *see* Council Recommendation on the 2023 National Reform Programme of Spain and delivering a Council opinion on the 2023 Stability Programme of Spain, SWD (2023) 609 final.
86. *See* Christian Wetz, *Towards a New Start for Social Dialogue? Collective Employment Relations: Q1 2015*, https://www.eurofound.europa.eu/observatories/eurwork/articles/industrial-relations/towards-a-new-start-for-social-dialogue-collective-employment-relations-q1-2015 (accessed 19 August 2024); ETUC criticised a lack of involvement of the social partners, ETUC, *3 Years of Youth Guarantee: What Next? A Follow-up Report*, 6 (Brussels 2016).
87. *See, e.g.*, Eurofound, *Involvement of the Social Partners in the European Semester: 2016 Update* (Publications Office of the European Union 2017); Eurofound, *Involvement of Social Partners in the National Recovery and Resilience Plans* (Publications Office of the European Union 2022); Eurofound, *Involvement of Social Partners in the Implementation of National Recovery and Resilience Plans* (Publications Office of the European Union 2023); and Sebastiano Sabato,

On the other hand, CSR used as instruments of the European Semester and financial policy seem to have rather discouraged the participation of social partners unless collective bargaining is used with the aim of promoting wage moderation or introducing more flexible working conditions. When it comes to collective bargaining or collective bargaining systems as aspects mentioned in the NRP or CSR, they usually seem to be considered a source of inflexibility and an obstacle to employment. At the beginning of the European Semester mechanism, there was a tendency to advise Member States to introduce more flexibility in collective bargaining systems, supposing that this could be reached by decentralising collective bargaining and by allowing deviation from legal rules or higher-level (i.e., on the national or sectoral level) agreements by lower-level agreements (i.e., respectively on the sectoral or company level).[88] This could be observed in the respective memorandums of understanding (e.g., for Greece and Spain) as well as in the CSRs of 2015 and 2016.[89] Today, the subject of collective bargaining does not seem to be specifically addressed by the CSRs. The recent CSRs (2023) all contain the very general phrase 'The systematic and effective involvement of local and regional authorities, *social partners* [emphasis added] and other relevant stakeholders remains important for the successful implementation of the recovery and resilience plan, as well as other economic and employment policies going beyond the plan, to ensure broad ownership of the overall policy agenda.'[90]

Angelina Atanasova, Ludovico Fiorucci & Slavina Spasova, *Monitoring the Quality of Public Consultations with Trade Unions on Implementation of the National Recovery and Resilience Plans* (ETUI 2023).

88. Bernadette Allinger, Jörg Flecker & Christoph Hermann, *Das Ende der Pfadabhängigkeit?: Umwälzungen in den industriellen Beziehungen seit der Krise*, (1/2) Sozialer Fortschritt, 5-13 (2014); Thorsten Schulten & Torsten Müller, *A New European Interventionism? The Impact of the New European Economic Governance on Wages and Collective Bargaining*, in David Natali & Bart Vanhercke (eds), *Social Developments in the European Union 2012* (OSE/ETUI 2013), 181-213; for an in-depth analysis, Aristea Koukiadaki, Isabel Távora & Miguel Martínez Lucio (eds), *Joint Regulation and Labour Market Policy in Europe During the Crisis: A Seven-Country Comparison*, 8-134 (ETUI 2016).
89. *See* Council Recommendation of 14 July 2015 on the 2015 National Reform Programme of Italy and delivering a Council opinion on the 2015 Stability Programme of Italy (2015/C 272/16), No. 19, OJ C 272, 64 and Recommendation for a Council Recommendation on the 2016 National Reform Programme of Italy and delivering a Council opinion on the 2016 stability programme of Italy as of 18.5.2016, COM (2016) 332 final, No. 16, 6; Recommendation for a Council Recommendation on the 2016 National Reform Programme of Spain and delivering a Council opinion on the 2016 stability programme of Spain as of 18.5.2016, no. 10, COM (2016) 329 final, 5; Council Recommendation of 14 July 2015 on the 2015 National Reform Programme of Portugal and delivering a Council opinion on the 2015 Stability Programme of Portugal (2015/C 272/25), OJ C 272, No. 10, 95 et seq. and Recommendation for a Council Recommendation on the 2016 National Reform Programme of Portugal and delivering a Council opinion on the 2016 stability programme of Portugal as of 18.5.2016, COM (2016) 342 final, No. 9, 5.
90. *See, e.g.*, Council Recommendation on the 2023 National Reform Programme of France and delivering a Council opinion on the 2023 Stability Programme of France, SWD (2023) 610 final, No. 27.

[B] Ban on Age Discrimination

When concluding collective agreements, the social partners are bound by the legal rules prohibiting age discrimination, particularly those implementing the Employment Equality Directive (2000/78/EC).[91] This does not mean that any age-specific rules in collective agreements are prohibited. Rules that apply to a certain age group are directly discriminating. Rules applying for apprentices or first-jobbers are likely to be considered indirect discrimination because the majority of apprentices or employees entering the labour market consists of younger employees and in reality, the rules will mainly apply to younger employees. But following Article 6(1) of the Directive, age discrimination may be justified as long as the measures follow the principle of proportionality.[92] In this regard, the European Court of Justice (ECJ) seems to leave a wide range of discretion to the social partners, relying on the collective bargaining process and the social partners' ability to reconcile interests.[93] It may be questioned for good reason if this is always the case when it comes to young people's interests.[94] More generally speaking, the grounds for justification of age discrimination by levelling down the employment conditions of younger employees are rather weak.[95] However, one would not suppose that the current legal situation actually forms an obstacle to collective bargaining with regard to young employees' matters.

[C] Trade Unions and Young Employees

When it comes to collective bargaining on young employees' matters, it also seems appropriate to give attention to the actors and especially to the trade unions. Among other factors,[96] trade union structures and functioning may also have an impact on the relatively low importance of collective bargaining with regard to young employees. First of all, it must be stressed that the fight against youth unemployment and decent

91. ter Haar & Rönnmar, *supra* n. 72, at 16 with further references.
92. For a critical analysis on age discrimination *see also* Julén Votinius, *supra* n. 37 at 292 and 295 and Julén Votinius, *supra* n. 45 and Christa Tobler, *EU Age Discrimination Law and Older and Younger Workers: Court of Justice of the European Union Case Law Development,* 93 et seq., in Ann Numhauser-Henning & Mia Rönnmar (eds), *Age Discrimination and Labour Law. Comparative and Conceptual Perspectives in the EU and Beyond* (Kluwer Law International 2015), as well as Dagmar Schiek, *Proportionality on Age Discrimination Cases: Towards a Model Suitable for Socially Embedded Rights,* 71, 79 et seq., in Ann Numhauser-Henning & Mia Rönnmar (eds), *Age Discrimination and Labour Law. Comparative and Conceptual Perspectives in the EU and Beyond* (Kluwer Law International 2015).
93. *See* examples given by ter Haar & Rönnmar, *supra* n. 72, at 19: *Palacios de la Villa v. Cortefiel Servicios SA,* Case C-411/05, para. 68 (2007); *Rosenbladt v. Oellerking Gebäudereinigungsges. mbH,* Case C-45/09, para. 67 (2010); *Hörnfeldt v. Posten Meddelande AB,* Case C-141/11, para. 32 (2012); *Johann Odar v. Baxter Deutschland GmbH,* Case C-152/11, para. 47 (2013).
94. In this sense *see also* Bram Foubert et al., *An EU Perspective on Age as a Distinguishing Criterion for Collective Dismissal: The Case of Belgium and The Netherlands,* 29(4) International Journal of Comparative Labour Law and Industrial Relations, 416, 430 et seq. (2013) https://doi.org/10.54648/ijcl2013026; ter Haar & Rönnmar, *supra* n. 72, at 19.
95. Julén Votinius, *supra* n. 1, at 387; Malcom Sargeant, *Young Workers and Age Discrimination,* 26(4) The International Journal of Labour Law and Industrial Relations, 467, 474 (2010).
96. Vandaele, *supra* n. 20, at 16, 34.

labour conditions for young employees is expressed as a major concern of trade unions. This is not only true for the European Confederation level[97] but can also be observed in the Member States, particularly at the confederation level.[98] Confederations often seem to play a more political role and to be more involved in campaigning than the single trade unions.[99] But this may vary, of course, depending on the different collective bargaining systems of the Member States.[100]

However, the importance of young employees and their interests are not reflected in the membership structure of trade unions. Data and research show that unionisation among young employees is particularly weak.[101] Unemployed people and employees on non-standard contracts are far less unionised than employees on standard contracts.[102] That said, young people in general are less unionised than older ones. The former are highly under-represented by trade unions all over Europe, regardless of the overall rate of unionisation.[103] This may be for various reasons, which can be more or less influenced by the trade unions.[104] It has been considered that 'young workers seem to be almost invariably the most problematic group of workers to unionise'.[105] Low unionisation among young people may depend on (little) knowledge about[106] and (negative) attitudes towards trade unions. It has been reported that young employees often do not see the personal benefits of trade union membership.[107] But it may also be a problem based on trade unions' structures, policies and communication.[108] Hence, trade unions at the European Confederation Level and in the Member States aim to

97. *See, e.g.*, Pavlovaite, *supra* n. 32; and industriAll, *Youth Action Plan: Trade Unions' Future at Risk?* Position Paper 2022/140 (Stockholm 2022), https://news.industriall-europe.eu/documents/upload/2022/6/637897673509877031_dopted%20-%20Youth%20-%20Trade%20unions'%20future%20at%20risk%20Building%20a%20future%20for%20trade%20unions%20through%20youth%20inclusion%20-%20EN.pdf (accessed 28 October 2024).
98. For the example of Sweden *see* Rönnmar, *supra* n. 36, at 14.
99. Torsten Geelan, *Responses of Trade Union Confederations to the Youth Employment Crisis*, 19(3) Transfer 399, 400 (2013) https://doi.org/10.1177/1024258913493702; Kurt Vandaele, *Youth Representatives' Opinions on Recruiting and Representing Young Workers: A Twofold Unsatisfied Demand?*, 18(3) European Journal of Industrial Relations, 203-218 (2012) https://doi.org/10.1177/0959680112452692.
100. *See* the various contributions in Jeremy Waddington, Torsten Müller & Kurt Vandaele (eds), *Trade unions in the European Union. Picking up the Pieces of the Neoliberal Challenge* (Brussels 2023).
101. *See* Kurt Vandaele, *Bleak Prospects: Mapping Trade Union Membership in Europe since 2000*, at 23 et seq. (ETUI 2019); and the various contributions in Waddington, Müller & Vandaele (eds), *supra* n. 100.
102. Keune, *supra* n. 16, at 2.
103. *See, e.g.*, Beck & Williams, *supra* n. 83, at 9; Rönnmar, *supra* n. 36, at 3 et seq. and at 15 with further references; as well as Roberto Pedersini, *Trade Union Strategies to Recruit New Groups of Workers*, European Foundation for the Improvement of Living and Working Conditions, 13 (2010), https://migrant-integration.ec.europa.eu/library-document/trade-union-strategies-recruit-new-groups-workers_en (accessed 19 August 2024) for an in-depth analysis, who stresses the exemption of Belgium, *ibid.*, at 14.
104. Vandaele, *supra* n. 20, at 395 stresses the influence of the specific national-economic context.
105. Pedersini, *supra* n. 103, at 13.
106. Vandaele, *supra* n. 20.
107. Hans Dietrich, *Youth Unemployment in Europe, Theoretical Considerations and Empirical Findings*, at 34 (2012), https://library.fes.de/pdf-files/id/ipa/09227.pdf (accessed 20 August 2024).
108. Vandaele, *supra* n. 20, at 384; Keune, *supra* n. 16, at 3.

attract young employees. As Vandaele puts it: 'deliberative vitality – defined here as the integration and participation of young members in union life and the internal union structure – is crucial to unions'.[109] But, as young members form a minority group inside trade unions, the organisational structures to attract and represent young people still seem to be rather weak.[110] Thus, trade unions try to build new internal structures to improve young employees' representation within trade unions and their politics and actions.[111] Various examples show that trade unions tend to attract younger employees in different ways. On the EU level, the European Trade Union Confederation (ETUC) nowadays has an established and well-set structure with its Youth Committee,[112] whereas the six Trade Union Federations on the European level have far less developed and more informal youth structures.[113]

Trade unions use different strategies to attract new members.[114] They may try to canvass them by special campaigns tailored to young employees' needs, and also by using new ways of communication such as social media.[115] They may approach young employees by organising exchanges about their needs and interests in structures other than the 'classical' trade union organisations.[116]

But for the time being, it must be assumed that young employees do not form an important subgroup within trade unions and that trade unions' internal structures do not facilitate the promotion of their interests.[117] Naturally, trade unions tend to represent the interests of their members.[118] The target group of collective bargaining is usually labour market insiders.[119] Thus, when it comes to collective bargaining, the

109. Vandaele, *supra* n. 20, at 16.
110. Rustico & Pedersini, *supra* n. 44, at 5; Tros, *supra* n. 14, at 11 et seq.
111. Vandaele, *supra* n. 20, at 16-36.
112. Despite important efforts to establish and institutionalise stable structures to represent youth and the interests of young employees, this is not the case for other trade union federations on the EU level, *see* Kurt Vandaele, *Youth Structures in Six European Trade Union Federations: A Short Overview*, 21(4) Transfer, 471-476 (2015) for an in-depth analysis. Note that industriAll European Trade Union set up a youth working group in June 2016, visit https://news.industriall-europe.eu/p/youth1 for further information.
113. Vandaele, *supra* n. 112.
114. Vandaele, *supra* n. 99.
115. *See* Vandaele, *supra* n. 99, at 203-218. Vandaele, *supra* n. 112, at 471.
116. The European Trade Union Federations have published a collection of best practices on involving young people in trade: European Federation of Building and Woodworkers (EF-BWW), *Just Go For It! A Compendium of Best Practices from all over Europe on Involving Young People in Trade Unions*, Chiara Lorenzini (ed.), https://www.etf-europe.org/wp-content/uploads/2018/10/Just_go_for_it_GB.pdf (accessed 19 August 2024).
117. *See* Vandaele, *supra* n. 112, at 203, 2011; Marcus Kahmann, *Confederal Youth Structures and Policies: The Case of CGT*, December 2015 (unpublished paper, by courtesy of the author), slides 'Representing and organizing young workers: The case of the French trade union confederation CGT, September 2016' available on http://www.ires.fr/component/k2/item/5197-representing-and-organizing-young-workers-the-case-of-the-french-trade-union-confederation-cgt (accessed 21 July 2017).
118. Bernhard Ebbinghaus, Claudia Göbel & Sebastian Koos, *Mitgliedschaft in Gewerkschaften und Wirtschaftsverbänden: Inklusions- und Exklusionstendenzen in der Organisation von Arbeitnehmerinteressen in Europa*, Mannheimer Zentrum für Europäische Sozialforschung – Working Papers Nr. 111/2008, http://www.mzes.uni-mannheim.de/publications/wp/wp-111.pdf (accessed 21 August 2024).
119. Brettschneider, *supra* n. 43, at 47.

influence of young members is weak.[120] Most of the members and those with influence are labour market insiders,[121] whereas young unemployed people are outsiders.[122] And even if the young people are already on the job, trade unions seem to rather protect the established position of the members with tenure/higher seniority than facilitate the intake or redistribution in favour of younger employees. Special contract types and internships may isolate young workers[123] and even exclude them from the application of collective agreements. Hence, trade unions cannot be conceived as guarantors of achieving distributive justice between insiders and outsiders.[124] In this sense, it has even been stated that trade unions' actions for insiders have negative effects when it comes to combating youth unemployment.[125] Furthermore, there have been incentives for the social partners introduced by statutory legal provisions in some Member States to bargain collectively in order to level down the working conditions for young employees, for example, to lower the legal minimum wages in order to make their intake more attractive for employers.[126] But downgrading labour conditions for young employees also 'threatens' the insiders. And even if this mechanism worked and trade unions agreed on the levelling down of labour conditions, they would lose some of their appeal for young (potential) members, who might see their proper interests concerning decent working conditions being either not represented or even betrayed.

[D] Labour Market Situation

In addition, the labour market situation has to be considered. With regard to young employees or job seekers, employability and qualifications are often described as problems and possible reasons for unemployment. Early school dropouts, low levels of education, problems with school-to-work transition and skills mismatch are major concerns in this regard.[127] A lack of qualifications aggravates individual risks to young employees and negatively influences their chances in the labour market. However, the problem cannot solely be described from an individual perspective.[128] But it must be stressed – as the numerous initiatives at EU and Member State level do – that the problem also has structural aspects. Thus, reforms in the educational systems,

---

120. Vandaele, *supra* n. 20, at 396, 211.
121. Vandaele, *supra* n. 99, at 209.
122. That said, intra-generational inequalities have to be taken into account, *see* Tros & Keune, *supra* n. 13, at 12.
123. Daniele Di Nunzio, *Working Conditions and Changes in Production Processes*, in: Daniele Di Nunzio (ed.), *Young People at Risk: How Changes in Work Are Affecting Young Italians' Health and Safety*, 10, ETUI Report 129 (2013).
124. Andreas Sachs & Werner Smolny, *Youth Unemployment in the OECD: The Role of Institutions*; 235(4 + 5) Jahrbücher f. Nationalökonomie u. Statistik, 403, 405 (Lucius & Lucius, Stuttgart 2015).
125. *Ibid.*, at 412, 415.
126. Schulten & Müller, *supra* n. 88, passim.
127. *See also* Dietrich, *supra* n. 10, at 312 with further references.
128. Julén Votinius, *supra* n. 1, at 373 et seq.

particularly secondary education and initial VET, seem crucial.[129] It cannot be doubted that the involvement of the social partners in approaching these tasks is a necessary but not sufficient condition. Parts of the problems may be addressed by collective bargaining and collective agreements; others need state-driven remedies, i.e., the structures, functioning and funding of public employment services.[130]

Moreover, only considering the supply side of the labour market, i.e., the young employees as part of the labour force, would draw an incomplete picture.[131] The employers' side has little motivation to bargain collectively with regard to young employees as long as there is no profit or need.[132] In times of high labour supply with high youth and overall unemployment rates, the possible profits of collective bargaining on young employees' matters for the employers' side seem limited. It may become attractive if it helps to get the qualifications that are needed or if it makes employment more cost-effective and flexible, i.e., by downgrading labour conditions, especially wages.[133] The latter only works when the legal frame allows it to do so.

§7.05 OTHER OPTIONS FOR SOCIAL PARTNERS' INVOLVEMENT

With regard to European policies, it seems that collective bargaining is not as relevant as other forms of social partner activities, at least concerning young employees' matters. Other ways of involving social partners may have become more important. This means especially consultation processes and participation in tripartite commissions or committees. An example can be taken from Portugal, where the social partners are members of the tripartite Economic and Social Council (ESC) and the Social Concertation Standing Committee (SPSC).[134] Other institutionalised forms of tripartite co-operation can also be found in the Netherlands, such as the Social and Economic Council (SER) that has advised the government since its establishment in 1950.[135] Rather than governing themselves in the framework of collective bargaining and 'traditional' collective agreements, social partners are involved in the policy-making process and the application of state law, including with regard to young employees' matters,[136] e.g., the implementation of the EYG.[137]

129. *See also* the initiative taken on EU-level, Council Recommendation of 24 November 2020 on VET for sustainable competitiveness, social fairness and resilience (2020/C 417/01).
130. Joachim Möller & Hans Dietrich, *Youth Unemployment in Europe: Business Cycle and Institutional Effects*, (1)13 International Economics and Economic Policy, 5, 22 (2016) https://doi.org/10.1007/s10368-015-0331-1.
131. Bussi & Geyer, *supra* n. 28, at 42.
132. *See also* Ales, *supra* n. 78, 122, 125 analysing the changing perception of the employers' role in European Employment policies.
133. *See* for the example of Greece, Papadopoulos, *supra* n. 21, at 415.
134. Isabel Távora & Pilar González, *The Reform of Joint Regulation and Labour Market Policy During the Current Crisis: National Report on Portugal*, in: Aristea Koukiadaki, Isabel Távora & Miguel Martínez Lucio (eds), *Joint Regulation and Labour Market Policy in Europe During the Crisis*, 321, 324 (ETUI 2016).
135. SER, *The Social and Economic Council* (2022), https://www.ser.nl/-/media/ser/downloads/engels/algemeen/informatiebrochure-en.pdf (accessed 19 August 2024).
136. Vandaele, *supra* n. 20, at 395. The SER also established a youth platform in 2015: visit https://www.ser.nl/nl/thema/jongeren/SERjongerenplatform (accessed 20 August 2024).

But this brings new challenges for the social partners: they are placed outside the conventional framework of labour law, as there are weak or non-existent legal foundations to these activities. Traditional modes of action developed for traditional collective bargaining may not be appropriate. And furthermore, the outcomes of consultation processes are usually not legally binding, unless explicitly foreseen by national legislation. Therefore, it is much more challenging to promote these activities to union members.[138]

§7.06 CONCLUSIONS

Collective bargaining with regard to young employees' matters can be considered circumstantial. It seems to be complex and difficult to produce win-win situations in reconciling employers' and trade unions' interests. As long as employers do not experience any need in terms of qualifications or attractive labour conditions for young employees, and see their needs fulfilled by the supply side of the labour market, there is little motivation for them to collectively bargain on these matters. However, it might be attractive for employers to collectively bargain to downgrade labour conditions for young workers, which is particularly unattractive and might be counterproductive for trade unions. The social partners' scope for action might be limited by of the current European or national political and legal framework. However, facing the risks of young employees in the labour market by contributing to qualification and good quality employment opportunities for young employees can be considered crucial for the future of social partnership.

137. ETUC, *The Youth Guarantee in Europe* (2014), https://www.etuc.org/sites/default/files/publication/files/ces-brochure_youth_guarantee_09pap.pdf (accessed 19 August 2024); Verónica Escudero & Elva López Mourelo, *The Youth Guarantee Programme in Europe: Features, Implementation and Challenges*, ILO Research Department Working Paper No. 4 (2015), https://ilo.userservices.exlibrisgroup.com/discovery/delivery/41ILO_INST:41ILO_V2/1252399060002676?lang=en&viewerServiceCode=DigitalViewer (accessed 19 August 2024), 11; and Verónica Escudero & Elva López Mourelo, *The European Youth Guarantee: A Systematic Review of Its Implementation Across Countries*, ILO Research Department Working Paper No. 21 (2017) (accessed 19 August 2024).

138. *See also* John Geary, *Economic Crisis, Austerity and Trade Union Responses: The Irish Case in Comparative Perspective*, 22(2) European Journal of Industrial Relations 131, 142 (2016) with further references https://doi.org/10.1177/0959680115616526.

CHAPTER 8

Multi-employer Situations and Collective Bargaining: The Hungarian Cases

Gábor Kártyás

§8.01 INTRODUCTION

There is a long-standing discussion in labour law literature concerning the notion of 'employer'. Numerous studies have challenged the unitary concept of the employer and pointed out situations where multiple entities exercise employer functions.[1] Yet the collective aspects of such scenarios have not gained as much attention as their effects on the individual employment relationship. This paper aims to discover the obstacles trade unions face in collective bargaining caused by the proliferation of employer positions. After an analysis of the most common cases of multiple employers, there are some concluding remarks and questions for the future.

The scope of the study is limited by two factors. First, in the settings assessed, employee status - the legal form of employment - is not questioned. Although employment rights beyond the employment relationship (including questions of collective labour rights)[2] are a major problem in contemporary labour law, especially as regards the gig economy,[3] this paper focuses only on situations based on the typical

1. *See*, for example: Paul Davis & Mark Freedland, *The Complexities of the Employing Enterprise*. In: Guy Davidov & Brian Langille (eds), *Boundaries and Frontiers of Labour Law: Goals and Means in the Regulation of Work* (Hart Publishing 2006); Jeremias Prassl, *The Concept of the Employer* (Oxford University Press 2015); Emiliano Maran & Elisa Chieregato, *Multiparty Work Relationships Across Europe: A Comparative Overview*. European Labour Law Journal, 2022/4 https://doi.org/10.1177/20319525221131173.
2. In the *FNV Kunsten* case the ECJ ruled that a collectively bargained minimum wage applicable for self-employed musicians may be contrary to the prohibitions of competition law (*FNV Kunsten Informatie en Media kontra Staat der Nederlanden*, C-413/13., ECLI:EU:C:2014:2411).
3. *See* especially: José María Miranda Boto & Elisabeth Brameshuber (eds), *Collective Bargaining and the Gig Economy* (Hart Publishing, 2022).

employment relationship. Nonetheless, it will be seen that even in this 'traditional' setting, multi-employer cases can challenge the very structure of collective labour law. Second, collective bargaining in temporary agency work is not tackled here. Agency work significantly differs from the cases analysed below, as the employer-like responsibility of the user company/non-contractual employer is recognized by law.[4] Needless to say, the division of the employer's position between the agency and user company still raises several questions on collective bargaining in the agency work sector.[5]

§8.02 A CASE STUDY: LOST BETWEEN FOUR 'EMPLOYERS'

The nature and complexity of multi-employer situations is well illustrated by the following case study. At the end of 2015, a leading Hungarian online media company was sold. The firm operated as a subsidiary of the biggest telecommunication service provider in Hungary (the mother company), while the whole group was controlled by a huge international company. The mother company had a long-standing history of developed social dialogue with two unions active within the organization. Both the mother company and the subsidiary had collective agreements. When the first rumours of the acquisition leaked out, the union represented in the subsidiary immediately started negotiations on the future of working conditions – and especially of the collective agreement. But no matter how desperately the union tried to find a partner to negotiate with, it faced closed doors.

First, the union officials approached the subsidiary, the legal employer with whom the collective agreement had been concluded. They were rejected, as the management felt no longer competent on future working conditions and said the mother company was responsible for conducting the vending process. When the union knocked on the mother company's door, the answer was negative again: the Hungarian management pointed to the group's international headquarters, as all questions relevant to the transition were determined there. On reaching the international managers, the union learned that the vending contract strictly stipulated that the vendor should not alter any working conditions prior to the acquisition taking place. Thus the union was politely referred to the buyer. As the final step, the new owner of the company expressed a warm welcome to the union and requested patience: the new management confessed that they needed at least a year to become familiar with the organization and did not wish to enter into negotiations on the working conditions until then.

4. *See* especially the user's right to supervise and direct agency workers and its obligation to offer equal working conditions as prescribed in directive 2008/104/EC of the European Parliament and of the Council of 19 November 2008 on temporary agency work, Arts 3 and 5.
5. James Arrowsmith, *Temporary Agency Work and Collective Bargaining in the EU* (European Foundation for the Improvement of Living and Working Conditions, 2008); Eurociett, *UNI-Europa: The Role of Temporary Agency Work and Labour Market Transitions in Europe – Institutional Frameworks, Empirical Evidence, Good Practice and the Impact of Social Dialogue* 54-63 (2013); Tamás Gyulavári & Gábor Kártyás, *The Hungarian Flexicurity Pathway? New Labour Code after Twenty Years in the Market Economy* 148-150 (Pázmány Press 2015).

After nearly eight months of chasing a competent bargaining partner, the union's overtures remained unanswered. In the event, the union was involved in the acquisition process only as far as was required by law, which meant merely formal consultations and no real influence. The employer's side of the bargaining table remained unoccupied during the whole process.

§8.03 GENERAL REMARKS: IS THIS JUST A QUESTION OF POWER?

Before turning to the specific cases involving more employers, some common features may be pointed out.

Such situations are always initiated or designed by the employer. It is never the employees' interests that drive these organizational changes, but rather it is within the employer's autonomy to shape the employing organization. This principle appeared in the European Court of Justice's (ECJ's) practice concerning the mass dismissals directive. In the *Fujitsu Siemens* case, the ECJ stated that the way the management of a group of undertakings is organized is an internal matter and that it is not the purpose of the directive to restrict the freedom of such a group to organize their activities as they think best suits their needs.[6] In most cases, the shaping of the employer's organization is not considered a labour law issue but rather handled as a transaction governed by civil law. Nonetheless, such civil law contracts have grave labour law implications, which are often seen as unintended side effects. The above-mentioned characteristics also explain the huge diversity of the cases.

Multi-employer situations mean at least a twofold challenge for unions. First, it is definitely more difficult to organize workers in complex organizations. Most employers are not structured as a sole legal person operating out of unitary physical premises and are led by one manager exercising and fulfilling the full range of employers' rights and obligations. Even a matter as simple as informing employees about the union's position on the current wage policy becomes a challenge if such workers are separated into small employing entities all acting as legally independent employers – or alternatively, controlled by a central body.

Second, as the above case study suggests, the real decision-maker might easily disappear in the maze of complex organizational structures, leaving the union without a partner to bargain with. The effectiveness of collective bargaining rights may depend on whether they are recognized in relation to the party which ultimately determines the worker's remuneration.[7] In contrast to the above-mentioned *Fujitsu Siemens* case, the European Court of Human Rights pointed out how employers might abuse their freedom to organize their business to escape some legal obligations in a case concerning the right to strike and a UK ban on secondary actions. Delocalising work centres, outsourcing work to other companies and adopting complex corporate structures in

6. *Akavan Erityisalojen Keskusliitto AEK ry and Others v. Fujitsu Siemens Computers Oy.*, C-44/08., ECLI:EU:C:2009:533, para. 59. *See also Rockfon A/S v. Specialarbejderforbundet i Danmark*, C-449/93., ECLI:EU:C:1995:420, para. 21.
7. Christina Hiessl, *Multiparty Work Relationships in Europe: Introduction to this Special Section.* European Labour Law Journal, 2022/4, 471 https://doi.org/10.1177/20319525221131161.

order to transfer work to separate legal entities or to hive off companies could make trade unions '*find themselves severely hampered in the performance of their legitimate, normal activities in protecting their members' interests*'.[8]

Before proceeding any further, some possible solutions can be highlighted. First, the problems of chasing the relevant bargaining partner can be overcome if the bargaining takes place at a higher level, e.g., for the whole sector or on a national level. In centralized bargaining systems trade unions can evade at least some of the challenges caused by multi-employer organizations, as the bargaining partner is an employers' organization and not a single employer with a possibly very complicated structure. Nonetheless, there are also some other organizational solutions – like subcontracting – that might be used to escape from the scope of sector-level agreements.

Second, the social partners concluding the agreement themselves can set barriers against fraudulent or proforma structures, purely designed to avoid responsibilities for employers covered by a collective agreement. This is the case in Denmark, where the social partners play a central role in enforcing such protection. The circumvention of a collective agreement is sanctioned as a breach of agreement, even if not expressly stated in the agreement.[9]

Finally, the power of the union could also make the present story very short. If the relevant union is strong enough and has sufficient members to ensure that its threat of a strike is taken with due seriousness, the employer will surely appoint a bargaining partner, no matter how complex the organizational structure. We can still agree with Otto Kahn-Freund that when employees negotiate with the employer, it is '*a negotiation between collective entities, both of which are, or may at least be, bearers of power*'.[10] While choosing this quick ending for the story is rather tempting, we might wonder whether today's unions are powerful enough to overcome the challenges of multi-employer structures. We might be rather doubtful. In my view, the least labour law can do is to eliminate the legal barriers blocking the route to the bargaining table.

In the following sections, some of the most common multi-employer scenarios are presented, mostly from the Hungarian experience, with a focus on the (legal) obstacles they imply for unions and some possible solutions.

§8.04 PUBLIC FUNDING ENTITIES

Probably the most common cases where other entities appear behind (or next to) the legal employer are those where employers do not enjoy financial independence. This occurs in public funding entities, where the legally independent employer has no or very limited competence over financial issues and such decisions are made by a sustainer that funds the employer, which results in a gap between those who negotiate

8. *RMT v. UK* (No. 31045/10), para. 98.
9. Natalie Videbaek Munkholm, *Multiparty Work Relationships in Denmark: The Active Role of Social Partners*. European Labour Law Journal, 2022/4, 528 https://doi.org/10.1177/20319525221131184.
10. Otto Kahn-Freund, *Kahn-Freund's Labour and the Law* 17-18 (Stevens & Sons 1983).

and those who provide the funds.[11] For example, a local government runs different institutions, such as a kindergarten, concert hall or museum. While these may have their own legal personality and act as employers of their staff, all decisions with financial implications require the consent of the town hall. In this setting, collective bargaining without the mayor's representative at the table is meaningless.[12] The issue is the same when the employer has a complex ownership background.[13]

It is obvious that there are always owners or shareholders behind an employer who in one way or another will have their say during collective bargaining. The issue becomes complex if the employer is not the owner's or sustainer's only business, meaning its decision does not reflect solely the interests of the relevant employer. The more complex the interests at stake become, the harder it is for the union to achieve its goals. For example, even if the museum supports the union's claim for a pay raise, the local government might reject it to allocate more budget for its other institutions. It is not rare in such cases for the employer and union to stand on common ground and bargain with joint forces against the sustainer. Here the factual bargaining situation (union + employer against the sustainer) is totally different from that mapped by labour law (union against the employer). Nonetheless, the International Labour Organization (ILO) supervisory bodies recognize that collective bargaining in public administration has important differences compared to the one that takes place in private undertaking, but this does not mean that their special characteristics, like the barriers imposed by the state budget, remove or prohibit the collective autonomy, only that they define limits.[14]

While it seems unrealistic to legally oblige the owner/sustainer to negotiate directly with the union if requested, such a concept appears partly in European Union (EU) labour law. Directives on mass dismissals and transfer of undertakings prescribe that the employer has to fulfil its obligation to inform and consult the workers' representatives irrespective of whether the relevant decision regarding the collective redundancy or the transfer is being taken by the employer or by an undertaking controlling the employer.[15] Nonetheless, the ECJ pointed out that even if these decisions are made by a separate entity, it does not have the status of employer and the

11. Clyde Summers, *Public Sector Bargaining: A Different Animal*. University of Pennsylvania Journal of Labour and Employment Law, 2003/3, 443.
12. This is exactly the case with Hungarian public employees. Public institutions act as the legal employer of their public employees; however, the financial background for their activity is guaranteed by the sustainer. As unions cannot negotiate directly with the sustainer, collective bargaining with the legal employer becomes rather formal, especially in the most important questions, such as wages. Csilla Lehoczkyné Kollonay, *A magyar munkajog* I-II. 82 (Vincze Kiadó 2001).
13. *See*, for example, Prassl's thorough analysis of the employer's functions in Private Equity Investments. Prassl, *supra* n. 1, at 73-80.
14. International Labour Office, *The Scope of Collective Bargaining in Public Administration,*. Sector working paper No. 329 (Geneva, 2019), 23.
15. Council Directive 98/59/EC of 20 July 1998 on the approximation of the laws of the Member States relating to collective redundancies Art. 2(4) and Council Directive 2001/23/EC of 12 March 2001 on the approximation of the laws of the Member States relating to the safeguarding of employees' rights in the event of transfers of undertakings, businesses or parts of undertakings or businesses Art. 7(4).

obligation to inform, consult and notify is imposed solely on the employer and not the controlling entity.[16] Thus, from a legal point of view, the two organizations are to be approached as different employers; however, EU law recognizes that certain decisions are made outside the unitary employer.

§8.05 COMPANY GROUPS

If different companies are connected by ownership, the identity of the union's bargaining partner might become blurred. *'Once the majority, or at least a significant proportion of voting rights, are vested in a single shareholder, it will be able to exert considerable power over management.'*[17]

In the *Albron* case,[18] the ECJ recognized that the employers' functions and responsibilities might rest beyond the party who signed the employment contract as employer. The case concerned a group of companies where all the staff were employed by one employer, which acted centrally and detached the staff from the group's various operating companies. One member provided catering services in various locations for the group's employees. These activities were outsourced to a third party. The ECJ had to decide whether such an arrangement constituted a transfer of an undertaking within the meaning of directive 2001/23/EC,[19] considering that there was no actual employment contract between the employees affected and the economic entity transferred.

Article 3(1) of directive 2001/23 requires an employment contract, or alternatively and thus as an equivalent, an employment relationship at the date of the transfer. From such wording, the Court concluded that a contractual link with the transferor is not required in all circumstances for employees to be able to benefit from the protection conferred by the directive. In its reasoning, the ECJ differentiated the 'contractual' from the 'factual' employer, where the former was not responsible for the economic activity of the economic entity transferred. The Court ruled that if there is a plurality of employers, the contractual employer must not systematically be given greater weight and take precedence, for the purposes of determining the identity of the transferor, over the position of a non-contractual employer who is responsible for that activity. The ECJ also referred to the aim of the directive – that is the protection of employees in the event of a change of the employer – and found that the above interpretation is in line with such an aim.[20]

One might wonder what message this ruling has for unions. The separation of the factual and contractual employer would be useful for unions to identify who to bargain with in multi-employer cases and there is little in the judgment to suggest that this

16. C-44/08., paras 57-58.
17. Prassl, *supra* n. 1, at 54.
18. *Albron Catering BV kontra FNV Bondgenoten and John Roest*, C-242/09., ECLI:EU:C:2010:625.
19. Council Directive 2001/23/EC of 12 March 2001 on the approximation of the laws of the Member States relating to the safeguarding of employees' rights in the event of transfers of undertakings, businesses or parts of undertakings or businesses.
20. C-242/09., paras 25-29.

purposive interpretation is limited to the transferor concept.[21] Nevertheless, such a functional approach can only be relied on if it is incorporated into national law; otherwise, it is less likely that courts will apply it to oblige employers to bargain with the union.

§8.06 LARGE EMPLOYING ENTITIES

The union's bargaining goals can be seriously hampered if a huge and diverse employing organization is centralized. Even numerous physically separated premises with diverse activities can come under the umbrella of one organization (one legal person) which acts as a sole legal employer. Only a very detailed collective agreement could cover all the various needs of the different divisions of such an organization, not to mention that these needs might contradict each other. The more diverse interests appear in the activities and workplaces to be covered, the more challenging it becomes to find the common ground to represent against the employer.

The collective agreement concluded in the public education sector in Hungary is a good example. In 2013 an umbrella organization called the Klebelsberg Centre for Public Education Institution Management (KLIK) was set up to centralize the operation of all public (primary and secondary) schools in the country. This meant an enormous reorganization, putting one government agency in the place of over 5,000 independent education institutions with their own legal personality.[22] In November 2013, KLIK concluded a collective agreement with the teachers' union.[23] While the union welcomed reaching such an agreement, a closer look at its content reveals that it is rather an empty shell. Most of the nearly ten-page document merely repeats the statutory regulation and contains but a handful of substantive provisions (e.g., on substitution fees, disciplinary actions or breaks). Nonetheless, one should not forget that the agreement is applicable to all schools maintained by KLIK. Both tiny village schools with only one teacher and prestigious urban secondary schools with laboratories and sports centres are covered, although they have little in common as workplaces. Considering such heterogeneity, it is not surprising that the bargaining partners could not touch upon more relevant issues.

Although Hungarian labour law traditionally builds on the system of multi-level collective agreements[24] – that is to say, it recognizes that agreements can be concluded at sector level, mezzo level (covering more employers) and employer level – it must be emphasized that KLIK acted as one unitary employer. Thus, legally all public schools had to be covered by one collective agreement. Nonetheless, court practice recognized the possibility of a collective agreement containing annexes applying only to specific

21. Prassl, *supra* n. 1, at 104.
22. 202/2012. (VII. 27.) Governmental Decree Art. 6.
23. Available in Hungarian at: http://klik.gov.hu/download/7/fe/80000/KLIK_PSZ%20kollekt%C3%ADv_1122.pdf.
24. Tamás Gyulavári, *The Hungarian Experiment to Promote Collective Bargaining: Farewell to 'Principle of Favour'*. In: Tamás Gyulavári & Emanuele Menegatti (eds), *The Sources of Labour Law*, 252 (Kluwer Law International 2020).

workplaces of the employer and which might prescribe special (even less favourable) rules to certain groups of employees.[25] This could have been a way to enrich the content of KLIK's collective agreement. Nonetheless, in 2017, KLIK was decentralized and around sixty 'school district centres' took over the employer's position in public education. Since then, around twenty collective agreements have been concluded by these district centres.[26]

§8.07 MICRO-EMPLOYING ENTITIES

The way a business is organized may be diametrically opposite to that described above; moreover, the disintegration of the employing organization is much more common. In this case, the separate divisions of the organization have a legal personality and act as the employer of their own staff. Although these 'cells' are independent (and could also appear as separate companies), they cooperate under the auspices of an umbrella organization. This is how a franchise system is usually structured. Numerous franchisees, acting on their own account as legal persons, contribute to the operation of the franchisor's business, retailing the latter's product or providing its service. Nonetheless, the franchise contract generally contains detailed provisions on how the franchisee can carry out its activities, in accordance with the franchisor's concept.[27] The franchisee's bounds can be as tight as between a division and the headquarters within one organization.[28]

In labour law systems based on the unitary concept of the employer, it can be difficult if not impossible for employees in small franchise outlets to organize and bargain effectively.[29] Separate legal persons mean separate bargaining partners for the union if it intends to conclude an agreement covering all workers. For example, if a restaurant chain operates on the franchise model, each restaurant will be approached to cover all staff in the chain. While it seems much more convenient to bargain with the franchisor directly, it can easily refuse the union's approach with the excuse of not being the legal employer of the workers affected. Moreover, the franchisor might organize its business precisely in this way to outsource employment risks and obligations to its partners.[30] While the franchisor may have little or no intent to

25. *See* Supreme Court decision No. Mfv. II. 11.082/2001/3.
26. Tamás Gyulavári & Gábor Kártyás (eds), *A kollektív szerződéses lefedettség csökkenése Magyarországon (2012-2023)* 10 (FES 2023); https://library.fes.de/pdf-files/bueros/budapest/20640.pdf.
27. Maran & Chieregato, *supra* n. 1, at 488.
28. Joellen Riley, *A Blurred Boundary Between Entrepreneurship and Servitude: Regulating Business Format Franchising in Australia*. In: Judy Fudge, Shae McCrystal & Kamala Sankaran (eds), *Challenging the Legal Boundaries of Work Regulation* 103-104 (Hart Publishing 2012).
29. Riley, *supra* n. 28, at 107.
30. The employment contract, understood as a bilateral relationship, 'allows (and, perhaps, invites) firms to shift the risks associated with employing labour' to various forms of intermediaries (Judy Fudge, *The Legal Boundaries of the Employer, Precarious Workers, and Labour Protection*. In: Guy Davidov & Brian Langille, *Boundaries and Frontiers of Labour Law: Goals and Means in the Regulation of Work* (Hart Publishing 2006)). Now, we can add, the burdens of collective bargaining may also be outsourced.

bargain, it is also burdensome to negotiate with the franchisees. Approaching separate employers requires a lot of time and resources the union might not have, and besides the franchisees can be small organizations where the union cannot attract members or meet the statutory criteria to be eligible for collective bargaining. Nonetheless, in some countries, national courts have recognized that the franchisor has some liabilities towards the franchisee's employees if the franchisee is not a genuinely economically independent undertaking.[31]

§8.08 EMPLOYEE SHARING

Employee sharing (or labour pooling, co-employment) is built on the clear multiplication of the employer's position. In this new form of employment, a group of employers hires workers jointly and is jointly responsible for them. The nature and regulation of employee sharing, however, vastly differs across states. It might be framed as a special form of long-term agency work, with an employer consortium regarded as the temporary work agency and the members of the consortium as the user undertaking (Austria). Differently, an employment contract can be directly concluded with two or more employers performing the same work function (Lithuania).[32] In this latter case, unlike agency work, the variations in employer status are not qualitative but quantitative. For example, each employer may give orders to the shared employee but has to respect the other employers' same right. Thus, the employers have to agree among themselves on how to split the employee's working time and define the time limits the employee is available for each of them. Joint employment also means that the employers bear the costs of employment together without a 'central' employer who would charge the others for the assigned workforce (as a temporary work agency would do with the user company).

Employee sharing is a rather rare but spreading phenomenon, which has not yet been regulated in most European countries. Shared employment is mostly used to cope with seasonal or unbalanced workforce needs (e.g., in ports or agriculture). It may also be favourable for small and medium enterprises (SMEs) to hire highly trained specialists (e.g., a tax lawyer or a marketing expert) jointly and split the costs or risks. From the employee's side, permanent joint employment is more advantageous than a set of consecutive short-term contracts with the members of the group would be.[33]

An employment relationship involving more employers leads to confronting collective agreements if more participating employers have agreements in force. At this point, legal regulation should step in and guide the parties as to which agreement to apply to the shared employee. As an illustration, the Hungarian Labour Code prescribes that the collective agreement concluded by the employer liable for wages shall apply to the shared employee, in the absence of an agreement to the contrary.[34] It is up to the

31. Maran & Chieregato, *supra* n. 1, at 488.
32. Maran & Chieregato, *supra* n. 1, at 490.
33. Eurofound, *New Forms of Employment* 11-13, 17 (Publications Office of the European Union 2015).
34. Act 1 of 2012 on the Labour Code Art. 279(4).

employers to decide which one of them is responsible for wages. Thus great discretion is offered to the parties. As collective agreements usually set out detailed rules on remuneration, it is a logical choice to follow the Labour Code rule and apply the collective agreement of the employer responsible for wages. However, the employers might specifically want to exclude the shared employee from its scope. For instance, where another employer's agreement offers less generous benefits, the parties might choose it for cost-cutting reasons. Nonetheless, it would clearly be an abusive exercise of rights[35] to select an employer where there is no collective agreement in force, and such an agreement is therefore void. Note that deviation from the statutory rule needs the agreement of all employers and the employee, and not just of the employers alone.[36]

§8.09 CONCLUSIONS AND QUESTIONS

'*Will the real employer please stand up?*' Unions could quote this smart title two British scholars used in their paper on the employer's rights and obligations in agency work.[37] In the cases presented, the difficulties unions face do not lie in the legal construction of employment, in the sense that they all involve employees in the traditional, typical employment relationship. In these scenarios, it is rather the employer who is atypical. While it is undoubtedly within the employer's autonomy to design its organization to best fit its activities, such freedom is not without boundaries. The chase after cost-effective business models cannot outsource the responsibilities an employer has towards workers' representatives to no man's land. '*No public or private entity should be permitted to profit from violations of the four core labour rights in the ILO's 1998 Declaration of Fundamental Principles and Rights at Work*', among them the denial of freedom of association.[38] The cases analysed show some of the examples of labour law stepping in to defend such basic principles. The number of similar multi-employer situations will surely grow in the near future. It remains to be seen whether and how labour law will follow.

35. Labour Code Art. 7.
36. This solution is similar to a previous but still relevant court practice, which recognized that parties may stipulate in the employment contract the application of a certain collective agreement, even if the employer falls under no collective agreement (Supreme Court, Mfv. II. 10.137/2001/5.).
37. Michael Wynn & Patricia Leighton, *Will the Real Employer Please Stand Up? Client Companies and the Employment Status of the Temporary Agency Worker*. Industrial Law Journal, 2006/35 https://doi.org/10.1093/indlaw/dwl023.
38. Alan Hyde, *Legal Responsibility for Labour Conditions Down the Production Chain*. In: Judy Fudge, Shae McCrystal & Kamala Sankaran (eds), *Challenging the Legal Boundaries of Work Regulation* 98 (Hart Publishing 2012). The freedom of association and the effective recognition of the right to collective bargaining are also recognized in the 2022 revised version of the ILO Declaration.

CHAPTER 9

Enhancing Working Conditions for Platform Workers Through Social Dialogue: The French Example

Cécile Nicod

In France, a worker is either classified as an employee or they are not. Those who are not classified as employees fall under the broad category of self-employed workers, to whom, in principle, the French Labour Code does not apply. The French legal system is therefore binary: it does not make provision for an intermediate category providing a third possible status for workers. Most of the time, platform workers are self-employed, so they cannot benefit from the regulations applicable to employees, such as a guaranteed minimum wage, regulated working hours, and occupational risk prevention measures. Neither do they benefit from social protections granted to employees, which include coverage for illness, accidents, and unemployment. Self-employed workers are instead subject to a distinct regime to which they contribute solely.

The situation is a familiar one, and platform workers' demands for better working conditions and greater protection are not limited to France. Litigation on this issue is constant throughout Europe,[1] and the French Court of Cassation frequently reiterates that an 'employment contract' is defined by law and is mandatory when certain conditions are met, irrespective of the name given to the contract by the parties. Hence, whatever name the parties give to a contract, a judge will examine the context and circumstances to determine whether that contract constitutes an employment contract. To do so, the judge establishes whether or not a subordinate relationship exists between the worker and the platform. If such a relationship is found to exist, the

1. J. Adams-Prassl, S. Laulom & Y. Maneiro Vázquez, *The Role of National Courts in Protecting Platform Workers: A Comparative Analysis*, in J.M. Miranda Boto & E. Brameshuber (eds), *Collective Bargaining and the Gig Economy: A Traditional Tool for New Business Models*, 75-97 (Oxford: Hart Publishing 2022).

contractual relationship is reclassified as an 'employment contract' and the worker is assumed to have salaried status even though the French Labour Code presumes non-employment status when an activity is carried out by a self-employed worker.[2]

The risks of litigation have become very real and have resulted in civil judgments from France's highest court[3] and subsequently in criminal proceedings. Concealing an employment contract by engaging a self-employed worker is a criminal offence because it results in the company avoiding social security contributions and the consequences are serious. Deliveroo was recently heavily penalised for this practice.[4] Although the penalties can be severe, such rulings have limited scope for claimants and are not automatically extended to cover all workers on a platform that has been found culpable.

However, due to the increasing number of such rulings, the French government fears that in France the operating model of such platforms will be called into question, particularly for drivers and delivery workers. French authorities are convinced that the platform business model would not function if workers were allowed to become salaried employees and benefit from the protections set down by the Labour Code. So far, the French government recognises the need for and value of preserving this existing business model. As a result, they have, over the last few years, made every effort to bolster self-employed status by protecting it from the risk of requalification, while also granting a number of guarantees for the working conditions and social rights of self-employed platform workers. As early as 2016, this political policy led to the introduction of specific rules into the Labour Code.[5] These rules are set out in Part 7 of the French Labour Code, which makes special provisions for certain categories of workers whose activities are characterised by a high degree of independence. Some of the provisions in Part 7 lead, under certain conditions, to the presumption of the existence of an employment contract or relationship, while others aim to ensure workers benefit from certain protective rules without calling their self-employed status into question. The French legislator has chosen to apply the latter option to delivery workers and drivers. These self-employed workers deserve protection; however, the legislator has chosen to leverage the platforms' 'social responsibility',[6] rather than their status as an employer. Thus, in 2019, platforms were invited to draw up unilateral 'Charters' defining their own rights and obligations and those of their workers.[7] The public authorities then again attempted to safeguard the platforms' operational model

2. Labour law code, Art. L. 8221-6.
3. There are now numerous decisions recognising the existence of an employment contract. *See*, Cass. Soc. 4 March 2020, Uber, n° 19-13.316, FP-P + B + R + I.
4. In April 2022, Deliveroo was fined EUR 375.000 by the 'Tribunal Correctionnel de Paris' for undeclared work (Trib. Corr. Paris 19 April 2022, Cah. dr. entr. n°3, 2022, p. 14). The same court then ordered the company to pay EUR 9.7 million in unpaid social security contributions. In April 2024, Deliveroo announced it had decided not to appeal this decision on the grounds that its relations with delivery workers have changed since and is no longer liable to prosecutions.
5. Labour law code, Arts L. 7341-1 et seq.
6. For instance, platforms must cover insurance contributions for work accidents (if subscribed to by the delivery worker) and guarantee the right to professional training, Labour law code, Art. L. 7342-1.
7. Labour law code, Art. L. 7342-9.

by stipulating that the creation of such a Charter may not be used as proof that a subordinate relationship exists and, therefore, that an employment contract is implicit. However, the Constitutional Council invalidated this provision[8] and the issue of litigating to reclassify contractual relationships between workers and platforms remained unresolved.

With unwavering determination, French public authorities then attempted to address the ongoing discontent of platform workers, who were beginning to organise collectively into associations and who were increasingly attracting the interest of trade unions. Their response was to create a framework for potential collective negotiations on platform workers' employment and working conditions.[9] The term 'collective bargaining' in French law is closely associated with salaried status, so, keen to avoid any assimilation, the legislator opted for the term 'social dialogue'. This term is somewhat vague and encompasses all rights to consultation, information, and collective bargaining, which sometimes fall under the purview of elected company representatives and sometimes under that of trade unions.

The social dialogue framework is, therefore, the direct result of a political desire to stop platform workers from obtaining legal recognition of their 'employee status'; as such it is one of the tools in a political strategy created by the French public authorities to avoid discussions about these workers' status (§9.01). However, can social dialogue to enough to provide precarious platform workers with decent working conditions? Does it not risk segmenting workers' rights? Lastly, does it truly protect platforms from the pressure on them to recognise employee status? These questions remain open to doubt. It is also important to consider the long-term viability of the system, especially given that a European directive is being adopted that makes provision for a presumption of employment for these workers(§9.02).[10]

§9.01 STRENGTHENING THE PRESUMPTION OF INDEPENDENCE BY ESTABLISHING A LEGAL FRAMEWORK FOR SOCIAL DIALOGUE

The collective organisation of workers has always begun as a spontaneous movement, and collective agreements preceded the provision of rights to collective bargaining. The organisation of platform workers into associations and trade unions has been similarly spontaneous. Likewise, platform workers have formed and organised themselves in groups in order to express and defend their own interests and to improve their working conditions. However, in France, as elsewhere, numerous challenges continue to

8. Constitutional Council n° 2019-794, DC of 20 December 2019, *RDT* 2020, 42, obs. Barbara Gomes.
9. Ordonnance n° 2021-484 of 21 April 2021 and ordonnance n° 2022-492 of 6 April 2022, S. Vernac et Y. Ferkane, *D.* 2022, p. 1280; A. Denizot, *'Le sucre serait trop cher si l'on ne faisait travailler la plante qui le produit par des esclaves'*, 714 RTDCiv (2022).
10. At the time of writing, the directive has been approved by the Member States and adopted by the European Parliament (European Parliament legislative resolution of 24 April 2024 on the proposal for a directive of the European Parliament and of the Council on improving conditions in platform work). It must be adopted by the Council before it comes into force. Member States will then have two years to ensure it is transposed into national law.

exist.[11] These challenges arise from, on the one hand, the workers' economic vulnerability, sociological categorisation, and isolation, which makes coordinating collective actions difficult; and, on the other hand, from the platform's reluctance to engage in discussions with them. These difficulties are structural, but there are also legal difficulties in France: even if the workers' representatives reached an agreement with the platforms, it would not be recognised as a collective agreement unless an express provision was made in law.

Indeed, France has a very limited conception of collective autonomy, which is understood as the ability of worker and employer representatives jointly to develop legally binding norms. This collective autonomy is only understood in a 'weak sense'. As such, the French concept of collective autonomy is itself an obstacle to the recognition of these apparently independent workers' right to bargain collectively [A]. Consequently, a specific system had to be constructed to provide these workers with the ability to bargain collectively [B].

[A] The French Conception of Collective Autonomy: Hindering Recognition of Collective Bargaining Rights for Platform Workers

In France, collective autonomy exists 'under the control of the State'.[12] This situation results from political choices debated and made at the beginning of the twentieth century.[13] At that time, the legislator had to determine the legal nature of collective agreements made between employers and workers, which resembled contracts between private parties but were intended to apply to groups of workers. Recognising that these agreements applied *erga omnes*, i.e., to others beyond the signatories and their represented parties, was not without difficulties.

The French State might have limited itself to merely recognising a form of self-regulation determined by the specificity of social relations within the professional sphere or the forms of action and representation used by workers and employers that were able collectively to express their interests, however, this was not the case. Instead, the State made choices that allowed recognised norms to be produced via conventions or agreements. The State thus produced the norms that endowed collective agreements with binding force and made them *erga omnes* rights or obligations.

In France, collective agreements apply to all employees, whether they belong to a signatory trade union or not. While the rules have evolved since the mid-twentieth century, the founding principles of collective bargaining have not changed: a collective agreement is only valid under the conditions set out by law and within the limits imposed by law. Outside this framework, any such agreement is considered to be a mere contract affecting solely those who signed it or who are formally represented by

11. On these questions, *see* a comparative approach examining France and the United Kingdom, M. Vicente, *Les droits collectifs des travailleurs de plateformes*, thesis presented at Strasbourg University, 2022, 125 et seq.
12. G. Borenfreund, *Pouvoir de négocier et négociation collective*, 1006, Dr. soc. (1997).
13. Claude Didry, *La naissance de la convention collective*, Préf. E. Serverin, Éditions de l'EHESS (2002).

the signatories. The French legislator therefore defines precisely which organisations can bargain and under what conditions the agreement shall be valid and applicable to all employees of the company or sector. In principle, a collective agreement is bargained and concluded with representative trade unions. However, a trade union is not qualified as a representative because the employer recognises the trade union's legitimacy. Instead, a trade union is considered to be representative when it meets seven conditions set out by law. One of these conditions is based on the number of employee votes[14] during the company elections held to set up work councils ('comités sociaux et économiques').[15]

This entire system was designed for salaried workers. Self-employed workers, even though they are sometimes covered by special provisions in the Labour Code, do not benefit. However, depriving platform workers of any means for participating in the collective regulation of their contractual relations with platforms means that their working conditions are governed entirely by the whims of the markets and the law of the strongest. Characterised by precarity, dependence, economic and physical risks, and a want of protection, the situation of platform workers is reminiscent of that of workers in the early days of industrialisation.[16]

However, platform workers have never been totally deprived of their rights to collective action. The right to unionise and the right to bargain collectively are fundamental rights under International Labour Organization (ILO) conventions,[17] the European Union (EU) Charter of Fundamental Rights[18] and the European Social Charter,[19] and, as such, they apply to all workers, regardless of status. Under French law, the freedom of association and principle of participation also apply to all workers, whether they are employees or not.[20] In practice, platform workers have always been able to join professional organisations that represent and defend self-employed workers. These organisations claim to be best suited to representing their interests.

14. Only trade unions can propose candidates on the first round of the CSE elections. Trade unions have sufficient representativeness if they reach 10% of the votes.
15. The 'Comité social et économique' is an elected body representing workers that is supposed to be informed and consulted about employer decisions that have an impact on the working and employment conditions of employees.
16. One important nuance relates to the existence of social protection systems covering all workers, and not just employees, but on condition that they are declared, which is not always the case for delivery drivers. Precariousness is at its worst when delivery drivers, often because they are not legally resident, sublet accounts to others who are registered legally.
17. The Freedom of Association and Protection of the Right to Organise Convention, 1948 (n°87), states that, 'workers shall have the right to establish and, subject only to the rules of the organisation concerned, to join organisations of their own choosing' (Art. 2). This includes the self-employed. The Right to Organise and Collective Bargaining Convention, 1949 (n° 98), states that, 'all workers, including platform workers, should also enjoy the right to bargain collectively'; World Employment and Social Outlook, *The Role of Digital Labour Platforms in Transforming the World of Work*, specific p. 205 (ILO flagship report 2021).
18. UE Charter of Fundamental Rights, Art. 28.
19. ESC, Art. 6. For a detailed analysis, *see* B. Kresal, *Collective Bargaining for Platform Workers and the European Social Charter*, in *Collective Bargaining and the Gig Economy: A Traditional Tool for New Business Models*, J.M. Miranda Boto & E. Brameshuber, 61-73 (Oxford: Hart Publishing 2022).
20. Paragraphs 6 and 8 of the Preamble to the 1946 Constitution.

However, the question of whether self-employed platform workers might join employee trade unions proved more problematic, because the statutes of such unions did not originally allow it. Moreover, traditional trade unions have been reluctant to accommodate the idea of improving the status of self-employed workers. It is hard to reconcile such a notion with their demands that these workers be granted employee status. Improving self-employed or independent status by according to it better protections would contribute to encouraging its use to the detriment of salaried employment.

Access to a collective voice is crucial for improving the working conditions of platform workers, just as it was for improving working conditions for workers at the time of the Industrial Revolution. Their demands can only be heard if they are collectively supported. The law of 8 August 2016 explicitly sets out their freedom to unionise and their right to form a coalition to stop work in support of their professional demands.[21] There is, therefore, express recognition of the collective interest of platform workers, or at least some of them (drivers and delivery workers), and they have been given the legal means to express and defend that interest.

This approach to addressing the issue of freedom of association and exercising the right to strike aligns with a well-defined legal tradition in France. While these rights hold constitutional value and are fundamental to international law, they can only truly be implemented when legal provisions are made for workers to mobilise. The recognition of these rights in law has facilitated collective organisation and helped assuage some of the trade unions' reservations.[22] However, while platform workers' right to unionise was confirmed by law, no specific measures were created to support that right. Platform workers are, therefore, legally protected against discrimination and cannot face reprisals for forming coalitions, but they lack support for such actions. Furthermore, while access to collective bargaining is not prohibited, it has long remained very difficult. In order to operate effectively, collective bargaining needs collective agreements to be legally recognised. However, a path to collective bargaining has been opened through the creation of a specific system for these self-employed workers, operating in parallel to the existing system for employees.

[B] Developing a Collective Bargaining System for Independent Platform Workers

The French government's preferred approach to resolving the issue of self-employed platform workers' condition has been social dialogue. Social dialogue does not necessarily require support from the law to be effective; nothing prohibits discussion, and nothing prohibits agreements. However, the structure of industrial relations in France is such that an agreement, if not reached under the conditions set out by law, remains a strictly contractual act and is not binding on any parties beyond its

21. Labour Code, Art. L. 7342-4 et L. 7342-5.
22. For a detailed review, not limited to France, of the different forms of collective organisation, Vicente, *supra* n. 11, pp. 100 et seq.

signatories. Collective autonomy may operate only within the legal framework and its outcomes may only be acknowledged by law if reached according to the provisions set out by law. Until the ordinance of 21 April 2021, such provisions only applied to salaried workers. In some neighbouring European states binding agreements can be concluded by the representatives of platform workers.[23] In France, the scope of any such agreement and the extent to which it is binding remained debatable.[24]

A second obstacle to collective bargaining for platform workers was European competition law, particularly Article 101 TFUE, which prohibits cartels.[25] The Court of Justice of the European Union (CJEU) has ruled that genuinely self-employed workers have no right to bargain collectively. They cannot, therefore, benefit from the exemption granted by the CJEU to workers and employers concluding collective agreements. If self-employed workers collectively agree to set prices for the services or 'undertakings' they provide, such an alliance would constitute a cartel. The key question was whether drivers and delivery workers were 'genuine' self-employed workers. If they were, in fact, 'false' self-employed workers, as defined by the FNV Kunsten ruling,[26] there was no reason for them not to be given the right to bargain collectively to reach agreements.

To combat significant legal uncertainty surrounding this issue,[27] reduce the risk of cartel convictions, and recognise the need to facilitate social dialogue to achieve valid collective agreements, the European Commission adopted guidelines on collective agreements for solo self-employed workers in September 2022.[28] These guidelines guarantee that European competition rules shall not apply to 'false' self-employed workers in weak positions, provided that those self-employed workers do not themselves have employees.

The Commission's position on this issue recognises a power imbalance between platform workers and platforms. It reaffirms the traditional purpose of collective rights and collective bargaining, which is to redress the balance of inherently unequal contractual relationships in which one party is economically dependent on the other. This emphasis on empowering collectives faced with economically stronger parties, thereby, represents a return to the original function of collective bargaining.[29]

---

23. On this question, J.M. Miranda Boto & E. Brameshuber (eds), *Collective Bargaining and the Gig Economy: A Traditional Tool for New Business Model*, (Oxford: Hart Publishing 2022); Daniel Dumont, Auriane Lamine, Jean-Benoît Maisin (eds), *Le droit de négociation collective des travailleurs indépendants – Cadrages théoriques et études de cas* (Larcier, 2020).
24. Beyond salaried employment, '*il n'existe point de salut pour la négociation collective, du moins en l'état actuel du droit*', Y. Ferkane, *L'accord collectif de travail. Étude sur la diffusion d'un modèle*, 312 (Paris: Dalloz, 2017).
25. E. Brameshuber, *A Fundamental Right to Collective Bargaining for Economically Dependent, Employee-like Workers*, in J.M. Miranda Boto & E. Brameshuber (eds) *Collective Bargaining and the Gig Economy: A Traditional Tool for New Business Model*, 227-257 (Oxford: Hart Publishing 2022).
26. CJEU, 4 déc. 2014, aff. C-413/13, FNV Kunsten Informatie en Media.
27. On the subtleties in CJEU case law concerning the criteria for classification as an undertaking and as a worker, *see* Vicente, *supra* n. 11, esp. pp. 411 et seq.
28. https://eur-lex.europa.eu/legal-content/FR/TXT/?uri=celex%3A52022XC0930%2802%29.
29. These considerations also justified the position of the European Committee of Social Rights in the *ICTU v. Ireland judgment*, complaint No. 123/2016. The Committee stated that Art. 6, §2 of

As competition law can no longer apply, it has now become possible to consider the negotiation and conclusion of collective agreements. To promote social dialogue with the aim of regulating the relationships between platforms and workers, the French government created a parallel system specifically for drivers and delivery workers. Although the law does not expressly refer to collective bargaining, it makes provisions to create 'a sectoral social dialogue'.[30] Despite similarities with provisions for employees, there is one key difference: in these negotiations, the employee representatives for self-employed platform workers may be either trade unions or associations.[31] In this way, the French government has attempted to rebuild a collective bargaining model within the market system.[32] There is, however, an obvious weakness in the approach: its failure to address the glaring power imbalance between workers and platforms. A sectoral approach alone will not resolve the ongoing debate on the status of platform workers.

§9.02 SECTORAL SOCIAL DIALOGUE: AN INADEQUATE SOLUTION TO THE STATUS OF PLATFORM WORKERS

Since the implementation of these provisions, social dialogue between platform workers and platforms has been conducted by different stakeholders under highly varied conditions. Throughout 2022 and 2023, representatives were appointed and discussions held which led to several agreements that helped improve platform workers' working conditions [A]. However, the situation remains unstable for various reasons including a crisis in the legitimacy of those bargaining, insufficient content in the agreements, and, now, the potential impact of a forthcoming European directive which is to introduce a presumption of employment for platform workers [B].

[A] Agreements Lightly Improving Working Conditions for Platform Workers

Starting in 2022, the French Administrative Authority for the Regulation of Platforms (ARPE) organised elections to designate representatives. These elections suffered extremely high abstention rates, for example, an abstention rate of 96.6% in the transport sector and 98.17% in the delivery sector. Possible reasons include the

---

the European Charter is not limited to workers and also applies to self-employed workers, given their particular weakness and vulnerable situation, with the only limit being the restrictions necessary in a democratic society. The *ICTU* decision accepts these restrictions but considers that the concept of 'commitment' should not be interpreted too broadly, thereby depriving self-employed workers of the power to negotiate even if they have no other means of discussing the price of their work.

30. Labour Code, Arts L. 7343-1 et seq., resulting from Order No. 2021-484 of 21 April 2021 and Order No. 2022-492 of 6 April 2022. These texts are intended to be supplemented by provisions relating to 'platform social dialogue', in other words company-level negotiations.
31. This may open up the possibility of representation by organisations of self-employed workers, or even organisations defending the interests of companies, Labour Code, Art. L. 7343-2.
32. J. Dirringer et Y. Ferkane, *Modéliser la négociation collective dans le champ économique*, 598 Dr. Soc. (2021).

exclusively online format and major reliability issues of the elections, the trade union's call for a social media boycott and, the fact that the elections were organised exclusively within companies.[33] However, no quorum was stipulated by law so, despite the very low turnout, representatives were appointed by the ARPE based on the votes cast. Associations of independent workers and traditional trade unions became the recognised representatives of drivers and delivery workers.[34]

Negotiations began between these representatives and the platforms' representatives in autumn 2022, resulting in several agreements for drivers (five agreements) and delivery workers (four agreements).[35] The scope of the agreements encompassed two key issues: remuneration levels for services provided, and conditions for terminating relationships with the platforms or deactivating accounts.[36] These agreements were approved by the administrative authority and are now applicable to all platforms within their respective sectors.

[1] Agreements Regarding Compensation

In January 2023, the first agreement was reached covering drivers working on e-hailing platforms. It granted them a minimum guaranteed payment per ride, regardless of the distance or duration of the ride.[37] This guarantee exceeded what had previously been offered by Uber, but was still considered to be insufficient for covering the costs of short rides, which drivers tend to refuse for this reason. Trade unions that have traditionally defended employees did not see this as major progress. However, negotiations resumed, and a second agreement in December 2023 established a minimum guaranteed rate of EUR 30 per hour worked. The time worked included not only 'ride time' (from picking a client up to dropping them off at their destination) but also 'approach time' (from the moment a ride was accepted to the moment the client was picked up). The agreement also included a guaranteed income of EUR 1 per

33. They also challenged these elections before the Court of Cassation, in vain: Cass. Soc. 18 Oct. 2023, No. 22-19.937, FS-B.
34. New elections were held at the end of May 2024. The turnout at these elections was better, particularly among drivers (19.96%). It remained very low among delivery drivers (3.9%).
35. On this topic, *see* B. Palli, *Les accords collectifs de secteur des plateformes d'emploi*, 679 RDT (2023).
36. *Remuneration*: Agreement of 20 April 2023, introducing a minimum income guarantee for self-employed delivery drivers using a matchmaking platform; agreement of 18 January 2023 creating a minimum income per journey for self-employed drivers, agreement of 19 December 2023 to improve the income of self-employed drivers using a matchmaking platform.

    Termination of contractual relations: Agreement of 20 April 2023 setting out the terms and conditions for the termination of commercial relations between self-employed workers and ride-hailing platforms; agreement of 19 September 2023 on transparency and deactivation in the drivers' sector, as well as an agreement of 19 December 2023 strengthening the freedom of drivers to choose their journeys.

    There are also two agreements on the terms and conditions for negotiating future agreements and one agreement preventing delivery drivers from *discriminations*, concluded in May 2024.

    All the texts are available on the ARPE website. https://www.arpe.gouv.fr/dialogue-social/les-accords/.
37. This guarantee per race has been re-evaluated at EUR 9 at the end of 2023.

kilometre. The agreements, signed only by independent workers unions, were hailed as proof of 'the strength of sectoral social dialogue in France', demonstrating that platforms were 'attuned to drivers' priorities' and that the reality was 'far from the false debates some try to impose regarding employment status, which the vast majority of drivers reject'.[38]

Delivery workers also benefited from a contractual remuneration guarantee, set at EUR 11.75 per hour of platform work. The duration of work is estimated in advance by the platform and lasts from the moment a delivery offer is accepted to when it is handed over to the final recipient. The guaranteed remuneration is aligned with the minimum hourly wage for salaried workers, which was spontaneously referenced by negotiators. However, any waiting time between two orders is not considered, significantly limiting the scope of the minimum remuneration.

[2] Agreements on the Termination of Contractual Relationships

Agreements specifically address the conditions under which accounts can be deactivated or terminated for both drivers and delivery workers. In both cases, the agreements define situations that may lead to termination and stipulate that any such termination must involve human intervention and not result from an algorithmic decision. A driver or delivery worker must receive prior notification of the decision to terminate, allowing them to comment. Additionally, a lapse of time must be observed between the notification and implementation of the platform's decision. However, this period is very short, potentially only twenty-four hours for delivery workers and forty-eight hours for drivers.[39]

The agreements also set out actions that may be taken by drivers and delivery workers in case of account deactivation or termination. Any appeal is made directly to the platform within a very brief window to time following termination or deactivation (seven days only for delivery workers, and a period determined by the platforms for drivers).

Drivers and delivery workers thus benefit from some guarantees which appear to align with French law and the forthcoming European directive. However, these guarantees fall significantly short of those provided to employees under the Labour Code. Additionally, procedures are implemented very rapidly, and the timeframes are very short. Delivery workers and drivers cannot receive support or assistance during the process and there is no provision for an 'in-person' meeting. Even though the final decision cannot be automated and must involve human intervention, the entire procedure is fully digitalised and does not facilitate any genuine exchange about the circumstances leading to potential account deactivation.

---

38. Y. Weisselberger, *Chairman of the Fédération française du transport de personnes sur réservation (FFTPR)*, quoted in '20 minutes': https://www.20minutes.fr/economie/4067568-20231220-vtc-chauffeurs-obtiennent-plateformes-hausse-remuneration.
39. The agreements also provide for the possibility of exceptional situations justifying the immediate termination of commercial relations and the possibility of precautionary suspensions.

[3] Agreements That Fail to Resolve All Difficulties

Although these collective agreements do now exist and have improved conditions for platform workers, they fail to satisfy all stakeholders. The organisations that signed them are recognised as representative and champion self-employed workers' rights, however, other organisations have been much more reluctant to endorse the agreements. They believe that these agreements strengthen the assertion that self-employed worker status is distinct from employee status while continuing to offer self-employed workers fewer protections.

There is a further issue concerning the recourse available to workers if a platform fails to comply with the terms of the agreement. As long as these workers are recognised as self-employed, the contractual relationship with the platform is a commercial one. Disputes do not, therefore, fall under the jurisdiction of the French labour courts (*Conseil de Prud'hommes*) that oversee employment contracts. Instead, they fall under the jurisdiction of commercial courts. This means that disputes between drivers or delivery workers and the platforms are adjudicated as disputes between merchants and resolved by other merchants. In practical terms, it also means that a delivery worker or driver cannot receive trade union-appointed assistance during the proceedings, which is permitted in the Labour Courts. Instead, such workers must use a lawyer or defend their case themselves, thereby incurring significant costs. The only alternative is to ask for the relationship to be requalified and recognised as an employment contract. The dispute may then fall under the jurisdiction of the Labour Courts.

Furthermore, although the way that social dialogue has been structured for platform workers is rooted in the traditional French process for producing state-regulated conventions, it is not rooted in the usual foundations. There is no organised mechanism for facilitating interaction between representatives and those they represent. This essential link relies solely on the ability of workers' organisations to contact workers by whatever means they see fit. Any action taken by platform workers' representatives is entirely aimed at facilitating participation in sectoral social dialogue. This is highly inadequate. Although provision has been made, the lack of well-structured worker representation within platforms remains a major issue. Platform workers have no guaranteed rights to information and consultation. Furthermore, no information is provided on the number of terminations of the contract or the reasons for them. The way in which the algorithms are configured also remains opaque.

Many collectives and trade unions are critical of the deficiencies in the system and refuse to engage in negotiations within the framework of this sectoral social dialogue. As a result, negotiations predominantly reflect the influence and position of organisations which defend the rights of independent workers and not the position of traditional trade unions now defending these workers.

Social dialogue is indeed constructed in a highly ambivalent way for platforms. While agreements do improve working conditions for platform workers, they fall far short of protections afforded to employees. Moreover, there is an inherent risk of creating a form of competition between salaried and independent workers operating within the same field. By setting out the conditions for social dialogue in these sectors, the legislator has facilitated collective bargaining within a highly precise and regulated framework, however, the process currently excludes any assertive action at the company level and thereby hinders the creation of authentic worker collectives.

Social dialogue was introduced by French public authorities to safeguard against requests to reclassify the working relationship between the platforms and their self-employed workers as an 'employment contract' or employee relationship. However, by adopting the European directive that establishes a presumption of employment the authorities have raised doubts about the effectiveness of this safeguard.

[B] A Safeguard Against the Presumption of Employment?

The directive adopted by the European Parliament in April 2024,[40] which mandates Member States to acknowledge the presumption of an employment relationship for self-employed platform workers within two years, could potentially impact the current framework for agreements in France. Both the French and German governments have actively opposed the adoption of the directive and only a last-minute change of position from Greece and Estonia, who were initially opposed to the directive, allowed their opposition to be overcome. However, between the first version of the proposed directive and the final adopted version major amendments were made. The directive establishes a presumption of subordination (i.e., presumes that a subordinate relationship exists), but this only applies when there are facts indicating control and direction of work. If such facts are proven to exist, the presumption of employment relationship applies, reclassifying self-employed workers and stating that an employment contract exists. In such cases, the burden of proof falls on the platform, which has to prove that an employment relationship does not exist.

The implications for French law of this presumption of an employment relationship remain uncertain. Indeed, the European directive does not give a specific definition of the employment contract but refers to '*facts indicating control and direction as defined by the law, collective agreements or practice in force in the Member States with consideration to the case-law of the Court of Justice*'.[41] The criteria on which such an assumption is based are similar to those that French law uses to determine employee status. Legal subordination is usually decisive in determining the existence of a misclassified employment contract, and in French law this '*is characterized by the performance of work under the authority of an employer who has the power to give orders and directives, control their execution, and sanction any failures by the subordinate*'.[42] In France, no employment contract exists without control and direction of work, and these elements are established based on the factual circumstances of the performance of work. When judges grant the reclassification request of an employment relationship, they have first clearly established that the platform controls and directs

40. https://www.europarl.europa.eu/doceo/document/TA-9-2024-0330_FR.html - def_2_1.
41. Article 5 of the Directive adopted the 24 April 2024 by the European Parliament.
42. Cass. soc. 13 November 1996, Société Générale, n° 94-13.187, Bull. civ. V, n° 386.

the work. These two elements are crucial and are combined with the power to impose sanctions, which might include deactivating a worker's account. Control is relatively easy to establish through the geolocation systems used for delivery workers and drivers.[43] However, the direction of work can be more challenging to prove, as platforms stress that workers are free to connect, or not, and to accept a ride, or not.

Additionally, the platforms' terms of use evolve, requiring constant reassessment of the factual conditions under which services are provided.[44] Ultimately, the presumption of an employment relationship as set out in the directive may have a limited impact under French law because the presumption of an employment relationship may be seen to exist only when the essential elements of the employment relationship are established.

Under current French law, all workers classified as independent workers, which includes platform workers, are presumed to have non-employee status. This presumption of non-salaried status will have to be rounded out by another, opposite presumption, specific to platform workers. The directive's presumption or an employment relationship could lead to a reversal of the burden of proof, but that depends on its scope. Currently, the presumption of non-salaried status in France is applied generally and is not specific to platform workers; indeed, it applies whenever a worker provides services while declared as an independent contractor. This presumption in France is simple in nature and can be overturned if evidence of an employment relationship is proved to a judge. In contrast, the presumption of an employment relationship under the European directive requires proof of control and direction of work. Thus, the French and European presumptions have different foundations and mechanisms. They are not, however, necessarily contradictory: a platform worker hired as an independent worker would be presumed to be independent unless it can be proven that the platform directs and controls his work. This proof would lead to a presumption of an employment relationship and a reversal of the burden of the proof.

Thus, when interpreted as narrowly as possible, the directive allows for a conditional presumption of salaried status based on the proof of control and direction. Subsequent action would depend on the national legal requirements for establishing control and direction of work, which might not be very different from those currently required for proving legal subordination in France. A more comprehensive interpretation of the directive might result in a general presumption of salaried status for platform workers, shifting the burden of proof onto platforms who would have to demonstrate they do not have control and direction over work. Such a generalised presumption, applicable to all administrative and judicial proceedings (but possibly excluding social security and criminal law), would mark a major advancement and provide a better guarantee that platform workers will benefit from employee status.

43. Cass. soc. 28 November 2018, Take it easy n° 17-20.079, FP-P + B + R + I.
44. The same platform, 'Le Cab', has been the subject of contradictory decisions: Cass. soc. 13 April 2022, Le Cab, No. 20-14870 FS-B (refusal to recognise the existence of an employment contract considering the Court of Appel motivation insufficient) and Cass. soc. 24 April 2024, Le Cab, No. 22-17995 D (recognition of the existence of an employment contract).

Finally, the presumption of an employment relationship established by the directive could facilitate the intervention of labour inspectors, thereby moving beyond the frequently individualised approach to legal proceedings. The Deliveroo case in France shows that collective action within a criminal law framework initiated by the labour administration can yield results. However, hopes may yet be dashed. In France, labour inspectors are mandated to ensure compliance with labour law, and their powers are linked to criminal offences. Should an employer commit a criminal offence a formal report may be drawn up which may lead to legal proceedings or administrative penalties. The directive, however, explicitly excludes applying the presumption of salaried status to the field of criminal law.

The conditions for the directive's presumption of an employment relationship do not directly call into question the social dialogue framework established by the French government. Collective agreements for platforms might also be used to confirm that national French law complies with the European directive. For example, collective agreements already guarantee a worker's right to receive information about decisions affecting them and prevent automatic contract termination without human intervention, thereby addressing the 'algorithmic management' of work relations. Thus, the French strategy of creating specific social dialogue for platforms might help them retain their economic model while guaranteeing the minimum rights granted by the directive. However, social dialogue requires the active participation of stakeholders, and they may be less active and involved if it is presumed that drivers and delivery workers are employees. Conversely, minor repositioning of the directive might also strengthen workers' resistance and encourage more robust forms of collective organisation, outside the framework established by the French Government.

While it seems plausible that new agreements further improving conditions for platform workers could be negotiated,[45] it remains uncertain at this stage whether any such measures would be sufficient to protect platforms from collective action seeking full recognition of their workers as employees, especially when the European directive will come into force.

45. Another agreement concerning delivery workers was signed in May 2024, covering the prevention of discrimination.

Part II National Perspectives

CHAPTER 10

The Continuous Importance of Sectoral Collective Bargaining in Austria

Elisabeth Brameshuber

§10.01 INTRODUCTION

Compared with other countries,[1] the Austrian labour law (relations) system has proved quite stable over the past decades, especially during the economic crisis of 2008/2009 as well as during the COVID-19 pandemic. As a result, there were no major systematic changes or amendments to the Austrian labour law system in general or to the system of collective bargaining in particular, not even with regard to the rise of platform- or gig-work.[2] One might therefore ask whether the Austrian system of collective bargaining is a 'miracle cure' for the erosion of collective labour relations. In other words, is the Austrian example a 'best practice model' that could be implemented in other countries as well? Examining how the Austrian system works – not only on paper but also in practice – might prove helpful in particular with a view to implementing Article 4 of the AMW-Directive 2022/2041 in those Member States where sectoral collective bargaining coverage is below 80%.[3] The aim of this chapter is to first demonstrate why collective bargaining at sectoral level is so important in Austria and to show, second,

1. *See* the reports regarding Spain or Portugal in this volume, or the systematic change in German labour law, where a national statutory minimum wage was introduced in 2015.
2. *See* Franz Marhold, et al., *Austria*, in Marie-Cécile Escande Varniol, Sylvaine Laulom & Emmanuelle Mazuyer (eds), *Quel droit social dans une Europe en crise?* (Bruxelles: Larcier 2012) 89 et seq., which shows that apart from some minor legislative changes regarding part time employment, short-time work and educational leave, no amendments were made to the labour law system; Rolf Gleißner & Thomas Stegmüller, 50 Jahre ArbVG: Die Sicht der Wirtschaft, in Rudolf Mosler (ed.), *50 Jahre Arbeitsverfassungsgesetz* (ÖGB Verlag 2024) 83 (95 et seq.).
3. *See* on Art. 4 of the AMW-Directive Antonio Lo Faro in Luca Ratti, Elisabeth Brameshuber & Vincenzo Pietrogiovanni (eds), *The EU Directive on Adequate Minimum Wages* (Hart 2024) 181 and in particular 191 et seq.

which systemic factors contribute to a collective bargaining coverage of nearly 100%. Therefore, §10.02 focuses on the functions of sectoral collective bargaining. Reference to current data and examples highlights that despite not having a national statutory minimum wage, if covered by a sectoral collective bargaining agreement, there are no employment relationships with a minimum wage of less than EUR 1,500/month[4] (for a fulltime position), a minimum threshold that the leading social partners agreed on in 2017.

But how does it work from a systematic legal point of view? In §10.03 we explore the functioning of the system of sectoral collective bargaining. Referring not only to the hard-law legal provisions but also to practice carried out over the past decades, it is argued that only because of that complex system of normative rules – auxiliary law according to Otto Kahn-Freund[5] – in combination with the de-facto practices, no erosion has taken place. However, as shown in §10.04, in the event of one of these systemic elements being abolished, the whole system as we know it today would collapse. The caveat when considering whether the Austrian system or one of its components could serve as a best practice model therefore lies in the fact that only the system as a whole can guarantee (relative) stability in the labour relations system.

§10.02 SECTORAL COLLECTIVE BARGAINING AS STABILISER

When referring to sectoral collective bargaining as a stabiliser, one cannot avoid digging a little into the history of Austrian labour relations. When the Austrian Constitution was adopted in 1920, collective bargaining agreements already existed and their application was widespread.[6] Thus, it can be safely argued that there has been a longstanding practice leading to a common consensus between political parties, social partners and economic players that there is no necessity for statutory national minimum wages.[7] This is displayed by an agreement concluded in June 2017 between the presidents of the social partners – Trade Union Federation, Economic Chambers,

4. *See* the respective agreement between the leading social partners, the Austrian Economic Chambers and the Austrian trade union federation, dating from 2017, http://www.ots.at/presseaussendung/OTS_20070702_OTS0138/hundstorfer-und-leitl-unterzeichnen-sozialpartner-vereinbarung-ueber-1000-euro-mindestlohn (8 August 2024).
5. Otto Kahn-Freund in P Davies and M Freedland (eds), *Kahn-Freund's Labour and the Law*, 3rd edn (Stevens, 1983) 60.
6. Florian Wenninger, Zur Genese des Arbeitsverfassungsgesetzes 1973 Ein historischer Rückblick aus Anlass des 50. Jahrestages der Beschlussfassung im Nationalrat, in Rudolf Mosler (ed.), *50 Jahre Arbeitsverfassungsgesetz* (ÖGB Verlag 2024) 19 et seq.; Franz Marhold, Elisabeth Brameshuber & Michael Friedrich, *Österreichisches Arbeitsrecht*, 508 et seq. (4th ed., Verlag Österreich 2021). *See* for the similar development in Germany and thus generally speaking, respectively, Volker Rieble, *Arbeitsmarkt und Wettbewerb*, §1122 (Springer 1996).
7. *See* Andrea Garnero, Minimum Wages in OECD Countries, in Luca Ratti, Elisabeth Brameshuber & Vincenzo Pietrogiovanni (eds), *The EU Directive on Adequate Minimum Wages* (Hart 2024) 87 et seq. *See also* the recent Eurofound publication on Minimum wages in 2024: Annual review. In twenty-two out of twenty-seven Member States, a generally applicable statutory minimum wage exists. Besides Austria, there is no general statutory minimum wage in Denmark, Finland, Italy and Sweden, although in the last four of these countries, the minimum wage level is de facto set in (sectoral) collective bargaining agreements; https://www.eurofound.europa.eu/en/publications/2024/minimum-wages-2024-annual-review(accessed 2 August 2024).

Chambers of Labour and Agricultural Chambers – to establish a minimum wage of EUR 1,500 in all collective bargaining agreements for all full-time employees until 2020. And indeed, as of 2024, there is no sectoral collective bargaining agreement with a minimum wage below that threshold, with most collective bargaining agreements providing for a minimum wage of at least EUR 1.700/month.[8] Back then, though, this agreement was concluded under pressure from the government only, because the latter had envisaged adopting a statutory national minimum wage in the case where the social partners would not agree upon such a minimum standard.[9]

Of course, sectoral collective bargaining agreements provide not only for minimum wages but also for standard employment conditions in other crucial areas, such as the length of notice periods for terminations. Yet, cartelising of working conditions is not the only function sectoral collective bargaining agreements in Austria fulfil.[10] The particularity of the Austrian system lies in further functions, and although these are – at least in some way – also acknowledged as general functions of collective bargaining systems,[11] the Austrian labour relations system provides for a quite strong shaping of them.

[A] Functions

Generally speaking, collective bargaining agreements are supposed to guarantee just and fair employment conditions, provided that the bargaining parties are – to a certain extent – 'socially powerful'.[12] This is particularly true when comparing collectively bargained employment conditions with those laid down by individual employment contracts. From a functional point of view, due to the structurally weaker position of employees, the collective bargaining agreement is deemed the better agreement: it is agreed between two relatively equal parties, so there is no need for any abuse control exercised by the state.[13]

8. https://www.wko.at/oe/news/position-mindestlohn (2 August 2024). *See also* the recent Eurofound publication on Minimum wages in 2024: Annual review, pp. 12 et seq., pointing to Collectively agreed average and median monthly wages in ten low-paid jobs, January 2024 (€), of EUR 2.255 and EUR 2.127, respectively (https://www.eurofound.europa.eu/en/publications/2024/minimum-wages-2024-annual-review) (2 August 2024).
9. Agenda of the Austrian Federal Government 2017/2018, 10, http://archiv.bundeskanzleramt.at/DocView.axd?CobId=65201 (accessed 2 February 2017). *See also* the printed version in Neue@Hochschulzeitung 2018, 19-24.
10. *See, e.g.*, Franz Marhold, Elisabeth Brameshuber & Michael Friedrich, *Österreichisches Arbeitsrecht* 509 et seq. (4th ed., Verlag Österreich 2021); Rudolf Mosler, Gibt es eine kollektivrechtliche Friedenspflicht?, in Rudolf Mosler (ed.), *50 Jahre Arbeitsverfassungsgesetz* (ÖGB Verlag 2024) 473 (475).
11. Cf. for Germany, e.g., Abbo Junker, *Arbeitsrecht*, paras 500 et seq. (23rd ed. C.H. Beck 2024), and §4a, I of the German *Tarifvertragsgesetz*.
12. Günther Löschnigg & Charlotte Reiff, in Günther Löschnigg & Nora Melzer (eds), *AngG* I §6, para. 191 (11th ed., ÖGB Verlag 2021); Rudolf Strasser, Juristische Methodologie und soziale Rechtsanwendung im Arbeitsrecht, DRdA 1979, 85 (95); *see also* Ruth Dukes, Constitutionalizing Employment Relations: Sinzheimer, Kahn-Freund, and the Role of Labour Law, Journal of Law and Society 2008, 341 (343) https://doi.org/10.1111/j.1467-6478.2008.00442.x.
13. Volker Rieble, *Arbeitsmarkt und Wettbewerb*, para. 1211 (Springer 1996).

[1] *Cartelising Function*

One of the functions of sectoral collective bargaining agreements is its cartelising function.[14] The first caveat lies in the fact that this must not be mistaken for a general regulatory function. It is not the purpose of the sectoral collective bargaining agreement to cater for the application of the same employment conditions in all the undertakings of one sector. The cartelising function aims at creating schematic minimum employment conditions which all employers and employees belonging to one specific sector of industry can trust.[15] Thus, a twofold understanding of this function is necessary. On the one hand, employers legitimately expect their fellow business owners in the sector to apply at least the employment conditions laid down in the sectoral collective bargaining agreement.[16] Because deviation from the sectoral collective bargaining agreement in the individual employment contract is only allowed to the employee's advantage in Austria,[17] no employer in the respective sector can adjust their production costs based on wage-cutting or reducing other employment rights provided for in the sectoral collective bargaining agreement. On the other hand, employees cannot dump their colleagues by offering their labour at a cheaper price.[18]

Apart from that very general assessment of the cartelising function of collective bargaining agreements, sectoral bargaining in the Austrian system also leads to a certain kind of market adjustment. Although there is no relevant data available, it is widely acknowledged that wage-setting in a specific sector is not oriented towards the most productive companies in that sector, but rather the most productive of the last third. So if a given sector comprises ninety companies, with company No. 90 the most and company No. 1 the least productive, collectively agreed wages will be oriented towards the productivity of company No. 30. In this way, 'low-performing' companies perish in the long run because they cannot compete with the other companies within their sector.

As we are going to *see infra*, the near 100%[19] coverage rate does provide for a very distinct cartelising function in Austria. Thus, it is hardly surprising that there is no

---

14. For example Franz Marhold, Elisabeth Brameshuber & Michael Friedrich, *Österreichisches Arbeitsrecht*, 510 (4th ed., Verlag Österreich 2021).
15. Volker Rieble, *Arbeitsmarkt und Wettbewerb*, §§1307 et seq. (Springer 1996).
16. Franz Marhold, Elisabeth Brameshuber & Michael Friedrich, *Österreichisches Arbeitsrecht*, *supra* n. 13; Tobias Hinterseer, Arbeitsverfassungsgesetz und Sozialpartnerschaft: Eine Bestandsaufnahme zum Jubiläum, in Rudolf Mosler (ed.), *50 Jahre Arbeitsverfassungsgesetz* (ÖGB Verlag 2024) 47 (57).
17. *See infra* §10.03[A][5].
18. Vera Glassner & Michael Mesch, Kollektivvertragliche Deckungsraten in Europa, in Rudolf Mosler (ed.), *50 Jahre Arbeitsverfassungsgesetz* (ÖGB Verlag 2024) 533 (535).
19. Ninety-eight per cent according to the OECD/AIAS ICTWSS database; *see also* Torsten Müller & Thorsten Schulten, The Collective Bargaining Directive in Disguise: How the European Minimum Wage Directive Aims to Strengthen Collective Bargaining, in Luca Ratti, Elisabeth Brameshuber & Vincenzo Pietrogiovanni (eds), *The EU Directive on Adequate Minimum Wages* (Hart 2024) 75.

substantive call for a statutory national minimum wage.[20] In addition, the strength of sectoral collective bargaining and its cartelising function strongly relies on the fact that the collective partners at the sectoral level may regulate any rights and obligations deriving from the individual employment contract, as long as they do not infringe mandatory statutory provisions.[21]

The distinctness from other systems of sectoral collective bargaining, leading to a very strong formation of the cartelising function, is also depicted by the definition of a sector or a branch. In the Austrian model, a branch is defined according to the production method and not the market outcome, i.e., the generated products. As we are going to *see infra*, this is strongly related to how businesses are registered, on the one hand, and on the other to their mandatory membership of the Economic Chambers, which are organised according to the production method. However, there is also de facto leeway regarding the setting of wages, even within collective bargaining agreements of very homogeneous sectors, as the following table of minimum wages extracted from the current (valid from 1 May 2024 onwards) collective bargaining agreement for white-collar employees in Hotels and Catering shows:

Category (First Six Years of Employment)	*Vienna*	*Upper and Lower Austria, Burgenland, Styria, Carinthia*	*The Tyrol, Salzburg, Vorarlberg*
0 (best)	EUR 2,678.00 (catering)/2,798.00 (hotels)	EUR 2,500.00	EUR 2,798.00
5 (worst)	EUR 1,910.00	EUR 1,910.00	EUR 1,910.00

Although the Hotel and Catering sector can definitely be described as homogenous in terms of the 'production method', taking into account the productivity level in different regions can be presented as a positive example of flexibility within a rather strict system. Yet this outcome is completely up to the collective partners and not provided for by law.[22]

Another specific phenomenon is the acceptance of so-called *Istlohnklauseln*/guarantee clauses:[23] according to these clauses, which might form part of the sectoral collective agreement, annual pay rises not only apply to the collectively

20. Andrea Garnero, Minimum Wages in OECD Countries, in Luca Ratti, Elisabeth Brameshuber & Vincenzo Pietrogiovanni (eds), *The EU Directive on Adequate Minimum Wages* (Hart 2024) 87 (92).
21. Cf. §2 para. 2 lit 2 of the Austrian Labour Constitution Act (Arbeitsverfassungsgesetz, ArbVG).
22. Cf. also https://kurier.at/wirtschaft/1500-euro-mindestlohn-in-der-gastronomie/246.389.427 (accessed 8 August 2024).
23. *See* for the following Franz Marhold, Elisabeth Brameshuber & Michael Friedrich, *Österreichisches Arbeitsrecht*, *supra* n. 13, pp. 564 et seq.; Christoph Kietaibl, Entgeltfragen im KollV und Verhältnis zur BV, in Rudolf Mosler (ed.), *50 Jahre Arbeitsverfassungsgesetz* (ÖGB Verlag 2024) 239 (241).

agreed minimum wages in the whole sector but also to individually agreed overpayments. According to the courts, employer and employee might deviate from these clauses to the employee's disadvantage. Yet if they do not reach an agreement, the overpayment is also adjusted automatically.

Example: the collectively agreed minimum wage in sector A for 2023 is EUR 2,000. The *Istlohnklausel* in the agreement provides that individual overpayments have to be adjusted in the same nominal way as the minimum wage. Employee X gets a monthly payment of EUR 2,200. In 2024, the collective partners agree on a minimum wage of EUR 2,600. Because of the clause, employee X gets EUR 2,800 in 2024.

In this way, the cartelising function of the collective agreement is guaranteed, but at the same time, the *Istlohnklausel* allows for specific circumstances of each undertaking in the sector to be taken into account. Where one employer can afford to pay more than the collectively agreed minimum, the *Istlohnklausel* provides for an automatic guarantee of purchasing power, an important factor regarding employee satisfaction, which also leads to a relatively low level of collective action.

[2] Peace Function

The importance of sectoral collective bargaining in Austria is also reflected in the strike statistics of recent years.[24] Overall, the strike minutes per employee[25] per year always amounted to less than one minute, with exceptions only in 2011, 2018, 2022 and 2023:

Year	*Participating Employees*	*Strike Days*	*Strike Minutes/Employee*
2009	0	0	0.0
2010	0	0	0.0
2011	87,034	56,670	7.9
2012	1,500	563	0.1
2013	5,529	3,277	0.5
2014	5,196	3,309	0.5
2015	0	0	0.0
2016	0	0	0.0
2017	0	0	0.0
2018	37,923	8,934	1.1
2019	5,262	1,973	0.2
2020	9,883	3,687	0.5
2021	5,032	1,421	0.2

24. http://wko.at/statistik/Extranet/Langzeit/lang-streiks.pdf (accessed 8 August 2024).
25. In 2023, there were on average 3,941,200 employees in Austria, https://www.statistik.at/fileadmin/user_upload/Arbeitsmarktstatistiken_2023_Webversion-barrierefrei.pdf, 19 (accessed 8 August 2024).

Year	*Participating Employees*	*Strike Days*	*Strike Minutes/Employee*
2022	15,336	14,711	1.8
2023	110,401	98,605	12.0

Whereas collective bargaining is supposed to contribute to collective peace in general, the Austrian example shows that a strong sectoral collective bargaining system establishes industrial peace most effectively.[26] It strengthens employers' and employees' positions to a much larger extent than bargaining at the company level, simply because united employers are more powerful. Employees do not or simply cannot legitimately take strike measures against one single employer because of the peace function inherent to the sectoral collective bargaining agreement: as long as the collective agreement is valid, collective action cannot be taken legitimately.

[3] Innovation Function

The third reason why sectoral collective bargaining is so important in Austria is that it is a driver for innovation in the field of labour legislation.[27] Contrary to regular labour legislation that is particularly resistant to modification in Austria, sectoral collective agreements are the ideal arena to test whether modifications to existing rules or new regulations should be adopted. Historical milestones are the forty-hour week and the regulations regarding a mandatory five weeks of holidays. Although these regulations have now been part of general labour legislation for a long time, the collective partners in specific sectoral collective agreements first tested their provisions. Over the past few years, whereas the federal government cannot come to an agreement regarding more flexible working time arrangements, some sectoral collective bargaining agreements have already established regimes that enable employees to take compensatory time off instead of having their wages adjusted or to opt for a four-day-working week (instead of the traditional five-day-working week). Thus, sectoral collective bargaining agreements allow for both more flexible bargaining conditions and an opportunity to test new regulations for a limited period and are therefore driving innovation in the field of labour legislation.

[B] Stabiliser in Times of Crisis

The Austrian system of sectoral collective bargaining and the corresponding strength of the collective partners was one main factor in the Austrian economy faring reasonably well during the 2008-2010 crisis. As outlined in the study carried out during the INLACRIS I-project on '*Quel droit social après la crise*', short-time work arrangements

26. Cf. Franz Marhold, Elisabeth Brameshuber & Michael Friedrich, *Österreichisches Arbeitsrecht,* 510 (4th ed., Verlag Österreich 2021).
27. *Ibid.*, pp. 510 et seq.; Christoph Kietaibl, *Arbeitsrecht I* 200 (12th ed., new academic press 2023).

were established within already existing sectoral collective bargaining agreements.[28] In this way, the needs of one specific sector could be addressed without having to wait for the government and eventually Parliament to decide upon any legislative measures. As a result, and because of the flexibility of the sectoral collective bargaining agreements, hardly any legislative amendments were necessary. Thus, sectoral collective bargaining agreements are an important stabilising factor in times of crisis. This also proved to be true during the COVID-19 pandemic, where short-time work was again used as a flexible instrument.[29] However, during the pandemic, not only social partners at the sectoral level but also social partners generally speaking contributed to introducing new and tailor-made rules rather quickly: In January 2021, a so-called general collective bargaining agreement[30] established, among others, that in specific fields of employment, mandatory COVID-19-tests were to be conducted during remunerated working time, and that employees who mandatorily had to wear masks were entitled to take that mask off for at least ten minutes after a working period of three hours.

This last assessment shows that the Austrian system of sectoral collective bargaining is obviously quite stable and reform-resistant, while at the same time apparently being flexible enough to cope with unpredictable developments. In the following chapter, we are going to explore its legal foundations and look at the legislative as well as the de facto pillars supporting the system.

§10.03 THE SYSTEM OF SECTORAL COLLECTIVE BARGAINING

The Austrian system of collective labour relations is often considered to be in breach of freedom of association,[31] above all because of the employer's mandatory membership of the Economic Chambers. However, the leading Austrian doctrine is that both the Act on the Economic Chambers and the Austrian Federal Constitution, according to which the Economic Chambers are public associations with public authority,[32] place the

28. Franz Marhold, et al., *Austria*, in Marie-Cécile Escande Varniol, Sylvaine Laulom & Emmanuelle Mazuyer (eds), *Quel droit social dans une Europe en crise?* (Bruxelles: Larcier 2012) 95 et seq.
29. Christoph Wolf, et al., Kurzarbeit und Kurzarbeitsbeihilfe, in Reinhard Resch (ed.), *Das Corona-Handbuch*, paras 1 et seq. (Manz 2021) with further references; Tobias Hinterseer, Arbeitsverfassungsgesetz und Sozialpartnerschaft: Eine Bestandsaufnahme zum Jubiläum, in Rudolf Mosler (ed.), *50 Jahre Arbeitsverfassungsgesetz* (ÖGB Verlag 2024) 47 (55 et seq.); Rolf Gleißner & Thomas Stegmüller, 50 Jahre ArbVG: Die Sicht der Wirtschaft, in Rudolf Mosler (ed.), *50 Jahre Arbeitsverfassungsgesetz* (ÖGB Verlag 2024) 83 (92 et seq.).
30. Concluded between the high-level social partner organisations and applicable to all undertakings for whom the Chambers of Commerce have the power to conclude collective bargaining agreements.
31. A mandatory membership of the employers' and employees' associations is deemed to be in breach of Art. 9, para. 3 of the German Basic Law (Grundgesetz, GG), according to which associations must not be established by mandatory membership, but only by members joining them voluntarily, Volker Rieble, *Arbeitsmarkt und Wettbewerb*, §1145 (Springer 1996). *See also* Abbo Junker, *Europäische Grund- und Menschenrechte und das deutsche Arbeitsrecht (unter besonderer Berücksichtigung der Koalitionsfreiheit)*, ZfA 91 (134) (2013) with further references.
32. ECtHR, 30 June 1993, Sigurjónsson/ISL, Nr 16130/90, para. 31.

Economic Chambers beyond the scope of Article 11 ECHR or Article 12 EU-CFR.[33] In addition, employers can always establish and join so-called voluntary business associations (*freiwillige Berufsvereinigungen*) that are also entitled to conclude collective bargaining agreements. The potential conflict between a collective bargaining agreement concluded by the Economic Chambers and an agreement concluded by a voluntary business association is resolved by the Labour Constitution Act (*Arbeitsverfassungsgesetz, ArbVG*). From that moment on, when an agreement concluded by the voluntary business association enters into force, the mandatory representative body (the Economic Chambers) loses its entitlement to conclude collective agreements for those employers who are members of the voluntary association.[34]

As regards potential conflicts between sectoral collective bargaining agreements and company agreements (concluded between a single employer and the works council), the Labour Constitution Act establishes clear rules which also contribute to the strength of sectoral collective bargaining: company agreements simply cannot stipulate rules on wages. In other words, the wage-setting competence remains with social partners at the sectoral level.

[A] Legal Background

The system of collective bargaining is laid down in the Labour Constitution Act, which was adopted in its current form in 1973 and came into force in 1974. However, not every aspect of the 'success' of the Austrian system of sectoral collective bargaining can be explained by referring to statutory law, as displayed by the de facto (and not *de iure*) bargaining monopolies of the Economic Chambers on the one hand, and the Austrian Trade Union Federation on the other.

[1] Registration of Business

In Austria, the registration of a business is the precondition for its exercise. The registration, though, leads *ipso iure* to automatic and mandatory membership of the Economic Chambers.[35] The Act on Economic Chambers further provides for automatic membership of one of the seven industry sectors within the Federal Chamber, as well as for automatic membership of one of the trade groups, according to the respective

33. Christoph Grabenwarter & Katharina Pabel, *Europäische Menschenrechtskonvention*, 470 (7th ed. C.H. Beck 2021).
34. *See* §6 Labour Constitution Act: 'Wird einer freiwilligen Berufsvereinigung die Kollektivvertragsfähigkeit gemäß §5 Abs. 1 zuerkannt und schließt diese einen Kollektivvertrag ab, so verliert die in Betracht kommende gesetzliche Interessenvertretung hinsichtlich der Mitglieder der Berufsvereinigung die Kollektivvertragsfähigkeit für die Dauer der Geltung und für den Geltungsbereich des von der Berufsvereinigung abgeschlossenen Kollektivvertrages.'
35. According to §2, para. 2 of the Act on Economic Chambers (Wirtschaftskammergesetz, WKG): 'Zu den Mitgliedern gemäß Abs. 1 zählen jedenfalls Unternehmungen, die der Gewerbeordnung unterliegen sowie insbesondere solche, die in der Anlage zu diesem Gesetz angeführt sind.' *See also* Torsten Müller & Thorsten Schulten, Collective Bargaining in Disguise, in Luca Ratti, Elisabeth Brameshuber & Vincenzo Pietrogiovanni (eds), *The EU Directive on Adequate Minimum Wages* (Hart 2024) 71 (80).

business licence. The crucial nexus with the Labour Constitution Act lies in the fact that: (1) the Economic Chambers are the statutorily provided association entitled to conclude collective bargaining agreements for the employer's side;[36] and (2) as soon as an employer is a member of the Economic Chambers or of a voluntary business association that has concluded a collective bargaining agreement, the agreement applies automatically.[37] In combination with the statutorily provided outsider validity for employees, the mandatory membership of the Economic Chambers and the nexus with the Labour Constitution Act as outlined above are the main contributing factors to the nearly 100% coverage[38] of collective bargaining agreements in Austria.[39]

Contrary to tendencies that existed some years ago, this system of business licences seems to be stable at the moment. Whereas past governments deemed the process of business registration to be too complex (with its more than 500 different business licences),[40] and therefore sought to make it more flexible, currently no one calls for a modification, eventually leading to a single business license to conduct any business. Thus, the current collective bargaining system can be described as secure.

[2] De Facto Bargaining Monopolies

Although there are the Chambers of Labour that are statutorily provided mandatory representation of employees, and therefore allowed to collectively bargain for the employees' side, the Austrian Trade Union Federation has a de facto monopoly on the conclusion of collective bargaining agreements.[41] In other words, the Chambers of Labour do not make use of their theoretical right to conclude collective bargaining agreements. Yet, the trade union monopoly is not provided for by law but has

---

36. *See* §4, para. 1 Labour Constitution Act: 'Kollektivvertragsfähig sind gesetzliche Interessenvertretungen der Arbeitgeber und der Arbeitnehmer, denen unmittelbar oder mittelbar die Aufgabe obliegt, auf die Regelung von Arbeitsbedingungen hinzuwirken und deren Willensbildung in der Vertretung der Arbeitgeber- oder der Arbeitnehmerinteressen gegenüber der anderen Seite unabhängig ist.'
37. *See* §8, para. 1 Labour Constitution Act: 'Kollektivvertragsangehörig sind, sofern der Kollektivvertrag nicht anderes bestimmt, innerhalb seines räumlichen, fachlichen und persönlichen Geltungsbereiches die Arbeitgeber und die Arbeitnehmer, die zur Zeit des Abschlusses des Kollektivvertrages Mitglieder der am Kollektivvertrag beteiligten Parteien waren oder später werden.'
38. Ninety-eight per cent according to the OECD/AIAS ICTWSS database; *see also* Torsten Müller & Thorsten Schulten, The Collective Bargaining Directive in Disguise: How the European Minimum Wage Directive Aims to Strengthen Collective Bargaining, in Luca Ratti, Elisabeth Brameshuber & Vincenzo Pietrogiovanni (eds), *The EU Directive on Adequate Minimum Wages* (Hart 2024) 75.
39. Rolf Gleißner & Thomas Stegmüller, 50 Jahre ArbVG: Die Sicht der Wirtschaft, in Rudolf Mosler (ed.), *50 Jahre Arbeitsverfassungsgesetz* (ÖGB Verlag 2024) 83 (88); Vera Glassner & Michael Mesch, Kollektivvertragliche Deckungsraten in Europa, in Rudolf Mosler (ed.), *50 Jahre Arbeitsverfassungsgesetz* (ÖGB Verlag 2024) 533 (536 et seq.); Torsten Müller & Thorsten Schulten, Collective Bargaining in Disguise, in Luca Ratti, Elisabeth Brameshuber & Vincenzo Pietrogiovanni (eds), *The EU Directive on Adequate Minimum Wages* (Hart 2024) 71 (76).
40. *See* for these past tendencies the first edition of this volume, p. 97.
41. Tobias Hinterseer, Arbeitsverfassungsgesetz und Sozialpartnerschaft: Eine Bestandsaufnahme zum Jubiläum, in Rudolf Mosler (ed.), *50 Jahre Arbeitsverfassungsgesetz* (ÖGB Verlag 2024) 47 (51).

historically grown, which makes it hard to integrate with any other system of collective bargaining.

However, this is only one of the reasons why the employees' position is deemed to be fairly strong in comparison with other countries. In contrast to Germany, for example, where it is quite usual for there to be more than one collective bargaining agreement applicable for comparable groups of employees working for the same employer,[42] such a situation has never arisen in Austria, because the Austrian Trade Union Federation is the only organisation bargaining for the employees' side. In other words, there is no other relevant employees' association that has been granted the right to conclude collective bargaining agreements.[43] Thus, there is no competition between trade unions, guaranteeing a strong employee position that cannot be undercut by competing associations. The de facto strength of the Austrian trade union federation is reflected in the size of its membership. Of the approximately 3.9 million employees in Austria, more than a quarter are members.[44]

The de facto bargaining monopoly on the employer's side derives from the fact that there are hardly any voluntary employers' associations that: (1) are granted the power to conclude collective bargaining agreements; and (2) actually make use of it if granted. Thus, because of mandatory business registration, the Economic Chambers exercise a de facto bargaining monopoly in most business sectors, too.[45]

[3] Mandatory Applicability to All Members of the Concluding Party

One particular feature of the Austrian system of collective bargaining providing for its high coverage rate is that according to §8, paragraph 1 of the Labour Constitution Act, all members of the concluding parties of a collective bargaining agreement automatically fall under its scope, irrespective of whether they were already members when the agreement was concluded or whether they joined the bargaining party at a later point in time. In other words, the legal system provides for a de facto automatic applicability of collective bargaining agreements, without granting an 'opt-out'. The only de facto possibility for employers to 'escape' the applicability of a collective bargaining agreement concluded by the Economic Chambers and the Austrian trade union federation is: (1) to establish a voluntary business association that, (2) fulfils all legal criteria to be officially granted the right to conclude collective bargaining agreements,

42. Cf. Abbo Junker, *Arbeitsrecht*, §§571 et seq. (23rd ed. C.H. Beck 2024).
43. There is the employees' association of dependent apothecaries and a trade union for employed medical doctors. However, the latter was not granted the right to conclude collective agreements because it had not fulfilled the statutorily provided criteria, the most important being a certain power within the groups of the employees represented; http://derstandard.at/2000030642011/Aerztegewerkschaft-darf-Aerzte-nicht-vertreten (accessed 8 August 2024); VwGH Ra 2018/08/0081 Arb 13.499; Franz Marhold, Elisabeth Brameshuber & Michael Friedrich, *Österreichisches Arbeitsrecht*, *supra* n. 13, pp. 485, 517.
44. In 2023, 1,212,990 employees were members of the Austrian trade union federation, ÖGB, *ÖGB Mitgliederstatistik*, https://www.oegb.at/der-oegb/der-oegb-in-zahlen (accessed 8 August 2024).
45. Franz Marhold, Elisabeth Brameshuber & Michael Friedrich, *Österreichisches Arbeitsrecht*, 487 et seq. (4th ed., Verlag Österreich 2021).

and (3) also achieves the conclusion of a collective bargaining agreement with the Trade Union Federation.

[4] Outsider Validity for Employees

The so-called outsider validity (Außenseiterwirkung) is provided for by the law itself: according to §12, paragraph 1 of the Labour Constitution Act, those employees who are not members of the concluding party, i.e., the Austrian Trade Union Federation, are automatically bound by the collective bargaining agreement applicable to their employer.[46] Although one might conclude that this outcome could be a violation of the state's monopoly on establishing generally binding law, the Austrian Constitutional Court's (Verfassungsgerichtshof, VfGH) line of argumentation shows that the Constitution is not violated. In other words, as long as the outsider validity is provided for by the legislator, and as long as the parties to the employment relationship may also deviate from the applicable collective bargaining agreement (to the employee's advantage), the state's monopoly in creating generally binding law is not violated.[47]

The reason for outsider validity being provided for by law is the Austrian legislators' realisation that especially without provision for statutory minimum wages, there was a need for equal treatment and protection of all employees, irrespective of their membership of the concluding party to the collective bargaining agreement.[48] In this way, employees are protected from wage dumping by their colleagues who are not members of the concluding party.[49] As a result, outsider validity only leads de facto to advantageous outcomes for the employees – and thus does not violate the Constitution.[50]

Compared with other legal systems, for example, the German one, where the application of a collective bargaining agreement to an employee who is not a member of the concluding party is guaranteed by so-called *Bezugnahmeklauseln* (reference clauses),[51] Austrian outsider validity provides for an application of a collective agreement without the need to declare its application in the individual employment contract. This outcome benefits the strong position of the only bargaining party for the employee's side, the Austrian Trade Union Federation, and although one might argue that outsider validity means that trade union federation membership rates are rather

46. Section 12, para. 1 Labour Constitution Act: 'Die Rechtswirkungen des Kollektivvertrages treten auch für Arbeitnehmer eines kollektivvertragsangehörigen Arbeitgebers ein, die nicht kollektivvertragsangehörig sind (Außenseiter).'
47. Cf. Reinhard Resch, in Peter Jabornegg, Reinhard Resch & Barbara Kammler (eds), *Kommentar ArbVG*, §12, paras 3, 5 (Manz 2019); Christian Holzner, 'Legitimationsprobleme' der Satzung?, 7(11) DRdA (1994).
48. *Ibid.*, 10 et seq.
49. Reinhard Resch, in Peter Jabornegg, Reinhard Resch & Barbara Kammler (eds), *Kommentar ArbVG*, §12, paras 3 (Manz 2019); Hans Floretta, Die Differenzierung nach der Gewerkschaftszugehörigkeit im deutschen Tarifvertragsrecht, 1(15) DRdA (1968).
50. Cf. Theodor Tomandl, *ZAS*, 14 et seq. (1995).
51. Abbo Junker, *Arbeitsrecht*, paras 538 et seq. (23rd ed. C.H. Beck 2024).

low, the opposite is, in fact, the case. Membership rates are at around a quarter of all employees.[52]

[5] *Deviation from the Collective Bargaining Agreement Only to the Employee's Advantage*

According to §3 of the Labour Constitution Act, deviation from the collectively bargained employment conditions in the individual employment contract or by company agreements (so-called *Betriebsvereinbarungen* concluded between one single employer and the relevant works council) is only possible where it is to the employee's advantage. Furthermore, it is crucial to note that the just-mentioned company agreements cannot regulate wages. Contrary to other countries,[53] there are no tendencies to abolish this fundamental feature of a functioning collective bargaining system. Apart from that rather general feature, the distinct feature of the Austrian system lies in the court-acknowledged possibility to include the already mentioned *'Istlohnklauseln'* in sectoral collective agreements. According to these clauses, which are part of the sectoral collective agreement, annual pay rises apply not only to the collectively agreed minimum wages in the whole sector but also to individually agreed overpayments. According to the courts, employer and employee might deviate from these clauses to the employee's disadvantage, as long as the collectively agreed minimum wages are not undermined. Yet if they do not reach an agreement, the overpayment is also adjusted automatically.[54]

[B] Critical Assessment

[1] *No Sectoral Bargaining: No Cartelising*

The CJEU's *ÖGB* case[55] shows that as soon as there is more than one collective bargaining agreement applicable in one rather homogeneous sector, the system falls apart. In the 1990s, the peak Austrian employers' organisation, the Austrian Economic Chambers, and the Austrian Trade Union Federation had concluded two separate collective agreements for the aviation sector, one for the company Austrian Airlines and one for the company Tyrolean, the latter being the subsidiary of the former. In addition, there was another collective agreement for Lauda Air, which was then the third aviation company in Austria. Over the years, the Austrian Airlines collective agreement proved to be too costly, especially because of rather generous company pension payments, automatic pay increases and automatic adaptation to inflation. Because neither side's representatives could agree upon a less expensive (to the employers) collective agreement within Austrian Airlines and because the collective

52. *See supra* §10.03[A][2].
53. Cf. Tamás Gyulavári & Emanuele Menegatti, Introduction, in Tamás Gyulavári & Emanuele Menegatti (eds), *The Sources of Labour Law* (Hart 2019) 1 (7).
54. *See* already under §10.02[A][1].
55. Case C-328/13, ÖGB, 11 September 2014, EU:C:2014:2197.

agreement applicable at Tyrolean was much cheaper from the employer's point of view, the parent company, Austrian Airlines, decided to take the curious step of transferring its business to its subsidiary in order to apply the cheaper collective agreement.[56] The outcome of the dispute before the CJEU was to the employer's disadvantage and shows that the co-existence of several collective agreements in one homogenous sector might easily lead to unwelcome results. The employer's defeat in the courts gave the employee's side much more leverage when bargaining for a new collective agreement (at last), enabling it to exert a lot of pressure on the employer's side.

Another conflict decided by the Austrian Supreme Court of Justice (*Oberster Gerichtshof, OGH*) regarding the applicability of different collective agreements in one homogeneous sector – banking – reveals that the existence of more than one collective bargaining agreement in one sector leads, when strictly sticking to the provisions of the Labour Constitution Act, to apparently undesirable outcomes. Specifically, there existed two collective agreements concluded with the Austrian Trade Union Federation by two different voluntary business associations, respectively. Several banking institutes were members of these voluntary business associations. At one point, one banking institute decided to change memberships. As a result, the other collective agreement became applicable, which was less advantageous for the employees regarding their wages. If the provisions of the Labour Constitution Act had been applied strictly, this would indeed have been the correct outcome. However, the OGH decided that the national provisions regarding a transfer of business had to be applied by analogy, resulting not only in the application of the new collective agreement but also in the preservation of the wage level according to the collective agreement concluded by the 'old' voluntary business association. According to the OGH, any other outcome would have been contrary to the employees' justified trust in the stability of their wages.[57]

This last example shows that in the end, from a systemic point of view, only the application of a single collective bargaining agreement in one sector can possibly prevent disputes over wages. It also shows that – at least when applying the provisions of the Labour Constitution Act – the Austrian system of sectoral collective bargaining might not guarantee wage stability in the event of employers (and employees) deciding to make use of their right to freedom of association. Yet even the Labour Constitution Act itself undermines the cartelising function of the sectoral collective bargaining agreement to some extent: the statutory provision for the collective bargaining power of public bodies/foundations under public law means there is a specific collective agreement for entities such as the Austrian Broadcasting Corporation (*Österreichischer Rundfunk, ORF*). Although this is advantageous for the ORF, as the relatively good employment conditions mean journalists are eager to work there, it is at the disadvantage of all other competitors in the TV and radio market. Due to the lack of public

56. Cf. Elisabeth Brameshuber, Balancing versus Preservation of Rights under the Acquired Rights Directive, 45 ILJ 443 (2016) https://doi.org/10.1093/indlaw/dww003.
57. OGH 9 ObA 128/04w ecolex 2006/95 = DRdA 2006, 149 = ZAS 2006/41 (Winkler) = SZ 2005/169 = DRdA 2006/42 (Grillberger).

funding, they cannot afford wages as high or employment conditions as generous as those granted to ORF employees.

[2] Deviation to the Employee's Advantage: Another Threat to the Cartelising Function?

On the one hand, the use of the so-called *Istlohnklauseln* guarantees the employees' purchasing power, yet on the other it can harm economically weak employers in particular. Since it is up to the parties to the individual employment contract to arrange for deviations from the *Istlohnklausel*, these clauses might harm employers in economically difficult periods: it is quite obvious that employees will not voluntarily agree to a lower rise in wages than provided for by the collective agreement and the *Istlohnklausel*. Thus, it is up to the employer's initiative to settle for a lower rise in wages. However, the balancing act between competing with the other employers in the sector and trying to keep employees by granting the same rise in payments as those other employers is not easy. Therefore, it is not at all surprising that in Germany the validity of the comparable so-called *Garantieklausel/Effektivklausel* is also highly contentious because of their threat to the cartelising function of collective agreements.[58]

[3] The Difficulty of Defining a Sector

Developments in the metal sector show that the Austrian system of sectoral collective bargaining is more fragile than expected prima facie, threatening its peace function especially. In 2012, for the first time, there were six collective bargaining agreements instead of one for the rather inhomogeneous metal sector.[59] Originally, the six different trade groups within the metal branch had decided to bargain together for one general collective agreement. Before 2002, there was even a seventh member of that bargaining group, representing the electro and electronic-industry employers. However, that employer's trade group decided to bargain its own collective agreement, resulting in a very distinct collective bargaining agreement when compared with the general one for the metal sector, especially regarding its structure. It was one of the first collective bargaining agreements that had overcome the anachronistic division between blue-collar and white-collar workers (which is still upheld in many statutes and collective bargaining agreements).

On the eve of the annual bargaining round on wages in 2012, the remaining six trade groups forming the employer's side decided to break apart and bargain separately for the six different groups of businesses within the metal sector. In the end, though, the current wage levels in the metal sector have proved to be more or less the same. In practice, one employer's trade group starts the bargaining process, with all other

58. Peter Löwisch & Volker Rieble, *Tarifvertragsgesetz*, §1 paras 2160 et seq. (4th ed. C.H. Beck 2017).
59. *See* for the currently applicable agreements https://www.wko.at/kollektivvertraege (accessed 14 August 2024). *See* for the following also Franz Marhold & Elma Osmanovic, *Ausstieg eines Fachverbandes aus einer Kollektivvertrags- Verhandlungsgemeinschaft*, ASoK 202 (2012).

employer's groups in the end following the example of the first trade group.[60] Thus, it is not quite apparent why the bargaining group was dissolved, although productivity in the foundry sector, for instance, is much lower than that in the metal industry.

One of the underlying questions was and remains how a sector should be defined. Generally speaking, there are two possible methods, one relying on the productivity of a group of businesses, and the other on their production methods. Defining a sector according to the productivity level or the outcome of the working process does not fit into a system where the applicability of a collective bargaining agreement strongly depends on the business registration and therefore the production method. This is illustrated by the example of textile fabrics, produced on the one hand by businesses that belong to the trade group of the textile industry, and on the other by businesses that, according to their registration, belong to the trade group of the chemical industry. As can be imagined, the collective bargaining agreement for the chemical industry is much more advantageous for the employees because of its higher wage levels but possibly creates a mismatch regarding the competition between the different employers. In other words, those employers that are members of the chemical industry trade group have to compete on wages with those employers that are members of the textile industry trade group, the latter needing to pay much lower wages than the former.

Solutions to overcome fragmentations within sectors have already been presented *supra*, one being the possibility of including so-called *Istlohnklauseln* in collective bargaining agreements. By including an *Istlohnklausel* in a collective bargaining agreement, collective wage increases also apply to individually agreed overpayments, unless the single employer agrees with the single employee that this wage increase should not take place. Another solution might be having one general collective bargaining agreement for one sector but adjusting the wage tables to a region's productivity level, as seen within the collective bargaining agreement for Hotels and Catering.

[4] The Limited Personal Scope of Application

The advent of platforms or gig work also brought along the question of whether collective bargaining should be possible for/on behalf of economically dependent self-employed, particularly in those cases where they face bargaining inequalities similar to those of employees. Whereas legislative developments or practices in other Member States of the European Union as well as the European Union (EU) Commission's Guidelines on collective bargaining for the solo self-employed[61] show that collective bargaining agreements for some non-employees actually exist and that they

60. *See* for recent developments Elisabeth Brameshuber & Felicia Kain, *Zur Zulässigkeit von Sympathiestreiks und zur Reichweite der kollektivvertraglichen Friedenspflicht*, ASoK 38 et seq. (2024).
61. Guidelines on the application of Union competition law to collective agreements regarding the working conditions of solo self-employed persons (2022/C 374/02), adopted by the Commission in 2022.

do not necessarily infringe antitrust law,[62] the Austrian system is more or less unimpressed. Although some scholars argue that the current provisions of the Labour Constitution Act might be interpreted in favour of application to certain economically dependent self-employed (with particularly strong economic dependency, such as (newspaper) deliverers, or teaching personnel),[63] the prevailing opinion is that the current provisions of the Labour Constitution Act do not cover an interpretation in favour of including economically dependent self-employed into the personal scope of application of collective bargaining agreements, neither *de lege lata* nor by analogous application:[64] Collective bargaining agreements are agreements concluded between employers' and employees' representatives,[65] regulating first and foremost rights and obligations of the employment relationship.[66] According to the prevailing opinion, the notions 'employees' representatives' and 'employment relationship' are to be interpreted narrowly. In short: The rules on collective bargaining agreements as established in the Labour Constitution Act only apply to employment relationships.[67]

Yet, outside of the Labour Constitution Act, there actually exist some protection tools for certain economically dependent self-employed: Special collective agreements that differ from collective bargaining agreements concluded under the Labour Constitution Act can be concluded for certain economically dependent journalists falling under the scope of the Law for Journalists (§§16 et seq. therein) and for certain economically dependent persons performing manual work at home under the so-called Heimarbeitsgesetz.[68]

In addition, although within the boundaries of the existing system (i.e., the bargaining agreement applies only to employees) Austrian social partners managed as one of the first ones worldwide to conclude a collective bargaining agreement for

62. *See* among others Elisabeth Brameshuber, A (Fundamental) Right to Collective Bargaining for Economically-Dependent, Employee-Like Workers, in José María Miranda Boto & Elisabeth Brameshuber (eds), *Collective Bargaining and the Gig Economy: A Traditional Tool for New Business Models* (Hart 2022), 227 et seq.; *see also* the contributions in this volume, in particular those by Marta Kozak-Maśnicka & Łukasz Pisarczyk, by Jeremias Adams-Prassl & Sylvaine Laulom & Yolanda Maneiro Vázquez and by Daniel Pérez del Prado.

63. In particular Rudolf Mosler, Anwendung des kollektiven Arbeitsrechts auf arbeitnehmerähnlich beschäftigte Selbständige?, DRdA, 100 (2012).

64. Amongst others Martin Risak, Kollektive Rechtssetzung auch für Nicht-Arbeitnehmer?, ZAS 165 (2002). *See* for a detailed overview also Christina Schnittler & Elisabeth Brameshuber, Kollektive Rechtsgestaltung im Wandel: Ist das ArbVG bereit für Arbeitnehmerähnliche?, in Rudolf Mosler (ed.), *50 Jahre ArbVG* (ÖGB Verlag 2024), 207 et seq.

65. *See* §2(1) Labour Constitution Act: 'Kollektivverträge sind Vereinbarungen, die zwischen kollektivvertragsfähigen Körperschaften der Arbeitgeber einerseits und der Arbeitnehmer andererseits schriftlich abgeschlossen werden.'

66. *See* §2(2) Ziffer 2 Labour Constitution Act: 'Durch Kollektivverträge können geregelt werden (...) die gegenseitigen aus dem Arbeitsverhältnis entspringenden Rechte und Pflichten der Arbeitgeber und der Arbeitnehmer.'

67. *See* §1(1) Labour Constitution Act: 'Die Bestimmungen des I. Teiles gelten – soweit im folgenden nicht anderes bestimmt ist – für Arbeitsverhältnisse aller Art, die auf einem privatrechtlichen Vertrag beruhen.'

68. *See* Elisabeth Brameshuber, in José María Miranda Boto & Elisabeth Brameshuber, *supra* n. 61, 238; *see also* Franz Marhold, Economically-Dependent Workers' in the EU Member States: A Austria, in Claudia Schubert (ed.), *Economically-Dependent Workers* (Hart Beck 2022) 9, (para. 5).

bicycle couriers. Two aspects seem worth mentioning in the context of this chapter. The first is the relatively narrow material scope of application: The collective bargaining agreement only applies to undertakings with a business licence for the delivery of goods with bicycles. The second is the fact that most delivery companies employ very few employees; the vast majority of their delivery personnel are freelancers/free service contractors or solo self-employed.[69]

Thus, despite the rise of platform and gig work, no legislative proposals have been brought forward to extend the Labour Constitution Act's personal scope of application to economically dependent self-employed. Out of several reasons, two can be singled out: On the one hand, when merely extending the personal scope of application, the question of who should represent those persons remains unresolved.[70] On the other, despite the fact that free service contractors enjoy only very few employment rights (e.g., antidiscrimination law applies) and that solo self-employed are completely exempt from the personal scope of labour law, both categories of working persons enjoy full mandatory social security protection. In other words, any working activity, irrespective of whether it is in dependent employment or in self-employment, falls under the scope of mandatory social security law (health, accident and old age; unemployment for employees and free service contractors, and for self-employed with an opt-in possibility). Thus, compared to other European countries,[71] the situation for persons not working in employment relationships can be assessed as less precarious, in particular in case of sickness or accident at work. This can safely be recognised as one reason for the Austrian system of collective bargaining not being adapted to these new realities.

§10.04 SECTORAL COLLECTIVE BARGAINING: 'BEST PRACTICE MODEL'?

As the previous chapters have made clear, the Austrian system of sectoral collective bargaining is fairly complex, both from a legal as well as from a de facto point of view. Although the current system works quite well, with a collective bargaining coverage of nearly 100%, making appeals for a national statutory minimum wage rather redundant,[72] attempts to copy only some features of the Austrian system should be watched most critically. Only the system as a whole with its legal and factual particularities has

69. Fairwork, Fairwork *Austria Ratings 2022: Labour Standards in the Platform Economy*, Vienna, Austria; Oxford, United Kingdom 10 et seq. (2022) https://fair.work/wp-content/uploads/sites/17/2022/05/Fairwork-Austria-Report-2022.pdf (21 August 2024).
70. Cf. Christina Schnittler & Elisabeth Brameshuber, Kollektive Rechtsgestaltung im Wandel: Ist das ArbVG bereit für Arbeitnehmerähnliche?, in Rudolf Mosler (ed.), *50 Jahre ArbVG* (ÖGB Verlag 2024), 207 et seq.
71. *See* Proposal for a Council Recommendation on access to social protection for workers and the self-employed, COM 2018/132 final; Council Recommendation of 8 November 2019 on access to social protection for workers and the self-employed, 2019/C 387/01; Report From the Commission to the Council on the implementation of the Council Recommendation on access to social protection for workers and the self-employed, COM/2023/43 final.
72. Cf. the assessment by Thomas Dullinger, Austria, in Luca Ratti, Elisabeth Brameshuber & Vincenzo Pietrogiovanni (eds), *The EU Directive on Adequate Minimum Wages* (Hart 2024) 339

proved to guarantee relative peace, cartelised wages and innovative solutions for emerging problems.[73] In other words, it is most crucial to take into account the whole legal and factual system when assessing whether some particularities could serve as a 'best practice model'. As the German example shows, mandatory membership of the Economic Chambers as provided for in Austria would be deemed unconstitutional under German law. Nevertheless, as we have seen, mandatory membership is one of the main pillars of the Austrian system. Although it appears hardly exportable, it follows from Directive 2022/2041 on adequate minimum wages in the EU, and more specifically from its Article 4(1)a) read in conjunction with its Recitals 16 and, that collectively agreed wages should ideally be set at sectoral level. The underlying premise is that in all Member States where minimum wages are set by collective bargaining agreement rather than by statute – i.e., except Italy, Austria, Denmark, Finland and Sweden – wages are deemed to be adequate. Thus, it comes without surprise that the European legislator seeks to promote collective bargaining at sectoral level, by obliging Member States to take respective action to "promote the building and strengthening of the capacity of the social partners to engage in collective bargaining on wage-setting, in particular at sector or cross-industry level" (Article 4(1)a) Directive 20224/2041).

§10.05 CONCLUSION

It was the aim of this chapter to show that up until the present, the Austrian system of sectoral collective bargaining has proved to be quite successful. It leads to a cartelising of wages, with hardly any sector of the industry currently offering a minimum wage of less than EUR 1,700/month for a full-time position. The regulatory function of the cartelised wages should not be underestimated either, leading to a de facto perishing of low-performing companies in the long run. By bargaining the wages and working conditions for one sector rather than just a single employer, the employer's position especially is reinforced, thus leading to relatively low strike rates. In this way, the Austrian system provides for a very distinct peace function. Another important feature is its innovation function, which was particularly visible during the crisis of the years 2009/2010 as well as during the COVID-19 pandemic where important decisions to stabilise the labour market were taken at the level of sectoral collective bargaining. Thus, it seems highly unlikely that the system is going to change in the near future. So far, there has been hardly any in-depth research on what alternatives to the current system would and should look like. Considering the sectoral collective bargaining agreement's main function of setting minimum wages, and taking into account the nearly 100% coverage rate, also the introduction of a statutory minimum wage – which

et seq.; cf. also Sophie Schwertner, The EU's New Minimum Wage Directive: Implications for Austria?, University of Vienna Law Review 35 (50 et seq.) (2022).

73. Cf. Stephan Kampelmann, Andrea Garnero & François Rycx, Minimum Wages in Europe: Does the Diversity of Systems Lead to a Diversity of Outcomes? ETUI 7 (2013) https://www.etui.org/publications/reports/minimum-wages-in-europe-does-the-diversity-of-systems-lead-to-a-diversity-of-outcomes (accessed 8 August 2024).

would certainly be a game changer – seems out of the question. Thus, although some features of the Austrian system are deemed to be the 'incarnation' of everything that under say German law would be regarded as unconstitutional,[74] the system of sectoral collective bargaining seems to be a valid way of regulating employment relations.[75]

74. Abbo Junker, Europäische Grund- und Menschenrechte und das deutsche Arbeitsrecht (unter besonderer Berücksichtigung der Koalitionsfreiheit), ZfA 91, 134 (2013) with further references. Junker even calls it *Teufelswerk – devil's work*.
75. Cf. also Torsten Müller & Thorsten Schulten, Collective Bargaining in Disguise, in Luca Ratti, Elisabeth Brameshuber & Vincenzo Pietrogiovanni (eds), *The EU Directive on Adequate Minimum Wages* (Hart 2024) 71 (76).

CHAPTER 11

Wage Moderation Measures in Times of Crisis: The Belgian Example

Fabienne Kéfer

The impact of crisis periods on social dialogue generally manifests in three ways: the increased role of the State, the concern of social partners with preserving employment and purchasing power as well as maintaining or restoring business competitiveness, and finally the decentralisation of negotiations.[1]

Belgian social dialogue has largely avoided the phenomenon of decentralisation observed elsewhere in Europe. However, it has experienced the effects of State interventionism, noticeable in various areas. Wage moderation is a particularly fitting example. Indeed, a government intervention mechanism, created in 1996 in view of preserving competitiveness, was only activated from – and because of – the financial crisis of 2008, which disrupted social dialogue. Since then, successive crises (health, energy) have made this mechanism continuously inescapable, except for the 2017-2018 period.

To make the demonstration easier, it is useful to first briefly describe the institutional setting of collective bargaining and the wage formation process (§11.01). Subsequently, it will be demonstrated that the crises have disrupted its usual functioning (§11.02).

§11.01 INTRODUCTORY CONSIDERATIONS

In comparison to other Western countries, Belgian social dialogue appears to be highly institutionalised and coordinated. The two party system is present at all levels of the

1. M. AJZEN & L. TASKIN, 'La concertation sociale au temps du coronavirus: enjeux et perspectives du premier confinement en Belgique', *Revue française de gestion*, Vol. 298 (2021), No. 5, pp. 82-83, https://doi.org/10.3166/rfg.2021.00549.

economy [A]. The way in which workers' wage is determined, as a consequence of this hierarchical arrangement, also presents some national specificities [B].

[A] Architecture of the Belgian Model of Social Dialogue

Belgian social dialogue is based on permanent consultation structures. It is also characterised by a high rate of membership in representative organisations, with a unionisation rate of between 50% and 55% of the working population.[2] Furthermore, it is estimated that 76% of employers are affiliated with an employers' representative organisation.[3]

The Belgian model of social dialogue was forged in the aftermath of the Second World War. In 1944, the representatives of employers and workers concluded a Draft Agreement on Social Solidarity, a genuine founding text of both a comprehensive system of social security and social dialogue. The parties agreed to request the government to implement a series of emergency measures as soon as the country returns to independence. The aforementioned measures were designed to address the hardship endured by the majority of wage-earners during the occupation, as well as to facilitate the emergence of a renewed trend of social progress, driven by both the economic development of a pacified world and an equitable distribution of the income generated by increasing production. These emergency measures primarily concern the wage regime, the establishment of a comprehensive system of social security for workers based on national solidarity, and the restoration or introduction of methods of collaboration, based on parity, between employers' and workers' organisations. These measures, which were designed to enhance the material and moral well-being of the workers and to establish peaceful relations based on justice between them and the business leaders, were initially of a temporary nature due to the urgency of the situation. However, the Legislative Chambers were requested to grant them a definitive status as soon as possible.[4] This status was granted in the following years.

The institutional architecture appears to be sophisticated. Belgian law promotes social dialogue at multiple levels. For the sake of simplicity, only some of the levels and bodies of negotiation and consultation will be discussed here.

At the top of the institutional hierarchy is the National Labour Council.[5] The members of the National Labour Council are delegates from the most representative organisations of employers and workers. Its scope of action extends to all the sectors of activity and to the whole country. Its collective labour agreements address social issues

---

2. European Committee of Social Rights, *Conclusions 2022, Belgium*, p. 26 (available on https://rm.coe.int/conclusions-2022-belgium-f/1680aa9c8f).
3. E. Léonard & F. Pichault, 'Belgique: l'adaptation d'un "modèlè de concertation sociale', *in* D. Andolfatto & S. Contrepois (dir.), *Syndicats et dialogue social. Les modèles occidentaux à l'épreuve*, Brussels, Peter Lang, 2016, pp. 55-75.
4. The full text is available on http://www.ccecrb.fgov.be/txt/fr/1944.pdf.
5. Act of 29 May 1952 setting up the National Labour Council (*Belgian Official Journal*, 31 May 1952).

that in principle concern all companies in Belgium.[6] Additionally, the Central Economic Council[7] and the High Council for Prevention and Protection at Work, which both play an advisory role, also do exist at an interprofessional level.[8]

At the next level, i.e., sectors of activity, joint committees have been established, with multiple competences. Their scope of action extends to a sector of activity previously defined by a Royal Decree.[9]

Finally, at the company level, negotiation and consultation take place, in particular, within the works council and the trade union delegation. The works council is a joint body, whose employee representative delegation is constituted following social elections. It should only be established in companies that usually employ an average of at least one hundred employees.[10] If this threshold is not reached, the employer is not legally obliged to set up a works council. However, if requested by one or more workers' organisations, it may be required from the employer to allow a trade union delegation to function. The status of the latter is determined by means of collective labour agreements adopted by the National Labour Council[11] and by the joint committee to which the company belongs. The employer's obligation to allow a trade union delegation to function is subject to a minimum number of workers, which varies from one sector of activity to another.

Belgian law is characterised by a plurality of trade unions. The freedom of association allows for the creation of numerous professional organisations. Nevertheless, only those who are deemed to be representative (for which several conditions

---

6. Article 7 of the Act of 5 December 1968 on collective labour agreements and joint committees (*Belgian Official Journal*, 15 January 1969).
7. Established by the Act of 20 September 1948 on the organisation of the economy, it comprises about fifty full members presented jointly by trade unions and employers' organisations, along with three experts (Art. XIII.2. of the Code of Economic Law and the *Arrêté du Régent* of 28 December 1948 fixing the number of members of the Central Economic Council and determining the modalities for their presentation). Its mission is to bring to the attention of the Legislative Chambers, the Council of Ministers, one or more ministers or any other federal public body, either on its own initiative or at the request of these authorities and in the form of written reports, any opinions or proposals concerning problems related to the national economy. These opinions or proposals shall be adopted by consensus. In the absence of consensus, the opinion includes the different points of view expressed by its members (Art. XIII.1).
8. Established by a Royal Decree of 27 October 2006, the Higher Council for Prevention and Protection at Work is mainly composed of an equal number of representatives of employers' and workers' representative organisations and civil servants. It has a broad advisory role in the field of health, safety and well-being at work.
9. For example, the ceramics industry sector, the clothing and garment industry employees' sector, the food industry employees' sector, etc. (The list is available on https://www.fedris.be/sites/default/files/assets/FR/Statistiques/rubriques_codes/commissionsparitaires.pdf).
10. Article 2 of the Act of 28 July 2011 determining the applicable threshold for establishing works councils or renewal of their members at the time of social elections in 2012 (*Belgian Official Journal*, 31 August 2011). This act derogates from Art. 14, §1, of the Act of 20 September 1948 on the organisation of the economy (*Belgian Official Journal*, 27 September 1948).
11. Collective Labour Agreement No. 5 of 24 May 1971 concerning the status of trade union delegations of company staff (available on https://cnt-nar.be/sites/default/files/documents/CCT-COORD/cct-005.pdf).

must be met)[12] are entitled to sit in the aforementioned bodies. In reality, only three trade union organisations are considered representative.[13]

One of the prerogatives of workers' representative organisations is the conclusion of collective labour agreements. These may be concluded at the various levels of social dialogue: the National Labour Council, the joint committee or the company. When an employer is bound by a collective labour agreement, the agreement binds it to all its employees, whether or not they are members of a representative trade union. The hierarchy of collective labour agreements is regulated by law according to a pyramidal system.[14] This system establishes that a collective labour agreement at the company level may not derogate from a sectoral collective labour agreement, which itself may not derogate from an intersectoral collective labour agreement. The French *principe de faveur* (principle of the most favourable treatment) does not exist in Belgian law. Nevertheless, in the overwhelming majority of cases, a collective labour agreement sets out a minimum level of rights for workers, which can be increased by lower-ranking norms (individual or collective agreement).

In addition to these bodies, whose composition, operating rules and powers are defined by law,[15] there is an informal body, called the *Groupe des dix* (Group of Ten). The latter plays a key role in coordinating social dialogue. Since the 1960s, the practice has been established whereby[16] the Group of Ten concludes interprofessional agreements (*accords interprofessionnels,* hereinafter 'AIPs') every two years. These AIPs aim to ensure the equitable sharing of the fruits of growth and to foster the country's economic development. They cover various areas: working hours, flexibility, wage increases, workers training, etc. While AIPs have no binding legal status, they significantly influence much of the content of sectoral negotiations. Indeed, they morally bind the signatory parties, who will then negotiate, in the joint committees, collective agreements complying with the minimum conditions set out by the Group of Ten. From the perspective of trade unions, this mode of operation enhances the protection of employees in sectors where unions are weaker, securing advantages that would otherwise be unattainable through negotiations conducted solely at the sectoral level. From the perspective of employers, it ensures stability and social peace.[17]

As a result, a two-party system has been established at every level of the economy. The social partners meet in full autonomy, at their own discretion, to discuss

12. Article 2, §4, of the Act of 29 May 1952 setting up the National Labour Council.
13. These three organisations are the General Confederation of Christian Trade Unions, the General Federation of Labour of Belgium and the General Confederation of Liberal Trade Unions of Belgium.
14. Articles 10 and 51 of the Act of 5 December 1968.
15. With a nuance for the trade union delegation, as indicated above.
16. On several occasions, this practice has experienced periods of difficulty and even suspension (J. Vilrokx, 'De interprofessionele arbeidsverhoudingen in België in de jaren '90: een keerpunt', *Liber amicorum R. Blanpain,* Bruges, Die Keure, 1998, pp. 503-506; I. Cassiers & L. Denayer, 'Concertation sociale et transformations socio-économiques en Belgique, de 1944 à nos jours', *in* E. Arcq, M. Capron, E. Léonard & P. Reman, *Dynamiques de la concertation sociale,* Brussels, CRISP, 2010, p. 88).
17. M. Capron & P. Reman, 'Flexibilité : vers un modèle belge?', *La revue nouvelle,* 2006, Nos 7-8, p. 54; Léonard & Pichault, 'Belgique: l'adaptation d'un "modèlè de concertation sociale', *supra* n. 3, pp. 55-75.

subjects that they have chosen themselves. The State authority refrains from interfering in the process. It only provides a legal framework for social dialogue and its outcome, i.e., collective labour agreements. It also provides a significant logistical support; indeed, both the presidents of the National Labour Council and the joint committees are civil servants, as are the social conciliators, genuine 'mine-clearers' of social conflicts. Finally, the social partners participate, on a parity basis, in the management of the main social security institutions. They are also involved in the development of the country's social and economic policy. No bill on social law shall be adopted without the consultation of the Group of Ten and the National Labour Council.

Since 2008, interprofessional social dialogue has been 'deadlocked'.[18] The AIP concluded on 22 December 2008 was the result of very difficult negotiations. Since then, no such agreement has been concluded, except for the 2017-2018 period. As a consequence, the State authority has been compelled to intervene directly in areas that, until then, had been subject, if not exclusively, at least mainly to collective bargaining. For example, it has on several occasions adopted restrictive measures in the wage formation process. The aim was to control the evolution of wage costs, considered disadvantageous for Belgian companies compared to competing companies in neighbouring countries. These measures are part of a government policy in line with the expectations of the European authorities[19] and have been welcomed by the Council.[20] Nevertheless, they have almost always been accompanied by strong protests from the trade unions denouncing, among other things, a challenge to the traditional model of social dialogue. It should be noted, however, that the intervention of the State authority has made it possible to unblock collective bargaining at the interprofessional level and therefore, to restore it at the lower levels.

[B] The Wage Formation Process

The wage formation process is mainly based on collective bargaining. (i) An intersectoral collective labour agreement[21] guarantees a minimum average monthly wage for full-time adult workers (i.e., workers over 18 years of age). (ii) Within each sector of activity, joint committees conclude collective labour agreements that determine the minimum wage according to the function, the qualification requirements, the work experience, etc. The amount of this wage should be higher than the guaranteed minimum average monthly income. (iii) Sectoral collective labour agreements also

18. M. Capron, B. Conter & J. Faniel, 'Belgique. La concertation sociale interprofessionnelle grippée', *Chroniques internationales de l'IRES*, No. 141, 2013, pp. 3 et seq.
19. Recommendation of the Council of 13 May 2015 on the National Reform Programme of Belgium for 2015 and delivering Council opinion on the Stability Programme of Belgium for 2015 COM(2015)252.
20. Recommendation of the Council of 11 July 2017 on the National Reform Programme of Belgium for 2017 and delivering Council opinion on the Stability Programme of Belgium for 2017 (2017/C 261/01), recital 13, available on https://eur-lex.europa.eu/legal-content/FR/TXT/PDF/?uri=CELEX:32017H0809(01)&from=NL.
21. Collective Labour Agreement No. 43 of 2 May 1988 (available on https://cnt-nar.be/sites/default/files/documents/fr/cct-043_1.pdf).

provide for the automatic indexation of wages based on the evolution of the price index (*see* below). (iv) Finally, companies can conclude collective labour agreements that provide for higher wages than those set by the sectoral collective labour agreement. The scope for individual autonomy is very limited: contractual clauses must, under pain of nullity, be compatible with the minimum amounts set at the collective level.[22]

The evolution of wages as a result of collective bargaining is essentially linked to three parameters:

(a) *Salary scale increases*: As a worker climbs the seniority and qualification ladders, his or her reference salary increases. These increases, known as 'scales increases', are compulsory for employers.
(b) *Automatic indexation*: Belgium is the only country, or one of the only countries, with a system of automatic, generalised wage indexation. According to our information, Denmark, the Netherlands, and France abolished automatic indexation systems for all wages in 1982-1983. Italy did the same in 1993. In France, Malta and Slovenia, indexation applies only to the minimum wages. In Luxembourg, it has been capped since 2022 while, in Cyprus, indexation has been partial since 2018.[23] Although the link between wages and the price index is widespread in Belgium, it is not imposed by a State regulation. It is the result of collective bargaining and is generally organised through sectoral collective labour agreements, which freely determine the frequency of indexation as well as its formula.[24] Its existence depends solely on the agreement of the social partners. Thus, to end it, it would be sufficient for a single signatory employers' organisation to withdraw from it.
(c) *Sharing the fruits of growth*: Other wage increases can be granted to workers, either on a one-off basis (extraordinary bonus) or on a recurring basis. These can be in the form of a sum of money or a benefit in kind (i.e., a non-monetary benefit). In Belgium, it is customary to negotiate a collective wage increase every two years, in order to share the fruits of growth.

This process must also consider the wage moderation scheme laid down in an Act of 26 July 1996.

§11.02 WAGE MODERATION

The supervision of collective bargaining had already been encountered in the past, in the context of the economic crisis following the first oil shock. The sharp increase in

22. Article 11 of the Act of 5 December 1968.
23. Central Economic Council, *Opinion of 20 December 2023 on the recommendations made to the Belgian government by the Committee on Freedom of Association of the International Labour Organization on the 1996 Act*, p. 4.
24. For illustrations, cons. B. Conter & J. Faniel, 'Hausse des salaires nominaux, aides publiques ponctuelles et perte de pouvoir d'achat', *Chronique internationale de l'Ires*, 2022/4, No. 180, pp. 4-5.

production costs, directly or indirectly linked to the price of oil, threatened the competitiveness of Belgian companies. This was due not only to the increase in energy costs but also to wage costs since, as a reminder, wages are linked to the evolution of the consumer price index, which includes fuels. The export-oriented Belgian economy has faced serious issues of underemployment. From 1976 onwards, the State authority adopted numerous measures to control wage amounts: wage freezes, indexation freezes or both simultaneously.[25] In 1982, in support of the devaluation of the Belgian franc, a competitiveness standard was adopted: wage costs could not increase by more than the weighted average of Belgium's main trading partners.

Although wage negotiations regained a certain degree of freedom from 1987 onwards, the idea of a framework for the wage formation process persisted. A first legal framework was provided by the Act of 6 January 1989 on the safeguarding of the country's competitiveness,[26] which laid down the criteria and procedure for the assessment of competitiveness by the social partners.[27]

This framework became obsolete by Belgium's entry into the monetary union, which deprived the authorities of the possibility to make macroeconomic adjustments by adjusting the exchange and interest rates. In order to prevent the lack of competitiveness from having a very negative impact on the employment rate, a policy designed to control wage costs[28] was implemented through the Act of 26 July 1996 on the promotion of employment and the preventive safeguarding of competitiveness.[29] The content of the law had been negotiated with the social partners and its main concern was to maintain employment, or even to create new jobs.[30]

---

25. Act of 30 March 1976 on economic recovery measures (*Belgian Official Journal*, 1 April 1976); Act of 23 December 1980 on precautionary and transitional measures for the moderation of all wages (*Belgian Official Journal*, 25 December 1980) and the Act of 10 February 1981 on the adjustment of wage moderation (Belgian *Official Journal*, 14 February 1981); Act of 2 February 1982 conferring certain special powers on the King (*Belgian Official Journal*, 4 February 1982) and Royal Decrees Nos 11 and 180 (*Belgian Official Journal*, 18 January 1983); Act of 11 April 1983 on fiscal and budgetary provisions (*Belgian Official Journal*, 16 April 1983) and Royal Decree No. 278 (*Belgian Official* Journal of 7 April 1984); Act of 22 January 1985 on recovery containing social provisions (*Belgian Official Journal*, 24 January 1985).
26. *Belgian Official Journal*, 31 January 1989.
27. Furthermore, a new index has been adopted as an instrument for wage indexation: the health index. It is obtained by subtracting certain products from the consumer price index basket, namely alcoholic beverages, tobacco, petrol and diesel (the effects of certain contributions and taxes are also excluded). Since then, individual or collective agreements providing for wage indexation must refer to this index (Art. 2 of the Royal Decree of 24 December 1993 implementing the Act of 6 January 1989 on safeguarding the country's competitiveness (*Belgian Official Journal*, 31 December 1993), confirmed by an Act of 30 March 1994).
28. *See* the graph reproduced *in* E. Doutrepont, *Formation salariale et concertation collective en Belgique*, Bruges, La Charte, 2009, p. 54, illustrating the fact that the employment rate in Belgium is directly dependent on the difference between the cost of Belgian labour and that of neighbouring countries, which are also our main competitors.
29. *Belgian Official Journal.*, 1 August 1996.
30. *Parl. Doc.*, Chamber, 1995-1996, No. 49-609/1, pp. 1 et seq. and No. 49-609/9, p. 205; R. Plasman, M. Rusinek, F. Rycx & I. Tojerow, *La structure des salaires en Belgique*, Novembre 2007, p. 61, available on https://www.researchgate.net/publication/4800931_La_structure_des_salaires_en_Belgique.

The means used is a mechanism which, through the coordination of social dialogue,[31] aims to preventively control the evolution of wages and to prevent the average hourly wage cost in Belgium from rising faster than in neighbouring countries (France, Germany, and the Netherlands). Since 2017, under the influence of the recommendations of the Council of the European Union,[32] these objectives have been supplemented by the objective of eliminating the wage gap with the aforementioned countries accumulated since 1996. The social partners are now obliged to ensure that real wage growth is lower than that of the reference countries until this wage handicap is eliminated.

The legality of this mechanism, which is quite elaborate [A], is challenged by the trade unions, which see it as an unjustified interference in the right to collective bargaining [B].

[A] Description of the Mechanism

[1] The Procedure

Every two years, the representative organisations, meeting at the interprofessional level, shall determine a margin for an increase in wage costs (hereinafter referred to as 'the margin').

The negotiations between the social partners are preceded by a report drawn up by the Central Economic Council.[33] This report is divided into two parts. The first part comes from the Council secretariat, an independent body composed of economists and accounting professionals (which means that the social partners are not part of it).[34] This part of the report contains an analysis of the wage cost handicap[35] as well as the maximum margin *available* for the evolution of wage costs. It is drawn up in accordance with the – highly technical – guidelines laid down in the law. To achieve this, the secretariat takes into account the forecasts for the evolution of wage costs in the reference States (France, Germany, and the Netherlands) over the next two years.

31. *Parl. Doc.*, Senate, 1995-1996, No. 1-386/4, p. 16; Doutrepont, *supra* n. 28, pp. 56 et seq.
32. Recommendation of the Council of 13 May 2015 on the National Reform Programme of Belgium for 2015 and delivering Council opinion on the Stability Programme of Belgium for 2015 COM(2015)252. Cons. F. Dorssemont, 'Wage setting and wage moderation in Belgium: A never-ending and already-old story in the wake of the "new European economic governance"', *European Labour law Journal*, Vol. 13 (2022), No. 2, pp. 156-169 https://doi.org/10.1177/20319525221093488.
33. Article 5 of the Act of 26 July 1996.
34. Article XIII.5 of the Code of Economic Law.
35. Wage costs are defined by reference to European Regulation 549/2013. They refer to the total remuneration, in cash or in kind, that employers pay to their employees for the work done during the accounting reference period, as mentioned in Annex A, Chapter 4, point 4.02 of Regulation 549/2013 of 21 May 2013 of the European Parliament and of the Council on the European System of National and Regional Accounts in the European Union (Art. 2 of the Act of 26 July 1996).

The second part of the report, which comes from employers' and workers' representatives, includes an analysis of the wage and employment policies of the reference States, as well as the factors that could explain any divergent evolution compared to Belgium. This section also addresses the structural aspects of competitiveness and employment.[36]

The report is then transmitted to the House of Representatives, the government, and the social partners.

Thereafter, the Group of Ten starts negotiations on the AIP, which must be concluded by 15 January of odd-numbered years at the latest. The AIP sets out, among other things, measures to promote employment as well as the maximum margin for the evolution of wage costs for the next two years, which may not exceed the available margin determined by the Central Economic Council. This margin is then transposed into a collective labour agreement of the National Labour Council, thus acquiring the value of a legal rule.[37]

If no agreement is reached within two months of the Central Economic Council report, or more precisely 'in the absence of consensus', the government attempts mediation. In the event of failure, the government itself decides on the margin, which cannot exceed the available margin determined by the Central Economic Council.[38]

As we have seen, during the bilateral negotiations, the social partners have the possibility to take the government out of the game, by reaching an agreement on the margin. The government cannot oppose the social partners' agreement; it can only compensate for the absence of an agreement. Furthermore, if the government itself sets the margin, it cannot affect indexation and scale increases that result from sectoral collective agreements.[39]

Once the maximum margin has been set, negotiations on the development of wage costs are then carried out at the lower levels. During the first year of the period covered by the AIP, collective labour agreements are concluded at sectoral or company level in order to decide on the evolution of wage costs - which may not exceed the negotiated margin - for a two-year period.[40,41]

36. Article 5, §3, of the Act of 26 July 1996.
37. Article 6 of the Act of 26 July 1996.
38. Article 6, §3, and Art. 7 of the Act of 26 July 1996.
39. Articles 7 and 8 of the Act of 26 July 1996.
40. Article 8 of the Act of 26 July 1996.
41. In the autumn of the first of the two years of application, the Central Economic Council updates its report on labour costs, which may lead to the obligation to apply a corrective mechanism if the development of wage costs in Belgium is higher than in our neighbours. This exceedance of the forecasts is noted by the social partners who apply the correction mechanism; if they fail to do so, the State again plays the role of mediator and, if this mission fails, it may itself impose the correction of the margin (Arts 11 to 13 of the Act of 26 July 1996).

[2] The Content of the Interprofessional Agreement

The AIP does not decide on the evolution of wages but on the margin of evolution.[42] Moreover, it is not the salary itself that is at issue but the 'wage cost', which includes, among other things, the charges that weigh on the salary.[43]

The margin is globally defined in the AIP. The same margin applies to all industries, regardless of their performance degree or exposure to international competition.[44] It is therefore a macroeconomic concept. Furthermore, it is not a percentage (or an amount) that has necessarily to be allocated.[45] Rather, it is a framework for wage bargaining: an envelope available to sectors and companies to negotiate wage increases and other one-off or recurring benefits, whether or not subject to social security contributions.

Although the margin is defined globally, it is generally accepted that compliance with it should not be assessed at the level of the private sector as a whole, nor at the level of the sector of activity or for each individual worker. Instead, it is at the company level that compliance with the margin must be verified, for its whole wage cost.[46]

Since 2017, the bargaining room for the social partners has been significantly reduced. Indeed, in order to lower the wage handicap accumulated since 1996, the available margin has been reduced by a safety margin of at least 0.5% to neutralise forecasting errors (i.e., higher inflation in Belgium or a lower-than-expected wage increase in neighbouring countries). In addition, a correction mechanism has been introduced. This mechanism results from a complex economic calculation that increases or decreases the maximum margin available depending on the extent of wage cost handicap.[47]

According to Article 6, §2 of the 1996 Act, the margin does not affect indexation or wage scale increases, i.e., those resulting from promotions or changes in individual categories. Even if the margin is set at 0%, the indexation and the wage scale increases resulting from collective labour agreements are preserved.[48]

42. The wage increase in Belgium and in the reference States is based on data and forecasts from the Institute of National Accounts and on available official national and international sources (Art. 2 of the Act of 26 July 1996).
43. Wage costs include not only gross salary but also bonuses, holiday pay, guaranteed wages in the event of sickness, meal vouchers, employer contributions, etc. Certain compensatory benefits are excluded from the concept of wage costs, such as profit-sharing (Art. 10 of the Act of 26 July 1996).
44. V. Bodart, L. Jacquet & B. Van der Linden, 'Salaires et norme salariale en Belgique', *Regards économiques*, 2002, n° 6, pp. 2 & 3.
45. Doutrepont, *supra* n. 28, p. 72.
46. Not. O. Debray, 'Les mesures de modération salariale', *Orientations*, 1997, p. 123; W. van Eeckhoutte & V. Neuprez, *Compendium social. Droit du travail*, Diegem, Kluwer, 2015-2016, t. 2, p. 1373, No. 2567. This is also the view of the administration (https://emploi.belgique.be/fr/themes/remuneration/norme-salariale).
47. Article 5, §2, of the Act of 26 July 1996.
48. The situation may be different when, as in 2015, the legislator itself derogates from this principle by organising an index jump (Arts 2 to 2*quater* of the Act of 23 April 2015 on the promotion of employment, *Belgian Official Journal*, 27 April 2015).

This guarantee helps to explain the recurrent difficulties in keeping Belgian wage costs close to those of the reference countries. It may seem paradoxical in some respects, or at least the source of a vicious circle. Automatic indexation, which preserves the purchasing power of workers has no equivalent in the three reference countries. This indexation has thus the effect of widening the gap between wage costs in these countries and those in Belgium. Moreover, in times of inflation, it reduces to zero the margin available for wage increases that would result from a sharing of the fruits of growth.

As we can see, the 1996 Act locks in wage collective bargaining, both upwards (principle of the maximum margin) and downwards (indexation and guaranteed salary scale increases).

[3] The Impact of Crises

The determination of wages under this framework proceeded nearly without a hitch until 2008. Negotiations almost always[49] resulted in an AIP.[50] It should be noted that, in many respects, the social partners have taken liberties with the law. In 1996, the margin was conceived by the legislator as a limit to be imposed on the sectors in wage negotiations and to which employers had to comply under the threat of repressive sanctions. In most cases, however, the interprofessional agreements have qualified the margin as indicative, giving the social partners the freedom to negotiate increases above the margin. It was more like a cautionary message in wage bargaining rather than a legal norm.[51]

It was also pointed out that, while the margin should be set uniformly for the whole private sector, the social partners had provided for two different margins for the period 2001-2002. The highest margin was for sectors that had performed well in the previous two years.[52]

This practice undermined the effectiveness of the Act of 26 July 1996. For a violation of the margin to be established, the margin must be a real limit. However, when it was declared 'indicative' by the authors of the agreement, it was conceptually

49. Social partners were unable to reach an agreement in the first period following the entry into force of the law; it was a Royal Decree of 20 December 1996 which fixed the margin for 1997 and 1998 (*Belgian Official Journal*, 31 December 1996, p. 32357). There was no interprofessional agreement in 2005-2006, but the government preferred not to take action to determine the margin, leaving sectoral negotiations free.
50. The texts are available on https://cnt-nar.be/fr/about-cnt/groupe-des-10-et-accords-interprofessionnels.
51. Bodart, Jacquet & Van der Linden, 'Salaires et norme salariale en Belgique', *supra* n. 44, p. 9; Doutrepont, *supra* n. 28, p. 58; K. Magerman, 'De maximale marge voor loonkostenontwikkeling voor 2011-2012', *Orientaties*, 2011/6, p. 173; I. Ficher, 'L'accord interprofessionnel a-t-il une place parmi les sources de droit du travail?', *Les sources du droit revisitées*, vol. 2, Bruxelles, Presses de l'Université Saint-Louis, 2012, pp. 426-427.
52. Bodart, Jacquet & Van der Linden, 'Salaires et norme salariale en Belgique', *supra* n. 44, p. 3.

impossible to establish an infringement.[53] The lack of effectiveness of the Act of 26 July 1996 that lasted for a dozen years can also be partly explained by the difficulty of punishing its non-compliance with civil law sanctions. The nullity sanction is difficult to handle, whether in the case of collective or individual agreements.[54] In cases where the margin is exceeded,[55] absolute nullity can only be invoked once it has been demonstrated, at the end of the two-year period, that the average cost per worker has increased. In the meantime, and unless the unlawfulness of the wage increase is obvious, which is not often, the employer is required to pay the benefits prescribed by the collective or individual norms.[56]

Since the economic crisis of 2008, the negotiation process has stalled.

[a] *The Impact of the Financial Crisis*

At the end of 2008, negotiations for the interprofessional agreement for the period 2009-2010 started. An agreement was finally reached only because the government agreed to inject a significant amount of money into the negotiations. The – very low – increase margin was declared mandatory and identical for all sectors ... but at least, there was an agreement.

Subsequently, despite government mediation,[57] the social partners were unable to reach a consensus. As provided for by law, the State authority took over. Two Royal Decrees were adopted on 28 March 2011 and 28 April 2013.[58] They set mandatory and uniform margins for all sectors. The first decree set the margin at 0.3% for 2011 and 2012, increased, where applicable, by indexation and scale increases, specifying that it corresponded to a margin of 0% for 2011 and 0.3% for 2012. The second decree set the margin at 0% for the years 2013 and 2014, also increased, where applicable, by indexation and scale increases. For the period 2015-2016, for technical reasons, the

53. Until March 2007, there was only one report, which was closed without further action (*Doc. parl.*, Chambre, 2006-2007, n° 51-3059/001, p. 248). It does not seem that there were any others thereafter.
54. J. Vanthournout & P. Humblet, *Loonmatiging en de loonnorm 2011-2012*, Ghent, Story Publishers, 2011, pp. 99-104.
55. M. De Vos, *Loon naar Belgisch recht arbeidsovereenkomstrecht: Rechtspositie, recht op loon, loonbegrip*, Antwerp, Maklu, 2000, pp. 218-227.
56. Rather, the administration exercises control over the conformity of sectoral collective agreements with regard to the margin by refusing to grant the extension of the binding force by Royal Decree that (P. Humblet, 'Het IPA: exponent van het tripartisme?', *Nouvelle Revue du travail*, 2012, p. 53).
57. The 2011-2012 draft agreement, drawn up by the Group of Ten, was rejected by the trade unions members. Two years later, the unions refused to enter into negotiations because the government itself had set a narrow framework in advance. For 2015-2016, the draft agreement of the Group of Ten was rejected by one of the trade unions and accepted by the others as well as by the employers' organisations. The Act of 28 April 2015 follows this draft agreement.
58. *Belgian Official Journal*, 1 April 2011 and 2 May 2013.

margin was set at 0% for 2015 and 0.8% for 2016[59] by law[60] rather than by Royal Decree.

Once this margin had been established by the State authority, wage negotiations could resume at the sectoral and/or company levels.

It can therefore be observed that the crisis has led to a freeze in interprofessional collective bargaining. The intervention of the State authority in wage bargaining made it possible to unlock the situation, thanks to an interventionist mechanism conceived long ago but which only had to be resorted after the economic crisis that began in 2008.[61]

On a more ad hoc basis, the State authority organised, through an Act of 23 April 2015,[62] an index jump of 2%, paralysing for a few months the operation of collective labour agreements related to the linking of remuneration to the price index. The purpose of this act was to reduce the wage gap that has widened compared to our neighbouring countries through wage indexation, which these reference States do not have - or at least not in the same way - and which has always been preserved since the Act of 26 July 1996 came into force.[63]

[b] A Glimmer of Hope in 2017-2018

Despite the legislative changes of 2017 providing a more structured framework for the negotiation of the margin, an agreement between the social partners was reached around a maximum margin of 1.1%.[64] This agreement offered a touch of optimism for a return to the 'Belgian-style' consultation. However, the optimism was short-lived as it was the last time the social partners managed to agree on a maximum margin. Since then, the revision of the law has been criticised by the trade unions, which have called for its repeal.

During the period 2019-2020, advanced negotiations were expected to lead to an agreement on a margin of 1.1%, following government mediation. Nevertheless, in the final stages, one of the three unions refused to agree, leading to the government setting the margin at 1.1% through a Royal Decree.[65]

59. The 0.8% corresponds to 0.5% of the gross wage bill increased by 0.3% of the net wage bill (Art. 2 of the Act of 28 April 2015).
60. Act of 28 April 2015 establishing the maximum margin for the evolution of wage costs for the years 2015 and 2016 (*Belgian Official Journal*, 30 April 2015).
61. Except for the very first period following the entry into force of the law; it was the Royal Decree of 20 December 1996 which set the margin for the years 1997 and 1998.
62. Act of 23 April 2015 on the promotion of employment (*Belgian Official Journal*, 27 April 2015).
63. National Bank of Belgium, *Indexation en Belgique: ampleur, nature et conséquences pour l'économie et alternatives possibles*, 28 June 2012; V. Bodart & F. Shadman, 'Indexation et compétitivité en Belgique', *Regards économiques*, 2013, No. 107, p. 4.
64. According to some observers, the success of this latest agreement is due to the need of the three unions to reaffirm the effectiveness of social dialogue (B. Conter & J. Faniel, 'Une sortie de pandémie sans modification du carcan salarial', *Chronique Internationale de l'IRES*, Vol. 177 (2022), No. 1, p. 30).
65. Royal Decree of 19 April 2019 implementing Art. 7, §1, of the Act of 26 July 1996 on the promotion of employment and the safeguarding of competitiveness (*Belgian Official Journal*, 24 April 2019).

[c] *Health and Energy Crises*

At the time of the preparation of the 2021-2022 AIP, the COVID-19 health crisis made it difficult for the Central Economic Council to forecast the evolution of wage costs in the reference States. In the end, the available margin was estimated at 0.4%. The small margin for negotiation has provoked strong protests from the trade union side. Despite government mediation, no agreement could be reached, leading the government itself to set the margin at 0.4%.[66] However, not all companies suffered from the health crisis and some of them even made profits (e.g., vaccine manufacturers). The law therefore allowed them to grant their workers an exceptional 'corona bonus'. Its amount could not exceed EUR 500 and was given in the form of a voucher to be spent in establishments particularly affected by the lockdowns (restaurants, wellness centers, cinemas, etc.).[67]

The social partners have also failed to reach an agreement for 2023-2024. The high inflation following the energy crisis has led to a historic loss of purchasing power in the eurozone[68] while in Belgium, it has led to a wage indexation of around 10%. The timing of indexation has varied according to the sector of activity, which depends on the applicable collective labour agreement.[69] Indexation has certainly - partially - reduced and delayed the loss of purchasing power of Belgian workers. Moreover, as in other countries, Belgian workers also benefited from one-off measures to reduce energy costs. However, the automatic indexation of wages has widened the competitiveness gap with neighbouring countries. In its report of October 2022, the Central Economic Council noted, by cross-referencing the macroeconomic forecasts of the central banks, that, over the period 2020-2024, the growth gap in hourly wage costs between Belgium and the reference States would be 5.7%. This suggests that it would be impossible to

---

66. Royal Decree of 30 July 2021 implementing Art. 7, §1, of the Act of 26 July 1996 on the promotion of employment and the safeguarding of competitiveness (*Belgian Official* Journal, 9 August 2021). Royal Decree No. 45 of 26 June 2020 issued pursuant to Art. 5, §1, 5° of the Act of 27 March 2020 granting powers to the King to take measures in the fight against the spread of the coronavirus COVID-19 (II) aimed at extending certain measures, specifying certain detailed rules of corona parental leave and consumption vouchers (*Belgian Official Journal*, 30 June 2020).
67. Articles 56 to 67 of the Act of 18 July 2021 on temporary support measures due to the COVID-19 pandemic (*Belgian Official Journal*, 29 July 2021).
68. A. Math, 'Inflation, salaires. Réponses des États, revendications des salariés', *Chronique internationale de l'Ires*, 2022/4, n° 180, pp. 3-36.
69. For example, for the Guaranteed Average Minimum Monthly Income, seven indexations of 2% were applied in 2022 and 2023, according to the following schedule:

    - 1/1/2022: 2%
    - 1/3/2022: 2%
    - 1/5/2022: 2%
    - 1/8/2022: 2%
    - 1/11/2022: 2%
    - 1/12/2022: 2%
    - 1/11/2023: 2%

    (*source*: European Committee of Social Rights, *Ad hoc report on the cost-of-living crisis submitted by the Government of Belgium*, 21 December 2023, p. 9, available on https://rm.coe.int/belgium-ad-hoc-report-on-the-cost-of-living-crisis/1680ae13fb).

negotiate wage increases for several years, unless German, French and Dutch wages rise sharply in the meantime. In this highly unfavourable economic context in terms of competitiveness, the Central Economic Council has set the available margin at 0%. In other words, there was no room for negotiations over wage increases. This led to a deadlock in collective bargaining. As a result, the State authority took over and imposed a margin of 0%, while maintaining indexation and scale increases.[70] However, some companies, far from suffering from the crisis, had made significant profits in 2022 and could – and sometimes even wanted to – offer wage increases to their employees in the following two years. The law therefore authorised the granting of an exceptional bonus known as 'purchasing power bonus' of a maximum amount of EUR 750. It could only be granted in the form of a voucher that had to be used for specific expenses, aiming to support consumption and contribute to the economic recovery from the energy crisis aggravated by rising inflation and the outbreak of the war in Ukraine.[71] Such a system has a limited impact in time, unlike a wage increase, which has a lasting effect.

Summary table:

Period	*Legal Standard*	*Margin*	*Remark*
2009-2010	AIP	EUR 250	
2011-2012	Royal Decree	0.3%	0% in 2011 and 0.3% in 2012
2013-2014	Royal Decree	0%	Royal Decree
2015-2016	Act	0.8%	0% in 2015 and 0.8% in 2016 Index jump of 2% in 2015
2017-2018	AIP and collective labour agreement of the National Labour Council	1.1%	
2019-2020	Royal Decree	1.1%	
2021-2022	Royal Decree	0.4%	Possibility of a 'Corona bonus' of up to EUR 500

70. Royal Decree of 13 May 2023 implementing Art. 7, §1 of the Act of 26 July 1996 on the promotion of employment and the safeguarding of competitiveness (*Belgian Official Journal* of 26 May 2023).
71. Act of 24 May 2023 on measures relating to wage negotiations for the period 2023-2024 (*Belgian Official Journal*, 31 May 2023) and Royal Decree of 23 April 2023 on the purchasing power bonus (*Belgian Official Journal*, 28 April 2023).

Period	Legal Standard	Margin	Remark
2023-2024	Royal Decree	0%	Possibility of a 'purchasing power bonus' of up to EUR 750

[B] Legality of State Intervention

The intervention of the State authority in wage negotiations has been criticised, particularly by the trade unions. They argue that it is an unjustified infringement of freedom of association. Indeed, according to them, collective labour agreements should be free to regulate wages and their evolution. By not giving the social partners exclusive competence to decide on wages and by allowing the State authority to do so itself, does the Belgian law violate the right to collective bargaining enshrined in supra-legislative rules, such as the Belgian Constitution and the law of the International Labour Organization (ILO) and the Council of Europe[72]? In its version prior to the 2017 amendment, the Belgian wage moderation system was considered compatible with the right to collective bargaining by all the bodies that evaluated it. However, it is questionable whether an opinion of the Committee on Freedom of Association that was issued in 2022 on the amendment made in 2017 could change the situation.

[1] Legality under ILO Law

Article 4 of the ILO Convention No. 98 on Right to Organise and Collective Bargaining (1949)[73] states that: 'Measures appropriate to national conditions shall be taken, where necessary, to encourage and promote the full development and utilisation of machinery for voluntary negotiation between employers or employers' organisations and workers' organisations, with a view to the regulation of terms and conditions of employment by means of collective agreements.'[74] The purpose of this provision is to prevent trade union action from being hampered by a systematic refusal by employers or employers' organisations to negotiate.[75]

The 1996 Act may be problematic on different points. First, this act forces the social partners meeting at the interprofessional level to negotiate a margin, under the

72. Compliance with Article 12 of the Charter of Fundamental Rights of the European Union or Art. 8 of the International Covenant on Economic, Social and Cultural Rights could also be examined.
73. This Convention does not have the same purpose as Convention No. 87 on Freedom of Association; the latter protects professional organisations vis-à-vis State authority, while Convention No. 98 aims to prevent interference by employers' and workers' organisations with each other (N. Valticos, *Droit international du travail*, 2nd ed., Paris, Dalloz, 1983, p. 256).
74. In 1981, the protection of Convention No. 98 was complemented by Convention No. 154 on Collective Bargaining and by Recommendation No. 163 concerning the Promotion of Collective Bargaining.
75. Valticos, *Droit international du travail*, *supra* n. 73, p. 258.

threat that the government will set it itself. In doing so, it undermines the voluntary nature of the negotiations, which can be seen as a violation – although not necessarily unjustified and disproportionate – of the 'voluntary' right to negotiate referred to in Article 4 of Convention No. 98.[76] However, this is not the element that attracts the attention of the supervisory bodies of the ILO Conventions.

The position of the Committee on Freedom of Association – which is not a court but whose positions are likely to influence States or the supervisory bodies of other instruments in their interpretative work – on wage moderation measures is as follows: 'If, as part of its stabilization policy, a government considers that wage rates cannot be settled freely through collective bargaining, such a restriction should be imposed as an exceptional measure and only to the extent that is necessary, without exceeding a reasonable period, and it should be accompanied by adequate safeguards to protect workers living standards.'[77] If these conditions are not met, the right of trade unions to negotiate freely with employers and their organisations would be unjustifiably restricted. As for the duration of the restriction, a period of three years seems to be the maximum.[78] The Committee adds that 'This principle is all the more important because successive restrictions may lead to a prolonged suspension of wage negotiations, which goes against the principle of encouraging voluntary collective negotiation.'[79] For example, in its 1985 report, the ILO Committee of Experts on the Application of Conventions and Recommendations observed, regarding Belgium, that government intervention in the field of collective bargaining, when it lasts for several years, impairs the rights of workers and employers to freely negotiate their terms and conditions of employment.[80] In 1987, the Committee noted with satisfaction that the social partners had regained their full freedom to negotiate since 1 January 1987.[81]

Subsequently, on several occasions (2011, 2013, 2014), workers' representative organisations submitted to the ILO bodies their comments on the determination of the maximum margin for wage increases under Belgian law. The Commission has addressed two direct requests to Belgium[82] but has not yet made any observations on the application of Convention No. 98.

---

76. On the substance of this right, *see*. B. Gernigon, A. Odero & H. Guido, 'ILO principles concerning collective bargaining', *International Labour Review*, Vol. 139 (2000), No. 1, pp. 40 et seq. https://doi.org/10.1111/j.1564-913x.2000.tb00401.x; C. Vargha, 'La négociation collective', *in* J.-M. Thouvenin & A. Trebilcock (dir.), *Droit international social*, t. 2, Brussels, Bruylant, p. 1047.
77. I.L.O., *Compilation of Decisions of the Committee on Freedom of Association*, 6th ed., Geneva, 2018, §1456, available on https://normlex.ilo.org/dyn/normlex/en/f?p=NORMLEXPUB:70002:0::NO:70002:P70002_HIER_ELEMENT_ID,P70002_HIER_LEVEL:3947747,1.
78. *Ibid.*, §1457.
79. *Ibid.*, §1461.
80. International Labour Conference, *Report of the Committee of Experts on the Application of Conventions and Recommendations*, Geneva, 1985, 71st session, Report III (Parts 1, 2 and 3), p. 216.
81. International Labour Conference, *Report of the Committee of Experts on the Application of Conventions and Recommendations*, Geneva, 1987, 76th session, Report III (Part 4A), p. 263. Q. Detienne, 'La Belgique et les conventions internationales du travail', *J.T.T.*, 2014, p. 335.
82. International Labour Conference, *Report of the Committee of Experts on the Application of Conventions and Recommendations*, Geneva, 2012, 101st session, Report III (Part II), p. 241, and 2014, 103rd session, Report III (Part II), p. 129.

At the end of 2021, the Committee on Freedom of Association received a complaint initiated by trade union organisations, which considered that, since the 2017 amendment, the law 'drastically limits the possibility for the social partners to freely negotiate wage increases for workers in the private sector', in violation of Conventions Nos 98 and 154. The Committee agreed with them on two points. First, while taking into account the tradition of social dialogue in Belgium, the Committee considers that the system in place significantly restricts the ability of the social partners to negotiate autonomously the evolution of wage levels in the private sector. Indeed, in the Committee's view, it is up to the parties to negotiate the criteria to be taken into account when setting wages (increase in the cost of living, productivity, etc.). Second, it considers that the temporary nature of the restriction is only apparent because, since the 2017 revision, the criteria for determining the wage margin are laid down by law for an indefinite period of time (i.e., until the wage handicap is eliminated). The Committee therefore recommended asking the Belgian government 'to take, in full consultation with the social partners, the necessary steps to ensure that the social partners are able to freely determine the criteria on which to base their negotiations on wage increases at the intersectoral level, and the results of those negotiations'.[83]

The government then sought the opinion of the social partners. Unsurprisingly, the trade union organisations agreed with the Committee's recommendations. On their side, the employers' organisations disagreed, attributing the criticised restrictions to the inflation crisis. Indeed, according to them, under normal economic conditions, the social partners will regain the freedom to negotiate a positive margin for wage evolution. However, they are open to a revision of the law – which also restricts their freedom to negotiate downwards – as long as it goes hand in hand with the deletion of the automatic nature of wage indexation. In this way, Belgian employers, like their counterparts in the reference countries, could negotiate an overall increase every two years that would cover both the maintenance of purchasing power and a real increase in wages.[84] It is already certain that the opening of such a legislative project – if it were to materialise – would lead to very significant social tensions that no government wishes to face.

[2] Legality under Council of Europe Law

Article 6, §2, of the Revised European Social Charter, seeks to ensure the effective exercise of the right to collective bargaining. In the view of the European Committee of Social Rights, the intervention of the State authority in the determination of wages is likely to jeopardise this right. However, in order to achieve a recovery for a particularly serious situation, the government must be able to impose certain restrictions on

83. I.L.O., 400th Report of the Committee on Freedom of Association, GB.346/INS/15, 9 November 2022, §§110-149.

84. Central Economic Council, Opinion Nos 2023-2925 of 20 December 2023, p. 10, available on https://www.ccecrb.fgov.be/home/fr. Cons. not. B. Van der Linden, 'L'inflation actuelle en Belgique requiert une réaction collective équilibrée', *Regards économiques*, 2022, No. 175, pp. 1-9.

collective bargaining, in particular on wage increases. Nevertheless, such restrictions should only be imposed following a wide consultation with all interested parties, including trade unions and employers' organisations. They must also be exceptional and temporary.[85] Additionally, they should only be used when there is evidence that other measures would not produce the same effects.[86]

The law of some countries has been declared by the Committee to be incompatible with Article 6, §2, because the implementation of the restriction was not preceded by consultations and has led to a total suspension of negotiations (Iceland)[87] or because the application of the law was not linked to a particularly serious economic situation and was not limited to a short period of time (the Netherlands).[88]

However, the Belgian situation, as it results from the application of the Act of 26 July 1996, was declared to be in conformity with Article 6, §2, of the Charter by the Committee in its conclusions of 5 December 2014.[89]

Subsequently, in the context of the national reporting procedure, the Committee requested information from the Belgian government on the revision of the act carried out in 2017. This request was not made on the basis of a specific question concerning Article 6, §2, but following observations made by third parties (trade unions) and in light of the above-mentioned conclusions of the Committee on Freedom of Association. Pending the information requested, the Committee postponed its conclusion.[90]

The freedom of association enshrined in Article 11 of the European Convention on Human Rights also includes the right to bargain collectively with the employer and to conclude collective agreements. This principle is illustrated in two judgments of the European Court of Human Rights, *Demir and Baykara v. Turkey* and *Sindicatul Păstorul cel Bun v. Romania.*[91] Although Belgian law has not yet been examined by the Strasbourg Court, domestic courts have ruled on the compatibility of the wage moderation scheme with Article 11. The Belgian Council of State held that the restriction of this right imposed by a Royal Decree fixing the margin and excluding a substantial part of collective bargaining was compatible with Article 11, §2, of the Convention. This is because such measures are prescribed by law, pursue a legitimate aim, and are considered necessary in a democratic society. In addition, the measures are proportionate to their aim: the State intervention is subsidiary, is effective for only two years and leaves room for collective bargaining at sectoral and company levels. The State authority has used its leeway to ensure Belgium's economic competitiveness,

85. The restriction must be limited to the time necessary to restore a normal situation in which the exercise of the right to collective bargaining would again be fully secured (COMMITTEE OF INDEPENDENT EXPERTS, *Conclusions XII-1*, 1988-1989, pp. 129-131).
86. European Social Charter, Committee of Independent Experts, Conclusions IX-1, 1985, pp. 55-56 and Conclusions XII-1, 1988-1989, pp. 127-129.
87. COMMITTEE OF INDEPENDENT EXPERTS, *Conclusions XII-1*, 1988-1989, pp. 127-129.
88. *Ibid.*, pp. 129-131.
89. EUROPEAN COMMITTEE OF SOCIAL RIGHTS, *Conclusions 2014, Belgique*, p. 24 (summary available on https://hudoc.esc.coe.int/fre/?i=2014/def/BEL/6/2/EN).
90. EUROPEAN COMMITTEE OF SOCIAL RIGHTS, *Conclusions 2022, Belgique*, p. 29 (available on https://rm.coe.int/conclusions-2022-belgium-f/1680aa9c8f).
91. Eur. Court D.H. (Grand Chamber), 12 November 2008, *Demir and Baykara v. Turkey*, §154; Eur. Court. D.H. (Grand Chamber), 9 July 2013, *Sindicatul Pastorul cel Bun v. Romania*, §135.

the preservation of which is part of the protection of rights and freedoms, such as the right to work and the right to a decent standard of living.[92]

The Constitutional Court came to the same conclusion in 2016. Regarding the proportionality between the measure and the objective it seeks to achieve, the Court draws inspiration from the view of the Committee on Freedom of Association. Indeed, the Court emphasised that a restriction must be applied as an exceptional measure, limited to what is necessary, must not exceed a reasonable period of time and be accompanied by appropriate safeguards to protect the workers' standard of living. Such a restriction must necessarily be preceded by consultations with workers' and employers' organisations in order to obtain the agreement of social partners. It must also be ensured that collective bargaining on non-monetary issues can continue.[93] After emphasising that, every two years, the negotiation of wage cost adjustment is primarily left to the social partners, with the State authority acting only subsidiarily to compensate for the lack of agreement, the Court notes that the law[94] fully supports the chances of collective bargaining.[95]

In the same vein, with regard to the Act of 23 April 2015 neutralising, up to 2%, sectoral collective labour agreements organising wage indexation, the Court ruled that the State authority had the right to oppose in this way what the social partners had decided, since the interference with the right to collective bargaining pursued a legitimate aim under Article 11 of the European Convention on Human Rights – to promote the competitiveness of companies by reducing the wage gap between Belgium and neighbouring countries and to keep public expenditure within reasonable limits – and appears necessary, in a democratic society, to achieve the legitimate objectives pursued. In other words, the interference did not constitute a violation of the right to collective bargaining.[96]

As mentioned above, the Act of 26 July 1996 was amended in 2017. No action for annulment has been brought against it, not even by the highly critical trade unions. An interprofessional agreement – the last to be concluded – was even based on the new legal framework. It was from the following period, when the projections of the Central Economic Council turned out to be pessimistic, that the opposition grew. As noted above, the Committee on Freedom of Association found that this legislative amendment was too restrictive of the freedom of collective bargaining. Is this likely to influence the position of the Constitutional Court? Although the latter can no longer be consulted on an action for annulment – as the time limits have expired – it could be asked for a preliminary ruling in the context of an individual dispute concerning a subjective right (such as a wage dispute). It is difficult to predict whether the Court would find it appropriate to consider the conclusions of the Committee on Freedom of

92. C.E., 27 September 2013, No. 224.863; C.E., 13 February 2015, No. 230.207.
93. I.L.O., *Freedom of Association International Labour Office Geneva Digest of decisions and principles of the Freedom of Association Committee of the Governing Body of the ILO*, 5th ed., Geneva, 2006, p. 199, §§999, 1024 and 1027.
94. In this case, it was a question of reviewing the constitutionality of the Act of 28 April 2015.
95. C.C., 1 December 2016, No. 152/2016, B. 11.
96. C.C., 13 October 2016, No. 130/2016, B. 27 and 28.

Association when assessing the proportionality of a restriction on freedom of association. Exploring the possible reasoning is beyond the scope of this study.

§11.03 CONCLUSION

In the land of consensus and surrealism, social dialogue has flourished like almost nowhere else in Europe. Even the wage moderation system is underpinned by social dialogue. The social partners, who are under a certain State constraint to negotiate every two years a margin for wage cost evolution for the upcoming two years, are sovereign in determining this margin when they reach an agreement (provided that this margin falls within the framework previously set by the Central Council for the Economy). The State authority may not oppose it. The architecture of the system and the structures set up on an autonomous basis and encouraged by the public authority have not been undermined by the successive crises. However, since the 2008 economic crisis, social dialogue has become so difficult that, except for the period 2017-2018, no more AIPs have been concluded since then. The stalemate at the intersectoral level has led to increased State interventionism in the decision-making process for wage evolution. A twofold movement, paradoxical, can be observed: on the one hand, wage negotiation is being placed under State supervision, on the other hand, this interventionism is helping to revive social dialogue; indeed, once the margin has been set by the government, the social partners, who have failed to reach an agreement at the intersectoral level, regain control to negotiate the new wage benefits at the sectoral and company levels within the limits of the margin, and this according to their particularities.

The legislative amendment of 2017, adopted to meet the wishes of the European Union and which resulted in a more rigid framework for wage negotiations, has further strengthened the unions' protests.

In addition, the high inflation to which Belgium is structurally exposed has the effect – via the automatic wage indexation mechanism – of increasing labour costs, which, through a spiral effect, reduces the social partners' room for negotiation regarding wage amounts. This margin is contained between, on the one hand, the minimum amounts resulting from the automatic indexation of wages and scale increases, which are maintained in all circumstances, and, on the other hand, the maximum margin, which has been reduced to almost nothing as neighbouring countries do not have automatic and generalised wage indexation.

For several years now, many social movements have been calling for the repeal of the Act of 26 July 1996. They are reinforced by the recommendations of the Committee on Freedom of Association, which considers the restriction on the freedom of the social partners to decide on the criteria for their wage evolution negotiations to be excessive.

One can imagine that, as in the 1980s, the recurrent intervention of the State will allow social dialogue, temporarily suspended, to survive the rough waters and then try to adapt it to a changed context.[97] The survival of the Belgian collective bargaining model depends on the ability of its actors to adapt to new challenges and their ability to actively redefine a common vision of economic and social progress.[98]

97. This is a paraphrase – taken out of its chronological context – of CASSIERS et DENAYER, 'Concertation sociale et transformations socio-économiques en Belgique, de 1944 à nos jours', *supra* n. 16, p. 92.

98. CASSIERS & DENAYER, 'Concertation sociale et transformations socio-économiques en Belgique, de 1944 à nos jours', *supra* n. 16, p. 92; LÉONARD & PICHAULT, 'Belgique: l'adaptation d'un "modèlè de concertation sociale', *supra* n. 3, p. 75.

CHAPTER 12

Is a Revival of Collective Bargaining Possible? Polish Way from Neoliberalism to the Welfare State*

Łukasz Pisarczyk

§12.01 OPENING REMARKS

The development of collective bargaining in Poland is an important part of the history of political, social and economic changes. In 1989, Poland chose democracy and a market economy.[1] At the same time, a neo-liberal agenda unfavourable to collective bargaining was implemented for many years.[2] The move towards the idea of a welfare state which occurred in recent decades[3] did not cause a fundamental change in the situation of industrial relations. Collective bargaining has been undergoing a deep crisis.[4] At the same time, however, there has been a significant change in European social policy. The European Union (EU) shifted from decentralization justified by the

* This article is co-financed by Narodowe Centrum Nauki (the National Science Centre in Poland), project No. 2019/33/B/HS5/02067.

1. M. Seweryński, *Polish Labour Law from Communism to Democracy*, Warszawa, Dom Wydawniczy ABC 1999.
2. *See, e.g.*, I.T. Berend, *Social Shock in Transforming Central and Eastern Europe*, Communist and Post-Communist Studies 2007/40(3), pp. 269-280 https://doi.org/10.1016/j.postcomstud.2007.06.007; M.A. Orenstein & B. Bugarič, *Work, Family, Fatherland: The Political Economy of Populism in Central and Eastern Europe*, Journal of European Public Policy 2020/29(2), pp. 176-195 https://doi.org/10.1080/13501763.2020.1832557.
3. T. Gyulavári & Ł. Pisarczyk, *Populist Reforms in Hungary and Poland: Same Song, Different Melodies*, International Journal of Comparative Labour Law and Industrial Relations 2023/39(1), pp. 49-70 https://doi.org/10.54648/ijcl2023004; J. Becker, *Governing Neo-nationalism, Trade Unions and Industrial Relations: The Cases of Hungary and Poland*, Transfer 2024/1, pp. 51-65 https://doi.org/10.1177/10242589231221518.
4. B. Mądrzycki & Ł. Pisarczyk, *Ekspertyza układy zbiorowe [Expert opinion on collective agreements]*, 2022, https://www.gov.pl/web/dialog/krajowy-plan-odbudowy.

global economic crisis to promoting collective bargaining and increasing their coverage.[5] Transposing the Minimum Wage Directive, Poland will have to answer the question about the future model of industrial relations.

The article is a continuation of the work included in the book *Collective Bargaining in Times of Crisis*.[6] Therefore, the text omits detailed characteristics of the collective bargaining system in Poland. The time caesura for the research presented in the article is the adoption by the Polish Parliament (Sejm), on 5 July 2018, the Law amending the Law on Trade Unions and some other laws.[7] However, some references to the previous development of collective bargaining and its legal framework are necessary to understand the reasons for the crisis and challenges faced by the Polish legislator. The article discusses the key elements of the 2018 reform and their legal consequences. Next, the analysis moves to the collective mechanisms adopted during the pandemic (2020-2021) as an element of anti-crisis policy. Both legal actions, i.e., the 2018 reform and the anti-pandemic legislation were perceived as an opportunity to revitalize collective relations. However, to-date results have been disappointing.

The situation changed with the adoption of a new European policy towards collective bargaining aimed at increasing their coverage. The key element will be again multi-company (e.g., sectoral) collective bargaining which in the past constituted a focal point of the European social model. The MSs are expected not only to promote and support collective bargaining but also to strive to achieve 80% coverage by collective bargaining. However, to strive to achieve and not necessarily to achieve.[8] As a result, the question arises whether the MSs, like Poland, where the coverage is very low are ready to rebuild their economic systems and undertake actions aimed at establishing a comprehensive system of collective bargaining based on branch (sectoral) negotiations. The article discusses first drafts submitted by the government to satisfy the requirements arising from the EU law.[9] Taking the AMWD seriously Poland would have to reconstruct the legal framework of collective bargaining profoundly. However, the question arises whether it is 'doable' and desired by Polish stakeholders.

§12.02 POLISH SYSTEM OF COLLECTIVE BARGAINING

Polish law distinguishes between regular collective bargaining aimed at concluding typical collective agreements (regulated in chapter eleven of the Law of 26 June 1974 – Labour Code),[10] the procedure of resolving collective disputes (regulated by the Law

5. E. Brameshuber, L. Ratti & V. Pietrogiovanni (eds), *The EU Directive on Adequate Minimum Wages. Context, Commentary and Trajectories*, Hart Publishing 2024.
6. S. Laulom (ed.), *Collective Bargaining Developments in Times of Crisis*, Bulletin of Comparative Labour Relations 2018, No. 99.
7. Journal of Laws 2018, item 1608. The law aimed at reforming and revitalizing collective labour law in Poland.
8. Report Expert Group Transposition of Directive (EU) 2022/2041 on adequate minimum wages in the EU, 2023, https://ec.europa.eu/social/main.jsp?catId=1539.
9. https://www.gov.pl/web/premier/projekt-ustawy-o-ukladach-zbiorowych-pracy-i-porozumieniach-zbiorowych.
10. Journal of Laws 2023, item 1465.

of 23 May 1991 on Resolving Collective Disputes)[11] and irregular collective bargaining aimed at concluding collective agreements limited to specific issues.[12] Typical collective agreements are of the widest application scope. They may regulate all issues that belong to competences of employers and trade unions[13] including working conditions as well as the relationships between social partners themselves (Article 240 of the Labour Code). The procedure of resolving collective disputes constitutes a legal framework for the organization of a strike. Regular collective bargaining and resolving collective disputes are formally independent procedures. Atypical collective bargaining is provided for to protect workers' interests in extraordinary circumstances (collective redundancies, transfer of undertaking), in organizational matters (reference periods of working, teleworking) or as a means to mitigate the consequences of a crisis and to protect jobs (anti-crisis agreements, including short-time).[14] Some Polish companies are covered by transnational (usually European) collective agreements. However, Polish law does not recognize transnational agreements as sources of law. To be binding they must be implemented by local social partners which is rather rare.[15]

§12.03 NEOLIBERAL AGENDA AND ITS CONSEQUENCES

Poland inherited from communism a developed system of collective acts formally called collective agreements. Sectoral agreements covered the vast majority of workers. However, they were concluded as an element of a centrally-planned economy, by public authorities and trade unions controlled by the state. Consequently, they could not be treated as a result of voluntary collective negotiations between management and labour in the meaning of international standards in particular Article 4 of the International Labour Organization's (ILO's) convention No. 98.[16] Nonetheless, the legislation adopted at the beginning of the transition period recognized their binding force. Moreover, the social partners (real employers and free trade unions) were entitled to enter the legal position of the parties to the agreements.[17] The inherited agreements could constitute a starting point for establishing a new, democratic system of industrial relations. In reality, they did not play this role. Since 1989, a constant trend in the development of collective bargaining in Poland has been a decreasing scope of negotiations and a decreasing number of collective labour agreements. This tendency has not been significantly affected by global phenomena such as the world economic

11. Journal of Laws 2020, item 123.
12. Z. Hajn & L. Mitrus, *Poland,* [in:] *International Encyclopaedia of Laws: Labour Law and Industrial Relations*, R. Blanpain (ed.), Kluwer Law International 2016.
13. Z. Hajn, *Collective Agreements in Poland in the Light of International Standards*, Studia z Zakresu Prawa Pracy i Polityki Społecznej (Studies on Labour Law and Social Policy), 2022/29(4), pp. 377-385.
14. K.W. Baran, *Outline of the Polish Labour Law System*, Wolters Kluwer 2016.
15. A. Boguska, *Europejskie układy ramowe* [*European Framework Agreements*], Warszawa 2022, pp. 84 et seq.
16. *See, e.g.*, M. Seweryński, *Polish Labour Law from Communism to Democracy*, Warszawa, Dom Wydawniczy ABC 1999.
17. The Law of 29 September 1994 amending the Law – Labour Code and some other laws, Journal of Laws 1994, No. 113, item 547, as amended.

crisis and economic recovery. The decreasing trend has remained stable during both economic slowdown and prosperity.

The decreasing tendency has been caused by various reasons, including historical development, the approach of the social partners but also the existing legal framework. During the transition period, Poland needed to attract foreign investments and presented itself as a cheap labour country (flexible working standards, low level of wages). Flexibilization and decentralization of working standards were also expected by Polish employers unable to compete with Western companies. Polish employers have not appreciated the advantages arising from cartelizing employment standards. Collective bargaining, in particular of a multi-company dimension, could constitute an obstacle to the neoliberal agenda.[18] As a result, the law did not introduce solutions which would stimulate collective bargaining and increase their coverage. Social partners are not obliged to initiate periodically collective bargaining at specific levels/on specific issues. Their no legal mechanism for setting up sectoral (branch) employment standards. Multi-company collective agreements could be negotiated by employers' organizations only and for their members. It is estimated that only 2%-3% of employers who employ 15%-20% of workers are unionized.[19] The generalization by the minister for labour (Article 241[18] of the Labour Code) requires an active role of social partners and has never been used in practice. At the same time trade unions, to perform their rights at a company level, are required to establish a formal structure – company trade union organization (CTUO) which unites at least ten members employed by a given employer. In Poland, where small and medium enterprises (SMEs) dominate, it is an important obstacle in developing collective bargaining. Although the law recognizes and allows inter-CTUO (covering more than one employer) in practice, in particular in the private sector, they are very rare. As a result, the legal access of trade unions to SMEs is actually limited.

Not surprisingly, the legal framework of collective bargaining has not been perceived as supportive of the development of collective bargaining at both: multi-company as well as company levels.[20] The law remains, at least apparently, neutral. However, the neutrality of the law in combination with passivity (trade unions) or reluctance (employers) to be involved in collective bargaining has contributed to the breakdown of industrial relations and can be called 'hostile neutrality'.[21] The state achieved its goal to flexbilize or even atomize working conditions.

In recent years, a visible shift from the neo-liberal agenda to a sui generis welfare state idea took place. However, it did not cause an increase in collective bargaining. The social agenda has been implemented by the state itself. The state developed social

18. B. Mądrzycki & Ł. Pisarczyk, *Ekspertyza układy zbiorowe [Expert Opinion on Collective Agreements]*, 2022, https://www.gov.pl/web/dialog/krajowy-plan-odbudowy.
19. https://www.oecd-ilibrary.org/docserver/1fd2da34-en.pdf?expires=1666950035&id=id&accname=guest&checksum=B6E879D468BF1F8C7C21DF1A47D3FCA7.
20. B. Mądrzycki & Ł. Pisarczyk, *Ekspertyza układy zbiorowe [Expert Opinion on Collective Agreements]*, 2022, https://www.gov.pl/web/dialog/krajowy-plan-odbudowy.
21. Ł. Pisarczyk, *Towards Rebuilding Collective Bargaining? Poland in the Face of Contemporary Challenges and Changing European Social Policy*, Industrial Relations Journal 2023/1 https://doi.org/10.1111/irj.12397.

transfers and interfered with working conditions, in particular by increasing the statutory minimum wage. At the same time, the re-nationalization of numerous strategic companies occurred.[22] The direct intervention of the state could be perceived as an element of centralizing the economy as well as a part of the populist agenda developed in various states including Poland.[23] No transfer of regulatory power to social partners took place. The law neither enhanced nor supported the social partners in negotiating working conditions. The state, although it has adopted a developed social agenda, was to remain the main donor of the welfare of workers. The political change which occurred in 2023 has not caused yet a significant improvement in the position of collective bargaining.

Transnational collective agreements have not had a major impact on the collective bargaining system either. A certain number of such agreements apply to Polish companies. Their practical significance, however, remains limited. This is the result of the passivity of both corporations and national social partners who do not press for the implementation of transnational standards. Multinationals were not really interested in raising employment standards and labour costs. There were cases of not informing Polish structures about the conclusion of an agreement. The approach of Polish employers was similar, while trade unions remained passive. At the same time, the law did not recognize TCAs and their legal nature.[24]

To summarize, the state, neither neo-liberal nor welfare, has been interested in supporting collective bargaining. Its approach towards collective bargaining, although for various reasons, can be called 'hostile neutrality'.

§12.04 EXTENDING PERSONAL SCOPE OF COLLECTIVE BARGAINING

An important example of legal obstacles in developing collective bargaining was the limitation of its personal scope. Since the 1990s, the right to bargain collectively has been restricted to employees only (with some lesser exceptions). At the same time, the number of people working outside the employment relationship has increased significantly reaching the level of 2 million. They worked on the basis of civil-law contracts (performing services). Some of them enjoyed the legal status of entrepreneurs (self-employed). Workers (non-employees) could be covered by collective agreements but did not participate in negotiating them. As a result, provisions of collective agreements concerning non-employees were very rare. The limitation of freedom of association of workers who were not employees was alleged as a violation of international standards

22. A. Åslund, *The Biggest Problem in Post-Communist Transition: The Privatization of Large Enterprises*, CASE Working Papers 2021/16(140), https://www.case-research.eu/files/?id_plik=6857.
23. T. Gyulavári & Ł. Pisarczyk, *Populist Reforms in Hungary and Poland: Same Song, Different Melodies*, International Journal of Comparative Labour Law and Industrial Relations 2023/39(1), pp. 49-70 https://doi.org/10.54648/ijcl2023004; J. Becker, *Governing Neo-nationalism, Trade Unions and Industrial Relations: The Cases of Hungary and Poland*, Transfer 2024/1, pp. 51-65 https://doi.org/10.1177/10242589231221518.
24. A. Boguska, *Europejskie układy ramowe* [*European Framework Agreements*], Warszawa 2022, pp. 84 et seq.

(ILO conventions Nos 87 and 98) as well as the Polish constitution (Article 59). The ILO's mission in Poland expected national authorities to recognize the collective rights of non-employees, to protect non-employees against discrimination based on trade union membership as well as to enable non-employees to participate in procedures aimed at setting up their working conditions. However, the ILO did not require a full uniformization of the collective rights of employees and other workers.[25] In 2015, the Polish Constitutional Court declared the limitation of personal scope of freedom of association to employees as a violation of constitutional guarantees.[26] It required the legislation to recognize the collective freedoms and rights of those who did not enjoy the formal status of employees but who perform paid work for others and whose collective interests can be represented by trade unions.

The ruling of the Constitutional Court challenging the personal scope of the freedom of association forced the legislator to reconstruct the legal fundaments of industrial relations. After a few years of preparatory work (2016-2018), the amending law was adopted in 2018.[27] The core of the reform is the recognition of freedom of association of non-employees who perform work for other persons or entities. The full recognition of collective freedoms and rights is not, however, open. It was limited to workers (non-employees) who perform work personally (not employing other workers); work in return for remuneration (paid work) and whose interests can be represented by trade unions. The criterion of collective interests can be associated with the deficit of bargaining power towards another party caused, *inter alia*, by economic dependency or even subordination to an employing entity (Polish law does not offer an efficient mechanism of reclassification of civil law into employment contracts if work is performed in conditions characterizing the latter).

The new category was called workers performing paid work (WPPW). The WPPW, similarly to employees, may form and join trade unions. They may also exercise functions in trade unions and, consequently, enjoy the rights conferred upon union officials: the right to time off to perform union activities as well as the right not to be dismissed by the employer without a trade union consent. People performing unpaid work (e.g., volunteers) and pensioners enjoy limited union rights. They are entitled to join (but not to form) trade unions. Last but not least, the amending law enlarged the personal scope of anti-discriminatory standards. Anti-union discrimination has been prohibited, combated and penalized if practised towards not only employees but also WPPW. It is a starting point for exercising further collective rights

25. Skarga (nr 2888) dot. prawa koalicji i ochrony związkowej osób świadczących pracę na podstawie umów cywilnoprawnych i samozatrudnionych [Complaint (No. 2888) concerning freedom of association employed under civil law contracts and self-employed] 2014, https://www.solidarnosc.org.pl/projekty-i-dokumenty/skarga-nr-2888-dot-prawa-koalicji-i-ochrony-zwiazkowej-osob-swiadczacych-prace-na-podstawie-umow-cywilnoprawnych-i-samozatrudnionych/.
26. The judgment of the Constitutional Court of 2 June 2015, K 1/13, Journal of Laws 2015, item 791.
27. M. Latos-Miłkowska, *The Right to Unionise in Poland after the Amendment of the Law on Trade Unions*, European Labour Law Journal 2023/14(1), pp. 108-113 https://doi.org/10.1177/20319525221148129.

including the right to collective bargaining (Article 21.3 of the Law of 23 May 1991 on Trade Unions).[28]

WPPW build up, next to employees, trade union capacity and bargaining position. After the reform both: employees and WPPW are taken into account when calculating the number of trade union members necessary to: (1) establish a CTUO; (2) acquire the status of a representative trade union at national/multi-company/company level (Article 25^{2} and 25^{3} of the Law on Trade Unions). However, in the case of company-level trade union structures which have to unite at least ten members to perform their rights, WPPW is taken into account if their seniority is of at least six months (Article 25^{1}.2 of the Law on Trade Unions). Conversely, the employees are taken into account from the first day of their employment. The difference can be justified by the non-permanent nature of civil-law contracts. The law associates trade union rights only with these workers who are integrated into the company structure.

The amending law strived to put the procedure of submitting data from CTUO to an employer in order. The idea was to improve the quality of interaction between trade unions and employers. Company trade union organizations were obliged to inform the employer twice a year about the number of members (employees and other WPPW) they associate with. The information concerns the status as of 31 December and 30 June and should be provided by 10 January and 10 July, respectively (Article 25^{1}.2 of the Law on Trade Unions). The amending law decided that the CTUO which has failed to submit the information loses its statutory competences. In particular, it cannot participate in collective bargaining. However, after submitting the information the CTUO recovers its status (Article 25^{1}.6 of the Law on Trade Unions). The problem in the past was the lack of a procedure enabling the verification of data submitted by trade unions. The amending law granted the employer the right to challenge the data by raising a so-called objection (Article 25^{1}.7 of the Law on Trade Unions). The same right may be exercised by other CTUOs. The challenged organization is obliged to verify its status via court procedure. The procedure has been designed so as to protect personal data of unions' members (they should not be revealed to employers). (Article 25^{1}.8-10 of the Law on Trade Unions)

At the same time, the law limits the right to collective bargaining in public administration. Collective agreements cannot be concluded for civil servants employed in governmental administration (Article 239, §3 of the Labour Code). The existing mechanisms of setting working conditions in this area cannot be treated as an appropriate equivalent for collective bargaining. Consequently, the law is problematic from the perspective of international standards (in particular Article 7 of the Convention No. 151). Surprisingly, the Constitutional Court did not find the limitation inconsistent with constitutional standards.[29] Moreover, the law deprives all the public employees from the right to strike (Article 19.3 of the Law on Resolving of Collective Disputes). Such a restriction may be perceived as excessive.

28. Journal of Laws 2022, item 854.
29. Judgment of the Constitutional Court of 17 November 2015, K 5/15, Journal of Laws 2015, item 1982.

§12.05 RECONSTRUCTING COLLECTIVE PROCEDURES

Recognizing the freedom of association of the WPPW the legislator needed also to adjust collective procedures to the extended scope of the freedom. Moreover, the reform offered an opportunity to modify also other regulations considered detrimental to industrial relations.

The ILO's mission expected Poland to recognize some forms of collective setting of employment conditions. Theoretically, the Polish legislator made, in fact, a step further and equalized the position of employees and WPPW within two main collective procedures (negotiating typical collective agreements and resolving collective disputes) which are rooted in the freedom of association. Provisions of chapter eleven of the Labour Code as well as the Law on Resolving Collective Disputes which concern employees apply *mutatis mutandis* to other WPPW (Article 21.3 of the Law on Trade Unions and Article 6 of the Law on Resolving of Collective Disputes). As a result, WPPW may, on the same basis as employees, participate in negotiating typical collective agreements and benefit from them.[30] The same is valid for the procedure of resolving collective disputes which may be finalized by the conclusion of a collective agreement.

The legislator did not, however, adjust collective procedures to the actual position of the WPPW. The finest example is the relationship between collective agreements and individual contracts. Labour law is based on the *favor laboratoris* principle which means that the provisions of individual employment contracts cannot be less favourable than those of statutes and collective agreements (Article 18, §1 of the Labour Code). This provision does not apply to civil law contracts. It could mean that workers who are not employees could waive their rights arising from collective agreements. However, such an interpretation would undermine the sense of the reform. Nonetheless, the extension of collective rights of the WPPW was of a mechanical nature and without any special solutions aimed at adjusting and supporting collective bargaining for non-employees. The legislator limited itself to eliminate formal restrictions to freedom of association found inconsistent with international and constitutional standards.

Other amendments to the legal framework of collective bargaining were implemented to a limited extent, too. One of the most important is the new (increased) threshold of representativeness of trade unions at a company level. The Polish system of collective bargaining is pluralistic at both: the company as well as sector (branch) levels. All unions representing affected workers may participate in negotiations (Article 241^{16}, §1 and 241^{25}, §1 of the Labour Code). However, the efficiency of bargaining may be affected by the segmentation and atomization of trade unions. Polish trade union movement, despite low level of unionization, is characterized by a large number of union organizations. In some companies, there are several unions. This not only leads

30. *See, e.g.*, K.W. Baran, *Model of Collective Labour Agreements in the Polish Legal System*, Praca i Zabezpieczenie Społeczne [Labour and Social Security] 2019/2, pp. 6-8.

to competition but also may paralyse the negotiation process.[31] If trade unions are unable to act together or to establish a common representation then the law, to break the deadlock, sets out the criteria of representativeness. In such cases, the negotiations may be continued with the representative units. The amending law increased the threshold for representativeness. The idea was to support the strongest unions, to enhance the consolidation of movement and, consequently, to facilitate the negotiations. Trade unions which are representative at national level to be representative at a company level are expected to unite at least 8% of workers: employees and WPPWs employed by a given employer (formerly 7%). For other trade unions, the threshold was increased from 10% to 15%, which means a significant increase in expectations.

Procedural amendments can be considered mainly as a simple extension of the recognition of the freedom of association of the WPPW with a number of lesser amendments concerning the capacity of social partners. The legislator eliminated the most obvious violations of freedom of association. At the same time, no significant changes in the procedure of negotiating collective agreements have been adopted. The legislator either considered the extension of freedom of association as a sufficient remedy to the crisis of collective bargaining or was not interested in developing industrial relations. The policy of 'hostile neutrality' remained in force.

§12.06 PRACTICAL IMPLICATIONS OF THE 2018 REFORM

Taking into account the weakness and passivity of trade unions and the reluctance of employers[32] one could expect any improvement in collective bargaining. It is valid, especially for collective bargaining for non-employees.

First, the reform has not caused a significant increase in the union membership. Traditional trade unions have not adopted any attractive offer for the WPPW. Five years after the reform took place non-employees account for ca 1% of trade union members[33] while their share in the labour market is around 20%. As a result, there is no union pressure on collective bargaining for non-employees. At the same time employers, who utilize civil-law employment as a means to reduce labour costs, are not interested in negotiating collective agreements covering workers. As a result, despite lifting formal limitations collective bargaining for non-employees has not been launched to a greater extent. No collective agreement addressed exactly to this group of workers has been concluded. More popular are collective disputes initiated to improve the working conditions of workers or employees and workers. Some of them

31. J. Czarzasty & A. Mrozowicki, *Poland. Trade Unions Developing after a Decline*, [in:] *Trade Unions in the European Union. Picking Up the Pieces of the Neoliberal Challenge*, J. Waddington, T. Müller & K. Vandaele (eds), Peter Lang 2023, pp. 833-869.
32. B. Mądrzycki & Ł. Pisarczyk, *Ekspertyza układy zbiorowe [Expert Opinion on Collective Agreements]*, 2022, https://www.gov.pl/web/dialog/krajowy-plan-odbudowy.
33. Główny Urząd Statystyczny [Statistics Poland], Partnerzy dialogu społecznego – organizacje pracodawców i związki zawodowe w 2022 r. [Social partners – organizations of employers and trade unions in 2022], https://stat.gov.pl/obszary-tematyczne/gospodarka-spoleczna-wolontariat/gospodarka-spoleczna-trzeci-sektor/partnerzy-dialogu-spolecznego-zwiazki-zawodowe-i-organizacje-pracodawcow-wyniki-wstepne-w-2022,16,2.html.

have been organized within the existing legal framework (the Law on Resolving Collective Disputes) some, like protests of couriers (Glovo, pyszne.pl), outside this framework. Nonetheless, collective bargaining for WPPW is still *in statu nascendi*.[34]

The general tendency of decreasing the scope of collective bargaining has not been reversed either. Since 2014, no multi-company collective agreement has been concluded. The number of workers covered by company-level collective agreements decreased from 1,648,245 in January 2023 to 1,643,097 in January 2024.[35] In the pre-election period (before October 2023) trade unions were more active in initiating procedures for resolving collective disputes. It was valid in particular for state-owned companies involved somehow in political disputes. Since the governing party did not want to heat up social sentiment the numerous collective actions were successful leading, usually, to an increase in wages. The revitalization of collective bargaining in the pre-election period did not lead to the establishment of stable industrial relations and an increase in coverage by collective bargaining.

To summarize, the 2018 reform, despite its scope and objective, has not caused an improvement in collective bargaining in Poland. Social partners remain active only at a company level and in specific types of companies. The coverage by collective agreements is still among the lowest in the EU. It is neither because of the global economic crisis nor of the pandemic but because of systemic features of collective bargaining as well as the approach of social partners in Poland.

§12.07 SHORT-TERM RECOVERY. COLLECTIVE BARGAINING DURING THE PANDEMIC

The pandemic, in particular in its first phase, came as a shock for the whole socio-economic system. After establishing necessary protective (hygienic) standards legislators started seeking measures aimed at protecting employers and workers against the consequences of lockdowns and economic slowdowns. The Polish legislator adopted the anti-crisis shield providing financial support for those who had been affected by the pandemic and its consequences. The central element of the shield was the system of short-time work. The law authorized employers who suffered from the closure/limitations of their activities either to suspend employment relationships or to limit the number of working hours. The adoption of short-time work required an agreement with workers' representatives. Employers who conclude such agreements could apply for support from the state budget. It encouraged companies to start negotiations. According to the data, around 27,000 agreements were concluded. Pandemic collective bargaining was, however, of a special character as regards its participants, objective, as well as application scope.[36]

34. Ł. Pisarczyk, *Uphill Struggle: Collective Bargaining for the Self-Employed in Poland*, Transfer 2023/4.
35. The data submitted by the State Labour Inspectorate.
36. B. Mądrzycki & Ł. Pisarczyk, *The Impact of the Pandemic of Industrial Relations in Poland*, Studia Iuridica 2022/95, pp. 354-374.

Pandemic agreements could be concluded with company-level trade union organizations or, due to their lack, with elected representatives. The law provided neither for the rules of election nor for the protection of elected representatives against employer's repressions. Representatives were elected among the staff without any requirements concerning their competences to participate in negotiations. As a result, elected representatives could not be treated as a real power able to balance the employer's potential. The vast majority of the pandemic agreements were concluded not with trade unions but with elected representatives. Moreover, the agreements were limited to very specific goals and matters. They could be treated as a response to an extraordinary situation aimed at rescuing businesses and jobs. They were boosted by the possibility of receiving the financial support (while concluding an agreement was a condition *sine qua non* of the support). At the same time, the pandemic has not caused any significant changes to typical collective bargaining. The trend of a gradual decrease in the scope of collective bargaining continued.[37]

§12.08 TRANSPOSING THE MINIMUM WAGE DIRECTIVE AS A GAME CHANGER FOR COLLECTIVE BARGAINING IN POLAND?

In mid-2010, the approach of the EU towards collective bargaining started changing once again. The Pillar of Social Rights could be perceived as a declaration of the will to restore the social model based on social dialogue. The EU expects the MSs to increase the coverage of collective bargaining in particular by supporting sectoral and cross-sectoral negotiations. A changing social policy was reflected by requirements formulated in national recovery plans for the EEC. Poland was expected to analyse the situation of collective bargaining and adopt a strategy to increase their scope. A real game changer was, however, the adoption of the Minimum Wage Directive in 2022.[38]

However, the question arises of how to reach the threshold of 80% coverage in a country when there is no system of multi-company negotiations and the current coverage remains under the level of 20%.

In 2024, the Government submitted a draft law on collective bargaining aimed at increasing its coverage.[39] First, the draft is to extend the negotiation room for social partners. The draft is intended to satisfy employers' needs to regulate employment standards, e.g., working time, in a more flexible way. However, collective agreements, as a rule, will not be allowed to depart from statutory standards to the detriment of workers. Second, collective agreements will be concluded only for a specific period of time – not longer than five years. Nowadays the vast majority of collective agreements are concluded for an indefinite term. As a result, employers have problems with modifying employment standards even if their situation changes. Moreover, employers

37. B. Mądrzycki & Ł. Pisarczyk, *The Impact of the Pandemic of Industrial Relations in Poland*, Studia Iuridica 2022/95, pp. 354-374.
38. E. Brameshuber, L. Ratti & V. Pietrogiovanni (eds), *The EU Directive on Adequate Minimum Wages: Context, Commentary and Trajectories*, Hart Publishing 2024.
39. https://www.gov.pl/web/premier/projekt-ustawy-o-ukladach-zbiorowych-pracy-i-porozumieniach-zbiorowych.

covered by multi-company collective agreements will have the right to renounce the agreement by means of a unilateral statement of intent. Both solutions are intended to mitigate employers' concerns about excessive petrification of employment conditions through collective agreements. Third, to increase employers' capacity the draft provides that a group of employers (not only employer's organizations) will be able to negotiate multi-company collective agreements. Fourth, the new law is to impose on employers who employ at least fifty employees and are not covered by any collective agreement an obligation to initiate, on a yearly basis, negotiations aimed at concluding a collective agreement (in the first version of the draft, under criminal liability of the employer). Fifth, when negotiating collective agreements social partners will be able to easily resort to the state-organized mediation. Sixth, the registration procedure, criticized by social partners as complicated, is to be replaced by much simpler notification. Seventh, the law will facilitate the generalization of multi-company collective agreements. Eight, the limitations on collective bargaining in the public sector are to be abolished.[40] Only uniformed services (like the army, police, border service) and some higher civil and municipal servants will be excluded.

The draft was criticized by both trade unions (the fixed-term nature of the agreements) and employers (the obligation to start negotiations). In the next version, submitted in November 2024[41], the government took into consideration some of the suggestions. On the one hand, the government resigns from a temporary nature of collective agreements. According to the decision of the social partners, the collective agreements will be concluded for a definite or an indefinite duration. On the other hand, employers not covered by collective agreements will be obliged to start the negotiations every two years. In the new draft the government has resigned, however, from the criminal responsibility of employers for breaching this obligation (only offence). At the same time the new draft provides for the action plan to support collective bargaining. The action plan will be adopted by the minister for labour on the basis of an agreement between the national social partners, at their joint request or after consulting them. The purpose of the action plan is to build the capacity of the social partners, to encourage them to bargain collectively and to promote the idea of the social dialogue. However, more precise solutions which would increase the collective bargaining coverage are missing. The idea of the action plan, needed and required by the EU law, in the Polish case seems to be too general to exert a real influence of the social dialogue practice. The action plan is going to be revised every five years by the Council of the Social Dialogue.

Proposed solutions may enhance the social partners' involvement in collective bargaining. Some hopes can be attached to the obligation to initiate negotiations which will remain, however, at a company level. Nonetheless, the proposed solution cannot be considered a turning point in the development of collective bargaining. The employers, as a rule, are not interested in concluding collective agreements since they

40. https://www.gov.pl/web/premier/projekt-ustawy-o-ukladach-zbiorowych-pracy-i-porozumieniach-zbiorowych.
41. https://legislacja.rcl.gov.pl/docs//2/12386550/13066374/13066375/dokument690640.pdf.

are willing to be flexible and competitive. Many of them are SMEs.[42] Collective bargaining, even in the form submitted by the government, does not offer much to improve their market position. For instance, the government has neglected preferences for employers covered by collective agreements while using public funds (e.g. training funds) or applying in the procedure of public procurement. Moreover, even if the obligation to negotiate periodically brings some results they will be limited to the company level. Last but not least, the state can play a more active role as an indirect employer (public administration, state-owned companies). The activity of public authorities may lead to an increase in coverage (the public administration)[43] as well as serve as an example for other employers in specific sectors and branches (state-owned companies). Of course, it can be just a trigger not a game changer in the whole system of industrial relations.

Finally, no significant improvement without developing multi-company bargaining is possible. The only chance for a real change of the situation in industrial relations is to provide for an *erga omnes* effect of multi-company collective agreements. Such a solution was proposed by trade unions (Solidarność). Collective agreements concluded by trade unions and employers' organizations representative at a national level would gain the value of general applicability.[44] This would lead, however, to a fundamental change in the economic model and unification of working standards. Polish employers having less potential than Western companies, affected by unstable economic situation and high inflation will not accept such a model. At the same time the state not only lacks enough power to implement such a solution, but it may also not be interested in waiving regulatory competences. The draft does not even provided for the obligation to bargain collectively at a higher (branch or sectoral) levels.

Some hopes were associated with the transnational collective agreements. Sometimes they are perceived as potential boosters in developing social dialogue. Unfortunately, the idea of transnational negotiations has slowed down for many reasons. European trade unions and employers' organizations are not interested any longer in developing this form of social dialogue. An obstacle is also the lack of legal incentives. A chance to support transnational collective bargaining could be a voluntary legal framework at the European level.[45] However, the prospect of undertaking an effective legislative action is doubtful.

42. B. Mądrzycki & Ł. Pisarczyk, *Ekspertyza układy zbiorowe [Expert Opinion on Collective Agreements]*, 2022, https://www.gov.pl/web/dialog/krajowy-plan-odbudowy.
43. I. Blaziene & J. Jasiuniene, *Collective Bargaining and Inequality in Lithuania*, (Deliverable 3.1 National report for Lithuania). Leuven: BFORE project VS/2021/0209, 2023.
44. https://www.tysol.pl/a37998-Nasz-wywiad-Piotr-Duda-W-przyszlej-kadencji-sejmu-emerytura-stazowa-i-uklady-zbiorowe.
45. Ł. Pisarczyk & A. Boguska, *European Framework Agreements in Multinational Companies: What Role of European Labour Law?*, International Journal of Comparative Labour Law and Industrial Relations 2023/39(2) https://doi.org/10.54648/ijcl2023017.

§12.09 CONCLUSIONS

The economic crisis that began in 2007 did not cause any major changes in the Polish collective bargaining system. This does not mean, however, that the situation of collective bargaining in Poland is satisfactory. On the contrary, collective bargaining has been undergoing a deep crisis. Since 1989, when the transformation began, the intensity and scope of collective bargaining have been significantly decreasing. The improvement of the economic situation did not change anything. Poland is among the EU countries with the lowest coverage by collective agreements. The reform of collective labour law, which took place in 2018, did not entail expected improvement while the increase in the activity of social partners due to the pandemic was temporary. The Polish legislator must face the problem of the deficit of democracy as well as the unfair distribution of the national income. The obvious impulse for the reconstruction of collective labour law in Poland was the adoption of the Minimum Wage Directive, in particular its Article 4.

Supporting the capacity of the social partners and facilitating negotiations are not enough when employers are reluctant to be involved in bargaining while trade unions are unable to adopt efficient strategies and insert necessary pressure on the other party. Revitalizing industrial relations requires, however, new strategies of social partners but also a fundamental reconstruction of the legal framework. The only solution leading to a significant increase in the coverage by collective agreements would be the obligation to bargain collectively at both: company and multi-company levels combined with the generally binding force of branch (sectoral) collective agreements. It would mean, however, a change of the whole economic model, a shift of the regulatory power from the state to social partners and a new model of redistribution based on limiting employers' profits. First, despite economic improvement Polish economy is still weaker than the economies of Western countries. Second, despite political changes after 2023, the question arises whether the state is ready to share its regulatory power with the social partners and to take the risk of confrontation with employers. Because of the above-mentioned a fundamental reconstruction of collective bargaining is rather unlikely. One can expect rather minor amendments as well as a more active approach of the state as an employer. It may improve the situation and cause an increase in coverage but not change the position of collective bargaining in a dramatic way. The threshold of 80% of workers covered by collective bargaining still seems to be very far.

CHAPTER 13

The Revival of Sectoral Collective Bargaining: The Portuguese Experience

Teresa Coelho Moreira

§13.01 INTRODUCTION

Collective bargaining is a fundamental instance of adapting labour legislation to the specificities of each sector and company, promoting social peace, improving working conditions and regulating competition and it is therefore a national and international desideratum. Collective bargaining is, however, subject to tensions, which although not new, have become more acute and may deepen in the future.

In Portugal, first, there is the slow erosion of collective bargaining coverage and union density, within a broader framework of weakening of the associative movement. Although this is not exclusive to the world of work, it finds added challenges in the more precarious segments of the labour market and the difficulty traditional associative structures have in ensuring representation of the new working arrangements.

The right of association is a fundamental right in Portugal, expressly provided for in the Constitution, and the right of association of workers and employers is a fundamental pillar not only of our system of labour relations but also of decent work. In turn, social dialogue at all levels, including tripartite social consultation and sectoral or company collective bargaining are widely provided for and densely covered by legislative sources, namely the Labour Code.

Thus, tripartite social dialogue, in the form of social consultation, has played a vitally important role in the formulation of public policies in different areas, including the areas of employment, training and labour relations through discussion and the search for consensus between the Government and Social Partners, reached in the Standing Committee for Social Consultation (CPCS).

§13.02 THE RIGHT TO NEGOTIATE

Collective bargaining is an employee's fundamental right, consecrated in Article 56 No. 3 of the Portuguese Constitution. According to this article, collective bargaining is a right that can only be exercised by trade unions and which has to be assured by law, determining a trade union monopoly on the workers' side as far as collective bargaining is concerned. As a result, workers' councils have no collective bargaining capacity in Portugal.

In 2012, the workers' councils were given, in Article 491 No. 3 of the Portuguese Labour Code, a chance to negotiate collective agreements at the company level, within legally defined and rather restrictive terms. Such terms included a delegation like empowerment by trade unions granted in the context and stated in the text, of a collective agreement of broader scope and a company size threshold of 150 or more workers. Since these company-level collective agreements are believed to either adjust or develop broader collective agreement discipline, their contents will comprise only the designated subjects where such tasks are deemed necessary. However, it must be noted that most companies in Portugal are small and medium enterprises (SMEs) and, therefore, the costs to employers of negotiating a company-level agreement are high.

Trade unions are also entitled, according to Article 56 of the Constitution, to participate in the creation of labour legislation, to express their opinion on any of the government's economic or social plans, and to participate in the management of social security institutions and company restructuring procedures.

On the employers' side, the freedom to set up employers' associations was introduced in 1975 by Decree-Law 215-C/75, although no reference was made to them in the Constitution. These provisions can be found in the Portuguese Labour Code from Article 440 onwards, regulating the freedom of association of both employers and employees as if they were equal.

Trade unions have the exclusive legal right to call strikes and to sign collective agreements.

§13.03 THE TRADITIONAL TRIPARTITE CONCERTATION

Portugal has a long tradition of social dialogue between the government and representatives of both employers and employees – especially at the highest level of representation.

This dialogue consists of regular consultations and active participation by the social partners in approving new legislation on employment and industrial relations, as imposed by the Portuguese Constitution, and in formulating the tripartite agreements concluded regularly over the years at the Standing Committee on Social Concertation.

It is important to note that in Portugal many subjects are discussed beforehand in the Social Concertation Standing Committee. The main tasks of this committee are to foster dialogue and social concertation so as to enter into agreements, offering opinions on restructuring and socioeconomic development policies, as well as their implementation; to provide solutions for the proper functioning of the economy, taking into account their social and labour impact; to regularly appraise the evolution of the country's social and economic situation; and to appraise legislation projects concerning social and labour matters - namely labour law, employment policies, vocational training, social welfare, tax and public administration policies, including active labour market policies.

From the mid-1970s onwards, collective bargaining developed largely according to the *favor laboratoris* principle, interpreted in the most traditional form. Collective agreements were seen as instruments planned only to improve legal provisions that were considered the minimum standard of labour protection, and a collective agreement in force could only be replaced by a more favourable one. Collective agreements therefore had the tendency to be more protective than the law and remained in force for a long time.[1]

The Labour Code of 2003 adopted new stipulations on the relationship between law and collective agreements, allowing the latter to establish less favourable conditions than those prescribed by the law. In addition, it adopted a set of provisions intended to favour the regular replacement of the old collective agreements by new ones. However, there was a huge fall in the number of collective agreements following these provisions and later on, in the Labour Code of 2009, a partial restoration of the previous provisions in this area. Since 2009 the general principle has remained the same: collective agreements can establish less favourable conditions than those prescribed by law, but there are some issues - such as, *inter alia*, equality and non-discrimination, personality rights, limits to the duration of working period, telework and use of algorithms, artificial intelligence and related matters, particularly in the context of working on digital platforms - that can only be established in a more favourable way than the law.

However, concerning the relationship between law and employment contracts, the principle continues to be the same - *favor laboratoris*, interpreted in the most traditional way - as it is for the relationship between collective agreements and employment contracts, according to Article 476 of the Portuguese Labour Code.

§13.04 SECTORAL COLLECTIVE AGREEMENTS IN PORTUGAL

In Portugal, collective bargaining has traditionally taken place at sectoral or multi-employer levels, with collective agreements extended to non-parties to the agreement to fill the gap caused by the low level of union membership in Portugal - i.e., less than 20%. Despite the general principle that they apply only to the members of the trade union or of the employers' association that signed the agreement based on the affiliation principle, in practice they are applied to non-affiliated workers and employers because the law has allowed the administrative extension of those agreements by extension ordinances and there is a strong tradition of the use of this tool. This

1. All this information can be seen in Maria Do Rosário Palma Ramalho, *Portuguese Labour Law and Industrial Relations During the Crisis*, in ILO Working Paper, 10, 2013.

administrative extension of collective agreements makes it possible for a large proportion of the labour force to benefit from collective agreements without belonging to the organisations that signed them.

Of course, one has to understand that this tradition has its roots in the type of enterprise that exists in Portugal. There are many SMEs with large numbers of low-skilled workers, so the sectoral collective agreements tend to offer more protection to unskilled workers. Also, as the International Labour Organization (ILO)[2] points out, it tends to offer more inclusive labour protection for vulnerable categories of workers, such as migrants, those in non-standard forms of employment or working in small firms. It can also help to establish minimum standards for working conditions in an industry or sector, taking these out of competition.

We think it is also important to bear in mind that there is a transversal movement involving the relative weakening of collective labour regulation systems: a movement that is visible not only in the decrease in membership rates (of workers and companies) but also in the loss of collective bargaining dynamism. That said, Portugal is unusual in having a significant starting point: at the end of the 1970s, even with the April 1974 revolution as a backdrop, close to 61% of Portuguese workers were unionised (above the 34% OECD average).

However, according to data from the International Labour Organisation, the trade union membership rate is around 16% in Portugal, and according to the information found in the Single Report, the percentage of unionised workers declared by companies dropped to 7.5% in 2018 (down from 10.6% declared in 2010), and this percentage is highly asymmetric, according to the incidence of permanent or non-permanent contracts in companies. Like the erosion of union density, declared business association membership has also declined (from 18.4% in 2010 to 15.4% in 2018).[3]

However, in Portugal, as a rule, there are no legal criteria to assess how representative trade unions are. As collective agreements may be extended to employers and employees that are not represented or affiliated respectively by employers' organisations or trade unions through administrative procedures, the government has a discretionary power to extend the personal scope of collective agreements even when the signatories of that collective agreement may be insignificant, having only a very small number of members. That is why the *Memorandum of Understanding* (MoU) in 2011 established that the Portuguese government 'should define clear criteria to be followed for the extension of agreements and commit to them and the representativeness of negotiating organizations and the implications of the extension for the competitive position of non-affiliated firms will have to be among these criteria'.

Regarding the restriction of extension ordinances, the *MoU* set the goal of defining criteria for issuing them that took into account the representation of the parties to collective bargaining agreements and their consequences to companies not covered by the collective bargaining agreement.

2. https://www.ilo.org/publications/tackling-jobs-crisis-portugal.
3. *See* all this in T. Coelho Moreira & G. Dray, *Green Paper on the Future of Work 2021*, GEP, Lisbon, 2022, p. 120.

After the third regular revision on 15 May 2012, it was established that the extension of collective bargaining agreements signed by employers' associations representing less than 50% of the workers in that sector would no longer be possible; however, even if that limit was reached, the government should always assess the consequences for the competitiveness of companies in that sector.

Council of Ministers Resolution No. 90/2012 of 31 October defined the following criterion for the issuing of extension ordinances: the employer that had signed the collective bargaining agreement should have in its service at least 50% of the workers in that sector of activity, within the envisaged geographic, personal and professional scope, except if the request for extension excluded micro, small and medium companies.

This decision had two important effects: a significant reduction in both collective labour regulation instruments and the number of workers covered, leading to wages and working conditions being increasingly determined by direct negotiation between employers and individual workers.

All social partners were against these changes in the extension ordinances.

This new situation also led to a change in the predominant type of collective agreement. The traditionally preponderant sectoral top-level branch and professional agreements (CCT and ACT), gave way to company-level agreements which also led to a decrease in the number of workers covered. The number of employees covered by collective agreements fell from almost 1.9 million in 2008 to some 246,643 in 2014.[4]

These developments show the difficulty that social partners were facing in reaching agreements during the crisis.

However, the low density of employer association membership led to concerns that the 50% representativeness criterion was too strict, and so, after the adjustment programme in 2014, Council of Ministers Resolution No. 43/2014 of 27 June created different criteria aimed at ensuring the representativeness of the parties. This change was necessary given paragraph 27 ('Labour Market Institutions') of the Letter of Intent of 26 May 2014, submitted by the Portuguese government to the International Monetary Fund, highlighting the policy steps to be taken in the months ahead and providing that the Government 'will encourage wage developments consistent with productivity, including by making collective bargaining more dynamic and fostering decentralization of wage bargaining'. The government's immediate priority in this area was to adjust the criteria for the extension of collective agreements, taking into account the representativeness of micro-, small- and medium-sized enterprises in the various sectors and maintaining the aim of the previous reform under the programme.

This resolution was enacted after the end of the adjustment programme and adopted to introduce flexibility into the principle for issuing extension ordinances.

Therefore, the employer need only to comply with one of the following criteria: to have in its service at least 50% of the workers of that sector of activity, within the envisaged geographic, personal and professional scope; or its associates must include at least 30% of micro, small and medium companies.

4. Data available in DGERT.

According to Article 100 of the Portuguese Labour Code, micro, small and medium-sized enterprises are defined as firms employing less than 250 employees.

Since this was likely to be the case for the large majority of employer associations, this mainly represented a return to the situation before 2011.

However, this decision by the Portuguese government was criticised by the IMF in January 2015 because they said that this option would 'undermine the progress towards a more dynamic and inclusive system of collective bargaining'.[5] Also the European Commission[6] in December 2014 wrote that this option *'is likely to hinder efficient wage adjustment at firm level. This measure represents a major setback in the reform of collective bargaining in Portugal'*.

We had our doubts about this, though. In our opinion, the new principle could allow a significant increase in the issuing of extension ordinances, without this meaning a return to the past, when extension ordinances were issued on a case-by-case basis and almost automatically.[7]

As the ILO[8] noted, a new approach to collective bargaining was needed. It was not a question of moving back to where the system was before the crisis, because that earlier system, among other limitations, was too focused on wages, with not enough attention devoted to skills development, mobility and competitiveness. Instead, the challenge was to build an environment that allowed wages and working conditions to move in line with productivity while supporting job recovery.

These new criteria resulted in a pick-up in the number of extensions issued in 2015 and 2016.

Finally, with a new political cycle, that started in 2015, in 2017, it was enacted another Council of Ministers Resolution, Resolution No. 82/2017 of 9 June. In this Resolution, we can read that *'The Government Programme of the 21st Constitutional Government, under the heading "Relaunching social dialogue and sectoral collective bargaining, articulating it with the level of companies, including in the public sector,"'* enshrined as an objective for the 2015-2019 parliamentary term the resumption of the dynamism of social dialogue at all levels, from social dialogue to collective bargaining at sectoral and company level.

To realise this goal, the government has set out to energise the publication of extension ordinances and establish clear provisions on reasonable legal deadlines for their publication.

It was agreed, as part of the 'Commitment to a Medium-Term Agreement', in the Standing Committee on Social Concertation, signed in December 2016, between the government and the majority of the social partners, to consider, on the basis of a government proposal, changes to the framework of extension ordinances and the

5. IMF Country Report No. 15/21, p. 12.
6. *Occasional Papers 208*, p. 30.
7. In the same sense D. Carvalho Martins, *Labour Law in Portugal Between 2011 and 2014, in ISL & ISSL European Regional Congress*, 25, 2014.
8. *Tackling the Jobs Crisis in Portugal*, Studies on Growth with Equity (ILO 2014) http://ilo.org/wcmsp5/groups/public/---dgreports/---dcomm/documents/publication/wcms_228208.pdf.

establishment legal deadlines for issuing notices and ordinances in the first quarter of 2017.

So, it was repealed the Council of Ministers Resolution of Ministers No. 90/2012, of 31 October, as amended by Resolution as amended by Council of Ministers Resolution No. 43/2014, of 27 June, was repealed and the criteria established on them disappeared.

The new criteria are established in Article 1 that states that '*the decision to issue the extension, taking into account the provisions of Article 514 and Article 515, both of the Labour Code, must be preceded by an analysis of the following indicators:*

a) Impact on the wage bill of the workers;
b) Impact on the wage bill of the workers covered and to be covered, with a view to gauging the possible economic impact of the extension;
c) Wage increase for the workers to be covered;
d) Impact on the wage range and the reduction of inequalities within the scope of the collective regulation instrument to be extended;
e) Percentage of workers to be covered (in total and by gender).
f) *Proportion of women to be covered*'.

This new criteria led to an increase in sectoral collective agreements.

In Portugal, despite the downward trend, there continues to be a high proportion of workers covered by collective agreements. According to data from DGERT,[9] despite fluctuations in the dynamics of the publication of collective agreements, the rate of coverage of collective bargaining has remained high, ranging from 91.4% in 2011 to 83.3% in 2023, although there has been a relative erosion of this indicator over the years, and the administrative extension of negotiating instruments is relevant for this purpose.

Recently, after years of marked loss of dynamism, the result not only of the difficult economic situation the country went through but also of the instability and unpredictability that marked that period, namely in matters of labour legislation, collective bargaining underwent a progressive and sustained recovery in the period following the crisis of 2008-2011, and before the pandemic. This was demonstrated not only by the number of agreements published annually but also, in particular, as regards their coverage.

In 2016, in a framework of specific enhancement of social dialogue at all levels, the number of agreements published increased by 6% and the number of workers potentially covered grew by 54%, approaching 750,000, moving further away from the minimum levels reached in the years 2013 and 2014. The number of published agreements grew again (+42%) in 2017, as well as their coverage (+10%), and in 2019 there was a further strengthening of collective bargaining, with published

9. https://www.dgert.gov.pt/relatorios-anuais-sobre-regulamentacao-coletiva-e-relacoes-profissionais-2012-2023.

agreements growing by 10% and the number of workers potentially covered approaching 1 million (+10% compared to 2017). These figures are closer to the levels prior to the financial crisis and the reforms of the adjustment period. Collective bargaining maintained significant momentum in 2019, with a total of 240 collective bargaining agreements published (+9% compared to 2018) and 883,727 workers potentially covered (–11% compared to 2018).

The COVID-19 pandemic interrupted this trajectory, resulting in an immediate contraction in collective bargaining. In effect, following a significant year-on-year increase in the number of bargaining agreements published (+16%) and their coverage (+156%) in the 1st quarter of 2020, there was an abrupt decrease in the 2nd quarter both in the number of published agreements (–62%) and in the number of workers potentially covered by them (–72%). This trend continued in the 3rd quarter, with decreases of 35% in the number of published agreements and 67% in the number of workers covered, and also in the 4th quarter, with a slight increase in the number of agreements (+3%) but with a loss of 63% in potential coverage. Thus, overall, 169 collective agreements were published in 2020 (–29% year-on-year) with a potential coverage of 488,482 workers (–45% year-on-year).

These data unequivocally show that collective bargaining is highly sensitive to the oscillations of the economy, to the uncertainty and unpredictability of the evolution of the pandemic and its economic and social effects. This fact reinforces the notion that the retraction of confidence and perspectives of economic agents in periods of crisis tends to translate into a lower propensity for negotiation and its renewal. The pandemic crisis differs from previous crises in that it incorporates a determining factor of uncertainty regarding its duration, the evolution of public health conditions associated with the pandemic and the way in which these restrict both economic and social activity and the expectations of different agents.

To value employers who had collective bargaining in 2021, the Government created an exceptional mechanism to support companies for salary increases minimum in 2022. The objective was to differentiate the companies that have increased the salary of workers above the minimum amount legally established in 2021, within the scope of collective bargaining, starting to receive EUR 112 for all workers who have salaries between EUR 665 and EUR 705 in 2021.[10]

Table 13.1 General Mapping of Collective Labour Regulation Instruments 2015 to 2022 (General Data: Collective Labour Regulation Instruments Published, by Type)

Negotiated Collective Labour Regulation Instruments									
Type	*2015*	*2016*	*2017*	*2018*	*2019*	*2020*	*2021*	*2022*	*2023*
Multiemployer agreements	20	19	21	26	30	11	20	31	32

10. All this can be seen in in Coelho Moreira & Dray, *supra* n. 3, pp. 121-122.

Negotiated Collective Labour Regulation Instruments									
Type	*2015*	*2016*	*2017*	*2018*	*2019*	*2020*	*2021*	*2022*	*2023*
Company agreements	53	58	96	98	105	97	109	112	156
Sectoral Agreements	65	69	91	96	105	61	79	97	111
Total (collective agreements)	**138**	**146**	**208**	**220**	**240**	**169**	**208**	**240**	**299**
Non-bargaining Collective Regulation Instruments									
Type	*2015*	*2016*	*2017*	*2018*	*2019*	*2020*	*2021*	*2022*	*2023*
Extension Ordinances	36	35	84	75	83	49	55	54	118
TOTAL	**174**	**181**	**292**	**295**	**323**	**218**	**263**	**294**	**417**

Source: DGERT – https://www.dgert.gov.pt/contratacao-coletiva-2 and Centro de Relações Laborais – https://www.crlaborais.pt/detalhe-noticia/-/asset_publisher/dF5FDptVm2T6/content/negociacao-coletiva-em-numeros-serie-2015-20-1.

§13.05 CONCLUSION

In conclusion, the legislative amendments and the historical resilience of collective bargaining in Portugal reflect a robust system designed to adapt to economic fluctuations and crises.

In Portugal, despite fluctuations in the dynamics of the publication of collective agreements, the rate of coverage of collective bargaining has remained high, ranging from 91.4% in 2011 to 83.3% in 2023 due to the high number of sectoral collective agreements signed along with the number of extension ordinances issued.

CHAPTER 14

Collective Bargaining in Romania: The Aftermath of an Earthquake – A Fresh Start for Social Dialogue?

Felicia Rosioru

As a post-communist country, in Romania there is a rather centralised approach; industrial relations are strongly regulated by the law and there is a quasi-inexistent tradition to 'solve' the different crises through social dialogue. For more than a decade, collective bargaining in Romania was rather weak and strongly decentralised as a consequence of a legislative reform. In fact, since 2011, social dialogue has been severely affected by a law adopted in the context of the economic crisis. In the previous edition of this book, we have assimilated its effects to those of an earthquake that has initially paralysed and subsequently weakened social dialogue. However, as catastrophes are usually followed by reconstruction, a relatively recent legislative reform,[1] the Social Dialogue Act, No. 367, was adopted at the end of 2022. The Act has aimed to improve 'collective bargaining and the overall functioning of social dialogue in the country',[2] in line with the recommendations of the International Labour Organization (ILO), giving hope to a new, fresh start of the social dialogue and to a more effective collective bargaining in particular. Several important measures were adopted to enhance the social partners' capacity to engage in collective bargaining, among which: the number of persons who can create a trade union, as well as the representativeness criteria were lowered compared to the previous thresholds; dependent, independent or unemployed workers (and not only employees, as previously) enjoy an effective trade union freedom and sectoral and cross-sectoral collective bargaining seem to have been

1. Law No. 367 of 19 December 2022 on social dialogue was published in the Official Journal No. 1238 of 22 December 2022 and it has entered into force on 25 December 2022.
2. European Commission, *Analysis of the recovery and resilience plan of Romania*, Brussels, 27.9.2021, SWD(2021) 276 final, p. 40.

revived. The reform of social dialogue was carried out, after several attempts, following the inclusion of this objective in Romania's Recovery and Resilience Plan and came into force on Christmas Day.

The main objectives of the Social Dialogue Act were to promote substantial and timely collective bargaining,[3] to strengthen the role of social dialogue, particularly in wage setting,[4] to encourage the participation of social partners in this process and to ensure consultations between the social partners and by the legislator.

The new regulation is too recent to assess its effectiveness or to highlight a visible improvement in social dialogue in Romania, a country where, currently, collective bargaining coverage is low and collective agreements usually contain very limited supplementary rights for the workers. Given the Social Dialogue Act's specific objectives to improve social dialogue and to enhance the capacity of social partners to engage in informed, substantial and timely collective bargaining, including on wage setting, the transposition of Directive 2022/2041 on adequate minimum wages in the European Union (EU)[5] might constitute the relevant test to assess the practical relevance of the new regulation on social dialogue. However, the collective bargaining coverage rates may be explained by several factors, including national traditions, practices and the historical context.[6] Having these aspects in mind, we shall analyse: the legislative changes in the context in which they were adopted (§14.01), and the historical background, as they are likely to play an important role in assessing the ability of the Romanian industrial relations to contribute to upward social convergence and reduce wage inequality through an effective involvement of social partners (§14.02).[7]

§14.01 THE NEW SOCIAL DIALOGUE ACT OF 2022: A STEP TOWARDS AN EFFECTIVE FREEDOM OF ASSOCIATION?

The Social Dialogue Act of 2022 was adopted quickly, given that milestone 449 of the National Recovery and Resilience Plan provided for its entry into force in 2022, and that the technical comments of the International Labour Office, requested by the Romanian Government, were received in October 2022. Given the considerable effect of the 2011 Law on social dialogue of weakening social dialogue and the role of the social partners, ever since, several reforms have been put forward in the field, without success. Law No. 367 of 2022 on social dialogue aimed to address all the deficiencies generated by

3. Recovery and resilience plan of Romania, Component C14, Good governance, Pillar V. Health, and economic, social and institutional resilience (aiming to reform public sector, enhance justice effectiveness and et reinforce the capacities of social partners), p. 37.
4. Recovery and resilience plan of Romania, Component C13 Social Reforms (Pillar V. Health, and economic, social and institutional resilience), p. 66.
5. Directive (EU) 2022/2041 of the European Parliament and of the Council of 19 October 2022 on adequate minimum wages in the European Union (OJ L 275, 25.10.2022, p. 33).
6. Preamble, §25 of Directive 2022/2041.
7. Council Decision (EU) 2020/1512(5) on guidelines for the employment policies of the Member States (OJ L 344, 19.10.2020, p. 22), Guideline 5 in the annex, according to which the effective involvement of social partners in wage-setting should be promoted also in Member States with statutory minimum wages.

the previous reform, adopted in the context of the economic crisis and to ensure, according to its explanatory memorandum, a collective bargaining coverage rate of 80% of workers. These objectives are in line with the obligations of the Member States, contained in Directive (EU) 2022/2041 on adequate minimum wages in the EU, to *'provide a framework of enabling conditions for collective bargaining, and establish an action plan to promote collective bargaining to progressively increase the collective bargaining coverage rate'*.[8] Basically, the framework for collective bargaining is established by Law No. 367/2022. Employees, workers, whether dependent or self-employed, civil servants, cooperative members, farmers and the unemployed have the right, without any limitation or prior authorisation, to create and/or join a trade union. The recognition of the right of all the workers, regardless of their statute - dependent or independent, employees or non-standard workers - to create or join a trade union marks an important step towards an effective freedom of association. Romania was one of the EU countries where unionisation, collective bargaining and the possibility to conclude collective agreements were recognised strictly to employees, contrary to the recommendations of the ILO Committee of Experts on the Application of Conventions and Recommendations (CEACR),[9] ILO Committee on Freedom of Association[10] and European Committee on Social Rights (ECSR).[11]

The new Social Dialogue Act of 2022 has genuinely aimed to improve the framework of collective bargaining, and it has introduced a series of structural changes that are likely to 'revive' social dialogue in Romania and empower the social partners to engage in genuine, substantial negotiations [A], in line with the specific recommendations in this field [B].

[A] Structural Changes of Social Dialogue in Romania

As already mentioned, Law No. 367/2022 has aimed to rebuild social dialogue through a series of measures guaranteeing freedom of association as a fundamental human right. Therefore, the changes are structural, and they address several weaknesses and deficiencies of social dialogue, mainly generated not only by the previous regulation of social dialogue, Law No. 62/2011 but also by the historical background. This part of

8. Preamble, §25 of Directive 2022/2041.
9. ILO, Report of the Committee of Experts on the Application of Conventions and Recommendations, Report III (Part 1A), 2011.
10. Committee on Freedom of Association, recommendations of 03/2012, case No. 2888, Poland, *Freedom of Association: Compilation of Decisions of the Committee on Freedom of Association*, ILO, 2018, p. 70.
11. European Committee on Social Rights, *Irish Congress of Trade Unions (ICTU) v. Ireland*, (8 August 2016) No. 123/2016, Case No. 1, §40. *Contra*, the European Court of Human Rights has ruled in the sense that there was no violation of Art. 11 European Convention of Human Rights in the case of Romanian farmers whose request to register a trade union was rejected by the courts as inadmissible on the grounds that, according to the law, only employees and civil servants could set up trade unions (ECtHR, 16 June 2015, Case of *Manole and 'Romanian Farmers Direct' v. Romania*, application No. 46551/06, §9 and 75). Law No. 367/2022 is silent on the situation of priests (ECtHR, [GC], 9 July 2013, Case of *Sindicatul 'Pastorul Cel Bun' v. Romania*, application No. 2330/09).

our study will focus only on the most important changes, as some of the details will be assessed in the section dedicated to the role of collective bargaining in wage-setting.

The first major change concerns the founding of trade unions, independent legal persons registered following a judicial procedure. At least ten employees/workers from the same company or at least twenty employees/workers from different employers of the same collective bargaining sector are necessary in order to create a trade union. A person may belong to only one trade union at the same time within the same employer, but the trade union itself is not strictly linked to an undertaking or employer, as previously.[12] However, certain categories of persons (such as magistrates, dignitaries, and persons having a military status) do not have the right to create or join a trade union.

The new Social Dialogue Act consolidates the information and consultation rights, as the employer is obliged to invite the representative trade union at the company level or, in the absence thereof, the person designated by the non-representative trade unions, to participate in the meetings of the board of directors or another similar body and to consult them on issues of professional, economic and social interest that impact employment. The law also provides for detailed procedures for informing and consulting employees/workers on the recent and probable developments of the employer's economic situation and activities, respectively on the decisions that may lead to significant changes in the organisation of work or in the employment relationships, including but not limited to transfers of companies, acquisitions, mergers, collective redundancies or closure of the company. The decisions adopted by the board of directors or similar bodies on these topics must be notified in writing within two working days to employees and workers, represented according to the law.[13] All the information that is necessary for collective bargaining also has to be provided by the employer, as a pre-condition for meaningful negotiations.[14]

The threshold to meet the representativeness criteria at the company level was lowered: the trade union must have among its members more than 35% of the employees or workers of the employer in question (compared to 50% of the employees, after the 2011 reform[15] and one-third of the employees, before the 2011 reform). At the

12. The existence of company level trade union was strictly related to a legal person according to Law No. 62/2011, as the founding fifteen members had to work for the same employer, whereas before 2011, fifteen persons working in the same sector or profession, albeit in different companies, were enough. In 2011, 90% of Romanian companies have employed only nine workers or fewer and a person could have belonged to only one trade union at the same time. While a minimum membership requirement is not in itself incompatible with Convention No. 87, the ILO Committee on Freedom of Association has stated that the number should be fixed in a reasonable manner so that the establishment of organisations is not hindered; therefore, the proportion of small enterprises in the country should be taken into account – ILO (2011) Memorandum of Technical Comments on the draft Labour Code and the Draft Law on Social Dialogue of Romania, Geneva, 17 January 2011 (hereinafter: ILO (2011) Memorandum of Technical Comments).
13. Article 30 of Law No. 367 of 2022 on social dialogue.
14. Article 98, §4 of Law No. 367 of 2022 on social dialogue establishes categories of information that have to be provided by the employer prior to collective bargaining.
15. The unionisation rate was approximately 24% in 2008.

company level, a trade union is representative also through affiliation to a sectoral-level representative federation.

Collective bargaining is mandatory at the company level for employers having at least ten employees or workers, as well as (for the first time in Romania) at the sectoral level. The new law grants the initiative for collective bargaining to the social partners, both the employer and the trade union, a provision that is particularly relevant, given the fact that the previous laws provided the right to initiate collective bargaining (except for the company level) only for employers, without any means to compel them to negotiate at sectoral or cross-industry level and without any possibility to declare a strike in case of refusal to negotiate.

The new Social Dialogue Act breaks another tradition, as now collective agreements may provide for the periodic renegotiation of any clauses agreed between the parties. Since 1929, the first regulation of collective agreements, in Romania there was an 'absolute' clause of social peace, in the sense that collective bargaining (and strikes) was prohibited when a collective agreement was in force, for the workers falling under its scope. The right to strike has always been strictly regulated in Romania, but now the situations giving the right to declare a strike have been extended. Previously, a strike could have been declared only if the employer refused to initiate collective bargaining at the company level or to negotiate or if the social partners couldn't reach an agreement. According to the new Social Dialogue Act, a strike can also be declared if the employer refuses: to periodically renegotiate clauses, if it has been agreed by the parties; to renegotiate the clauses declared void by the courts; to join the sectoral level collective agreement signed by the trade union representing workers performing work for that employer.

Collective bargaining may take place at the level of the company, of voluntary groups of employers, of the sector of activity and at the national level. Only one collective agreement can be concluded at each level and only the company-level collective agreement produces *erga omnes* effects (i.e., for all the employees or workers of the company, whether they are unionised or not). The sectoral level and the cross-industry (national) level collective agreements produce effects only for workers or employees who perform work for the employers represented by the signatory employers' organisations (federations or confederations). There is a favourability principle, in the sense that collective agreements can only contain rights that are more favourable to workers, compared to the statutory rights (representing the minimum level) and to collective agreements concluded at a geographically higher level (i.e., a company level collective agreement can only provide for supplementary rights compared to the applicable sectoral level collective agreement); derogation *in pejus* is not admitted by the law and any contrary clause is rendered void by the courts.

Adopted by the end of 2022, the new Social Dialogue Act could only start to be implemented six months later, because of the uncertainty regarding the collective bargaining sectors, which were established only in March 2023,[16] and the inconsistencies between some of its provisions, making necessary its revision by the Government's Emergency Ordinance No. 42 of 24 May 2023.

[B] Weaknesses and Deficiencies of Social Dialogue in Romania

Many of the weaknesses and deficiencies of social dialogue in Romania were generated by the former Law on Social Dialogue, No. 62/2011, adopted in the context of the economic crisis. The declared purpose of the 2011 legislative change was of a 'noble' and neutral nature: the need to unify terminology, the legal and procedural aspects related to social dialogue in general, to collective bargaining in particular, aspects that were formally expected to ensure its efficiency. The law was adopted without a direct or express link to the economic and financial crisis, but the Romanian Government had admitted that it would be promoted 'according to the commitments undertaken by Romania under the Stand-by arrangement concluded with International Monetary Fund (IMF)'.[17] The law intended '*to rationalize wage bargaining in the private sector*' (emphasis added), according to the Memorandum of Understanding signed in June 2011,[18] in order to render more flexible the system of wage setting and the settlement of labour disputes.

The criteria for trade union representativeness were amended, being stricter at the company level (more than half of the company's employees had to be members of the union for it to be recognised as representative, compared to only one-third in the previous regulation). In the absence of a representative trade union, collective bargaining took place with elected staff representatives, to the exclusion of non-representative

16. Government Decision No. 171 of 1 March 2023, published in the Official Gazette No. 190 of 7 March 2023 establishes fifty-eight sectors of activity for collective bargaining.
17. https://legislatie.just.ro/Public/DetaliiDocument/109133.
18. Memorandum of Understanding, signed on June 2011, p. 5. On the 6 May 2009, the Council adopted a Decision (2009/459/EC) to make available to Romania medium-term financial assistance for a period of three years. The accompanying Memorandum of Understanding, signed on 23 June 2009, and its successive supplements have settled the economic policy conditions on the basis of which the financial assistance was disbursed. The structural reform measures required by the European Community referred mainly to the need to tackle undeclared work, to establish a unified, simplified pay scale, through the elimination of most bonuses or rolling them in the base wage and to reform of the pensions systems. Romania has successfully implemented the programme, but, given remaining structural weaknesses in Romania's labour markets, the Council adopted a Decision (2011/288/EU) to make precautionary medium-term financial assistance available to Romania for a period of three years. https://eur-lex.europa.eu/legal-content/EN/ALL/?uri=CELEX:32011D0288. The new accompanying Memorandum of Understanding was signed in June 2011 on the conditions that the Romanian Government continues to reform the labour market through the adaption of the flexicurity principle (especially to widen the situations when the use of fixed-term labour contracts is legally allowed). This Memorandum of Understanding was followed by another one, signed 6 November 2013, for precautionary financial assistance, but the only mention on labour market reforms has concerned the need to equalise the pensionable age between man and women.

unions existing in the company.[19] The possibility of concluding cross-sectoral (inter-professional) agreements (called in Romania 'national level collective agreement') was abolished and the effects of the sectoral level collective agreements were limited, as they were biding only for the employers affiliated to the signatory employers' federations (compared to the previous *erga omnes* effects – all the employers in the sector). A mechanism for extending their effects to the level of the entire sector was provided for by law, but it was never used in practice. In addition, the representativeness threshold for trade unions was considered to be too high, and in only six out of twenty-nine sectors representative trade unions (federations) could have engaged in collective bargaining.[20]

In this context, several recommendations were addressed to Romania by the ILO, in 2015, 2018 and 2022, concerning in particular the need for adequate protection against acts of anti-union discrimination, provided by law and in practice; the exclusive negotiator system (which leads, in the collective bargaining process, to the exclusion, by the elected representatives of workers, of trade unions that do not reach the threshold of representativeness) and the minimum conditions for union membership.

Regarding the minimum conditions for membership, the 2011 law imposed a minimum requirement of fifteen founding members, employees of the same company, to form a trade union, while most employers in Romania are small and medium-sized enterprises (i.e., in 2022, a very high percentage – 92.5% of all companies in Romania – employed fewer than fifteen workers). According to statistical data, this requirement had deprived more than 42% of employees of the right to unionisation.[21] At the time of joining, membership in the union was strictly linked to the status of employee of the employer where the union was created or in the process of being created. In addition, self-employed workers and non-standard workers (including voucher-based workers or platform workers), as well as bogus self-employed and undeclared workers did not have the right to create or join a union;[22] they could only create civil law associations, without any role in social dialogue.[23] Thus, the 2011 law created the context for a sharp decline in collective bargaining coverage in the country, from 100% in 2010 (due to the

19. According to a national trade union confederation (Blocul National Sindical), although a minority of employers have signed collective agreements in 2021 (15,204 out of 734,507), most of them were negotiated with elected workers' representatives (12,835 out of 15,204, or 85%) – ECSR, Conclusions 2022, Romania, p. 25.
20. *Ibid.*
21. Observation (CEACR) – adopted 2022, published 111st ILC session (2023), *Freedom of Association and Protection of the Right to Organise Convention, 1948, (No. 87)*, Romania (Ratification: 1957).
22. Independent and non-standard workers represented, in 2022, about 25.5% of the total active population in Romania – Observation (CEACR) – adopted 2022, published 111st ILC session (2023), *supra* n. 21.
23. Despite of the fact that self-employment was one of the main sources of flexibility in employment in Romania – R. Rodríguez Contreras & Cl. Emmanuel Triomphe (eds), *The Impact of New Forms of Labour on Industrial Relations and the Evolution of Labour Law in the European Union*, European Parliament, 2008, p. 112.

erga omnes effect of the cross-sectoral collective agreement) to about 15% in 2017.[24] Negotiation was provided for at the level of companies with twenty-one or more employees but, given the number of small and medium enterprises (SMEs), in more than 90% of all the employers in Romania, collective bargaining didn't take place at the company level. In addition, the employer's decision to leave the employers' organisation had rendered inapplicable the sectoral level collective agreement.

The high threshold for company-level representativeness of trade unions had led, in practice, to an overwhelming majority of collective agreements signed by elected employees' representatives: 86% of all collective agreements were signed by elected representatives of the workers and only 14% by trade unions.[25] In addition, the principle of the exclusive negotiator allowed only the organisation representing more than half of the employees of the enterprise to negotiate collective agreements having an *erga omnes* effect. Otherwise, it was the elected representatives of the workers who had the right to collective bargaining, to the detriment of minority trade union organisations that could only negotiate voluntary agreements applicable only to their members (*inter partes*). This situation was contrary to ILO Convention No. 135 concerning Workers' Representatives, ratified by Romania, according to which recourse to elected representatives cannot be used to weaken the position of workers' organisations. The 2011 law was amended in 2016, and, in the absence of a representative trade union, a non-representative trade union could participate in joint negotiations with the elected workers' representatives, but only if the trade union was affiliated with a representative sectoral trade union (federation). In the event of disagreement between the trade union and the elected representatives, the collective agreement was not concluded. Exclusive representation of workers by their elected representatives was only possible if no trade union was established in the company. However, trade unions often claimed that it was impossible to control the transparency of the election of employees' representatives process, organised by the employer.

In addition, the low coverage of collective agreements, especially at the sectoral level, was also explained by the definition of economic sectors, which did not cover all economic activities carried out in Romani. The timely and substantial participation of social partners in matters related to social policy and reforms was limited;[26] consultations took place formally, within the Economic and Social Council and the social dialogue committees, but the stability and role of these institutions have been weakened. This institutional framework for consultations was not used adequately and did not involve sufficiently the social partners in the design and implementation of reforms.[27] According to ILO Convention No. 154 on collective bargaining, ratified by Romania, the measures taken within this framework must ensure that 'collective

24. Committee on Freedom of Association, 393rd report, March 2021; OECD and AIAS (2023), Institutional Characteristics of Trade Unions, Wage Setting, State Intervention and Social Pacts, version 1.1, OECD Publishing, Paris www.oecd.org/employment/ictwssdatabase.htm, p. 19.
25. A. Trif & V. Paolucci, *Romania: From Legal Support to Frontal Assault*, in T. Müller, K. Vandaele & J. Waddington (eds.), *Collective Bargaining in Europe: Towards an Endgame*, Volume III, ETUI, Brussels, 2019, p. 511.
26. Country Specific Recommendation 2019 (Brussels, 5.6.2019 COM(2019) 523 final), §16, p. 6.
27. Country Specific Recommendation 2020 (Brussels, 20.5.2020 COM(2020) 523 final), §25, p. 8.

bargaining is not hindered by the lack of rules governing its conduct or by the inadequacy or inappropriateness of such rules'; the government has an important responsibility to establish an environment conducive to social dialogue.[28]

§14.02 COLLECTIVE BARGAINING ON WAGE SETTING: EXISTING FRAMEWORK AND CHALLENGES IN THE TRANSPOSITION OF THE EU DIRECTIVE ON ADEQUATE MINIMUM WAGES

As already mentioned, the new Social Dialogue Act has set, in line with Directive 2022/2041 on adequate minimum wages in the EU, the specific objectives to improve social dialogue, to enhance the capacity of social partners to engage in informed, substantial and timely collective bargaining, including on wage setting and to reach a collective bargaining coverage rate of 80% of workers. As the law is too recent, it is difficult to assess its practical relevance. A recent major success is represented by the signature of the collective agreement for the (private) banking sector, given the fact that, since 2011, only a few sectoral collective agreements were signed and only in the public sector (for activities supported by public funds), where bargaining on wages is legally prohibited.

The Directive establishes a framework for promoting collective bargaining on wage-setting; for that purpose, Member States, with the involvement of the social partners, must adopt a series of measures to ensure meaningful collective bargaining, especially at sectoral and cross-industry levels, levels where collective bargaining is very weak in Romania. Or the starting point is that 'strong and well-functioning collective bargaining together with a high coverage of sectorial or cross-industry collective agreements strengthen the adequacy and the coverage of minimum wages'.[29]

[A] National Legal Framework and Positive Obligations under the Adequate Minimum Wages Directive

Romania is one of the countries where sectoral and cross-industry level collective bargaining came under pressure in the context of the 2008 financial crisis, therefore the measures to promote the building and strengthening of the capacity of the social partners to engage in collective bargaining on wages[30] should apply especially at sectoral and cross-industry level. Romania was one of the two countries (alongside Ireland) where the prevalent regime has shifted from multi- to single-employer bargaining. Coordination across sectors was weakened by the fact that the national

28. Individual Case (CAS) – Discussion: 2021, Publication: 109th ILC session (2021), *Right to Organise and Collective Bargaining Convention, 1949, (No. 98), Romania (Ratification: 195).*
29. Preamble, §§22-23 of Directive 2022/2041.
30. Article 4, §1 of Directive 2022/2041.

(cross-sectoral) agreement was abolished, and wage bargaining has largely moved to the company rather than to the sector level.[31]

The adopted measures should encourage 'constructive, meaningful and informed' negotiations of wages through access granted to both parties to the relevant information for collective bargaining on wages and they should protect both the exercise of the right to collective bargaining on wage-setting and the workers and trade union representatives against any discriminatory act in respect of their employment on the ground of collective bargaining on wage setting and of any acts of interference by the employers' organisations.[32]

The decentralisation of social dialogue had a significant impact on wage-setting mechanisms in the private sector in Romania, from 2011 until the present. Before the reform operated in May 2011, collective agreements were concluded at the national (cross-sectoral) level, at the sectoral level and at the company level. Only one collective agreement could have been concluded at each level and it had *erga omnes* effects, covering all the employees at that specific level and thus covering a large number of employees. At the national (cross-sectoral) level, collective agreements were always concluded and the rights they provided for had to be respected by all the employers. As a result, all the Romanian employees were covered by collective agreements and had a collectively negotiated level of rights, higher than the statutory minimum level. The possibility of concluding a cross-sectoral collective agreement was abolished in 2011 and reinstated, to some extent, in 2022, and the *erga omnes* effects of the collective agreements were severely restricted at the sectoral level. Sectoral-level collective agreements provide rights only for the employees of the employers belonging to the signatory parties (to the employers' organisations having signed the collective agreement). As a result, the easiest way for employers to 'escape' the effects of sectoral-level collective agreements was to quit or refrain from joining employers' organisations.[33]

The effects of the sectoral-level collective agreements, as well as the possibility of employers to 'escape' such effects are the same in the 2022 Act as in the 2011 regulation. However, as sectoral and cross-industry level collective bargaining represents an essential factor for achieving adequate minimum wage protection,[34] the possibility to initiate collective bargaining at the sectoral level and cross-sectoral level is recognised for both the trade unions and the employers' organisations (federations and confederations). In all cases, collective bargaining may be initiated sixty days prior to the expiry of the applicable collective agreement.

At the sectoral level, the trade unions' federations, meeting the legally established representativeness criteria, will notify the employers' federations of their intention to initiate collective bargaining at the level of the economic sector, mentioning the undertakings where the represented trade unions have members. The employers'

31. P. Marginson & C. Welz, *Changes to Wage-Setting Mechanisms in the Context of the Crisis and the EU's New Economic Governance Regime*, 3 (Eurofound 2014), https://www.eurofound.europa.eu/sites/default/files/ef_files/docs/eiro/tn1402049s/tn1402049s.pdf.
32. Article 4, §2 of Directive 2022/2041.
33. The number of nationally representative employers' associations has decreased from thirteen in 2010 to six in 2015 (Trif & Paolucci, *supra* n. 25, at 507-508) and to only two in 2024.
34. Directive 2022/2041, Preamble, §22.

federations shall invite to take part in the collective bargaining those employers belonging to the economic sector who are not affiliated to an employers' organisation. After having signed the collective agreement, the trade unions may ask in writing the non-affiliated employers employing their members to adhere to the sectoral-level collective agreement. If the employer disagrees or refuses to answer within ten days, the trade union may declare a strike. Unlike the previous regulation, Law No. 367/2022 provides trade unions with the means to engage employers in collective bargaining and establishes the sectoral level as a mandatory level of bargaining.

At the cross-sectoral level, the representative trade union confederations will notify their intention to initiate collective bargaining at this level to the representative employers' confederations. It is important to mention that the cross-sectoral level collective agreement cannot contain clauses related to minimum wages, as they can be exclusively established by the decision of the Government. The agreement is registered[35] at the cross-sectoral level only if the employees and workers employed by the employers affiliated with the signatory confederations represent more than 20% of the total number of employees/workers in the national economy, with the exclusion of the employees in the public sector. The cross-sectoral level collective agreement might be extended to all the employers and employees in the country, through the decision of the Government, with the mandatory opinion of the National Tripartite Council.

The obligation to encourage informed negotiations on wages through equal access to the relevant information was put into practice by the employer's duty to provide at least data referring to the economic and financial situation of the undertaking, and its potential development over the next twelve to twenty-four months;[36] the situation, the structure of the workforce and the eventual measures that might affect it; measures related to the organisation of work and of working time; the proposed measures to protect employees in the case of transfer of undertakings or of parts of it and to improve workplace health and safety.

A specific aspect is linked to collective bargaining in wage setting at the company and at the sectoral levels. This possibility is expressly recognised by the 2022 Social Dialogue Act, according to which collective agreements may also refer, without affecting the principle of contractual freedom, to the following elements: the minimum wage-ranking coefficients by categories of employees/workers, taking into account the occupational standards; counselling and professional assessment measures for employees/workers; work-life balance, working time and rest time, working conditions and occupational safety and health of employees/workers aspects and supplementary information and consultation measures, exceeding the legal obligations of the employer.

However, collective bargaining on wage setting is legally prohibited in the public sector (including civil servants[37] and employees, paid of public funds), and any such clause exceeding the legal level of wages is declared void by the courts.

35. In Romania, collective agreements become binding only upon registration.
36. For the duration of a collective agreement.
37. For the civil servants, collective agreements are called 'acorduri colective'.

The directive on adequate minimum wages has not been transposed so far; there is only a proposal of law aiming to amend the provisions of the Labour Code related to wages. Romania has chosen to continue the tradition of setting statutory minimum wages and collective agreements can only complement them. They are established by the decision of the Government, after consulting the representative trade union and employers' confederations (at the national level), and it is updated once a year. A procedure 'of application of the mechanism for establishing and updating the guaranteed gross minimum basic salary per country in payment' is to be approved by a decision of the Government, upon the proposal of the Ministry of Labour and Social Solidarity and with the consultation of the National Tripartite Council for Social Dialogue. The procedure is supposed to assess the degree of adequacy of the statutory minimum wage, compared to its share in the average gross wage and it will include the methods and the criteria for establishing and updating the statutory minimum wage. In line with the directive, the criteria will include: the purchasing power of the minimum wage, taking into account the cost of living; the general level of wages and their distribution; the growth rate of wages; the long-term national productivity levels and developments. The procedure will also include a set of annual indicators for monitoring and evaluating the impact of the statutory minimum wage on the economic and social environment and the way of carrying out support analyses and monitoring the evolution of the statutory minimum wage, The indicative reference value of the statutory minimum wage chosen by Romania is the level of 50%-52% of the gross average wage.

It is unclear how the social partners are to be involved in the setting and updating of statutory minimum wages, including their voluntary participation in the discussions throughout the decision-making process;[38] only the designated consultative body – the National Tripartite Council for Social Dialogue – is regulated. According to the 2022 Social Dialogue Act, the Council is formed of the presidents of the trade unions and employers' confederations, meeting the representativeness criteria at the national level, the representatives of the Government, from each ministry and from other public structures, as agreed with the social partners; the president of the Economic and Social Council and other members agreed with the social partners. Given the fact that, in June 2024, there were only five representative trade union confederations and only two representative employers' confederations, but eighteen ministries, it is obvious that the social partners are outnumbered by the representatives of the state.

The legislative proposal also states that the promotion of the tripartite social dialogue at the national level is carried out by the Council National Tripartite for Social Dialogue, with a consultative role between the Government and the social partners, but it is not clear how the social partners are going to be involved.

38. According to Art. 7 of Directive 2022/2041.

[B] Collective Bargaining Coverage: Challenges and Potential Remedies

The directive on adequate minimum wages highlights the role of high collective bargaining coverage in ensuring a decent standard of living, as it is associated with high levels of minimum wages.[39] Therefore, an additional obligation is established for Member States in which the collective bargaining coverage rate is less than 80% to provide for a framework of enabling conditions and to establish an action plan to promote collective bargaining, with a clear timeline and concrete measures to progressively increase the rate of collective bargaining coverage, after consulting the social partners or by agreement with them or as agreed between the social partners.[40]

The framework for enabling conditions for collective bargaining seems to be the new Social Dialogue Act of 2022. As mentioned, the law structurally changes the social dialogue and creates the conditions for the social partners to engage in collective bargaining.

Because of the 2011 reform, the collective bargaining coverage has considerably decreased and only a small proportion of employees are covered by a conventional minimum pay, set by the applicable collective agreement.[41] Mainly employees in large- or medium-sized companies tend to be covered, because of the forced shift to single-employer bargaining,[42] but the great majority of Romanian companies are small- and medium-sized companies.[43] The decentralisation of collective bargaining, led, in 2011 to a decrease in the number of company-level collective agreements, followed by a fluctuating trend an and important decrease in 2020.[44]

Higher collective bargaining coverage can be achieved through different legislative options. The first option could be a reinstatement of the *erga omnes* effects of the

39. Preamble, §25 of Directive 2022/2041.
40. Article 4, §2 of Directive 2022/2041.
41. The collective bargaining coverage rate was estimated to 35% for Romania – J. Visser, S. Hayter & R. Gammarano, *Trends in Collective Bargaining Coverage: Stability, Erosion or Decline?*, Issue Brief No. 1 – Labour Relations and Collective Bargaining 5 (2015), https://researchrepository.ilo.org/esploro/outputs/encyclopediaEntry/Trends-in-collective-bargaining-coverage-stability/995218767102676.
42. F. Rosioru, *El Salario En Rumania: The Myths Behind the Facts*, 108 Documentacion Laboral 132 (2016).
43. In December 2015, in Romania there were 41,976 such undertakings. In 2020, out of 624,206 active companies, 566,735 were small and medium enterprises (SMEs) employing less than 10 employees; 47,852 SMEs employing 10 to 49 employees (representing 8% of the SMEs) and 7,947 SMEs employing 50 to 249 employees (representing 8% of the SMEs) – A.D. Chirescu & S.R. Patarlageanu, *Analiza situației IMM-urilor din România*, Romanian Statistical Review – Supplement 107 (2022)).
44. According to the National Institute of Statistics, 7,473 company-level collective agreements were registered in 2011 by the Labour Inspectorates, compared to 2010, when there were 7,718 such agreements; in 2012, 8,783 company-level collective agreements were registered; in 2013, 8,726 such agreements; in 2014, 9,477 company-level collective agreements; in 2015, 8,702 such agreements. In 2016, there was an increase in the number of company-level collective agreements – 9,366 – as trade unions were considered to be representative if affiliated to a representative federation of trade unions. Afterwards, the new collective agreements concluded at the company level were: 13,359 new agreements in 2017, 10,708 in 2018, 8,233 in 2019, and 5,742 in 2020.

cross-sectoral collective agreement, that would, thus, cover all the workers in Romania. This wasn't the legislator's choice, as this collective agreement is binding only for the employers affiliated to the signatory parties and, according to the law, it cannot contain clauses setting minimum wages. The second choice is linked to a reinforced sectoral collective bargaining, and this seems to be the legislator's choice. The effects of the sectoral level collective agreement are only biding for the employers who were represented during the negotiations (members of the signatory employers' organisation), but the law expressly stipulates the possibility of trade unions to initiate collective bargaining (with the consequence of declaring a strike in the case of refusal) and to request the employer's adhesion to the sectoral collective agreement that the trade unions (through their federation) have signed (again, with the possibility to declare a strike in case of refusal). Collective bargaining at the sectoral level has been rendered mandatory; however, due to the new redefinition of sectors and the representativeness criteria, there might be sectors without representative federations. In this case, the law provides that the national-level representative confederations can take part in the sectoral-level collective bargaining if they have employers, trade unions or federations as affiliates, upon request and based on their mandate.[45]

In addition, if the signatory employers' organisations employ more than 35% of the employees/workers in the collective bargaining sector, the collective agreement can be extended at the level of the whole sector (and become binding for all the employers in the sector) by decision of the Government, with the mandatory opinion of the National Tripartite Council.

The third option could be represented by a high collective bargaining coverage at the company level, but strong trade unions are necessary. A sufficient membership base, organisational capacity to negotiate, legal recognition and the workers' confidence in the trade union are considered to be key preconditions 'for a strong and functional social dialogue',[46] that are not necessarily met, for the moment being, by the Romanian trade unions. The new Law No. 367/2022 has lowered the number of the founding members (from fifteen to ten employees or workers working for the same employer) and it had created the conditions for trade unions to be created even in very small companies (as founding members can consist of twenty employees or workers in the sector). In addition, the possibility of creating a trade union was recognised also to workers, dependent or independent, and not just to employees, as the previous option, according to ILO, was too narrow and did not 'capture the variety of emerging patterns of work organization', nor the disguised employment relationship.[47]

The elected representatives of the employees can negotiate the collective agreement only if there is not any trade union at the company level; representative federations can negotiate at the company level upon request of their non-representative members.

According to the new legislative project aiming to transpose Directive 2022/2041, the Government, by decision and at the proposal of the Ministry of Labour, approves an

45. Article 103 of Law No. 367 of 2022.
46. Eurofound, *Collective Bargaining in Europe in the 21st Century*, 11 (2015).
47. ILO (2011) Memorandum of Technical Comments, *supra* n. 12.

action plan to promote collective bargaining, with precise timeline and measures in favour of the progressive increase in collective bargaining coverage, to improve the conditions of work and livelihood of employees. This action plan is established with the consultation and/or agreement with the social partners in the National Tripartite Council for Social Dialogue and it is revised periodically or at least once every five years, having as its objective to support the increase of the rate of collective bargaining coverage to the value of 80%. The same Government's decision will include monitoring and evaluation procedures, as well as revision and reporting of the action plan to the European Commission.

However, collective bargaining coverage is influenced by different factors, among which national practices and the historical context play an important role [1]. In addition, as industrial relations are strongly regulated, it is important to assess the influence of legislative changes on collective bargaining coverage [2].

[1] The Potential Influence of the Historical Background on the Collective Bargaining Coverage Rate

Industrial relations in post-socialist countries were seen to have many important things in common at the moment of joining the EU, including the predominance of decentralised wage bargaining.[48] However, until 2011, 'decentralisation' was not the keyword for the Romanian collective bargaining system.[49] Industrial relations were strongly regulated and legislative reforms have weakened or strengthened the capacities of trade unions to defend the interests of their members, with a direct influence on collective bargaining coverage and the content of the collective agreements. This direct influence is highlighted by the historical background, characterised by two contradictory trends in the evolution of the collective bargaining system in Romania during the last thirty years[50].

The first trend (1991-2011) has aimed to encourage social dialogue and collective bargaining, after forty years of communism, when collective bargaining was rather formal and ineffective. As a result, in Romania collective bargaining was rendered compulsory, but only at the company level in companies with a workforce of at least twenty-one employees (at that moment, more than 24,000 companies). This trend was manifested not only in the context of relatively high trade-union density (similar to the unweighted average for the EU's fifteen Member States) but also of structural changes in the economy, involving a high rate of company closures and company start-ups.[51]

48. L. Funk & H. Lesch, *Industrial Relations in Central and Eastern Europe: Organisational Characteristics, Codetermination and Labour Disputes*, Intereconomics 264 (2004).
49. Al Athanasiu & L. Dima, *Dreptul Muncii*, 284-287 (All Beck 2005); I.T. Stefanescu, *Tratat teoretic şi practic de drept al muncii*, 168-172 (2nd ed., Universul Juridic 2017); Al. Ticlea, *Tratat de dreptul muncii*, 316-325 (2nd ed., Universul Juridic 2017); M. Tichindelean, *Dreptul colectiv al muncii*, 142-144 (Universul Juridic 2015); C.-A. Moarcaş Costea, *Dreptul colectiv al muncii*, 200-202 (C.H. Beck 2012).
50. The historical background is presented in more detail in our contribution to the previous edition of this book, focusing on the analysis of Law no 62 of 2011 on social dialogue.
51. Funk & Lesch, *supra* n. 48, at 264.

During the communist regime (1947-1989) trade union membership and collective bargaining were rather formal. The high rates of unionisation can be explained by the fact that all the employees were trade union members and, formally, trade union representatives were involved in decision-making at the undertaking level; in reality, undertakings were integrated into a centralised system and the most important decisions were taken at the central level. Given the public ownership and communal control of the major means of production and of the natural resources of a society, formally there were not any antagonist interests between the workers and the employers, as, ideologically, undertakings themselves served for the well-being of the working class.[52] Collective agreements were mandatory in every state-owned company, but have contained general, impersonal provisions, linked to the 'superior organization of work' and to the achievement of the economic goals of the centralised 'plan', as all the aspects of the employment relationship were regulated by the law. Collective agreements were signed by the employer and the representatives of the trade union, but they had to be previously approved by the general assembly of the employees. On the one hand, trade unions were involved to some extent in the distribution of benefits to the workers;[53] on the other hand, during the communist regime, trade unions had stopped playing their traditional role, linked to collective bargaining and collective action. The second trend (2011-2022) has aimed to 'discourage' collective bargaining by using the socio-economic context created during the financial crisis. Legislative measures were adopted to decentralise collective bargaining, seen as one of the ways to mitigate the effects of the financial crisis, by reducing the pressure in wage setting at the company level. However, collective bargaining was 'hit' in several ways, as decentralisation was combined with a higher percentage of membership required to trade unions to meet the representativeness criteria at the company level[54] and a limitation of the *erga omnes* effects of sectoral level collective agreements.

These aspects are useful to explain the high rates of unionism and collective bargaining coverage in the 90s; however, they also explain why today there is a certain lack of confidence on behalf of the workers in the role of trade unions and collective bargaining. It also explains the limited role of collective actions, the limited number of strikes and the rather passive attitude towards major legislative reforms impeding social dialogue. However, even after thirty-five years since the fall of communism, the

52. In this context, collective agreements were seen to be 'essentially different' than the ones concluded in 'capitalist countries', where collective agreements were 'the legal tool (...) to fight against exploitation' – S. Ghimpu, et al., *Dreptul muncii. Tratat,* vol. I, 107 (Editura Stiinţifica şi Enciclopedica 1977).
53. Trade unions were involved in allocating resources to providing workers with holidays for themselves and their families, housing, and money when they had particular needs – R. Croucher & M. Rizov, *Union Influence in Post-socialist Europe*, 65 ILR Review 630-650 (2012), https://journals.sagepub.com/doi/10.1177/001979391206500307.
54. Between 2011 and 2015, company-level collective bargaining took place only in a few large multinational companies, as the 50% density for trade unions was difficult to achieve; In 2016, just four companies were covered by collective agreements (Carrefour, Selgros, Metro and Real) – Trif & Paolucci, *supra* n. 25 at 516.

Government is still expected to and undertakes the role of solving, through normative measures, the different 'crisis' that may occur.

[2] *Are Legal Measures Adequate to Improve the Collective Bargaining Rate in Romania?*

The new Social Dialogue Act of 2022 has adopted a series of measures to promote social dialogue and to (potentially) enhance collective bargaining and the role of social partners in wage setting, in line with Directive 2022/2041. In this context, the question is whether the law is a suitable solution to promote social dialogue and improve collective bargaining coverage or whether a high degree of autonomy of the social partners would have been more adequate for that purpose. We argue that the answer depends on the historical background and the existing collective bargaining traditions. Therefore, a legislative overview is useful to assess the effectiveness of the measures adopted by Romania in the field of social dialogue.

After the fall of the communist regime, two laws – adopted in 1991 and 2003, aimed at reviving pre-communist trade union traditions, by rendering mandatory collective bargaining in larger companies and by establishing an annual obligation to periodically re-negotiate wages, working conditions, working time and schedules. At the company level, the employer had the obligation, according to the law, to initiate the negotiation process; in case he fails to do so, a formal request can be addressed by the trade union(s) or, in the absence thereof, by the workers' elected representatives. Thus, industrial relations were regulated by different laws adopted after the change of the political regime,[55] but in the context of a Labour Code adopted during the communist regime.[56] In 1996, Law No. 130 on Collective Agreements continued the tradition initiated by the first Romanian regulation, a law of German inspiration, adopted in 1929;[57] thus, these agreements have regained their traditional functions, but the clause of social peace was restrictively regulated: collective disputes could be triggered only in the context of collective bargaining and strikes couldn't be declared while a collective agreement signed by the parties was in force.

Law No. 62/2011 on Social Dialogue was seen as a major reform, as it had regrouped five existing laws, elaborated in different social-economic contexts,[58] as well as the previous legislation on the functioning of social dialogue committees organised at central and local levels in the public administration authorities. Its most obvious change consisted in the decentralisation of collective bargaining, giving a more

55. Law No. 13/1991 on Collective Agreements, Law No. 15/1991 on Labour Disputes Resolution, Law No. 54/1991 on the Organisation and the Functioning of Trade Unions; Governmental Decision No. 503/1991 on the Organisation and the Functioning of the Employers' Associations.
56. Law No. 10/1972, the Labour Code, in force until 2003.
57. J. Moscovici, *Lege asupra contractelor de munca*, 217-228 (Socec & Co S.A 1937); Tichindelean, *supra* n. 49, at 18.
58. Law No. 130/1996 on Collective Agreements; Law No. 109/1997 on the Organisation and the Functioning of the Economic and Social Council; Law No. 168/1999 on Labour Disputes' Resolution; Law No. 356/2001 on the Employers' Associations; Law No. 54/2003 on the Organisation and the Functioning of Trade Unions.

prominent role to enterprise bargaining compared to sectoral or group of undertaking bargaining; but, at the same time, sectoral-level collective bargaining was seriously undermined; there was no longer a compulsory agenda for negotiations; the sectors were established by the Romanian Government only in December 2011[59] and, as already mentioned, new company level representativeness criteria were adopted for trade unions. In addition, a collective agreement could have been registered at the sectoral level, producing *erga omnes* effects, only if the signatory employers' organisations were employing more than half of the total number of employees in that sector. If this condition was fulfilled, the collective agreement could have been extended to the whole sector, on the signatory parties' demand, by the decision of the Labour Minister, with the approval of the National Tripartite Council, but this extension procedure was never used. As a result, company-level collective bargaining has become the usual (and almost exclusive) level of collective bargaining. However, in this context, the European Commission and International Monetary Fund (IMF)[60] manifested their concern about 'loosening procedures in the existing legislation that are intended to avoid the proliferation of strikes', even if the number of strikes is very limited in Romania.[61]

Only a very limited number of sectoral collective agreements were signed. For example, in 2013, 2014, 2017 and 2021, only one sectoral collective agreement was signed each year; in 2012, 2019 and 2023, there were two sectoral agreements signed each year, but, except for the 2013 sectoral agreement for veterinary activities, all the others were applicable in the public sector, without any such agreement having been signed in 2015 or 2016.[62] The first sectoral agreement concluded after the 2022 reform was signed in April 2024 in the banking sector.

Thus, one of the persisting effects of the social dialogue reform consists of an important decline in collective bargaining coverage, as employees working in small and medium companies are, most often, totally uncovered. In addition, because of the former company-level representativeness criteria, most of the collective agreements

59. The Governmental decision, establishing twenty-nine sectors, was published only on 29 December 2011.
60. This 'behind-the-scenes pressure to halt the restoration of core labour rights' was strongly condemned by the International Trade Union Confederation (ITUC) – ITUC News: *IMF and EC Apply Behind-the-Scenes Pressure on Romania to Halt the Restoration of Core Labour Rights*, ITUC Press release, 21 November 2012, http://www.ituc-csi.org/imf-and-ec-apply-behind-the-scenes.html,.
61. The right to strike is strictly regulated and related to collective bargaining; as a result, less social dialogue in practice means that the possibilities to declare a strike are diminished. For example, in 2015, out of 41,976 undertakings having more than 21 employees, only 35 conflicts of interests were registered (compared to only 33 out of 42,645 undertakings in 2016) and there are no clear statistics as to the number of strikes that were subsequently declared (http://www.mmuncii.ro/j33/index.php/ro/transparenta/statistici/buletin-statistic/4391). A strike could be declared only in the context of collective labour disputes ('conflicts of interests'), occurring in the following situations: the employer or employers' organisation refuses to start the collective bargaining, while not having signed a collective agreement or the previous one having ended; the employer or employers' organisation does not accept the claims made by the employees; the parties don't reach an agreement until the date agreed to end the negotiations (usually sixty days). There is a mandatory dispute resolution mechanism (called conciliation); a strike may be declared only afterwards.
62. https://dialogsocial.gov.ro/sector-de-activitate/.

were concluded by elected employees' representatives,[63] deemed to be weaker, less experienced and less informed than the trade unions. The situation has led often to very diverse and 'weak' collective agreements, providing for only a limited number of rights, as usually there wasn't any higher-level collective agreement. As a consequence, there was a decreasing trend in certain extra salary benefits, such as social benefits and allowances (meal tickets, transport), insurance benefits (life insurance, medical, private pensions' schemes), statute benefits (car, phone) or benefits related to lifestyle (sports and recreation, childcare).[64]

The forty years of break – during the communist regime – in collective bargaining and collective action, as well as the communist era itself, has played and still plays an important role in explaining the weaknesses of social dialogue. The legislative overview highlights the fact that industrial relations are strongly regulated in Romania, and they limit or enhance the social partners' bargaining capacity, in a society where trade unions are still seen with certain scepticism and employers are, usually, not willing to undertake more obligations than the statutory level. It can also be noticed that, due to these particularities, the collective bargaining coverage rate still depends largely on the legal framework, that empowers or undermines the trade unions' prerogatives in representing and defending workers.

§14.03 THE IMPACT OF THE SOCIAL DIALOGUE REFORM: THE AFTERMATH OF THE EARTHQUAKE

Similar to the financial crisis,[65] different crises have struck European countries in different ways and, usually, collective bargaining and social dialogue are seen as means to circumvent their effects. After the financial crisis of 2008, the general trend in Europe was to decentralise collective bargaining, with new possibilities of opting-out or *in pejus* derogation at the enterprise level. Sometimes decentralisation was adopted by way of collective bargaining, by the social partners themselves; in other cases, opting-out possibilities were seen as ways of proving the social partners' capacity to manage the effects of the crisis, offering 'custom fit' solutions, adapted to the particular situation of a certain company and of a certain country. The legislation adopted in many EU Member States has changed the way of adopting collectively bargained rules, establishing a different hierarchy of the sources of social (labour) law and new representativeness criteria that have to be met by the trade unions in order to render the outcome of collective bargaining more 'legitimate', and Romania was a part of the trend.

---

63. Trif & Paolucci, *supra* n. 25 at 512.
64. PayWell Romania: *Salariile din sectorul privat au crescut in medie cu 4,1% in 2014. Studiul confirma tendința de scadere a tuturor tipurilor de beneficii extra salariale*, 2014, http://economie.hotnews.ro/stiri-finante_banci-18035723-paywell-romania-salariile-din-sectorul-privat-crescut-medie-4-1-2014-studiul-confirma-tendinta-scadere-tuturor-tipurilor-beneficii-extra-salariale.htm.
65. S. Laulom, E. Mazuyer & C. Escande Varniol (sous la direction de), *Quel droit social dans une Europe en crise?* (Bruxelles: Larcier 2012).

As 'crisis seems to be everywhere',[66] the economic crisis turned out to be a crisis in law and institutions,[67] followed by the pandemic, the energy crisis, the environmental crisis, and more generally, the Ukrainian war crisis affecting the sources of supply and leading to the suspension of the activity of companies owned by Russian oligarchs and, more generally, the inflation that affected Romania. In all these cases, the general answer consisted of protective measures adopted by the State, due to the many features of social dialogue imprinted by the historical background. The systematic assault over trade unions may have reduced the pressure on wage setting during the financial crisis, but it has structurally weakened them and ruined the system the social partners have managed to build in two decades (from 1990 to 2011). Decentralisation of collective bargaining to the lowest level has weakened the social acquis achieved so far by the trade unions at the national level and affected sectoral collective bargaining. It has also lowered the standard of rights recognised so far, anchored in higher-level collective agreements. The forced decentralisation of collective bargaining and the criteria for the extension procedure introduced in legislation were accompanied with the replacement of the automatic continuation of collective agreements beyond expiry with the requirement of an express agreement between the parties, limited to one year.

Besides the significant decrease in the number of Romanian employees covered by collective agreements, in many cases collective wage bargaining was absent or irrelevant, providing for a slightly higher level of wages than the statutory minimum pay and rights. The reform has affected the very structure of trade unions as well as their institutional means of protecting and representing workers. New topics that arise out of the organisation of the labour market, in the context of globalisation and the use of technology, were usually not covered through social dialogue. Collective bargaining in Romania does not substantially contribute to the search for solutions to youth and/or senior unemployment, to precarious situations of 'outsiders', 'para-subordinate', platform workers or independent workers, nor for the issues of complex organisations.

Steps towards recentralisation and towards effective, meaningful collective bargaining were made by the 2022 Social Dialogue Act. The legislative changes are very complex and, usually, in line with international standards, aiming to grant an effective exercise of the freedom of association as a fundamental right. The typical 'outsiders' can now be integrated into social dialogue, an aspect that is particularly important given the rising number of platform and third-country nationals' workers in Romania. Independent workers may have a stronger voice and their interests can now be more effectively represented. However, this is just the beginning of a new era, as in many cases trade unions still have to gain a sufficient membership base, the organisational resources and the capacity to negotiate and, more importantly, the workers'

66. L. Henderson, *What It Means to Say 'Crisis' in Politics and Law* (2014) http://www.e-ir.info/2014/03/05/what-it-means-to-say-crisis-in-politics-and-law/.
67. A. Supiot, *A Legal Perspective on the Economic Crisis of 2008*, 149 International Labour Review 151, 153 (2010).

confidence, the necessary power to fight the employers' passivity and engage in meaningful collective bargaining. After the 'earthquake' generated by the 2011 reform, social dialogue in Romania was rebuilt on stronger and more democratic pillars, giving hope for a fresh start for collective bargaining and a stronger protection of workers.

CHAPTER 15

Collective Bargaining in Spain: The Road Goes Ever On

Yolanda Maneiro Vázquez & José María Miranda Boto

§15.01 COLLECTIVE BARGAINING'S REGULATION IN FORTY-FIVE YEARS: A SHORT STORY

Traditionally, statutory law has been the core of labour law in Spain, due to historical circumstances. The Constitution of 1978 did not greatly change this panorama, although it contained the foundations of a new, democratic system of industrial relations. In this context, the last forty-five years have seen a legal and political debate about the role of collective bargaining and its articulation with statutory law.

Immediately after the Constitution, in the development of its Article 37, the new system of collective bargaining was established in 1980, with the first version of the *Estatuto de los Trabajadores* (ET, Workers' Statute). Nonetheless, it clearly drew on the system of the Franco's regime that preceded it.[1] The general efficacy of collective agreements remained a landmark of the Spanish system.

Thus, agreements bargained according to the rules of Title III of ET (that deals with bargaining agents, contents, procedures, etc.) are entitled to general efficacy. All employers and all employees under the scope of a collective agreement are bound by the employment conditions established in it. All the contents of collective agreements must bring an improvement of the *minima* imposed by statutory legislation unless *in peius* derogations are expressly allowed by it, a rare feature in Spanish law.

In more than four decades, the main labour law reforms have tried to enhance and redefine the role of collective bargaining. However, it is an unfinished task. The structure of collective bargaining in Spain is hard to understand, as there are thousands of collective agreements in force and their organisation is not centralised. In this

1. F. Valdés Dal-Ré, *La negociación colectiva, entre tradición y renovación*, Comares, Granada, 2012.

panorama, there is a remarkable fragmentation, as we can point out the existence of State-level, regional (seventeen regions) and provincial collective agreements (and there are fifty provinces). The problems of their co-existence have a big importance in the Spanish system, not only legally but also politically, as we will explain later.

In 1994, the first major reform took place, giving more competences to collective bargaining and thus trying to limit the role of state legislation.[2] From that date, there was no further change until the economic crisis of 2008. Then there were two major reforms, in 2011 and 2012, the first under a Socialist government, and the second under a Conservative one.[3] Both of them followed the path of flexibility.

They did not all arise exclusively from the ideologies of the governing parties. There is no doubt that the changes were promoted from the outside, with the European Commission playing its part. Through Commissar Rehn, the Commission was a strong promoter of the austerity measures implemented. With regard to other driving forces of these reforms, there was strictly speaking no memorandum in Spain similar to the one in Portugal. However, a secret letter from the ECB dating from 2011 was published by former President Rodríguez Zapatero in 2013 and declassified in December 2014 by the ECB.[4] The great lines of reform had been drawn in Frankfurt and not in Madrid.

The impact of these reforms was smaller than expected, however. The most successful tool of the reforms, perhaps, was the possibility of opting out of an existing agreement, that will be explained later. It was rigorously employed in 2013 (2.512 times, affecting 159,550 workers), but with reducing frequency in the following years (544 times in 2023, affecting 24,538 workers).[5] Company-level bargaining did not have the expected development: there was significant growth until 2019, but the numbers in 2022 are very similar to those in 2010.

As of January 2024, the current state of the legislation has been established by the previous and the incumbent coalition government, of a progressive sign, integrated by PSOE and Podemos (2019-2023) and PSOE and Sumar (from the end of 2023). In 2021 and 2023, it implemented some counter-reforms that tried to change the model. The first one had the clear support of social partners, as it was preceded by a strong social dialogue. This was one of the lodestars of the government in the preceding four years, looking for solid support for its reforms, even if, when necessary, the government has shown independence of criterium.

The 1980 legislative decision has led, nowadays, to the paradox of one of the widest coverage rates of collective bargaining in Europe (more than 1.2 million companies and more than 12 million workers), with one of the lowest affiliations to

2. J. Rivero Lamas, 'Estructuras y contenidos de la negociación colectiva en la Ley 11/1994 (una aproximación interpretativa)', Documentación laboral, 43, 1994, pp. 35-92.
3. An analysis of these reforms can be found in the first version of this paper, 'The Spanish Example', in S. Laulom (ed.), *Collective Bargaining Developments in Times of Crisis*, Wolters Kluwer, 2018, pp. 117-128.
4. On the impact on public administrations, the first version of this paper, *supra*.
5. https://www.mites.gob.es/ficheros/ministerio/sec_trabajo/ccncc/B_Actuaciones/Boletin/No_88_-diciembre_2023.pdf.

trade unions (about 12.5%[6] in 2020). As a collective agreement will be applicable to all employees working in the branch or the company, and security clauses such as *closed shop* are forbidden, there is no incentive for many employees to join a trade union.[7]

The debate about the general efficacy of collective agreements, thus, could be approached from opposite views. On the one hand, there are liberal academic opinions that ask for a limited, contractual interpretation, on the grounds of a free market.[8] On the other hand, according to the opinion of some trade unions, never expressed in scientific literature, the end of their general application could bring higher rates of affiliation and a greater commitment to the organisations. In any case, this debate is not a priority either in the political or in the academic debate.

§15.02 THE AGENTS OF COLLECTIVE BARGAINING: THE DOUBLE CHANNEL

Since 1985, no changes have taken place concerning this issue. Workers' representation is, perhaps, the most stable part of Spanish labour law. As a result of history and the clash of political circumstances, the Spanish representation system is based on a double channel.

On the one hand, there is the so-called legal representation, established in the ET, that we can mainly summarise as works councils ('*comités de empresa*') and staff representatives ('*delegados de personal*'), depending on the size of the establishment and endowed with the same powers. Both of them represent all the employees in an establishment.[9] As they represent establishments, and not whole companies, the classic principle of 'unity of company' is no longer in force, and different establishments within the same company can have different agreements. On the other hand, the Supreme Court has ruled that a single works council cannot bargain on behalf of the others ('principle of correspondence').

On the other hand, there is the so-called representation by trade unions, based on the *Ley Orgánica de Libertad Sindical* (LOLS, or Organic Act on Trade Union's Freedom). Its main manifestations are the trade union sections within the enterprise, voluntary in their creation and only representing their own members.[10] Both bodies have the legitimacy to bargain, according to Article 87 ET, and have the same competences and powers when doing so. Since the reform of 2011, trade unions have priority in bargaining, if they represent the majority of posts in the works council. Thus, both channels are clearly interlinked. In any event, case law has ruled that *hybrid*

6. According to the OECD statistics: https://stats.oecd.org/Index.aspx?DataSetCode=TUD&fbclid=IwAR0EODM8R80NjMwbV2OJ5nJrPf1-9B209YTC_8JPxKRw40TNVeH4uVzqc6E.
7. One possible counterbalance for this situation was established in Art. 11 LOLS. It allows trade unions to collect fees as a canon for the task of collective bargaining. Doubts about its constitutionality were cleared by STC 89/1985, but this measure is never enforced, as it is obviously unpopular, and the Constitutional Court made compulsory the individual agreement of each payer, which leads to a difficult implementation.
8. J. Lahera Forteza, *Normas laborales y contratos colectivos*, Reus, Madrid, 2008.
9. J. Gárate Castro, *Derecho Sindical. Volumen I. Los actores*, Bomarzo, Albacete, 2023, pp. 186 ss.
10. *Ibid.*, pp. 258 ss.

bargaining bodies are not possible. In order to negotiate an agreement for a company with multiple establishments, trade union sections have been shown by case law as the only suitable body.

In the vast majority of cases, works councils have a very close bond with trade union organisations. In fact, the Spanish trade union model is based more on representation through the works council structure than on membership. However, as EIRO highlights, in sectors with high union membership – for example, the automobile or chemical industries – the works councils, though remaining unionised, lose much of their 'prominence'. In these cases, the protagonists of trade union activity and organisation within enterprises are the workplace sections of the different unions, marshalling their own members.

Trade union members predominate within the works councils, as they are the source of legitimacy to obtain the category of 'most representative' trade union.[11] This is a legal status in Spain conferring many legal privileges, guarantees and access to public funding. Nonetheless, individual workers can be members of works councils and thus participate in collective bargaining (though that is not the rule).

Above the company level, the only bargaining agents recognised by Spanish law are trade unions. On the employers' side, for this type of agreement, only organisations have the right to bargain. At these higher levels of bargaining, in order to respect the rules of the *Estatuto* and thus have general efficacy, it is necessary to achieve certain majorities. Any trade union holding 10% of the posts in works councils or staff representatives of a given geographical and functional scope can bargain, as well as those trade unions with the 'most representative' status in the whole country or a region.[12] It is necessary to have at least 50% of all representatives to conclude a valid collective agreement. For employers' organisations, the rate is calculated by taking into consideration the number of workers within the scope of the agreement.

§15.03 THE STRUCTURE OF COLLECTIVE BARGAINING: THE TENSION FOR DECENTRALISATION

The predominance of branch agreements in a context of intense business fragmentation has been a defining characteristic of the Spanish bargaining structure, giving priority to intermediate levels of negotiation and province-level agreements especially.[13] However, political interests, both internal and external (mainly, the influence of the European Commission), have introduced a tension pulling for decentralisation.

The first dimension of decentralisation in collective bargaining is linked to territorial issues: State-wide versus regional agreements. Politics have played an important role in the configuration of the balance of powers between these possibilities, as legal reforms have had sometimes their roots in the interest of enhancing the

11. J.L. Monereo Pérez, 'La mayor representatividad sindical como eje del sistema de relaciones laborales en España', *Revista española de Derecho del trabajo*, 10, 2016, pp. 283-327.
12. H. Álvarez Cuesta, *La mayor representatividad sindical*, Universidad de León, León, 2006.
13. J.R. Mercader Uguina, 'La estructura de la negociación colectiva', *Temas laborales: Revista andaluza de trabajo y bienestar social*, 76, 2004, pp. 113-134.

regional spaces of industrial relations, especially dealing with the regions with nationalist governments, such as the Basque Country and Catalonia, and in a lesser way, Galicia. This is a very Spanish problem, where many sources of discussion come together and the courts have not been able to find equilibrium between all those interests.

The last proposed reform, as of 20 December 2023, derives directly from the pact between the PSOE and the PNV (Basque Nationalist Party) and has been rejected firmly by the employers' organisations and mildly by the trade unions. It was rejected by Parliament in that moment, but passed in 2024 in a different political scenario.

As a rule, Article 83.2 ET gives social partners the power to decide the structure of collective bargaining, even modifying some statutory rules that will be exposed in the following paragraphs. These are the most *political* collective agreements, but their real efficacy was severely reduced by the reform of 1994.[14]

With the new legal modification, the social partners in regions have the power to bargain branch collective agreements that could derogate the State-wide branch agreements (Article 84.3 ET), if they had the majorities established in the ET and "their regulation is more favourable to workers than that laid down in state agreements or conventions". The possible limits to this freedom established by an agreement passed according to Article 83.2 ET are not an obstacle any more. The clear, explicit goal of this reform was to enhance the Basque framework of industrial relations. Furthermore, provincial agreements, that had never had any sort of preference, can, under the new legislation, be declared as prevalent by an agreement under Article 83.2 ET, in the regional framework, and derogate from State-wide agreements. (Article 84.4 ET).

In any case, there are several issues that can only be regulated in State-wide agreements. These are: probation period, labour contract modalities, professional classification of workers, maximum yearly working time, disciplinary regime, minimal dispositions on occupational risk prevention and geographic mobility (Article 84.5 ET).[15]

Thus, regional agreements receive a new dose of encouragement. Will it be enough to defeat the incumbent paradox of the system? The provincial agreement, that until now had no priority at all over other levels, nor formal competences reserved to it, has turned out to be the most important collective agreement in the last decades.[16] The proximity of bargaining agents, inertia or pure conservatism in the bargaining process has led to the survival of the weakest. 'Stability' is the most suitable word to describe the panorama of the practice of collective bargaining in Spain.

14. F. Valdés Dal-Ré, *Estructura contractual y concurrencia entre convenios colectivos*, in *La reforma laboral de 2012 en materia de negociación colectiva*, La Ley – Wolters Kluwer, Madrid, 2012, p. 84: social partners 'were deprived of the freedom to establish an articulated system of bargaining'.
15. On the territorial and political problems of the articulation of State-wide and regional agreements, T. Sala Franco & E. López Terrada, 'La negociación colectiva', in *Propuestas para un debate sobre la reforma laboral*, Francis Lefebvre, Madrid, 2018, pp. 57-58.
16. https://www.mites.gob.es/es/estadisticas/condiciones_trabajo_relac_laborales/CCT/welcome.htm. According to the official statistics from the Ministry, in respect to the agreements signed in 2017, 3,472,290 employees worked under a provincial agreement, 3,170,200 under a State-wide, 1,958,755 under a regional and 704,578 under a company agreement.

The second source of decentralisation comes from the conflict between branch agreements, of any geographical level, and company agreements. The change in the priority between them was the most remarkable innovation in collective bargaining in these decades. It appeared shyly in the reforms of 2011, made by the PSOE, and again more clearly in 2012 made by the Popular Party.

The 2012 reform provisions generated a landslide in the equilibrium between collective agreements. The will of the legislator was clear, as this reversal of forces was considered 'the most radical and devastating reform ever since 1980'.[17] According to the new law, company agreements may derogate *in peius* branch agreements, whatever their territorial scope, for the first time in history. In this context, prior to the reform introduced in 2011, Article 84.1 ET ensured the enforcement of any existing agreement, which could not be affected 'by the content of agreements with a different scope' unless otherwise stated in a cross-industry agreement reached according to Article 83.2 ET.

On this basis, the 2012 reform introduced the imperative rule for all purposes, unalterable by any agreement reached by the autonomy of the negotiating parties. Thus, absolute priority was given to company agreements over the state-level, regional or lower-level branch agreements on issues such as the basic wage and supplementary payments, or compensation for overtime, specific payment schemes for shift work, working time and work time distribution, shift work schemes and annual planning of rest periods, etc. Case law from the Supreme Court declared that agreements below company level do not enjoy this particular position of privilege.[18] However, this preference does not mean exclusivity. All these issues can be negotiated at other levels than company, in the absence of a company-level regulation.

This list must be understood as closed, a matter of public order, and subject to restrictive interpretation by the courts.[19] There are some other nuances that must be made to this affirmation. It is a list that can be expanded by the above-mentioned agreements on structure according to Article 83.2 ET. But, it cannot be limited by them. This prohibition of modification of the list was seen as a severe attack on the foundations of collective autonomy, as it denied any capacity of auto-structuration to the social partners:[20] statutory law kept being the organiser of collective bargaining.

Thus, the major reform in these years was the shift of power from the sectoral agreement to the company agreement. The Spanish legislative tradition in these matters was the pre-eminence of the sectoral agreement. Since 2012, as stated above, the company agreement has had preference. However, according to the data provided by the employers' organisations, this option is not being really used in Spanish enterprises. Their size makes conducting collective bargaining difficult and the fear of legal problems usually stops employers from using this tool. As pointed out by law

17. Miguel Rodríguez-Piñero y Bravo-Ferrer, 'Presentación', in *La reforma laboral de 2012 en materia de negociación colectiva*, La Ley – Wolters Kluwer, Madrid, 2012, p.17.
18. ECLI:ES:TS:2016:4385, ECLI:ES:TS:2017:2098.
19. For example, a recent decision established that the priority is only applicable to company-level agreements, not to establishment-level agreements.
20. F. Valdés Dal-Ré, 'Estructura contractual y concurrencia entre convenios colectivos', *Relaciones Laborales*, 2, 2011, p.59.

academics, having such a structure is a problem as most enterprises are small-scale (nine out of ten Spanish enterprises have ten employees or fewer), so there is usually no representation to negotiate a company agreement.

In 2021, a counter-reform on this topic arrived. But it was softer than expected. Even if the political programmes of the coalition had made a bid to annulate the reform of 2012, pragmatism imposed itself through social dialogue. Only one issue was derogated, the possibility of altering the basic wage and supplementary payments. It was, certainly, the most important one, as it introduced a factor of economic competition within a branch. It broke the cartelisation of salaries. Thus, it was in the interest of both workers and (some) companies that it was sacrificed in the reform.

§15.04 THE LEGAL EFFECTS OF COLLECTIVE AGREEMENTS: THE OPTING-OUT AND *ULTRACTIVIDAD*

The general efficacy (*erga omnes*) of collective agreements is still the rule in Spanish labour law, for those agreements bargained according to the rules of Title III of the *Estatuto*.

However, the possibility of opting out from an existing collective agreement has been greatly strengthened in the last years, to the detriment of general efficacy. Legislation nowadays offers the possibility of amending the employment conditions established in an agreement, especially concerning wages, by means of agreements reached at the company level, based on exceptional causes and through a formal procedure. A detailed reform in 2010 was the first response to the economic crisis in the sphere of labour law. It significantly accelerated and simplified opting-out procedures in those cases where an enterprise's situation could be damaged because of a wage scheme established through a collective agreement.

Similarly, the conservative reform in 2012 went further in this legal flexibilisation by enlarging the scope of the grounds on which opting out was possible to include most employment conditions, and by establishing a looser regulation of the economic, technical, organisational, or productive reasons justifying the opting-out process.[21] Economic causes are deemed sufficient when business figures show a negative economic situation: for instance, current or expected losses or a continuing loss of income level or sales.[22] In any case, a decrease will be considered to be continuing if it takes place over two consecutive quarters. It should be pointed out that since the amendment was introduced in 2010, legitimacy to negotiate an opting-out agreement has been extended to the workers' representatives authorised to negotiate an *erga omnes* applicable collective agreement and, in the absence of such representatives, a council appointed ad hoc and made up of three members, who can be company

21. C. Martínez Moreno, 'Impugnación de medidas de modificación sustancial de condiciones de trabajo y de inaplicación de convenios', *Derecho de las Relaciones Laborales*, 4, 2016, pp. 323-345.
22. J.M. Goerlich Peset, *Régimen de la negociación colectiva e inaplicación del convenio colectivo en la reforma de 2012*, Tirant lo Blanch, Valencia, 2013.

workers or members of trade unions with representation in the sector to which the company belongs.[23]

Lastly, the opting-out procedure includes a consultation period. The reform established that if such a period ends without agreement or without the parties submitting voluntarily to procedures to settle such differences, compulsory arbitration is enforced by the National Consultative Commission on Collective Agreements. The most recent reforms, those of the coalition government, have not dealt with this issue. The liberal approach, thus, remains.

However, the issue of the so-called ultra-activity (*'ultractividad'*), the effects of the agreement after its termination, has been a battlefield for reform and counter-reform in a decade. This institution, regulated in Article 86 ET, tries to overcome the legal void that occurs during the process of collective bargaining, encouraging the parties to regulate employment conditions anew in the corresponding sphere.

Traditionally, labour legislation in Spain sought to protect the stability of collective agreements. This conservationist approach was primarily articulated through legal references contained in Article 86 ET, according to which whenever a collective agreement ceased to have force, a new stage of negotiations was started with the aim of signing a new agreement. During this time, enforcement of the so-called legal content of the agreement was guaranteed (e.g., all provisions establishing and regulating working and employment conditions at the negotiating level of the agreement). The reform undertaken in 2011 opened up the autonomy of the negotiating parties, making the extended validity of the agreement a subsidiary issue.

The earthquake came in 2012. The extended validity of agreements was severely limited by the reform, which established that '*one year after a collective agreement has been contested without a new agreement or arbitration decision being reached, the former agreement will no longer be enforced unless otherwise agreed. In such case, the applicable collective agreement at a higher level will be implemented*'.[24]

One of the main concerns among academics and social partners once the reform was passed was that limiting the enforcement of an agreement would lead to a void in negotiation. As an immediate remedy, the social partners signed an Interconfederal Agreement establishing that '*before such term comes to an end, the negotiating parties must commit to continue negotiating, guaranteeing that the collective agreement will continue to be enforced during the duly-agreed duration of the process*'. Later on, several court decisions have allowed the continuation of legal clauses in collective agreements that contained their own validity scheme prior to the reform. In any case, as pointed out by several authors, this mechanism must be understood in the context of norms that

23. P. Nieto Rojas, 'Comisiones *ad hoc* y reorganización productiva empresarial: una solución para las empresas sin representación legal de los trabajadores', *La negociación colectiva en las reformas laborales de 2010, 2011 y 2012*, Cinca, Madrid, 2012, pp. 57-86.
24. C. Martínez Moreno, 'Revisitando as regras sobre a vixencia e a ultractividade do convenio colectivo', *Revista Galega de Dereito Social – 2ª etapa: (RGDS)*, Vol. 1, N°. 1, 2016, pp. 79-120.

aim to regulate collective bargaining in Spain (Articles 37.1 and 28.1 Spanish Constitution) in accordance with its true structure.[25]

A remarkable ruling by the Supreme Court[26] was the pioneer in the interpretation of the new Article 86 ET. According to that article, one year after the end of the validity of a collective agreement, the higher-level agreement enters into force. The problem raised in that ruling was the situation where there was no higher agreement. The enterprise had answered the question by applying the legal provisions, including those on wages. The Supreme Court ruled, in a very polemical decision (with two dissenting opinions from six Magistrates out of fourteen), that the working conditions existing in a collective agreement should effectively become contractual conditions in the situation described.[27]

This issue was one of the main points of the counter-reform of 2021. The coalition government brought back the *ultra-active* indefinite validity of the collective agreement, rebalancing the contractual power of the parties involved in the bargaining processes. Without denying its dispositive nature, the current rule preserves the clauses of the agreement during the time in which a new one is negotiated, overcoming the regulatory gaps that could arise from the non-application of the agreement whose validity has ended.

Starting from the end of the validity, after one year without a new agreement, the parties must submit to the mediation procedures provided for in interprofessional agreements, to put an end to the specific situations of bargaining impasse that prevent them from signing a new agreement. Mediation, clearly highlighted in the legal text, can only be displaced by arbitration when there is an agreement between the parties in this regard. It must be an express agreement, which, according to the legal provision, may be prior - not necessarily incorporated into the agreement - or contemporary - the latter term giving way to different options.

In conclusion, the version of Article 86 ET established in 2021 recovers the legal model of indefinite *ultra-activity* with the goal of recovering the lost balances and amending the distortions created by the 2012 reform. This is a legal model, as always, in the absence of regulation by a collective agreement, so it may be agreed that the agreement loses its validity upon the end date, or it may also freely reproduce the legal regime of ultra-activity, as well as its consequences and effects. Although directly aimed at covering regulatory gaps, it also provides the parties with a climate conducive to 'calm' or 'tranquillity' to negotiate.[28]

---

25. C. Martínez Moreno, 'La vigencia del convenio colectivo estatutario, problemática general y análisis en particular de la ultraactividad', in *El sistema de negociación colectiva en España. Estudio de su régimen jurídico*, Thomson Reuters Aranzadi, Cizur Menor, 2013, pp. 587 625.
26. ECLI:ES:TS:2014:5504.
27. L.E. de la Villa Gil, et al., 'Reflexiones acerca de la sentencia del Pleno de la Sala de lo Social del Tribunal Supremo de 22 de diciembre de 2014, sobre ultractividad de los convenios colectivos', *Revista General de Derecho del Trabajo y de la Seguridad Social*, 40, 2015.
28. C. Saéz Lara, 'Prohibición de concurrencia y vigencia ultraactiva del convenio colectivo', *Revista de Estudios Jurídico Laborales y de Seguridad Social*, 5, 2022.

§15.05 CONTENT OF COLLECTIVE AGREEMENTS

As a trend, collective bargaining in Spain lacks creativity and is mainly governed by inertia. Contents repeat themselves throughout the years, even making reference to derogated norms.

The contents of collective bargaining have not changed in their essentials since 2007.[29] That year, compulsory bargaining on gender and reconciliation issues was imposed in all company agreements applying to more than 250 workers.[30] In 2022, the threshold was altered, and this procedure became compulsory in all companies with more than fifty workers.[31]

In 2023, a new obligation was created. Companies with more than fifty workers must have a planned set of measures and resources to achieve real and effective equality for LGTBI people, which includes an action protocol to address harassment or violence against this group. The measures will be agreed upon through collective bargaining and agreed with the legal representation of the workers (not with the trade unions).

In the last years, however, it is possible to point out a slow development of digital content.[32] The passing of the GDPR and of the subsequent Ley Orgánica de Protección de Datos has led to a growing role of collective bargaining in the regulation of issues such as the right to disconnection or the private use of digital tools, for example.

Concerning the right to disconnection, it is subject to '*what is established in the collective bargaining or, failing that, what is agreed between the company and the workers' representatives*'. The provision, however, has been the subject of very reasonable criticism, which calls for the inclusion of this duty in the minimum content of collective agreements and the consideration of disconnection as a matter of health and safety which would require authentic consultation with the representation of working people.[33]

Without needing to explore beyond the first quarter of 2023, it can be seen that the matter is gaining its space. The clauses are very similar to each other and no great

29. For the creation in that year of the 'professional interest agreements' for economically dependent workers, *see* the first version of this paper, *supra*.
30. On its initial implementation, R. Menéndez Calvo, 'Estudio de la reforma de 2010 desde la perspectiva de género: clasificación y promoción o ascensos en la negociación colectiva', in *La negociación colectiva en las reformas laborales de 2010, 2011 y 2012*, Cinca, Madrid, 2012, pp. 361-382.
31. P. Nieto Rojas, 'El complicado entramado normativo de planes de igualdad y protocolos en las empresas. Algunas reflexiones sobre protocolos anti-acoso y de gestión de la diversidad', *Labos: Revista de Derecho del Trabajo y Protección Social*, Vol. 4, Extra 0, 2023, pp. 122 ss.
32. With more extension, J.M. Miranda Boto & E. Brameshuber, 'El impacto de la digitalización en la representación de las personas trabajadoras: posibilidades y desafíos para los derechos de información y consulta y la negociación colectiva', *Revista de Trabajo y Seguridad Social*, 478, 2024, pp. 21 ss.
33. C. Aragón Gómez, 'El tiempo de trabajo ante las nuevas formas de organización empresarial', in *Cambio tecnológico y transformación de las fuentes laborales. Ley y convenio colectivo ante la disrupción digital*, Tirant lo Blanch, Valencia, 2022, pp. 125 ss.

signs of originality are detected, confirming a 'poor'[34] balance in this area that had already been detected some time ago. But the first steps are already being taken, making effective the participation of representation in the protection of the right to disconnection. Now we need to improve the results and make said participation truly effective.

In this framework, collective bargaining may be called upon to play a great role in the surveillance of algorithms.[35] Legislatively, there is no basis for this, but it has already been seen throughout this work that there are calls for its intervention in other digital fields. The inclusion of precepts that provide a legal basis for this action, even making it mandatory, could be a new stage in the gradual regulation of digitalisation in the company. In any case, this basis is not necessary if the social parties consider it necessary to address the regulation of their reinforced protection within the framework of their negotiating freedom.

The LOPD, for example, calls for collective bargaining to optionally regulate the personal use of the equipment made available by the company. Beyond the indication of 'the social uses of said media', the mention of 'collective agreements or agreements' is very relevant. With this, the dialogue between the company and representatives becomes more flexible, along the lines noted above. This is one of the fields in which the possible advantages of a negotiated regulation have been pointed out: '*a policy agreed upon with workers' representatives through a negotiation process can obtain greater recognition, which will facilitate its effective compliance, especially if the representatives have good communication with their constituents. Thus, for example, if workers have felt in some way involved in the negotiation of the 'code of conduct' or 'protocol' for the use of the employer's devices, it is very possible that they are better informed of its content and that they are more capable of understanding its implications*'.[36]

34. F.A. Valle Muñoz, 'La regulación de las tecnologías de la información y de la comunicación por la negociación colectiva', *Temas laborales: Revista andaluza de trabajo y bienestar social*, 149, 2019, pp. 13 ss.
35. A. De la Puebla Pinilla, 'La negociación colectiva ante la disrupción digital: retos y respuestas', in *Cambio tecnológico y transformación de las fuentes laborales. Ley y convenio colectivo ante la disrupción digital*, Tirant lo Blanch, Valencia, 2022, pp. 337 ss.
36. A. Álvarez del Cuvillo, 'El papel de la negociación colectiva en la regulación del uso de los dispositivos digitales puestos a disposición de los trabajadores', in *Cambio tecnológico y transformación de las fuentes laborales. Ley y convenio colectivo ante la disrupción digital*, Tirant lo Blanch, Valencia, 2022, pp. 381 ss.

CHAPTER 16

A Retrospective Look at Turkish Decentralized Collective Bargaining: A Solution to Various Crisis?

Kübra Doğan Yenisey

§16.01 INTRODUCTION

The recognition of collective labour rights as fundamental rights does not shield collective agreements from criticism, particularly from perspectives that view them as contributing to labour market rigidity.[1] Critics argue that collective agreements, in particular sectoral ones, can have adverse effects on economic efficiency, potentially leading to reduced flexibility for employers, higher labour costs, and difficulties in adapting to changing economic conditions. However, company-level collective agreements were expected to provide firms with greater flexibility compared to branch-level agreements by increasing tailor-made anti-crisis measures, thereby enhancing the company's competitiveness. Thus, the literature shows an ongoing discourse from the 1980s onwards about the decentralization of collective bargaining. Many authors have observed the shift from industry-level to lower-level (i.e., company or plant) collective agreements due to the economic situation.[2]

1. S. Hayter (ed.), *Introduction, The Role of Collective Bargaining in the Global Economy: Negotiating for Social Justice* (ILO and Edward Elgar, 2011), 7-10.
2. For example, F. Traxler & B. Brandl, *Collective Bargaining, Inter-sectoral Heterogeneity and Competitiveness: A Cross-National Comparison of Macroeconomic Performance*, 50(1) British Journal of Industrial Relations, 73 (2012) https://doi.org/10.1111/j.1467-8543.2010.00804.x; C. Crouch, *Industrial Relations and European State Traditions* (Oxford University Press, 1993), 260 et seq.; T. Treu, *General Report, Procedures and Structures of Collective Bargaining at the Enterprise and Workplace Levels*, 7 Comp. Lab. L., 219 (1986); H.C. Katz, *The Decentralization of Collective Bargaining: A Literature Review and Comparative Analysis*, 47 Industrial and Labour

The economic crisis of 2008 once again highlighted the importance of decentralization, primarily to improve the efficacy of collective bargaining systems. The assumption was that the level at which collective agreement bargained is a key determinant affecting the content and outcomes of collective agreements. Decentralized collective bargaining shifts the focus of decision-making on wages and working hours down to the individual enterprise level.

However, a growing trend shows that the decentralized bargaining model does not meet all expectations in every case. There are numerous other factors, beyond the bargaining level, that influence the overall effectiveness of the bargaining system.[3] In the OECD's *Employment Outlook 2018*,[4] unlike the *Employment Outlook 1994*, the evaluation of collective bargaining regimes highlighted the importance of these systems in contributing to inclusive growth and labour market performance. The results show that fully decentralized systems give the worst results in terms of employment rate, inclusiveness, the protection of vulnerable groups, and wage inequality.

In the first edition of this article, we examined how Türkiye's mandatory decentralized model responded during an economic crisis to shed light on the question of whether the decentralized model per se brings flexibility to the system. Wage increase rates and working time clauses in enterprise and group collective agreements were analysed. An enterprise collective agreement represented a single-employer, one-level bargaining model, while a group agreement exemplified a multi-employer bargaining model. The metal industry was the only sector where both enterprise and group agreements were regularly concluded over a ten-year period.[5]

In this article, I aim to analyse whether the pandemic has influenced the content of collective agreements in Türkiye, specifically to determine if these agreements were used as a tool to regulate working conditions during the pandemic period or in the long term. So the focus will be on analysing clauses related to working time and health and security measures in enterprise collective agreements concluded between 2019 and 2025. This is because to analyse wage-setting clauses effectively, a successive series of collective agreements is required. Due to the strong rivalry between unions, social

---

Relations Review, 3 (1993) https://doi.org/10.2307/2524228; R. Blanpain, *Recent Trends in Collective Bargaining in Belgium*, 123 Int. Lab. Rev, 319 (1984) https://doi.org/10.1111/j.1468-2338.1984.tb00855.x.

3. For example, F. Tros, *Decentralisation of Collective Bargaining Comparing Institutional Change and Company Practices* in Europe, in *Pathways in Decentralized Collective Bargaining in Europe* (ed. F. Tros) (Amsterdam University Press 2023); P. Marginson & C. Welz, *European Wage Setting Mechanisms under Pressure: Negotiated and Unilateral Change and the EU's Economic Governance Regime*, 21(4) Transfer, 429 (2015) https://doi.org/10.1177/1024258915602638; N. Braakmann & B. Brandl, *The Efficacy of Hybrid Collective Bargaining Systems: An Analysis of the Impact of Collective Bargaining on Company Performance in Europe*, MPRA Paper No. 70025, posted 16 March 2016 00:21 UTC, https://mpra.ub.uni-muenchen.de/70025; J. Visser, *What Happened to Collective Bargaining During the Great Recession?*, 5(9) IZA Journal of Labour Policy (2016) https://doi.org/10.1186/s40173-016-0061-1.
4. OECD, *Employment Outlook 2018*, 73-110 (Paris, OECD Publishing, 2018), https://doi.org/10.1787/empl_outlook-2018-en.
5. K. Dogan Yenisey &B. Ataman, *Decentralized Collective Bargaining: A Solution to economic Crisis? – The Case of Turkey*, in *Collective Bargaining Development in Times of Crisis* (ed. S. Laulom), 169 (Kluwer Law International 2018).

partners often avoid sharing collective agreements with the public, making it difficult to examine wage issues during this period. As a result, wage increase rates for this period have been left unexamined.

In the first part of this article, I will provide a legislative overview of the Turkish collective bargaining system, along with a summary of the findings from the first edition related to wage-setting clauses, to offer a better understanding of how industrial relations systems react. Second, drawing from the North American collective bargaining culture embedded in Turkish law, I will explore whether the pandemic has influenced the content of collective agreements, particularly in terms of incorporating more health and safety measures or addressing flexible working hours and short-time work issues. Finally, I will briefly analyse other possible factors that could affect these outcomes.

§16.02 MANDATORY DECENTRALIZED MODEL: WAGE SETTING CLAUSES

Türkiye originally had a multi-level bargaining model, similar to many European countries, but in 1982, it shifted from a two-level to a one-level system, making the workplace the only level at which a collective agreement could be concluded. Act No. 6356 on Trade Unions and Collective Bargaining was adopted on 18 October 2012, with the aim of introducing legislation that meets the needs of a democratic society and aligns with International Labour Organization (ILO) Conventions Nos 87 and 98, as well as Articles 5 and 6 of the Revised Social Charter. However, regarding the bargaining level, the legislator adopted a simpler single-level bargaining model in 1982 and maintained this system in 2012. Collective agreements are to be concluded at the workplace level, with no industry or upper-level bargaining in the system.

Thus, even though unions are established at the industry level, they lack the legal tools to regulate working conditions at higher levels. To meet the requirements of the ILO supervisory organs, framework agreements were introduced into the system by Act No. 6356 in 2012. A framework agreement is an agreement at the branch level between an employees' union and an employers' union, both of which are members of confederations represented in the Economic and Social Council (Article 2/1, b of Act No. 6356). These agreements may regulate policies concerning vocational training, health and safety at work, social responsibility, and employment practices. Framework agreements apply to members of the confederations, meaning the unions (Article 33/1, 3 of Act No. 6356). However, unlike collective agreements, framework agreements have no binding effect.

At the workplace level, three different types of collective agreements can be concluded: First, a workplace collective agreement with a labour union established at the industry level, which must have as members at least 1% of the workers engaged in the same industry and represent more than half of the workers in the workplace. Second, an enterprise collective agreement covers all workplaces in the same branch of activity. For an enterprise agreement to be valid, the union party to the collective agreement must represent 40% of the workers, based on the total number of workers, regardless of the number of workers in each workplace. Since the company agreement may cover several workplaces established in different branches of activity, the scope of the enterprise agreement is narrower. And lastly, to address the need for industry-wide collective agreements, the legislature allows unions to have group collective agreements. A group agreement, concluded between a labour union and an employer's union, covers workplaces and enterprises established in the same industry branch that belong to more than one employer (Article 34 of Act No. 6356).

One of the most distinctive features of the system is that social partners have no authority to choose either the level of collective bargaining or the bargaining unit. The industrial relations system is primarily regulated by mandatory statutory provisions. Therefore, a mandatory one-level decentralized model has been in practice since 1982. This model has been severely criticized by ILO supervisory bodies, which have been urging the Government, in consultation with social partners, to ensure that social parties wishing to engage in cross-sector, regional, and national agreements can do so without impediments for a long time.[6]

In the first edition of this article, we analysed twenty-three different enterprise collective agreements covering the years 2005-2017. Additionally, we examined thirteen group collective agreements concluded between 2002-2014. The wage increase rates in enterprise and group collective agreements concluded with the same trade union could provide insights into whether the enterprise level offers the presumed flexibility during economic crises. The results showed that, with some exceptions, wage increases at the firm level were higher than or nearly equivalent to those at the group level. At both levels, a slowdown in wage increases after 2008 was evident, likely due to the economic crisis. Since inflation was considered in all collective agreements, real wages appeared to be protected. After the 2008 economic crisis, GDP fell sharply by 4.7%. Given that 50% of Turkey's exports go to the European Union (EU), the decline in external demand led to a decrease in employment levels. The European financial crisis turned into an employment crisis in the Turkish economy, with the unemployment rate rising dramatically to 14%.[7] Nevertheless, our data indicated a low sensitivity of collective bargaining to the crisis.

Both centralized and decentralized collective agreements protected employees' rights, as wage levels did not decrease significantly despite the crisis. The annual earnings of employees in firms covered by collective agreements were approximately 60% higher than those not covered by a collective agreement.[8] It should be noted that collective bargaining coverage was only 4.6% at that time. Therefore, collective agreements, whether enterprise or group, provide better wage levels to unionized

6. CEACR, 103rd ILC session (2014); CEACR, ILC 112th ILC Session, (2024).
7. S. Erdogdu, *Küresel Krizin Istihdama Etkileri ve Kriz Karşıtı Işgücü Piyasası Önlemleri,* 5(12) Siyaset ve Yönetim, 142 (2010).
8. Monthly average income in 2014 was TL 2,319, which was more than twice the minimum wage (TL 891). For more information about the wage structure in Türkiye *see* O. Tezgel, *An Assessment on Minimum Wages in Turkey,* in *From an Inequality Perspective During the 2000s, in Employment and Equity* (eds B. Ceylan Ataman & R. Lieberwitz) 133-150 (ILO Publications, Ankara-Geneva 2015).

employees, which is not a surprising result. Nevertheless, the data did not show a meaningful relationship between wage flexibility and the level of collective bargaining.

§16.03 COLLECTIVE AGREEMENTS DURING THE PANDEMIC

[A] Overview of Labour Law During the Pandemic

The first COVID-19 case in Türkiye was announced on 11 March 2020. Approximately one month later, Act No. 7244, which includes employment measures to address the pandemic, was adopted. The main policy of the Turkish government was to avoid an increase in unemployment by prohibiting dismissals and to protect companies by easing the suspension of employment contracts.[9]

All dismissals were prohibited for a period of three months, except those related to just causes due to employees' immoral or malicious conduct; the expiration of the time limit of fixed-term contracts; the closure of the workplace for any reason or suspension of business activities; and the termination of the business in all kinds of service procurements and construction works. The President of the Republic extended these periods several times, each extension lasting for a maximum of three months, until 30 June 2021.

Since layoffs were banned, employers were permitted to suspend employment contracts unilaterally. Employers could place employees on unpaid leave, either wholly or partially, without the employees' consent. This unpaid leave did not give employees the right to terminate the contract based on just cause. (Prov. Article 10 of the Labour Act).

Short-time work allowances and a wage support system were introduced to provide income protection. Short-term work allowances were granted based on the employer's declaration, without waiting for the completion of the eligibility assessment. To benefit from these allowances, the employer had to either temporarily reduce the weekly working hours at the workplace by at least one-third or stop the activity in the workplace completely or partially for at least four weeks. Additionally, the employment contract should have been in effect for the previous 60 days (instead of the usual 120 days), and the insured employee should have paid at least 450 days of social security contributions within the last three years (instead of 600 days).

Between March 2020 and June 2021, 506,624 companies declared short-time work and 3.7 million employees benefited from short-time work allowances. Additionally, 3.1 million employees benefited from the wage support system.[10]

9. For all policies and measures implemented during the pandemic *see* ILO, *Covid-19 Country Policy Responses* (2023), 275-298, https://webapps.ilo.org/static/english/covid-19/country-policy-responses/covid-country-response-EuropeCentralAsia-2023-03-01.pdf.
10. csgb.gov.tr/haberler/bakan-bilgin-kisa-calisma-odenegi-nakdi-ucret-destegi-ve-issizlik-pdenegi-kapsaminda-8-milyon-kisiye-57-milyar-TL-odeme-yapildi/.

[B] Data and Methodology

Given the well-known impact of the pandemic on working time in many companies, it can be expected that flexibility in working time clauses could benefit both employers and employees. Health and security were also critically important topics during the pandemic, so more regulations related to health and security were likely included in collective agreements. In both cases, tailor-made solutions are expected to be found in enterprise collective agreements, as these are shaped by considering the particularities of individual companies. This is why the research covers more enterprise agreements than group agreements. Also, we examined many additional protocols concluded during the pandemic, especially in the public health sector.

The list of collective agreements and their validity periods are given in the table annexe. Collective agreements are classified based on their content as follows:

- Neutral: An agreement is classified as neutral if the parties to the agreement refer to or repeat legislative provisions.
- Flexible: An agreement is classified as flexible if it includes a clause related to the balancing period or short-time work.
- Rigid: An agreement is classified as rigid if daily working time is strictly regulated without leaving any managerial prerogatives to employers, or if working over the daily working hours instead of the weekly working hours is defined as overtime work.

Similarly, for health and security measures, an agreement is classified as neutral, if social partners are satisfied by repeating or referring to legislative provisions; and if there are more detailed rules, classified as detailed. This classification helps in understanding how different agreements address working time issues and health and security measures.

[C] Working Time Clauses

Starting from the 1990s, one of the main areas requiring flexibility was working time regulations. In 2003, Labour Act No. 4857, based on the model of the EU Directive 93/104, introduced a balancing period opportunity, allowing working time to be distributed over the days of the week in different forms, provided that the daily working time does not exceed eleven hours. This balancing period may be extended up to four months through collective agreements (Article 63/II of the Labour Act).

In the first edition of this article, we analysed whether social partners implemented balancing periods in collective agreements and examined any differences (if exist) between enterprise and group agreements concerning working time regulations. None of the analysed collective agreements included a regulation about a balancing period that would reduce employers' overtime payments. Additionally, we found that enterprise collective agreements contained more rigid clauses than legislative provisions. The collective agreements concluded across various sectors also show that the pandemic has had no significant effect on the social partners' approach to working time. Only three out of the twenty-six collective agreements, two enterprises and one group, include a clause related to the balancing period, and one of these clauses is valid for only one year within a two-year collective agreement. In addition, there were no explicit clauses related to short-time work.

It appears that during the 2021-2022 period, despite the pandemic, the social partners did not explicitly address pandemic-related concerns in their collective bargaining agreements, even in the health sector. Their focus seemed to remain on traditional economic issues, such as wage increases, without introducing special regulations or measures in response to the pandemic's challenges. Even in the additional protocols concerning hospital personnel, the negotiations were limited to wage issues, indicating a narrow scope that possibly overlooked broader pandemic-related needs. This might suggest that the collective bargaining process in this context prioritized immediate economic considerations over more comprehensive responses to the unique challenges posed by the pandemic.

It has also been observed that these enterprise-level collective agreements did not inherently offer increased flexibility to firms. This lack of flexibility might be attributed to legislative interventions that facilitated unilateral short-time work arrangements, bypassing the need for negotiated solutions within the framework of collective bargaining. Additionally, unions perceive flexibility as a deregulation process that favours employers, and they often try to avoid such derogations.

[D] Occupational Health and Security Clauses

The health and security of employees are among the fundamental rights recognized by the ILO Declaration on Fundamental Principles and Rights at Work. Taking necessary health and security measures was one of the fundamental requirements not only to protect public health but also to continue production at the workplace during the pandemic. Social partners' involvement constituted a crucial resource to promote consensus and increase the efficacy of policies, both at the decentralized workplace level and the centralized national level.

According to research conducted among 998 employees and 201 employers or employer representatives working in various sectors such as ministries, banks, call centres, universities, insurance companies, etc., during the pandemic, 89.78% of respondents answered 'Yes' to the question of whether additional Occupational Health and Safety (OHS) measures had been taken against COVID-19 in their workplace. To prevent COVID-19, the Ministry of Family, Labour and Social Services has introduced guidelines that should be followed by all employers. These include creating a team to prepare for emergencies at work, introducing an emergency plan and risk assessment, controlling the spread of the pandemic through prevention, maintaining personal hygiene and protective equipment, and knowing what to do if an employee exhibits symptoms of illness. Nevertheless, the survey showed that new risk assessments specific to the pandemic were carried out in very few workplaces. Only 11.62% of the employees surveyed stated that the risk assessment was updated in their workplace after the pandemic began.

The formation of a pandemic board or a pandemic representative, which should include senior managers, consultants, worker representatives, and responsible OHS personnel, was one practice to ensure dialogue at the workplace. However, only 8.71% of employees reported that a pandemic committee was established in their workplace, and 4.70% stated that only a pandemic representative was appointed. Similarly, only 7.96% of employers reported establishing a pandemic committee in the workplace, while 5.47% appointed only a pandemic officer. Among the workplaces that established a pandemic committee, 62.5% were banks, 18.8% were public institutions, and 18.8% were universities, according to the statements of employers and employer representatives.[11] This research shows that there was insufficient social dialogue between employers and employees in terms of coming together and implementing the necessary measures during the pandemic.

The same attitude is reflected in the analysed collective agreements. In general, the occupational health and safety clauses in these agreements refer to the provisions of Act No. 6331 on Occupational Health and Safety. Also, specific clauses related to how wages during sickness will be paid, references to medical and health committees, medicine cabinets, etc., exist. Notably, only one collective agreement includes a specific provision stating that in the event of an epidemic that seriously endangers public health locally or nationally, or in the workplace, or in the case of crises such as earthquakes, floods, or fires, a 'Crisis Desk' shall be established. This crisis desk, consisting of employer and union representatives and experts determined according to the specific crisis conditions, is to advise on the measures to be taken and implemented regarding occupational health and safety and arrangements concerning working conditions.

It is interesting to note that even during a humanitarian crisis like the pandemic, the content of collective agreements appears largely unaffected. Remarkably, only one collective agreement included the provision for a crisis desk to regulate working conditions in the workplace. This does not imply that there was no dialogue during the pandemic at workplaces; however, it seems these practices did not lead to permanent changes in the attitudes of social partners. Even occupational safety and health measures are not regulated in detail.

§16.04 OTHER POSSIBLE FACTORS

Decentralization is assumed to bring the required flexibility to companies during times of crisis. However, our findings do not fully confirm this assumption. Nevertheless, it would be far-fetched to attribute all our findings solely to the bargaining level. Other factors should also be considered and discussed.

11. G. Baycık, Ö. Türkşen & I.C. Dinç, *COVID-19 Salgınında Alınması Gereken Iş Saglıgı ve Güvenligi Önlemleri, Sosyal Güvenlik Dergisi,* 11(1) Journal of Social Security, 17 (2021).

[A] Power Relations and the Size of Companies

In the literature, some authors argue that the difference between industry unions and local trade unions may impact the content differences between enterprise and group collective agreements.[12] However, under Turkish law, the parties to both types of agreements are the same. Both employers' and employees' unions can only be established at the industry level. Even if union density is decreasing at the industry level, trade unions maintain an absolute majority in workplaces, with 40% of employees as members in enterprises. Therefore, they remain quite strong at the bargaining table.

The size of companies may also affect wage-setting clauses. In an enterprise collective agreement, the parties must consider the financial power of a single employer, whereas group agreements cover many employers of different sizes. Therefore, social partners may feel obliged to consider smaller-sized employers when fixing wage increases in group agreements. Unionists also confirm such a policy.

Nevertheless, if the size of the company plays a role in wage setting, it is hard to explain the rigidity of working time clauses and the absence of OHS measures by the size of the company. The factors contributing to these rigidities and omissions likely extend beyond the financial considerations related to company size. Other influences, such as the industrial relations culture, negotiation dynamics, and the specific needs and priorities of the workforce, must be considered to understand these differences comprehensively.

[B] Union Rivalry

One notable characteristic of Turkish trade unionism is the presence of intense inter-union rivalry.[13] Over 90% of trade unions are affiliated with one of three main confederations – Türk-İş, DİSK, and Hak-İş – each aligned with distinct political views. As a result, the deep political divisions among these confederations extend to unions within the same industry.

This rivalry is further intensified by the system which requires the recognition of a trade union as an exclusive bargaining agent to negotiate. This recognition typically requires that the union demonstrates majority support (more than 50% at the workplace, 40% in enterprise) among the employees in that unit. When a union secures this status, it gains the sole right to represent all the employees in the bargaining unit, even those who are not affiliated with the union. This exclusivity can lead to competition among unions to win the majority's favour, sometimes resulting in rivalry and division within the workforce. Unions may focus intensely on securing majority support to obtain or retain their position as the exclusive bargaining agent,

12. A.R. Cardoso & P. Portugal, *Contractual Wages and the Wage Cushion under Different Bargaining Settings*, 23(4) Journal of Labour Economics, 875 (2005) https://doi.org/10.1086/491608.
13. B. Uçkan, *Türkiye'de Sendikalararası Rekabet* (Istanbul 2002), 123.

which can impact the issues they prioritize. This dynamic may contribute to explaining the differing attitudes of the same trade union in enterprise and group agreements.

Additionally, trade unions rely heavily on membership fees as their primary source of income. Workers who do not see a financial benefit from a collective agreement are often reluctant to pay union fees. Unions only collect these fees when they successfully conclude a collective agreement; otherwise, they risk losing their members. Therefore, maintaining a majority in the workplace is not only crucial for union influence but also for their financial stability.

Moreover, this rivalry makes the use of legal extension mechanisms extremely difficult. Although the legislation allows for the extension of a collective agreement concluded by the labour union with the highest number of members in the relevant branch (Article 40 of Act No. 6356), in practice, very few extensions occur.[14]

Such a hostile atmosphere prevents unions from implementing certain adjustments that an enterprise might need during a crisis. In our interviews, some union representatives mentioned that if an enterprise were at risk of closing, trade unions would be willing to make concessions, such as moderating wage demands. However, even in such situations, these agreements would be kept confidential out of concern that any written document could be obtained and exploited by rival unions. Thus, the legislative peculiarities of the collective bargaining system contribute to the heightened rivalry among unions.

[C] Weak Social Dialogue and Limited Coverage of Collective Agreements

ILO Social Dialog Report shows that the pandemic period has paved the way for more effective social dialogue channels in many countries, leading to measures adopted through collective bargaining agreements to address COVID-19-like hazards in the long term. However, in countries where the state plays a significant role in labour markets, this role became even more pronounced during the pandemic.[15] The case of Türkiye confirms this observation.

The weakness of social dialogue mechanisms in Türkiye has been highlighted by numerous studies.[16] The Economic and Social Council, a constitutional institution, has not convened since 2009. The Tripartite Consultation Board met only once during the pandemic. It is difficult to claim that these boards function consistently in accordance with legal regulations. At the workplace level, there exist few participation mechanisms, and the coverage of collective agreements is limited.

---

14. G. Baycık, *Avrupa Birligi Üye Devletlerinde Teşmil Uygulaması ve Türkiye Için Öneriler, ILO Calışma Hayatında Sosyal Diyalogun Geliştirilmesi Projesi* (Ankara 2019).
15. ILO, *Social Dialogue Report 2022, Collective Bargaining for an Inclusive, Sustainable and Resilient Recovery* (ILO 2022).
16. F. Adaman et al., *Perception on Social Dialog in Turkey: The Viewpoints of General Public, Employees and Relevant Actors, ILO Improving Social Dialogue in Working Life Project* (Ankara 2018); E. Bedir et al., *Analysis and Evaluation of Social Dialogue Mechanisms in Turkey, ILO Improving Social Dialogue in Working Life Project* (Ankara 2018).

During the pandemic, social partners primarily sought to mitigate its social and financial impacts by issuing separate statements or joint declarations.[17] Employees and employers organizations released statements in response to the government's Economic Stability Shield program, urging the government to act swiftly to mitigate the negative effects of COVID-19 measures on the labour market and economy. Their demands included protecting workers' income, supporting enterprises, preventing unfair dismissals, ensuring safe working conditions, providing assistance to small business owners, offering paid time off for workers, paying unemployment benefits without conditions, and ensuring free access to the healthcare system without restrictions. Trade unions also called for COVID-19 to be recognized as an occupational hazard, leading to its classification as an occupational disease for healthcare workers in Türkiye. However, it was interesting to see that social partners did not participate in determining which specific measures at the workplace should be taken. Instead, these measures were decided by the government with advice from a board composed of medical scientists.[18]

The coverage of collective bargaining also is a crucial component of industrial democracy. In highly coordinated multi-level bargaining systems, collective agreements play a significant role in shaping social policy. However, in countries with a single-employer collective bargaining model, collective agreements often lose their broader institutional function.[19] Without the practice of extension, one-level small bargaining units tend to have limited coverage, diminishing the institutional role of collective agreements.

Figure 16.1 displays union density and bargaining coverage from 2013 to 2021. Due to the decentralized collective bargaining model, only union members working within the territorial scope of a collective agreement benefit from it. Unlike in France, the extension of collective agreements is seldom used. As a result, the number of employees covered by a collective agreement is lower than the number of those who are union members. When collective bargaining agreements cover only a small portion of the workforce, their ability to set standards or influence broader economic and social conditions is limited. Low coverage of collective agreements can indeed affect their efficiency as a tool to address various crises.

17. ILO, *supra* n. 9, 291-296.
18. C. Kasım, *Covid-19 and Labour Law: Turkey*, 13(3) Italian Labour Law e-Journal, Special Issue 1 (2020).
19. V. Glassner & M. Keune, *The Crisis and Social Policy: The Role of Collective Agreements*, 151(4) ILR, 369 (2012).

Figure 16.1 Union Density and Collective Bargaining Coverage, 2013-2023 (% of Employees)

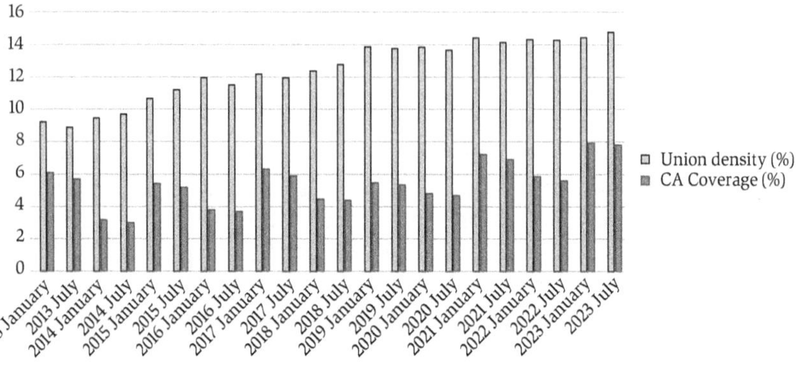

Source: The Ministry of Labour and Social Security, Working Life Statistics.

R-The research shows that during the pandemic, social discourse followed established national patterns and emerged in response to a general European trend of declining social concertation, particularly in institutionalized tripartite settings.[20] The situation in Türkiye indeed aligns with this observation. These mechanisms, which typically involve collaboration between government, employers, and workers (tripartite) or just between employers and workers (bipartite), are designed to foster cooperation and ensure that all parties have a voice in addressing labour issues. Their non-utilization during the pandemic suggests a missed opportunity for a more inclusive and cooperative approach to managing the crisis.

§16.05 CONCLUSIONS

A general overview reveals that decentralization does bring neither flexibility nor tailor-made solutions *per se*. The legal structure of collective bargaining, as well as industrial relations culture, determine how the bargaining system works.

In Türkiye, the primary focus of unions has traditionally been on negotiating collective agreements, with wage settlements being a key priority.[21] Nevertheless, despite Türkiye experiencing several economic crises – in 1994, 1999, 2001, 2009, and 2018 onwards it is notable that over the past forty years, collective agreements have not been considered either among the reasons for or the solutions to, the economic crisis. During the 1970s, high union wage demands and large-scale strikes were often cited as

20. B. Ebbinghaus & J.T. Weishaupt, *Postscript: Social Partnership Facing the 2020 Coronavirus Pandemic*, in *The Role of Social Partners in Managing Europe's Great Recession*, 279 (Routledge 2021).
21. M. Kutal, *Türkiye'de Toplu Iş Sözleşmesi Düzeninde Ücret Politikası, in Türkiye'de Işçi ve Işveren Ilişkileri* (Istanbul 1974), 33.

contributing factors to rising unemployment and economic problems. Although economic motivations were part of the rationale behind the 1982 reform, it's important to emphasize other factors, such as the goal of reducing conflict-driven industrial relations and simplifying the complex legal process.

This outcome is also linked to the limited coverage of collective agreements and the prevailing culture of industrial relations. Despite the legislative framework enabling the possibility of broader framework agreements since 2012, no such agreements have been reached between confederations. This suggests that trade unions have remained largely focused on securing immediate monetary benefits for their members, rather than addressing a broader range of issues. As a result, important topics like migration, and the specific needs of younger and older employees have been neglected in collective bargaining processes.

The Turkish experience further illustrates how the one-level bargaining with exclusive agent model has reinforced a form of unionism primarily focused on economic issues, often referred to as 'bread-and-butter' unionism. When all working conditions are negotiated within small bargaining units, that encourages unions to concentrate on the immediate welfare of their members within the workplace. In a system where union rivalry is prevalent, unions tend to adopt aggressive wage policies and a more rigid stance against flexible working hours. This is because moderate gains achieved through a collective agreement might be leveraged by rival unions.

However, in Türkiye, as in the UK and USA,[22] the alternative to negotiated wage setting is the non-unionized market. Since legislation and individual employment contracts are the primary sources of wage determination, the alternative to a collective agreement is the individual employment contract, unlike in countries with sectoral agreements that provide a default wage structure. It is important to note that the single-employer bargaining model creates strong incentives for pursuing anti-union policies, which is not the case with the multi-employer bargaining model. The fact that some other employers in the industry are also subject to the same working conditions may mitigate their hostile attitude towards unionization.[23]

In the *Employment Outlook* of the OECD[24] it is emphasized that analysing the role of collective bargaining in labour market performance requires a holistic approach, involving an examination of several key dimensions of bargaining systems: the degree of coverage, level of bargaining, degree of flexibility, and wage co-ordination in the sense of coordination between sector-level (or firm-level) agreements, such as the setting of common wage targets, to take account of macroeconomic conditions. Türkiye is categorized within the group of fully decentralized collective bargaining systems. Other countries that shared this fully decentralized approach included Canada, Chile, the Czech Republic, Estonia, Hungary, Korea, Latvia, Lithuania,

22. D. Card & S. de la Rica, *Firm-Level Contracting and the Structure of Wages in Spain*, 59(4) Industrial and Labour Relations Review, 573, 588-589 (2006) https://doi.org/10.1177/001979390605900403.
23. F. Traxler, Bargaining *(De)centralization, Macro Economic Performance and Control over the Employment Relationship*, 42(1) British Journal of Industrial Relations, 7 (2003)
24. OECD, *supra* n. 4, 73-110.

Mexico, New Zealand, Poland, the United Kingdom, and the United States in 2015. In these countries, like Türkiye, collective bargaining is largely confined to the firm level, resulting in a highly fragmented system with limited scope for coordinated wage-setting or broader labour market interventions. This structure often leads to significant variations in wages and working conditions across different firms and sectors, reflecting the unique circumstances of each workplace rather than broader economic or social goals. Thus, decentralization approaches that merely substitute sector-level bargaining with firm-level bargaining, without any coordination between sectors, are generally linked to somewhat worse labour market outcomes. However, organized decentralization tends to result in higher wages for covered workers, better productivity outcomes, and good employment performance.[25] Organized decentralization occurs within the framework provided by sector-level agreements, while explicitly allowing elements of working conditions and work organization to be negotiated or determined at the company or even workplace level under certain conditions through specific procedures. In principle, the sector-level framework should preserve collective bargaining coverage and give firms and workers more freedom to set working conditions.

In countries like the United States and Canada, where collective bargaining traditionally occurs at the workplace level, there is also a growing trend toward expanding collective agreements to sectoral and group levels.[26] Proponents of this approach argue that such agreements could yield more socially egalitarian outcomes. This shift is driven by concerns over increasing income inequality and the declining share of wealth accruing to workers over the past fifty years. It should be noted that the decline in unionization has led to a situation where collective bargaining agreements are limited to a number of workplaces. This reduction in coverage has contributed to a system that lacks effective mechanisms to address wage inequalities. Additionally, the complexities of the modern economy, particularly those related to global supply chains, multi-tier contracts, outsourcing, franchising, and independent worker arrangements, present significant challenges that shop-floor collective agreements are ill-equipped to address. As a result, the bargaining system struggles to counteract broader economic trends that have led to increased income disparity and a weakening of workers' bargaining power. By covering a broader workforce, these agreements could help reduce wage disparities, improve working conditions across entire industries, and provide stronger protections for vulnerable groups, such as low-wage workers, minorities, and women. This approach would potentially lead to a more inclusive and equitable labour market, where the benefits of economic growth are

25. OECD, *supra* n. 4, 75.
26. *See* S. Block & B. Sachs, *Clean Slate for Worker Power: Building a Just Economy and Democracy*, Lab. & Worklife Program, Harv. L. Sch. 1-125 (2020), American Compass, *Sectoral Bargaining's Promise and Peril*, https://americancompass.org/sectoral-bargainings-promise-and-peril/#top, *Sectoral Bargaining: Principles for Reform*, https://concerned-sectoral-bargaining.medium.com/sectoral-bargaining-principles-for-reform-7b7f2c945624; D. Madland, *Re-Union, How Bald Labour Reforms Can Repair, Revitalize, and Reunite the United States* (ILR Press, 2022); The Future of Worker Voice and Power, https://www.americanprogress.org/article/the-future-of-worker-voice-and-power.

more widely shared among all workers, rather than being concentrated in the hands of a few.

The case of Türkiye confirms these observations. In the absence of extension practice, one-level small bargaining units are associated with narrow coverage and result in a reduction of the functions of collective agreements as an institution. Addressing the socio-economic impact of the pandemic required a big effort, a great deal of responsiveness, and the capacity to take rapid decisions on potentially highly controversial issues, such as those limiting personal mobility and imposing lockdowns and closures, in a context of significant uncertainty. The pandemic, which highlighted the need for more comprehensive and adaptive labour relations, further exposed the limitations of a unionism approach that centres almost exclusively on economic concerns.

Another noteworthy point of interest is that in theory, decentralized bargaining should enable firms to negotiate agreements that reflect their unique circumstances, which could be particularly beneficial during times of rapid change. Instead, the situation in Türkiye reveals a disconnect between the potential flexibility of decentralized bargaining and the reality of rigid structures within the industrial relations framework. The industrial relations framework in Türkiye appears to be more rigid and less adaptive than the decentralized model would imply.

To conclude, the role of collective agreements as a key institution shaping social policies has been influenced by various factors, including the legal and sociological culture of each system. Türkiye's experience with the one-level, single-employer bargaining model demonstrates that the 'collective voice'[27] tends to diminish, and collective agreements often fail to provide the necessary adaptability in workplaces. While the level of collective agreement cannot be solely blamed for the current situation, it is evident that the decentralized model plays a significant role. In the ongoing debate over bargaining levels, it may be time to reconsider adopting a multi-level bargaining model for Türkiye.

27. Hayter, *supra* n. 1, 9.

ANNEX

Table 16.1 List of Collective Agreements

Validity Period of Collective Agreements	*Enterprise Collective Agreement*	*Group Collective Agreement*	*Degree of Flexibility of Working Time Clauses*	*Health and Security Measures*
1.7.2019-28.2.2022	Press and broadcasting		Flexible	Neutral
1.7.2021-1.7.2023	Press and broadcasting		Neutral	Neutral
1.1.2023-31.12.2025	Press and broadcasting		Neutral	Neutral
1.3.2021-28.2.2023	Commerce, clerical works, education and fine arts		Rigid	Neutral
1.1.2021-31.12.2022	Commerce, clerical works, education and fine arts		Neutral	Neutral
1.3.2023-28.2.2025	Agriculture, forestry, hunting and fishing		Rigid	Neutral
1.3.2023-28.2.2025	Agriculture, forestry, hunting and fishing		Rigid	Detailed
1.1.2023-31.12.2024	Mining		Neutral	Detailed
1.1.2019-31.12.2021 1.1.2022-31.12.2023		Glass	Rigid	Neutral
1.3.2021-28.2.2023		National defence	Flexible	Detailed
1.4.2022-31.3.2024	National defence		Rigid	Neutral
1.2.2021-31.1.2023	Inland transportation		Flexible – Neutral	Detailed

Validity Period of Collective Agreements	*Enterprise Collective Agreement*	*Group Collective Agreement*	*Degree of Flexibility of Working Time Clauses*	*Health and Security Measures*
1.3.2019-28.2.2021	Rail transportation		Neutral	
1.1.2023-31.12.2024	Health		Neutral	Neutral
1.7.2023-30.6.2025	Accommodation and entertainment		Rigid	Detailed
1.1.2024-31.12.2025	General services		Neutral	Neutral
1.1.2024-31.12.2026	General services		Neutral	Neutral
1.1.2020-31.12.2022	Petroleum, chemicals and rubber		Rigid	Detailed
1.1.2024-31.12.2025	Petroleum, chemicals and rubber		Rigid	Neutral
1.1.2024-31.12.2024	Petroleum, chemicals and rubber		Rigid	Neutral
1.1.2023-31.12.2024	Petroleum, chemicals and rubber		Rigid	Detailed
1.1.2023-31.12.2024	Petroleum, chemicals and rubber		Rigid	Neutral
1.1.2022-31.12.2024	Petroleum, chemicals and rubber		Rigid	Neutral
1.1.2021-28.3.2023	Construction		Neutral	Neutral

BCLR - BULLETIN OF COMPARATIVE LABOUR RELATIONS

Vol. Author/Title/Year/ISBN

1. Roger Blanpain, *Individual Employment Contracts: Collective Agreements,* 1970.
2. Roger Blanpain, *Social Planning,* 1971 (ISBN 90-312-0018-2).
3. Roger Blanpain, *Guaranteed Income Funds,* 1972 (ISBN 90-312-0019-0).
4. Roger Blanpain, *Employee Participation at the Level of the Enterprise,* 1973 (ISBN 90-312-0020-4).
5. Roger Blanpain, *Vastheid van Betrekking: Staking en Bezetting,* 1974.
6. Roger Blanpain, *Labour Law and Industrial Relations (International Bibliography),* 1975 (ISBN 90-312-0023-9).
7. Roger Blanpain, *Multinational Enterprises,* 1976 (ISBN 90-312-0024-7).
8. Roger Blanpain, *Worker's Participation in the European Company,* 1977 (ISBN 90-312-0044-1).
9. Roger Blanpain, *Women and Labour,* 1978 (ISBN 90-312-0077-8).
10. Roger Blanpain, *European Conference on Labour Law and Industrial Relations: Multinational Enterprises,* 1979 (ISBN 90-312-0091-3).
11. Roger Blanpain, *Job Security and Industrial Relations,* 1980 (ISBN 90-312-0147-2).
12. Roger Blanpain, Greg Bamber & Russell Lansbury, *Technological Change and Industrial Relations: An International Symposium,* 1983 (ISBN 90-312-0205-3).
13. Roger Blanpain, James Janssen van Raay & A. Moulty, *Worker's Participation in the European Community: The Fifth Directive,* 1984 (ISBN 90-654-4187-5).
14. Roger Blanpain, *Equality and Prohibition of Discrimination in Employment,* 1985 (ISBN 90-654-4215-4).
15. Roger Blanpain, *Restructuring Labour in the Enterprise: Law and Practice in France, F.R. of Germany, Italy, Sweden and the United Kingdom,* 1986 (ISBN 90-654-4283-9).
16. Roger Blanpain & E. Kassalow, *Unions and Industrial Relations: Recent Trends and Prospect: A Comparative Treatment,* 1987 (ISBN 90-654-4294-4).
17. Roger Blanpain & Marco Biagi, *Trade Union Democracy and Industrial Relations,* 1988 (ISBN 90-654-4394-0).
18. Roger Blanpain & Jelle Visser, *In Search of Inclusive Unionism,* 1990 (ISBN 90-654-4439-4).
19. Roger Blanpain, *Flexibility and Wages: A Comparative Treatment,* 1990 (ISBN 90-654-4461-0).

20. Roger Blanpain, Stephen Frenkel & Oliver Clarke, *Economic Restructuring and Industrial Relations in Industrialised Countries,* 1990 (ISBN 90-654-4488-2).
21. Roger Blanpain & Friedrich Fürstenberg, *Structure and Strategy in Industrial Relations,* 1991 (ISBN 90-654-4559-5).
22. Roger Blanpain, Amira Galin & Ozer Carmi, *Flexible Work Patterns and Their Impact on Industrial Relations,* 1991 (ISBN 90-654-4572-2).
23. Roger Blanpain, *Workers' Participation: Influence on Management Decision-Making by Labour in the Private Sector,* 1992 (ISBN 90-654-4600-1).
24. Roger Blanpain, Brian Brooks & Chris Engels, *Employed or Self-Employed,* 1992 (ISBN 90-654-4613-3).
25. Roger Blanpain & Tiziano Treu, *Industrial Relations Developments in the Telecommunications Industry,* 1993 (ISBN 90-654-4642-7).
26. Roger Blanpain & Marco Biagi, *Industrial Relations in Small and Medium Sized Enterprises,* 1993 (ISBN 90-654-4696-6).
27. Roger Blanpain & Marco Biagi, *Participative Management and Industrial Relations in a Worldwide Perspective,* 1993 (ISBN 90-654-4769-5).
28. Roger Blanpain, Jacques Rojot & Hoyt N. Wheeler, *Employee Rights and Industrial Justice,* 1994 (ISBN 90-654-4804-7).
29. Roger Blanpain & Ruth Ben-Israel, *Strikes and Lock-Outs in Industrialized Market Economies,* 1994 (ISBN 90-654-4841-1).
30. Roger Blanpain, Kazuo Sugeno & Yasuo Suwa, *The Harmonization of Working Life and Family Life,* 1995 (ISBN 90-411-0064-4).
31. Roger Blanpain & Laszio Nagy, *Labour Law and Industrial Relations in Central and Eastern Europe,* 1996 (ISBN 90-411-0298-1).
32. Roger Blanpain, *Labour Law and Industrial Relations in the European Union,* 1997 (ISBN 90-411-0527-1).
33. Taco Van Peijpe, *Employment Protection under Strain,* 1998 (ISBN 90-411-0528-8).
34. Roger Blanpain, Takashi Araki & Ryuichi Yamakawa, *The Process of Industrialization and the Role of Labour Law in Asia,* 1999 (ISBN 9-041-1104-7-X).
35. Roger Blanpain & Marco Biagi, *Non-standard Work and Industrial Relations,* 1999 (ISBN 90-411-1117-4).
36. Roger Blanpain, *Private Employment Agencies: The Impact of ILO Convention 181 (1997) and the Judgment of the European Court of Justice of 11 December 1997,* 1999 (ISBN 90-411-1118-2).
37. Roger Blanpain, *Multinational Enterprises and the Social Challenges of the XXIst Century: The ILO Declaration on Fundamental* Principles *at Work, Public and Private Corporate Codes of Conduct,* 2000 (ISBN 90-411-1280-4).
38. Roger Blanpain, Ryuichi Yamakawa & Takashi Araki, *Deregulation and Labour Law: In Search of a Labour Concept for the 21st Century,* 2000 (ISBN 90-411-1370-3).
39. Roger Blanpain, *The Council of Europe and the Social Challenges of the XXIst Century,* 2001 (ISBN 90-411-1543-9).

40. Roger Blanpain, *On-Line Rights for Employees in the Information Society, Use & Monitoring of E-Mail & Internet at Work,* 2002 (ISBN 90-411-1626-5).
41. Roger Blanpain, *The Evolving Employment Relationship and the New Economy: The Role of Labour Law & Industrial Relations,* 2001 (ISBN 90-411-1691-5).
42. Roger Blanpain, *Involvement of Employees in the European Union, Works Councils, Company Statute, Information and Consultation Rights,* 2002 (ISBN 90-411-1760-1).
43. Michele Colucci, *The Impact of the Internet and New Technologies on the Workplace: A Legal Analysis from a Comparative Point of View,* 2002 (ISBN 90-411-1824-1).
44. Roger Blanpain, *White Paper on the Labour Market in Italy: The Quality of European Industrial Relations and Changing Industrial Relations,* 2002 (ISBN 90-411-1841-1).
45. Roger Blanpain, Russell D. Lansbury & Young-Bum Park, *Impact of Globalisation on Employment Relations: A Comparison of the Automobile and Banking Industries in Australia and Korea,* 2002 (ISBN 90-411-1850-0).
46. Roger Blanpain & Antoine Jacobs, *Employee Rights in Bankruptcy: A Comparative-Law Assessment,* 2002 (ISBN 90-411-1942-6).
47. Roger Blanpain, Takashi Araki & Shinya Ouchi, *Corporate Restructuring and the Role of Labour Law,* 2003 (ISBN 90-411-1949-3).
48. Roger Blanpain, *Collective Bargaining, Discrimination, Social Security and European Integration,* 2003 (ISBN 90-411-2010-6).
49. Roger Blanpain & Luis Aparicio-Valdez, *Labour Relations in the Asia- Pacific Countries,* 2004 (ISBN 90-411-2239-7).
50. Roger Blanpain & Ronnie Graham, *Temporary Agency Work and the Information Society,* 2004 (ISBN 90-411-2252-4).
51. Roger Blanpain, *The Actors of Collective Bargaining: A World Report,* 2004 (ISBN 90-411-2253-2).
52. Roger Blanpain & Michele Colucci, *The Globalisation of Labour Standards: The Soft Law Track,* 2004 (ISBN 90-411-2303-2).
53. Roger Blanpain, Takashi Araki & Shinya Ouchi, *Labour Law in Motion: Diversification of the Labour Force & Terms and Conditions of Employment,* 2005 (ISBN 90-411-2315-6).
54. Roger Blanpain, *Smoking and the Workplace,* 2005 (ISBN 90-411-2325-3).
55. Roger Blanpain, *Confronting Globalization: The Quest for a Social Agenda,* 2005 (ISBN 90-411-2381-4).
56. Roger Blanpain, Thomas Blanke & Edgar Rose, *Collective Bargaining Wages in Comparative Perspective: Germany, France, the Netherlands, Sweden and the United Kingdom,* 2005 (ISBN 90-411-2388-1).
57. Roger Blanpain & Anne Numhauser-Henning, *Women in Academia & Equality Law: Aiming High - Falling Short?,* 2006 (ISBN 978-90-411-2427-6).
58. Roger Blanpain, *Freedom of Services in the European Union: Labour and Social Security Law: The Bolkestein Initiative,* 2006 (ISBN 978-90-411-2453-5).
59. Roger Blanpain, Frans Pennings & Nurhan Sural, *Flexibilisation and Modernisation of the Turkish Labour Market,* 2006 (ISBN 978-90-411-2490-X).

60. Roger Blanpain & Boel Flodgren, *Corporate and Employment Perspectives in a Global Business Environment*, 2006 (ISBN 978-90-411-2537-X).
61. Roger Blanpain, Shinya Ouchi & Takashi Araki, *Decentralizing Industrial Relations and The Role of Labor Unions and Employee Representatives*, 2007 (ISBN 978-90-411-2583-3).
62. Roger Blanpain, *European Framework Agreements and Telework: Law and Practice: A European and Comparative Study*, 2007 (ISBN 978-90-411-2560-4).
63. Roger Blanpain, Jim Kitay, Leanne Cutcher & Nick Wailes, *Globalization and Employment Relations in Retail Banking*, 2007 (ISBN 978-90-411-2620-1).
64. Roger Blanpain, Russell Lansbury, Jim Kitay, Nick Wailes & Anja Kirsch, *Globalization and Employment Relations in the Auto Assembly Industry: A Study of Seven Countries*, 2008 (ISBN 978-90-411-2698-6).
65. Roger Blanpain & Michele Tiraboschi, *The Global Labour Market: From Globalization to Flexicurity*, 2008 (ISBN 978-90-411-2722-8).
66. Roger Blanpain, Michele Colucci & Frank Hendrickx, *The Future of Sport in the European Union: Beyond the EU Reform Treaty and the White Paper*, 2008 (ISBN 978-90-411-2761-7).
67. Roger Blanpain, Linda Dickens, *Challenges in European Employment Relations: Employment Regulation, Trade Union Organization, Equality, Flexicurity, Training and New Approaches to Pay*, 2008 (ISBN 978-90-411-2771-6).
68. Roger Blanpain, Hiroya Nakakubo & Takashi Araki, *New Developments in Employment Discrimination Law, 2008* (ISBN 978-90-411-2782-2).
69. Roger Blanpain, Andrzej Marian wiątkowski, *The Laval and Viking Cases: Freedom of Services and Establishment v. Industrial Conflict in the European Economic Area and Russia*, 2009 (ISBN 978-90-411-2850-8).
70. Roger Blanpain, William Bromwich, Olga Rymkevich, Silvia Spattini, *The Modernization of Labour Law and Industrial Relations in a Comparative Perspective*, 2009 (ISBN 978-90-411-2865-2).
71. Roger Blanpain, Juan Pablo Landa & Brian Langille, *Employment Policies and Multilevel Governance*, 2009 (ISBN 978-90-411-2866-9).
72. Roger Blanpain, European Works Councils; *The European Directive 2009/ 38/EC of 6 May 2009, 2009* (ISBN 978-90-411-3208-6).
73. Roger Blanpain, William Bromwich, Olga Rymkevich & Silvia Spattini, *Labour Productivity, Investment in Human Capital and Youth Employment: Comparative Developments and Global Responses*, 2010 (ISBN 978-90-411-3249-9).
74. Greg J. Bamber & Philippe Pochet, *Regulating Employment Relations, Work and Labour Laws: International Comparisons between Key Countries*, 2010 (ISBN 978-90-411-3199-7). General Editor: Roger Blanpain.
75. Roger Blanpain, Desislava Nikolaeva Dimitrova, *Seafarers' Rights in the Globalized Maritime Industry*, 2010 (ISBN 978-90-411-3349-6).
76. Roger Blanpain, Hiroya Nakakubo & Takashi Araki, *Regulation of Fixed- Term Employment Contracts*, 2010 (ISBN 978-90-411-3356-4).

77. Roger Blanpain, William Bromwich, Olga Rymkevich & Iacopo Senatori, *Rethinking Corporate Governance,* 2011 (ISBN 978-90-411-3450-9).
78. Roger Blanpain & Frank Hendrickx, *Labour Law between Change and Tradition: Liber Amicorum Antoine Jacobs,* 2011 (ISBN 978-90-411-3424-0).
79. Roger Blanpain, Thomas Klebe, Marlene Schmidt & Bernd Waas, *Trade Union Rights at the Workplace,* 2012 (ISBN 978-90-411-3460-8).
80. Roger Blanpain, William Bromwich, Olga Rymkevich & Iacopo Senatori, *Labour Markets, Industrial Relations and Human Resources Management: From Recession to Recovery,* 2012 (ISBN 978-90-411-4004-3).
81. Roger Blanpain, Hiroya Nakakubo & Takashi Araki, *Systems of Employee Representation at the Enterprise: A Comparative Study,* 2012 (ISBN 978-90-411-4080-7).
82. Roger Blanpain & Frank Hendrickx, *Temporary Agency Work in the European Union and the United States,* 2013 (ISBN 978-90-411-4769-1).
83. Roger Blanpain, Toker Dereli, Y. Pınar Soykut-Sarıca & Aslı en-Tabaı, *Emerging Patterns of Work and Turkish Labour Market Challenges under Globalization: Readings on Labour and Employment Relations,* 2014 (ISBN 978-90-411-4983-1).
84. Roger Blanpain, Pablo Arellano Ortiz, Marius Olivier & Gijsbert Vonk, *Social Security and Migrant Workers: Selected Studies of Cross-border Social Security Mechanisms,* 2014 (ISBN 978-90-411-4770-7).
85. Roger Blanpain & Nikita Lyutov, *Workers' Representation in Central and Eastern Europe: Challenges and Opportunities for the Works Councils' System,* 2014 (ISBN 978-90-411-4746-2).
86. Roger Blanpain, Ulla Liukkunen & Chen Yifeng, *China and ILO Fundamental Principles and Rights at Works,* 2014 (ISBN 978-90-411-4984-8).
87. Roger Blanpain, *The Use of Languages and Employment Relations,* 2014 (ISBN 978-90-411-5606-8).
88. Roger Blanpain, Hiroya Nakakubo & Takashi Araki, *Protection of Employees' Personal Information and Privacy,* 2014 (ISBN 978-90-411-5608-2).
89. Roger Blanpain, Jan Wouters, Glenn Rayp, Laura Beke & Axel Marx, *Protecting Labour Rights in a Multi-polar Supply Chain and Mobile Global Economy,* 2015 (ISBN 978-90-411-5662-4).
90. Roger Blanpain & Stefania Marassi, *Globalization and Transnational Collective Labour Relations: International and European Framework Agreements at Company Level,* 2015 (ISBN 978-90-411-4748-6).
91. Roger Blanpain, Frank Hendrickx & Petra Herzfeld Olsson, *National Effects of the Implementation of EU Directives on Labour Migration from Third Countries,* 2016 (ISBN 978-90-411-6257-1).
92. Roger Blanpain, Frank Hendrickx & D'Arcy du Toit, *Labour Law and Social Progress: Holding the Line or Shifting the Boundaries?* 2016 (ISBN 978-90-411-6747-7).

93. Roger Blanpain & Frank Hendrickx, *Reasonable Accommodation in the Modern Workplace: Potential and Limits of the Integrative Logics of Labour Law*, 2016 (ISBN 978-90-411-6258-8).
94. Roger Blanpain, Frank Hendrickx & Bernd Waas, *New Forms of Employment in Europe*, 2016 (ISBN 978-90-411-6239-7).
95. Roger Blanpain, Frank Hendrickx, Hiroya Nakakubo & Takashi Araki, *The Notion of Employer in the Era of the Fissured Workplace: Should Labour Law Responsibilities Exceed the Boundary of the Legal Entity?*, 2017 (ISBN 978-90-411-8470-2).
96. Elena Sychenko, *Individual Labour Rights as Human Rights: The Contributions of the European Court of Human Rights to Worker's Rights Protection*, 2017 (ISBN 978-90-411-8629-4).
97. William Bromwich & Olga Rymkevich, *Improving Workplace Quality: New Perspectives and Challenges for Worker Well-Being*, 2017 (ISBN 978-90-411-8628-7).
98. Sarah De Groof, *Work-Life Balance in the Modern Workplace: Interdisciplinary Perspectives from Work-Family Research, Law and Policy*, 2017 (ISBN 978-90-411-8630-0).
99. Sylvaine Laulom, *Collective Bargaining Developments in Times of Crisis, Second Edition*, 2025 (ISBN 978-94-035-0628-9).
100. Frank Hendrickx & Valerio De Stefano, *Game Changers in Labour Law: Shaping the Future of Work*, 2018 (ISBN 978-90-411-9953-9).
101. Ivana Palinkaš, *The Legal and Institutional Framing of Collective Bargaining in CEE Countries: Between Europeanisation and Decentralisation*, 2018 (ISBN 978-90-411-9199-1).
102. Jeremy Waddington, *European Board-Level Employee Representation: National Variations in Influence and Power*, 2018 (ISBN 978-90-411-9202-8).
103. Jan Pichrt & Kristina Koldinská, *Labour Law and Social Protection in a Globalized World: Changing Realities in Selected Areas of Law and Policy*, 2018 (ISBN 978-94-035-0093-5).
104. Matthew W. Finkin, *American Labor and the Law: Dormant, Resurgent, and Emergent Problems*, 2019 (ISBN 978-94-035-0654-8).
105. Giuseppe Casale & Tiziano Treu, *Transformations of Work: Challenges for the Institutions and Social Actors*, 2019 (ISBN 978-94-035-0891-7).
106. Miguel De la Corte-Rodríguez, *EU Law on Maternity and Other Child-Related Leaves: Impact on Gender Equality*, 2019 (ISBN 978-94-035-1452-9).
107. Valeria Pulignano & Frank Hendrickx, *Employment Relations in the 21st Century: Challenges for Theory and Research in a Changing World of Work*, 2020 (ISBN 978-94-035-1764-3).
108. Matteo Bottero, *Posting of Workers in EU Law: Challenges of Equality, Solidarity and Fair Competition*, 2021 (ISBN 978-94-035-2860-1).
109. Bernd Waas & Christina Hießl, *Collective Bargaining for Self-Employed Workers in Europe: Approaches to Reconcile Competition Law and Labour Rights*, 2021 (ISBN 978-94-035-2373-6).

110. Mathias Wouters, *International Labour Standards and Platform Work: An Analysis of Digital Labour Platforms Based on the Instruments on Private Employment Agencies, Home Work and Domestic Work*, 2022 (ISBN 978-94-035-4024-5).
111. Luca Ratti, *In-Work Poverty in Europe: Vulnerable and Under-Represented Persons in a Comparative Perspective*, 2022 (ISBN 978-94-035-4996-5).
112. Silvia Rainone, *The Role of the Court of Justice in EU Labour Law: A Case Study on the Transfer of Undertakings Directive*, 2023 (ISBN 978-94-035-2896-0).
113. Frank Hendrickx, Elena Gramano & David Mangan, *Privacy@work: A European and Comparative Perspective*, 2023 (ISBN 978-94-035-3106-9).
114. Elena Sychenko & Adalberto Perulli, *Employment Law and the European Convention on Human Rights: The Research of the Recent Jurisprudence of the ECtHR Related to Employment Law (2017-2021)*, 2023 (ISBN 978-94-035-3556-2).
115. Ilda Durri, *Casual Work Arrangements and Platform-Based Work: The Casual Work Agenda as a Way to Enhance the Labour Protection of Platform Workers*, 2023 (ISBN 978-94-035-3107-6).
116. Charalampos Stylogiannis, *Collective Labour Rights for Self-Employed Workers: A Human Rights-Based Approach of Platform Work*, 2023 (ISBN 978-94-035-0667-8).
117. Heather Kurzbauer, *Employment Vulnerabilities in the World of Orchestral Musicians: Symphonic Metamorphoses*, 2023 (ISBN 978-94-035-2737-6).
118. Natalie Videbæk Munkholm, Vincenzo Pietrogiovanni & Karsten Engsig Sørensen, *Managers in European Law: Rights and Duties of Executive and Non-executive Managers in a European Perspective*, 2024 (ISBN 978-94-035-3286-8).
119. Frank Hendrickx & Christina Hiessl, *The Meaning of Work: A Labour Law Perspective*, 2024 (ISBN 978-94-035-0579-4).